Foundations of
Developmental Psychology

Foundations of

Developmental Psychology

Richard C. LaBarba

University of South Florida

Academic Press
New York /London /Toronto /Sydney /San Francisco
A Subsidiary of Harcourt Brace Jovanovich, Publishers

Cover and chapter opening art by Paula Goodman.

Academic Press, Inc.
111 Fifth Avenue, New York, New York 10003
United Kingdom Edition published by

Academic Press, Inc. (London) Ltd.
24/28 Oval Road, London NW1

ISBN: 0-12-432350-2
Library of Congress Catalog Card Number:
80-615

Printed in the United States of America

. . . to my family.

In tracts of fluent heat began,
    And grew to seeming-random form,
    The seeming prey of cyclic storms,
Till at the last arose the man;
    Who throve and branched from clime to clime,
The herald of a higher race,

. . .

    Move upward, working out the beast,
And let the ape and tiger die.

                                        Tennyson

Preface

Developmental psychology is ready to assert its position within the developmental sciences, and indeed must do so if a full understanding of human development, normal and abnormal, is to be attained. The acceptance of developmental psychology as a significant contributor to the study of human development requires recognition of its interdisciplinary nature and the scope and complexity of its subject matter. Most importantly, developmental psychology must be accepted as a science, whose data bases have applied professional significance for clinical psychologists and other practitioners in the helping professions. Unfortunately, this acceptance has not always come easily. Many students are so motivated to contribute to the solution of human problems that they have difficulty perceiving the value of a firm scientific foundation. Sometimes this attitude leads to the point of view that a scientific approach to psychology is inimical to applied psychology and to the human condition. Nothing could be further from the truth, and such distortion and misunderstanding have been particularly costly for applied psychology.

Currently, developmental psychology is among the most rapidly growing areas in psychology. Child development is attracting more students than ever before, and research projects in this area are at their peak. Predictably, introductory developmental psychology textbooks have appeared at a startling rate. These books are useful in arousing and maintaining interest in the area, but the need for a different level of basic study in developmental psychology seems apparent. This text is designed for the student seeking a comprehensive introduction to developmental psychology as a developmental science.

The intent is to introduce the field in a manner comparable to the introductory courses that college students take in biology, chemistry, or physics. The emphasis is on the empirical and theoretical foundations of fundamental human development. Because this is a first course in the scientific bases of developmental processes, little attention is directed toward applied concerns in child development or practical applications in clinical, educational, or school psychology. These are seen as more advanced pursuits, which must be based on an understanding of their scientific foundations.

The decision to write this book was prompted in part by the vigorous emergence of the developmental sciences and the growing prominence of developmental psychology. Although this text is written for undergraduate students in psychology, it can be understood by students in any discipline who have a grasp of introductory psychology and biology. One theme of this book is the attempt to trace the origins and processes of various developmental events. Mere description of child development and behavior has been avoided whenever possible. Therefore, discussion of developmental phenomena ends with the establishment of basic developmental processes, since discussion beyond that point is of more descriptive than etiological significance, and this would be more appropriate for advanced courses in developmental psychology.

Developmental phenomena are presented by topics rather than by chronological, age-related patterns of development. I believe this arrangement of the subject matter provides for more efficient study, integration, and synthesis of the material, along with a more organized view of development. The sequence of chapters presents various developmental considerations in an order that will, I trust, seem reasonably logical. Finally, I have made an effort to discuss both the factual and the controversial, the clear and the unclear, for I know of no other way to convey the state of the science—or of the art—in developmental psychology.

I am indebted to a number of people for their contributions during the preparation of this book. Foremost is Professor Joseph D. Matarazzo, of the University of Oregon Health Sciences Center, whose support and encouragement over the years are largely responsible for the completion of this project. Dr. Matarazzo's skill and endurance in reviewing the manuscript truly make him an author's friend. I would like to express my gratitude to Dr. Richard K. Lore of Rutgers University for his critical review of the manuscript. Dr. Lore's sobering comments greatly contributed to the accuracy and clarity of the manuscript. I would also like to thank Dr. Dorathea Halpert of Brooklyn College for her helpful review of several chapters.

I also owe a great deal of thanks to all my graduate students, both past and present. Their talent and interest were a continual source of comfort and encouragement. I would especially like to thank Christine Kimpel Cross for her critical review of portions of the manuscript and Dr. Michael Cross for his thoughtful contributions to the content of Chapter Ten. I am particularly indebted to Joseph Sclafani for his untiring efforts in every phase of this project, from library research to final draft preparations.

Finally, special acknowledgement is due the editorial and production staff of Academic Press for extending a publisher relationship that places the author first. I sincerely thank James D. Anker, Sponsoring Editor, for his cooperation and help in preparing the manuscript. To Allan Forsyth, Managing Editor, I express my appreciation and admiration for the editing skills that translated my manuscript into readable English. And to Richard Christopher, Project Editor, my thanks for ushering the manuscript through the many stages to final book form.

Contents

Chapter

INTRODUCTION TO DEVELOPMENTAL PSYCHOLOGY

One

INTRODUCTION

The emergence of the developmental sciences during the past 15 years marks an important trend in our efforts to understand human behavior. Increasing awareness of research findings in developmental biology, developmental genetics, developmental neurophysiology, and developmental medicine has spurred the growth of developmental psychology. More important, perhaps, is the growing awareness that the biological, medical, and behavioral sciences must ultimately focus on developmental phenomena in order to achieve a true understanding of human behavior.

Scientific explanation requires the interpretation of an event and some statement of the reasons for its occurrence. Scientific knowledge requires an explanation based on the etiology of the phenomenon under investigation. The singular importance of etiological considerations in the developmental sciences derives from the nature of the phenomena being studied, and from the obvious concern with organic and behavioral development. Any such interests in development must necessarily deal with origins and causes since events, conditions, and processes have a beginning, no matter how obscure. Complex biological and behavioral phenomena develop from less complex phenomena. The discovery and understanding of these "simpler" events lead, theoretically, to an explantion of normal developmental processes and events. Also, knowledge of the etiology of a particular developmental event holds the promise for the prevention of various abnormal patterns of growth and behavior.

Developmental psychology is a branch of the general science of psychology. Unlike the other major branches, developmental psychology is characterized by a distinct point of view rather than by specific content areas. The subject matter of developmental psychology encompasses most of the basic areas within traditional psychology. However, developmental analysis of these topics goes beyond descriptive and comparative treatments of various psychological phenomena, which usually focus on relatively static, isolated adult states and individual differences.

The developmental perspective emphasizes the search for trends of development. It is an attempt to understand the origins, emergence, and course of psychological processes. Etiology is the scientific study of causes, origins, or reasons. Therefore, the concept of etiology is inherent in all scientific studies, but it is the focal point of the developmental sciences. Thus, a developmental approach to such topics as learning or emotion involves the analysis of these behavioral dimensions in terms of their possible origins, appearance, and elaboration. It would range from simple behavioral displays in the infant to the more complex levels of functioning seen in late childhood or early adolescence. All the major dimensions of psychological functioning are similarly treated in developmental psychology.

A second major difference in the developmental approach is the attempt to integrate and synthesize various components of developmental phenomena as they occur in behavioral development. In other words, to understand the development of any behavioral dimension, we must appreciate the contributions of other psychological processes that may be emerging at the same time.

An integrated approach to developmental psychology also recognizes that the biological sciences contribute to the understanding of developmental psychology. This interdisciplinary approach to developmental psychology is a reasonable one to take regardless of one's special field of interest. Students tend to become absorbed in particular aspects of behavioral development. But such interests, no matter how intense, should not obscure the fact that all organisms have a biology, and that biological events have great import for behavioral outcomes. An interdisciplinary approach does not diminish the contribution of environmental factors to developmental events. Nor are environmental determinants relegated to the passive role of merely providing a support system for a biologically programmed individual. Rather, a competent and effective approach to developmental psychology assumes a sensitivity to biological as well as environmental factors having potential etiological significance. The development of a multidisciplinary attitude is just as important for educators, social workers, and other professionals and paraprofessionals who deal with human development in one capacity or another.

THE STUDY OF DEVELOPMENTAL PSYCHOLOGY

As we shall see, the nature and scope of developmental psychology has been somewhat of an issue. The resolution of this problem concerns us less than the recognition of the basic themes which underly these discussions. Students and psychologists alike often identify developmental psychology and child psychology as dealing with the same subject matter and so they use these terms interchangeably. But despite the considerable overlap between the two, there are some differences between developmental and child psychology. Developmental psychology is a broad, inclusive field of study dealing with the course of behavioral and psychological change. Various subdisciplines with developmental psychology are identified by such terms as "child psychology," "child development," and "life span" developmental psychology, the broadest extension of the field, covering developmental phenomena from conception to death.

We differentiate developmental psychology, not by its content, but by its more restricted, basic etiological research approach to fundamental developmental processes. We see these developmental processes and events as occurring from conception through middle adolescence, by which time they are fairly well established and matured. This approach draws freely from infrahuman developmental studies in the search for analogs to potentially basic processes that may have import for human development. Child psychology, on the other hand, is usually a more descriptive study of the behavioral and psychological characteristics of children at various ages. It tends to emphasize the clinical and practical applications of available data and theories to the rearing, education, and psychological treatment of children.

Reese and Lipsitt (1970) have summed up various attempts to differentiate developmental psychology, child psychology, and child development. They define developmental psychology as the study of behavioral changes associated with age changes in humans. Then they describe the study of behavioral development during childhood as that part of developmental psychology called child psychology. They note that child psychology also can be defined as the study of child behavior and psychological processes. In contrast, child development generally is considered to focus on the child as a developing person.

After describing several efforts to make such distinctions on the basis of research interests, methodological approaches, theoretical preferences, and philosophical orientations, Reese and Lipsitt conclude that such attempts fail to distinguish child psychology from child development. Nonetheless, Reese and Lipsitt go on to differentiate between experimental child psychology and other branches of developmental psychology. They define experimental child psychology as the study of child behavior and development, distinguished by (1) the study of basic process rather than the whole child (2) basic theoretical research in contrast to applied research, (3) etiological research instead of descriptive research, and (4) the use of scientific methodology.

Munn (1974) has described developmental psychology as a broad, generic discipline within psychology. He divides developmental psychology into two major branches: phylogenetic psychology and ontogenetic psychology. Phylogenetic psychology covers the evolution of psychological processes in organisms, from the simplest to the most complex on the phylogenetic scale. The prefix *phylo* is derived from the word phylum, which denotes the basic divisions in the taxonomic classification of the animal kingdom. Phylogenetic psychology, then, searches for developmental trends in the evolution of behavior across phyla. The attempt is to trace the etiology of some particular behavioral capacity, observed in an organism at any phylogenetic level, by comparing it with analogous capacities in organisms at other phylogenetic levels. Such research efforts by phylogenetic psychologists enable us to record the appearance of a specific behavioral capacity in its most primitive form and to follow its development into more elaborate and sophisticated behavioral systems. Increasingly complex behavioral capacities always reflect the evolution of more complex sensory capacities, and of more complex and sensitive organ systems such as the central nervous system. Therefore, phylogenetic psychology theoretically permits us to compare organic evolution with behavioral evolution.

The second major branch of developmental psychology is referred to as ontogenetic psychology. The term, ontogenetic, is derived from the word ontogeny, a biological term denoting the growth and development of individual organisms. Ontogeny is in contrast to phylogeny, which refers to the evolutionary development of animal species. Thus, ontogenetic psychology deals with trends of growth and development in individual organisms. The individual organism chosen for ontogenetic study may be from any animal group but, in fact, is most commonly humans. The ontogenetic psychologist, then, is typically a child psychologist or a developmental psychologist specializing in some aspect of human development. Such psychologists seldom, if ever, refer to themselves as ontogenetic psychologists.

Clearly, ontogenetic psychology is less broad than phylogenetic psychology because a single species is the focus of study. Within ontogenetic psychology, human developmental concerns range from conception to old age. This range of subject matter is much too extensive for any psychologist to acquire full expertise in all parts of it. Therefore, the field of ontogenetic psychology is segmented into age-related developmental periods that represent areas of specialization. These developmental periods are usually categorized broadly as childhood (birth to 13 years), adolescence (13 to 18 years), and senescence or the onset of old age (approximately 60 years).

During the period of childhood, developmental processes are at their peak of activity. But the period from early adulthood to the onset of old age is relatively stable in terms of developmental events. Moreover, it is extremely difficult to investigate developmental phenomena in the mature human adult. Often, research findings merely describe individual differences—events that have little implication for developmental psychology, although they are important for other areas of psychology. This does not mean that adolescents and adults do not show behavioral changes. They do, of course.

But some researchers argue that what are often viewed as true developmental changes are in fact *differential* behavioral variables or events (Wohlwill, 1970). That is, individual differences that inevitably appear in all behavioral phenomena may be mistaken for developmental changes. Although such confusion between developmental and differential variables may occur at any period along the continuum of development, it may be especially noticeable in adolescence and adulthood. Thus, we must emphasize that the origins and establishment of behavior are quite a different matter from the stability and maintenance of behavior. While the former will be characterized by developmental explanations and laws, the latter will undoubtedly be explained and governed by different psychological phenomena and underlying mechanisms (Endler, Boulter, & Osser, 1976). Behavioral change can occur as a function of the operation of developmental processes and events or as a consequence of differential environmental experiences, such as learning or special training. But the latter variables qualify as differential, not developmental variables.

We will have more to say about this issue later. Our principal point here, and a somewhat controversial one, is that after the period of adolescence, it is difficult to see any *new* developmental changes (Bower, 1979). Some changes in motivation, personality functioning, and general social adjustment are often seen during the period of adolescence, but these are differential changes rather than developmental ones. Similarly, certain physical changes and improvements in motor skills are also associated with adolescence. Although cognitive processes and intelligence continue to grow and improve, many psychologists suggest that no notable changes occur in basic cognitive processes beyond middle adolescence. For example, Piaget (1950) believes that the last stage of cognitive development, which he calls formal operations, first appears in early adolescence and matures to adult levels of intelligence by about age 15. (We will consider these data on cognitive development in much more detail in Chapter Six.

Our treatment of developmental psychology, therefore, assumes that maturation of the basic structural and functional systems of behavioral development has been virtually completed by approximately the middle period of adolescence. Since the span of human life from this point to the beginning of old age seems to lack developmental activity, our treatment of ontogeny ends at about the time of midadolescence.

From the onset of old age to death, a number of developmental changes may occur, including the decline of mental and physical skills and capacities. But unlike positive developmental changes, which always occur among normal individuals between birth and maturity, mental and physical decline are not inevitable developments of old age. Such regressive changes are neither universal in the aged nor predictable. Normal individuals entering old age do not share any common set of characteristic changes in basic skills and capacities.

While many old people suffer psychological and physical declines, many others do not. When such declines do occur, we often see differential patterns of decline rather than uniform losses across the various dimensions of functioning. In positive developmental change, we find commonality and predictability among all normal children as they acquire increasing competence. It would be unusual, for example, to see dramatically different patterns of cognitive, language, or emotional development among normal children. For these reasons, regressive developmental changes that may accompany old age represent a special problem in developmental psychology, one which has taken on increasing social and scientific significance as our population of older people increases. Recognition of these special problems has given rise to a new area of psychology—gerontological psychology—and developmental specialists with both basic and applied interests.

We must make one final point in our discussion of the study of developmental psychology. Earlier, we mentioned that developmental psychology is an interdisciplinary science, requiring the integration and analysis of data from various other scientific disciplines. At the same time, developmental psychology is also an intradisciplinary science, incorporating all the basic areas and subspecialties in psychology. If we are to investigate the development and growth of human behavior, we need to know something about sensation and perception, learning, language, cognition, motivation, emotional behavior, personality, social development, and physiological psychology. In short, development deals with all dimensions of psychological phenomena. Though students learn about each area in psychology in a relatively segmented fashion, in reality each area and the behavioral processes it represents are inextricably intertwined in a dynamic network with every other behavioral system. So, for example, it is misleading and simplistic to attempt to understand intellectual development without the perspectives of motivation, learning, emotional development, and personality–social development. All these developmental patterns must be considered and synthesized in terms of intellectual development.

In summary, the student of developmental psychology uses a different perspective than most other psychologists. Rather than isolating events and processes, as is often the case in standard psychological research, the developmental integrates many diverse observations to assemble an accurate picture of a developing organism. By acquiring this perspective early in the study of developmental psychology, students can dismiss any narrow, naive preconceptions of developmental psychology. They may also acquire a broader appreciation of the many topics they will encounter in both introductory and advanced study in psychology.

THE CONCEPT OF DEVELOPMENT

Development refers to maturational changes or changes that occur in organisms over the course of life. To study such changes, we must investigate three broad areas within developmental psychology (Langer, 1969): the genetic origins of behavioral systems, the psychological organization of behavioral systems, and the progressive and regressive transformations that occur in behavior with increasing age. Obviously change occurs over time. However, time itself is not a causal or independent variable effecting change (Bijou, 1968; Wohlwill, 1970). Time is merely an inherent dimension within which biological and psychological events take place. Time does not cause anything. Instead, events happen in time and we are provided with a convenient vessel for analyzing the critical antecedent variables producing change.

In this context, we may think of time or age as an index or carrier variable having no causal significance (Lewis, 1972). As Lewis puts it, developmental psychology deals with the delineation of psychological processes, but commonly investigated variables such as age, social class, and sex are *not* psychological processes. They are, rather, index variables containing sets of independent variables within which psychological processes occur. Time and the related dimension of age do not specify and isolate the independent variables producing changes in the individual. For example, it is not time or age, acting as an independent variable, that produces the emergence of the fear response in infants. The appearance of this response as a developmental phenomenon is dependent upon the maturation of certain response systems such as perception, cognition, and emotion, and their functional interaction with the infant's environment. Increasing age or the simple passage of time will not produce expected developmental changes if the structures and mechanisms underlying those psychological changes are arrested or altered by some abnormal condition.

Denenberg (1972) has clarified this issue by differentiating between chronological age and ontogenetic age. Denenberg asserts that the use of chronological age (time) as a scale of development is deceptively simple and promotes false categorization of age-related behaviors. Denenberg argues that time is biologically and psychologically meaningless, and that what is important in understanding and predicting behavioral development are the biological events and the psychological experiences of the individual. In response to the need for a more meaningful developmental scale, Denenberg employs the concept of ontogenetic age to denote the biobehavioral events of an organism. As he sees it, ontogenetic age focuses on psychobiological characteristics and clearly stresses that current developmental status is largely attributable to the accumulation of experiences unique to the individual organism. If we could learn the ontogenetic age of individuals, our understanding and prediction of behavioral patterns of development could be based on known differential experiences. An ontogenetic age scale requires a detailed history of an organism, from genetic to experiential.

Meier (1975) has also called for a different research approach focusing on the individual developing organism and its behavior relative to its environment. Meier calls for functional analysis of the ontogeny of behavior in specified environments. He asserts that we have the basic experimental methods but have failed to apply them to developmental concerns and problems.

Time and chronological age, then, should not distract us

from the developmental phenomena underlying behavioral transformations. The task of developmental psychology is to establish etiological principles and laws that will describe and explain development. The use of time and age as the descriptive basis for development does not appear to be an efficient strategy toward these ends. The status of age as a developmental concept and its use as an independent variable have been criticized by a number of developmentalists. Wohlwill (1970) has clearly expressed the general dissatisfaction with developmental research based on the Behavior = f(Age) paradigm (behavior is a function of age). Recognizing the important role of descriptive research in developmental psychology, Wohlwill nevertheless points out that the widely used B = f(A) paradigm cannot reveal functional relationships between independent and dependent variables. Discovering such relationships is a critical requirement for scientific understanding.

Wohlwill suggests that rather than treating age as an independent variable, we should reduce it to the status that a time variable assumes in other areas of psychology. Namely, age or time is simply a dimension along which developmental changes are studied. Wohlwill states that this approach to the age variable is applicable only when true developmental variables are under consideration. Behavioral variables that qualify as developmental are those for which the general course of development remains uniform, consistent, or invariant across a broad range of individuals and environmental and genetic conditions. Thus, developmental phenomena are identified by their common emergence under nonspecific experiential and environmental conditions. Such developmental variables include sensory–perceptual, linguistic, cognitive, motor, and emotional development.

Wohlwill notes that this experiential nonspecificity does not rule out environmental influences on the rate and terminal level of developmental change (differential variables leading to individual differences). It only implies that no single environmental situation constitutes a necessary condition for the emergence of developmental changes. This position resembles the notion of Hebb (1949) that the immature organism requires a minimally adequate stimulating environment to ensure normal development and maintenance of the central nervous system and subsequent normal functional development. But

Wohlwill considers consistent, age-related behavioral changes directly related to specific, unique experiences as nondevelopmental variables. Therefore, Wohlwill describes responses acquired through special training, unusual opportunities, and unique learning experiences (such as athletic coaching or specific academic achievements) as differential variables or dimensions of individual differences. These differences represent differential terminal levels of expression of developmental phenomena rather than true developmental changes. The nature of these *situationally determined* changes may either facilitate, retard, or otherwise alter the behavior patterns that individually characterize us as adults.

MODELS OF DEVELOPMENT

A model is a structure of ideas, designed to help us test scientific principles and understand empirical events. Models are convenient, systematic representations of phenomena, stated in logical, mathematical, or physical terms. Thus, models help us to organize and understand empirical events by comparing such events to the operation of the model. For example, computer construction and operation are often employed to model the functioning of the human brain; the camera is used as a model for describing the operation of the eye; mathematical formulas also serve as models to describe learning principles and to predict probabilities of learned responses occurring. Typically, models are generated by, or are part of, a particular theory. They are much more specific and less broad than the theory they represent. As Shontz (1965) puts it, a model is a "permanently tentative construct which provides us with a 'quasi-real' structure, the value of which serves methodological purposes for the investigator" (p. 16).

Developmental models may be presented in different ways and at different levels, depending on whether the approach one takes is global or specific. At a broad level, models of development can represent continuous or discontinuous phenomena. A continuity model describes development in terms of psychological changes emerging in a quantitative fashion, with the elaboration of function increasing in complexity by small degrees. Both general and specific developmental patterns are assumed to have primitive precursors. From these precursors, the patterns grow in smooth, uninterrupted transition to increasingly complex levels, which are cumulative and which maintain the essential integrity of the organism. Developmental continuity of structure and function is seen as analogous to the biological continuity of evolution.

Decrement of functioning is similarly viewed. Decreases in behavioral efficiency also present a picture of gradual, quantitative changes in behavioral capacity and integrity. The basic argument is that we seldom see sudden, dramatic behavior changes in development, where functions appear or disappear with no evidence of transitional stages. The exception to this general rule occurs when severe biological damage or disease processes suddenly disrupt the biological integrity of an organism and abruptly halt one or more behavioral systems.

Discontinuous models of development reflect qualitative changes, which tend to occur in a relatively discrete manner. This view of development sees developmental changes in ontogenesis as a series of segmented events whose basic elements and structures are unrelated to each other. These separate developmental events generate discontinuous behaviors that appear to have different properties.

Discontinuity models are often described as a stage progression of behavioral development. That is, the sequence of stages never varies. The emergence of each successive stage depends upon the appearance of the preceding stage level. The progression is from simple to more complex behavior and then to global psychological integration. According to the discontinuity model, development emerges in a series of abrupt changes that reflect structural and functional reorganizations of the organism. The behaviors associated with these changes are different in kind and quality from lower and higher stage changes. Note that these assumed changes are not gradual, accumulated alterations of degree in which basic properties and characteristics are retained, as is assumed in continuity models. Rather, discontinuous changes are qualitative in nature, representing the appearance of new kinds of elements and their reorganization with previously existing processes. Presumably, these integrative changes account for the increased complexity in behavior observed at a higher stage level. The notion of major alterations and reorganizations occurring in development is inherent in discontinuity models of development.

If in fact development occurs as a continuous process, then the same general laws or developmental variables should describe and explain developmental phenomena at any point in ontogenesis or phylogenesis, since psychological reorganization and its attendant functional changes at different stages of development would not be present. Alternately, if discontinuity describes general development, then different laws or sets of laws will be required to account for behavioral development during different periods of ontogeny or phylogeny because we would be dealing with new and different psychological structures and functions controlled by different principles. If there is a set of general laws controlling development, the degree of stability and applicability of those laws over time will determine the validity of the continuity or discontinuity of development.

We are not obliged to view development in terms of one or the other of these antithetical positions. The capacity for accomodating polar opposite positions by synthesizing and integrating elements of two or more theories is a critical attribute. We must draw upon that capacity in dealing with the continuity–discontinuity issue. The recognition that different kinds of events may be occurring simultaneously or at different times in a developing organism reflects an appreciation of the complexity of organic and psychological phenomena.

In short, developmental change may be characterized by both continuous and discontinuous events, or some processes may proceed in a continuous fashion while others occur in a discrete manner. Just because one behavioral system may reflect developmental continuity or discontinuity does not mean that all behavioral systems develop in the same way. An integrative or synthesis approach is a viable alternative, one in which both continuity and discontinuity are recognized as aspects of development. The argument that only one universal law must exist to account for development does not receive much support from most developmentalists. The many years spent in attempts to empirically resolve the continuity–discontinuity issue have been in vain. To proclaim either position as the only true model of development is to declare one's faith or theoretical bias. There are data and theoretical arguments to support both positions independently, and also their simultaneous existence and operation in both ontogenetic and phylogenetic development (Bitterman, 1975; Carmichael,

1970; Kendler & Kendler, 1962; Langer, 1970; Werner, 1957). Even Piaget (1950), a staunch proponent of discontinuity, does not deny the existence of continuity phenomena. As Langer (1969) has pointed out, the question of continuity versus discontinuity is a theoretical, logical, and interpretive issue, not an empirical and statistical one. Actual observation of these processes cannot be demonstrated at this time, but one's theoretical bias can lead to the interpretation and presentation of data to fit expectancies. Instead of finding behavioral development occurring in a continuous pattern or segmented into stages, psychologists may represent development in one of these models for reasons of convenience and theory construction.

Models and theories should be evaluated on the basis of their utility in generating testable hypotheses and stimulating further research and understanding. It is futile to attempt to evaluate them on the basis of their existence in reality or whether they are true or false. However, the implications and derivations of models and theories may be true or false. Their validity depends on the data generated by the predictions of certain events that are inherent in the model or theory in question (Hall & Lindzey, 1975).

To illustrate our discussion of models employed as a non-specific approach to developmental psychology, we will consider the major theories that have produced the central pool of knowledge and ideas about development. Langer (1969) has synthesized and critically reviewed the major contemporary theories of development. He identifies the three approaches that have dominated the research and thinking in developmental psychology as (1) psychoanalytic theory, (2) the mechanical mirror, and (3) the organic lamp. A brief presentation of these approaches to development will provide a theoretical perspective of the field, which should clarify your thinking about the subject matter to follow.

Sigmund Freud's psychoanalytic theory of human development is deeply rooted in evolution and biological, instinctual drives. These inborn, instinctual impulses continually strive for expression and satisfaction. They soon come into conflict with other psychic components, which emerge and develop in response to environmental pressures, societal controls, and cultural restrictions. Ultimately, compromises are made that presumably reduce internal conflict and lead to more or less healthy development. The psychosexual stages of development, which are discontinuous events, are crucial to personality development in traditional psychoanalytic theory. Basic, enduring developmental patterns and outcomes are said to be formed during the period of early childhood. While Freud had little, if any, direct clinical contact with children, he devoted much of his writings to infant and child development, particularly personality development. His theory of ontogeny was derived from observations of his own children and reports of childhood memories from his patients in analysis. Freud did treat one disturbed child. This was the famous case of Little Hans, who was analyzed by Freud via the boy's father, and not directly.

The psychoanalytic theory of development, while highly influential, has been of questionable value to our understanding of development, and has stirred much dissension and acrimony among psychologists. Essentially, psychoanalytic theory is a theory of psychopathology, lacking precision about the nature of its basic concepts and their relationship to actual events and behavior. As a theory, its vague structure and multiple interpretations of behavioral development generate serious difficulties for understanding and explaining developmental phenomena. The psychoanalytic view of ontogenesis is one of abstract clinical inferences and complex interpretations that cannot be measured or verified. Additionally, psychoanalytic descriptions of development attribute to the infant and young child a degree of complex thought processes whose existence is improbable. Despite the ease with which psychoanalytic theory can describe virtually all aspects of behavior, one fails to find any scientifically robust predictions of behavior.

Despite its shortcomings, psychoanalysis has made three major contributions to developmental psychology. It has drawn attention to the effects of early childhood experiences on ontogenesis, launched the idea of ontogenetic determinism, and attempted to provide a rational, causal interpretation of human development. Freud has generated more ideas and stimulated more research inquiry than any other figure in the history of psychology. His contributions remain controversial and sometimes bitterly disputed, a state of affairs well summarized by Pratt (1939):

Freud will be remembered long after the names of most scientific psychologists have been forgotten. . . . The tremendous sweep of his imagination has enabled him to see connections where narrower minds see nothing. Whether the connections are really *there or not, no one knows, not even Freud himself; or if he does, he has committed an unpardonable scientific sin by not revealing to the rest of the world the secret of his knowledge. Many generations of psychologists will spend their lives trying to translate the poetry of Freud into the prose of science. (p. 164)*

In later chapters we will examine further the empirical basis of psychoanalytic approaches to developmental problems.

The mechanical mirror is Langer's phrase for a learning approach to development. This theory states that behavioral development is controlled by, and is a function of, the physical and social environment. An organism's development is viewed as simply a reflection of the environmental reinforcement history of that organism. It is also an automatic, almost mechanical process, which is why Langer called it a mechanical mirror. This strict learning theory approach stems from the work of B. F. Skinner, a psychologist of undisputed influence throughout psychology.

Learning theorists view development as a continuous, gradual accumulation of behavior responses that develop from a set of basic reflexes present at birth. Conditioning phenomena resulting from interactions with the environment begin almost immediately, inexorably shaping the ontogenetic patterns of the individual by the continuous, quantitative acquisition of learned behaviors. Conditioning, whether classical (respondent) or instrumental (operant), is the process underlying the development of all dimensions of behavior and psychological functioning. Thus, response patterns are acquired, modified, and remodified; they grow increasingly complex in a continuous process of learning and reinforcement. The so-called S–R (stimulus–response) approach has generated a good deal of data related to development, but as Langer (1969) points out, the emphasis has been on demonstrations and research programs rather than on theory building. In his evaluation, Langer (1969) states:

The search for the mechanisms that govern the acquisition and modification of behavior is an important part of psychology. The question that arises with respect to the mechancial mirror view is whether it actually looks for mechanisms of acquisition and modification or whether it merely applies the preconceived notion that the growth of all behavior is caused by conditioning and thereby overlooks the actual mechanisms governing acquisition and modification. A less biased investigation might well reveal that the mechanisms are different for different species and for humans of different ages. (p. 85)

We will be dealing with learning approaches to development in more detail in later chapters.

Langer (1969) describes the theoretical positions of Piaget (1950) and Werner (1957) as representative of what he calls the organic lamp theory of development. Such an approach emphasizes that development proceeds in a direction determined by the individual's own actions. This is an autogenetic position, one which views development as an unfolding of inherent characteristics and potentials in a predetermined direction of stable, complex psychological organization. Transformations of psychological organization occur in a sequence of stages from simple to complex. Behaviors and thought processes (cognition) are spontaneously initiated by infants who strive for organization and meaning.

Although this and all other stage theories of development strongly stress qualitative, discontinuous events as characterizing development, there is no explicit denial of quantitative, continuous changes. Such continuous changes, however, are given little significance for development. Similarly, biological–environmental interaction is viewed as an inevitable process contributing to development, but autogenous or self-initiating factors play a larger theoretical role than environmental factors. Langer (1969) stresses that "the environment . . . in organic lamp theory is merely the occasion for a scene of, and not the cause or agent of, development" (p. 157).

There is a complex technology attached to organic lamp theories. A vast amount of research has been stimulated by such theories, particularly that of Jean Piaget. The findings are not entirely clear or consistent, but the impact of Piaget's theory on psychology has been both extensive and influential. These theories also are subject to serious criticism with regard to clarity, assumptions, and prediction, and we will be examining this approach in more detail in Chapter Six.

It should be apparent by now that there are widely disparate and incompatible approaches to development. Controversy, both rational and irrational, should be expected and even welcomed, for controversy breeds new and more vigorous research that, in turn, establishes a science.

RESEARCH METHODS IN DEVELOPMENTAL PSYCHOLOGY

*O*ur discussion to this point should have emphasized the need for adequate research methodology in developmental psychology. The current state of the art in developmental psychology is partly a reflection of inadequate research design or the failure to recognize the limitations of various methodological strategies. Competence in experimental design and methodology is not a skill required exclusively by students interested in research or academic pursuits. The argument that such research skills are irrelevant to people interested only in clinical psychology, psychotherapy, or the other helping professions is an empty one. Indeed, the awesome complexities and lack of adequate knowledge in the applied areas of psychology require an even greater degree of analytical sophistication and methodological prowess than so-called "laboratory" psychology. An interest in applied psychology does not rule out the need to know how to critically evaluate research programs, demonstration projects, and the subsequent findings.

Familiarity with research methods is no less important to the applied professional whose practices and procedures derive from research findings in laboratory science. Intelligent and responsible clinical applications of laboratory findings demand the practitioner's critical evaluation of the validity of those findings before they are put into effect with people. Responsible practicing psychologists, however far removed from the university setting, continue to read psychological journals in order to maintain their activities at the most current level of available knowledge. The credibility and acceptance of new procedures and techniques must be based on the critical analysis and evaluation of the research design and methodology employed. Research findings and conclusions generated by faulty design cannot be accepted as scientific data, and potential clinical implications or applications must certainly await further empirical investigation and justification.

At all levels of involvement, from the laboratory to the clinic, a sophisticated evaluation of research is an absolute requirement. The uncritical, indiscriminate acceptance of data reported in the literature probably has done more to impede the growth of psychology than any other factor. Our discussion of research methods is, of course, only part of a general introduction to developmental methodology. We want to acquaint you with the basic approaches to developmental problems in the hope that an analytical perspective will emerge, facilitating creative study of the material to follow. If you acquire an appreciation of methodology in the context of developmental problems and interests, then advanced study in research design should take on more meaning as a relevant component of training. Keep in mind that questions and ideas about development can only be answered and clarified by sound scientific approaches and procedures.

Experimental and Quasi-Experimental Approaches

There are a number of research methods and approaches available to the developmental psychologist, depending on the kind of information sought, the organisms being studied, and the experimental environment within which one has to work. These various methods are more or less efficient in producing acceptable scientific information. We can place all research efforts and approaches into one of two general categories: experimental and quasi-experimental designs (Campbell & Stanley, 1963). Experimental designs are characterized by the manipulation of independent variables and the observation of their effects on some dependent variable or variables. Manipulation refers to the ability of the researcher to isolate, control, and systematically vary some environmental condition, process, or event (the independent variable) in order to observe its impact or effect on some behavioral event or response (the dependent variable). This methodology is the classic independent variable design that describes laboratory science, regardless of the discipline or field of study.

This experimental procedure is seldom as easy as it sounds, and there are many situations in which this ideal scientific methodology cannot be reasonably attained. In such situations, the best alternative is the quasi-experimental design. Here, the experimental setting may be a natural, social, or clinical situation in which the investigator is unable to manipulate the independent variable, as required for a "true" experiment. However, the experimenter is still interested in the potential relationship between an independent variable and some aspect of behavior, the dependent variable. Moreover, the nonmanipulable independent variable already exists in different degrees in the natural setting, or else has existed in the past. There are two minimal criteria for such an independent variable. The experimenter must be able to measure the level at which it exists or has existed, or at least be able to sort the variable into qualitatively different categories. We are referring to a quantifiable independent variable in the former case, and a nonquantifiable independent variable in the latter case. An independent variable that cannot be measured and quantified must at least be identifiable, so that we can recognize it as existing at different levels, strengths, or categories.

Suppose, for example, that we want to determine the relationship between low birth weight in newborn infants and later learning difficulties in school. We cannot manipulate the independent variable of low birth weight. It is an independent variable that already exists or has existed in a natural setting. However, we can identify and quantify low birth weight by using hospital and pediatric records. Then we can select a large sample of schoolchildren, some with a history of low birth weight and some with normal or average birth weight. We can evaluate school performance under controlled conditions (dependent variable) and establish relationships between low birth weight conditions and normal weight conditions.

This approach to investigating the relationship between birth weights and subsequent learning problems is an example of a quasi-experiment. Note that in this example our independent variable of interest, birth weight, can be quantified by hospital records. What if we were interested in the relationship between maternal emotional patterns during pregnancy and some aspect of infant development, such as infant feeding problems? We might be dealing with a nonmanipulable independent variable such as anxiety, general adjustment, attitudes toward pregnancy, neurosis, or the like. In this case, our task would be to reliably identify and differentiate such emotional patterns into arbitrarily determined levels such as high and low or positive and negative. Then we would try to relate certain aspects of feeding problems to these two categories of maternal pregnancy states. Differentiation of high and low or positive and negative emotional patterns represents qualitative levels of the independent variable rather than quantitative measures.

In each of these examples, we have conducted controlled observation of our dependent variables. Without control over our independent variables, however, we cannot draw conclusions about causal events between the independent and dependent variables. That is, in the examples given above we would be unable to claim that low birth weight or maternal pregnancy state has a direct, causal effect on later learning problems or infant feeding difficulties. There may be many other uncontrolled independent variables operating that contribute to, or have more causal significance for, the behaviors observed.

Classical Designs in Developmental Research

The term "classical" refers to standard, traditional research designs that have long been employed in the study of developmental psychology. Two classical research designs have characterized developmental research over the years. These are the cross-sectional and the longitudinal designs. The cross-sectional method is a basic research design in general psychology. It becomes a developmental paradigm when some dimension of behavior is measured over several age-groups. The intent in this or any other developmental design is to obtain information about trends of development.

The cross-sectional method involves randomly selecting different groups of subjects across a range of age levels and then comparing the performance of each group on some dependent variable. The use of different subjects in different age groups, all of whom are exposed to the independent variable of interest and observed at the same time on some dependent measure, provides information about developmental trends. A basic assumption in this design is that developmental trends are revealed if the age-group samples are truly representative and no serious sampling errors have occurred. In many instances of developmental research, the independent variable in cross-sectional designs is chronological age—the age-group itself. This nonexperimental approach has generated most of our normative, descriptive data on the age-related emergence and growth patterns of various behaviors in infants and children. But the use of age as an independent variable is a purely descriptive approach, revealing nothing about functional relationships with the dependent variables.

In cross-sectional designs, the investigator measures the average performance within each of the age-groups. These averages can then be plotted on a graph to obtain a picture of trends in developmental patterns of behavior. Since the end result is a group average, the importance of representative sampling and control over other independent variables becomes obvious. As a simplified example of a cross-sectional study, let us suppose that a psychologist is interested in the emergence and development of the fear response in infants. The researcher might decide to obtain random samples of infants ranging in age from 4 to 12 months, separated by spans of 1 month. The total group of infants would then be composed of, say, thirty 4-month-old infants, thirty 5-month-old infants, and so on up to 12 months of age.

The experiment is conducted under controlled laboratory conditions. The independent variable is systematically varied by presenting unfamiliar adults to the infants and observing signs of a fear response such as crying, avoidance, and struggling to escape. The experiment could be made more complex by introducing additional independent variables such as presence or absence of mother, distance from mother and unfamiliar adult, and comparative reactions to unfamiliar adults and children. Overt fear responses could then be noted under each experimental condition and combination of independent variables. Observations of fear responses are recorded for each age group and averages computed for each group.

The investigator might end up with data suggesting the average age at which fear to strangers appears in infants, its intensity as a function of presence or absence of mother, distance or other factors, and at what age the response disappears, if at all. By taking the averages for each group and plotting the data points, the researcher would probably develop a graph like the one shown in Figure 1-1.

The cross-sectional approach is a fast and relatively inexpensive way to obtain developmental data. These practical considerations are the major advantages of the cross-sectional designs. There are, however, serious limitations on cross-sectional

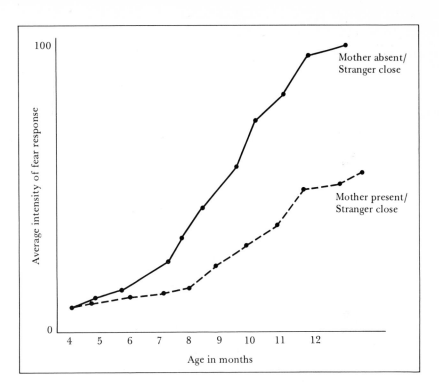

Figure 1-1
Fictitious data on the relationship between fear and age.

studies. These limitations will be discussed in the next section.

In longitudinal designs, a single sample of subjects is selected and their responses are measured two or more times at different ages. The same subjects are studied over an extended time period by collecting repeated measurements of the dependent variable. The longitudinal design offers some advantages over the cross-sectional method. For instance, the longitudinal method enables an investigator to examine individual subject changes over a period of time, the rates of these changes, and how behavioral patterns are affected by other known independent variables. This information cannot be obtained with the cross-sectional design because of its use of group averages and the loss of individual subject identity. Longitudinal designs are expensive and take a relatively long time to complete—practical considerations that may be a limiting factor in their use.

The research problem of the development of infant fear responses can also provide an example of the longitudinal design. Instead of selecting different groups of subjects at different ages, a single sample of 4-month-old infants is selected. The experimental procedures remain the same as described above, but the entire group of infants is observed under each experimental condition at predetermined time periods of 1 month. The result is repeated measurements of each infant's fear responses, taken once a month from 4 months of age through 12 months of age.

Thus, when this study utilizes a longitudinal design, it will take at least 8 months to complete, whereas the cross-sectional approach might enable the completion of the research project within a 1- or 2-month period. Unquestionably, the longitudinal approach to this particular research problem would provide us with much more information on the trend of development of fear responses in infants. But it involves much more time, and much more effort in keeping track of the subjects' whereabouts, obtaining parental cooperation, scheduling tests, and so on. Under ideal conditions, the data should be comparable, but often this is not the case. As with cross-sectional designs, there are difficulties and limitations involved in the use of the longitudinal method.

Methodological Inadequacies of Classical Designs

Historically, classical design approaches to development have done much to advance our knowledge of developmental psychology. However, inherent methodological deficiencies in these research approaches have made their almost exclusive use in developmental research a barrier to more unequivocal and significant progress, and may also have led us down some wrong paths. Methodological problems in research designs lead to inconsistent data and incorrect conclusions concerning development. These kinds of problems contribute to the conceptual difficulties and issues discussed earlier in this chapter.

There is a substantial collection of criticisms directed at the classical developmental designs. Friedrich (1972) has presented a cogent review of the literature arguing against the use of classical designs, citing a number of developmental psychologists who have challenged the validity of classical approaches. Most of these critics complain that classical designs cannot identify other, uncontrolled factors influencing research outcomes, and so they concentrate too much on age as the main

Table 1-1
Methodological Deficiencies in Classical Designs

LONGITUDINAL DESIGNS	CROSS-SECTIONAL DESIGNS
1. Selective sampling biases (non-representative samples) which weaken comparability of results obtained.	1. Selective sampling biases.
2. Selective survival in which group composition changes over time as a result of death or incapacitation.	2. Selective survival effects.
3. Selective drop-out due to subjects' loss of interest, change of residence, etc., during the course of the study. Sampling bias is the result.	
4. Testing effects due to repeated measurements result in contamination of dependent variable.	
5. Generation effects arising from cultural differences, background, etc. in different age groups.	3. Generation effects.

factor in development. For example, Friedrich (1972) cites Kessen's (1960) description of the weaknesses of cross-sectional and longitudinal designs. Kessen argues that classical approaches fail to provide the following critical information that should characterize developmental research: (1) age interacting with particular populations, (2) age interacting with environmental change, and (3) age interacting simultaneously with environmental and population differences. More specifically, Baltes (1968, cited in Friedrich, 1972) has detailed the methodological shortcomings of classical developmental designs. Baltes' basic arguments are presented in Table 1-1. Friedrich concludes his critical evaluation by emphasizing that neither classical design yields unambiguous data and that, at best, they are to some extent invalid.

There are alternative research methods, now available to developmental scientists, that compensate for the inadequacies of classical methods. These new methods promise to produce significant advances in development research. They include the use of multidimensional developmental design components (variables associated with ontogenesis) in multivariate research designs and analysis. These methods abandon simple, unidimensional approaches to development, and consider instead several basic developmental parameters and their differential contributions to development. Such multivariate designs require variables that are individually relevant and reliable. The selection and use of several variables that are likely to have little effect on a dependent variable does not produce more powerful results than procedures that study variables individually. The utility of multivariate designs lies in the intelligent selection of the variables to be combined.

Schaie (1965) has also described "sequential strategies" of developmental designs, which combine longitudinal and cross-sectional methods and permit sophisticated, complex, multivariate analyses of factors contributing to developmental change, while avoiding confounding effects of classical designs.

There have been some attempts to diminish the inherent methodological deficiencies of classical research designs. One such effort is that of Bell (1953, 1954), who has proposed a research approach that combines the components of the cross-sectional and longitudinal designs. This procedure has been offered as an alternative to classical designs. Bell describes this technique as a convergence approach, accelerated longitudinal design, or short-term longitudinal design. It combines the cross-sectional procedure of sample selection with the longitudinal feature of individual subject follow-up over time. For example, the convergence approach to our study of infant fear responses would involve the random selection of two groups of infants—one group of 4-month-old infants and one group of 8-month-old infants. The experiment would be conducted as previously described, but over a time period of 4 months.

The result would be to obtain 9 months of data over a 4-month period. In addition, this design allows us to compare the original group of 8-month-old infants at the start of the experiment with the 8-month-old infants who were 4 months old at the beginning of the experiment. This comparison would enable us to learn about the similarity of these two groups and about the possible effects of the experiment on the development of the fear response. That is, does the experimental condition alter the course of fear development relative to naive subjects? The accelerated longitudinal approach to this particular problem can be presented as follows:

```
CROSS-SECTIONAL AGE SAMPLES     LONGITUDINAL
                                MONTHLY
                                DATA
        4 months                5   6   7   8
                                         ╱
        8 months ◄──────────────         9  10  11  12
```

Bell's alternative design reduces, but does not eliminate, the difficulties of classical designs. However, the convergence approach is a better choice of design in many instances of developmental research. A comparison of conclusions drawn from the use of different developmental designs is shown in Table 1-2. We will explore the reasons behind these differing conclusions in later chapters. For the present we will merely point out the fact that different experimental designs may produce contradictory answers to the same questions.

Table 1-2
Comparison of Inferences Drawn From Cross-sectional,
Longitudinal, and Short-term Longitudinal Studies

VARIABLE	CROSS-SECTIONAL	LONGITUDINAL	SHORT-TERM LONGITUDINAL
Verbal meaning	Sharp decrement from middle adulthood to old age	Modest gain throughout life from young adult plateau	Modest decrement from young adult plateau
Space	Sharp decrement from young adult peak to old age	Modest decrement from adult plateau	Almost no decrement until advanced age
Reasoning	Sharp decrement from young adult peak to old age	Modest gain from young adult plateau till old age	Modest decrement from middle adulthood to old age
Number	Modest gain and loss before and subsequent to mid-life plateau	Modest gain from early adulthood to plateau at advanced age	Very modest decrement from plateau in middle adulthood
Word fluency	Moderate decrement from plateau extending over major portion of adulthood	Moderate gains from young adult levels	Sharp decrements from young adult levels

(Adapted from Friedrich, 1972.)

Experimental versus Nonexperimental Research Methods in Developmental Psychology

While experimental methods of research are the principal procedures for functional analysis and theory construction, other methodologies also are employed in developmental research. The major nonexperimental approaches include research designs using correlational methods, normative methods, and the method of naturalistic or controlled observation. We will look at each of these methods in this section.

CORRELATIONAL METHODS Experimental research methods involve the systematic manipulation of independent variables. In correlational research methods, by contrast, no attempt is made to manipulate independent variables or to change the conditions in which particular phenomena occur. Rather, the researcher simply attempts to measure the relationship between two or more occurrences, events, conditions, or situations. In this approach, information is sought about how two variables vary in relation to each other. Correlational methods provide a numerical value that describes the degree of relationship between two variables and the direction of the relationship. Numerical values of correlations are called correlation coefficients and range from +1.00 to −1.00. If no relationship exists, the value of the correlation cofficient is zero. If two variables vary together in the same direction, they are positively correlated. Negative correlations reflect relationships that vary in opposite directions.

Correlational data are important to the extent of their predictive value, their usefulness in determining the reliability and validity of psychological tests and measuring instruments or procedures, and their heuristic value in pursuing experimental tests of suggested hypotheses and cause-and-effect relationships. Correlational data, however, also have limitations. They cannot generate the kinds of conclusions that controlled experimental research produces. A relationship between A and B may mean that A is caused by B, B is caused by A, or that A and B are both influenced by some third, unknown variable C. It is important to understand that correlations do not imply causation, where experimental data do suggest cause and effect situations. Correlations between events may be due to any number of uncontrolled variables, and it is impossible to attribute causality to such relationships. A correlation between low birth weight and subsequent poor school performance does not imp y that low birth weight causes later learning problems. Other uncontrolled and unknown variables entering into the situation include genetic considerations, maternal age and health, intrauterine conditions, fetal characteristics, postnatal environmental factors, and socioeconomic characteristics. Each of these is a global stimulus complex—that is, each contains a host of variables also related to low birth weight.

NORMATIVE METHODS   Normative approaches to development are characterized by descriptive, detailed observational data on age-related appearance of various behaviors. Normative studies can be conducted within the framework of either cross-sectional or longitudinal designs. Generally, the purpose of this approach is to establish a set of expectancies about the average ages at which certain behaviors first appear in normal children. These normative data provide guidelines for normal patterns and sequences in motor, cognitive, language, and personal–social development. By furnishing data on the average age of appearance of these behaviors, along with normal limits of variability, norms may serve as a basis for clinical and educational applications and assessment. Significant developmental deviations from normative expectancies may signal clinical problems or abnormality, particularly of central nervous system development.

Normative data must be used cautiously and with special awareness of normal variability in age-related behavioral development. Because of individual differences in rates of maturation and psychological development, the limits of normal variation from "average" are rather broad. Therefore, the observation that an infant is several months behind the average age in displaying a particular behavior may have no clinical or diagnostic significance. Also, the bulk of normative data is at least 30 years old, and it is unlikely that norms remain constant from one generation to another, particularly when significant changes occur in socioeconomic conditions, rearing practices, and medical and health technology. Normative research was a dominant activity during the first four decades of the twentieth century, but there is little current research that can be described as classical normative research.

NATURALISTIC METHODS   In the method of naturalistic or controlled observation, natural settings are used to study behavior. Under realistic, nonlaboratory conditions, investigators meticulously observe and record every behavioral event that occurs. Although there is no manipulation of variables, the environmental conditions for specific target behaviors are selected for observation and description. The purpose of the naturalistic approach is to study individual development as it occurs in, and interacts with, a normal environment. This approach is sometimes referred to as an ecological approach (Barker & Wright, 1949). It resembles the naturalistic studies of ethologists, who study species-specific behaviors of such creatures as insects, birds, fishes, and apes. While the method of controlled observation may reveal behavior patterns not observed under laboratory conditions, it is a purely descriptive technique. Of course, experimental laboratory procedures can also be conducted under conditions that are natural or normal to the individual organism being studied. Laboratory investigations need not be totally artificial.

A HISTORICAL SURVEY OF DEVELOPMENTAL PSYCHOLOGY

*T*he appreciation of developmental psychology as a scientific discipline is heightened by a historical perspective on its emergence and its struggle for scientific status. The evolution of thought that forged contemporary developmental psychology emanated from nineteenth century science. Evolutionary doctrine was the single most important scientific event for the developmental sciences, for it served as both the vehicle and propellant for the emergence and growth of what is now recognized as developmental psychology. By the nineteenth century, the organic sciences had already been inexorably led to the study of human origins and development. But prescientific, doctrinaire, and exotic proclamations of organic life forms lingered until they were exposed to the withering light of Darwin's proposals. The following historical survey is heavily based upon Robert Grinder's (1967) excellent, scholarly book, *A History of Genetic Psychology,* which is required reading for serious students of developmental psychology.

What we now call developmental psychology was historically known as "genetic" psychology, a term referring to genesis, or the beginning or origin of something. It should not be con-

A graduate student from Stanford University takes notes on children at play at the nearby Bing Nursery School in Palo Alto, California. The naturalistic method allows the researcher to observe subjects in a familiar, nonlaboratory setting. As such, individual observations may be more accurate than those obtained in a controlled laboratory setting, but these observations can only describe behavior; causal relationships cannot be determined.

(Photo by Van Bucher/Photo Researchers, Inc.)

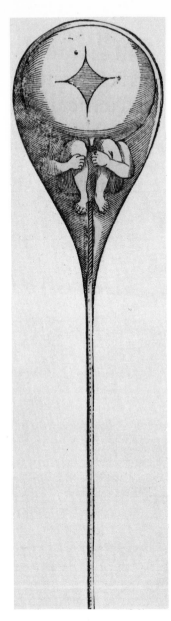

Figure 1-2
A preformationist view of a "Homunculus" in a human sperm cell.

(From Hartsoeker, 1694. Reproduction courtesy of the National Library of Science.)

fused with genetics, a branch of biology that deals with the study of heredity and variation in plants and animals. The term genetic was apparently first used in 1831 to describe growth, variation, and heredity, following Karl von Baer's discovery of mammalian egg cells (Grinder, 1967). Von Baer later did much to establish the science of embryology and encourage research and thinking in the developmental sciences. His influence on the nineteenth and twentieth century pioneers of developmental psychology was powerful and persuasive.

Prior to von Baer's discoveries, the organic sciences were dominated by the doctrines of special creation and preformationism. These theological beliefs reached their heights in the work of Charles Bonnet, an eighteenth century philosopher. Bonnet disavowed all ideas of formation and development, declaring instead that all the generations of individuals who were destined to exist until the end of time were produced at the moment of creation. The preformationists believed that special creation therefore fixed the kind and number of living things on earth, and that embryonic life forms were already complete, with growth representing simply an enlargement of the parts already present. The invention of the microscope merely strengthened preformationism. Grinder (1967) states that "the early microscopists, with fallible instruments and fertile imaginations, thought they saw a minute, preformed 'homunculus' neatly encased within the sperm cell" (p. 2). Such were the bonds from which the sciences had to escape in the nineteenth century (Figure 1-2).

The tenacity of dogma and the resistance to new scientific discovery is legendary in the history of science. The triumph of evolutionary theory over prescientific doctrines was undoubtedly not attributable to scientific discovery alone. Max Planck's (1949) bitter comment on the history of science is probably even more discriptive of the nineteenth century than the twentieth. Planck (1949) remarked that "a scientific truth does not triumph by convincing its opponents and making them see the light, but rather because its opponents eventually die and a new generation grows up that is familiar with it" (p. 33). This was the climate in which the first advances toward developmental theory and knowledge were made. But if evolutionary theory set the stage for developmental science, it was

The last known photograph of Charles Darwin (1809–1882) taken at his country home. Although Darwin did not originate the theory of evolution, the volume of his observations on the mutability of species and his development of the concept of natural selection, that is, "survival of the fittest," did much to win serious general acceptance of evolution as nature's way of life.

(Photo courtesy of the Bettmann Archive, Inc.)

unable to provide the script for its direction, for the dissolution of special creation and preformation swept away the only available explanation of organic development.

Jean Baptiste Lamarck, the French zoologist, was among the first to present a reasonable alternative to the doctrine of special creation. In 1809, Lamarck published *Zoological Philosophy*, in which he described his theory of evolution. Seeing the continuity of relationships along the phylogenetic scale of plants and animals, Lamarck attempted to explain life-form variations with "two laws of nature which are always verified by observation." These were (1) the law of use and disuse and (2) the law of inheritance of acquired characters. Lamarck stressed the role of environmental pressures in determining the shape and organization of life forms, and declared that environmental changes produced changes in organic life. The law of use and disuse stated that the presence, size, and strength of any organ is dependent upon the length of time over which it is used and the degree to which it is used. The law of acquired characters stated that all environmentally produced organic acquisitions or losses are preserved by hereditary transmission to the offspring, provided that such modifications are common to the parents. Specific structure was seen by Lamarck as shaped by the environment and by learned behavior patterns or habits. It should be pointed out that Lamarck viewed the operation of his basic laws as producing gradual, permanent changes only when the environmental pressures existed over hundreds of generations. Failure to recognize this aspect of Lamarckian theory was to play a role in twentieth century genetic psychology, as we shall see.

Fifty years later, Darwin published his *Origin of Species*, launching phylogenetic, ontogenetic, and comparative psychology as scientific disciplines. Unlike Lamarck, Darwin had amassed a prodigious amount of data and evidence for his theory of evolution. The next challenge for Darwin was to develop a theoretical explanation of heredity transmission and species variation. (Mendel's particulate theory of heredity, published in 1866, remained unknown until the twentieth century.)

Darwin adopted the Lamarckian theory of acquired characters as a factor in natural selection, since there was no other available theoretical explanation compatible with his theory of evolution. To describe the hereditary mechanism reponsible for variation and natural selection, Darwin derived his provisional hypothesis of pangenesis. Pangenesis proposed that reproductive cells were composed of atomic sized "gemmules" that originated from all body cells. These gemmules were capable of reproducing the cells from which they arose. They reached the ovaries and testes by migrating through the blood stream. Various other pangenetic theories followed during the second half of the nineteenth century, and all of them were discredited with the discovery of Mendel's principles of hereditary transmission. Grinder (1967) points out that theories of pangenesis are today viewed as sheer speculation, but he goes on to say that "the important fact is obscured that Lamarckianism, hence genetic psychology, could not have survived without them" (p. 78).

Darwin's proposals stirred whirlpools of activity among sci-

The Austrian monk Gregor Mendel (1822–1884) cultivating garden peas, his partners in pioneering the field of genetics. Mendel, having failed to become a teacher within his Augustinian order, devoted 8 years to studying the effects of crossbreeding on seven characteristics of the pea plant and published his findings in 1866. Two years later he was elected abbot of his monastery and abandoned his scientific studies. Although disregarded at first, his work was rediscovered by the scientific community in 1900, laying the foundation for modern genetic research.

(Photo by Abigail Heyman/ Magnum Photo Library Print.)

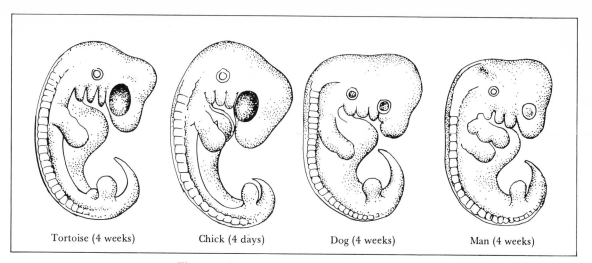

Tortoise (4 weeks)   Chick (4 days)   Dog (4 weeks)   Man (4 weeks)

Figure 1-3
Embryos of four vertebrates, from Haeckel's *The History of Creation,*
1906. Haeckel and others saw these close similarities as persuasive evidence in support of the recapitulation theory.

entists and philosophers. Among those rallying to Darwin's
support were paleontologists and biologists, who embraced the
young science of embryology not only as a way of verifying
Darwin's theory of evolution but also as a way of establishing
a new science of individual development. Earlier in the nineteenth century, von Baer had begun his studies in embryology,
comparing embryological development in different animals.
Von Baer found that he could not clearly differentiate between
various animal embryos during their early stages of development. His report inspired a series of publications on the
relationship between ontogeny and phylogeny, culminating in
the theory of recapitulation: Ontogeny recapitulates phylogeny—the development of the individual repeats the development of the race. Led by Haeckel, the proponents of the
concept declared that it was the key to understanding individual human development, and that the unfolding of human
behavior patterns would reflect the evolution of human existence (see Figure 1-3). Early in the twentieth century, G. Stanley
Hall accepted recapitulation theory as the first principle of
genetic psychology. But recapitulation theory was discredited
shortly thereafter with the recognition that ontogeny reveals
nothing more than gross, obvious clues to phylogeny. In short,

the application of this principle as an explanatory concept of evolution and human development turned out to be little more than sheer speculation.

The rediscovery in 1900 of Mendel's publication marked a significant advance in biology and tightened Darwin's grip on the natural sciences. Scientific interest focused more and more on the psychological evolution and development of man. The previous concentration on phylogenesis was of little value to understanding human consciousness, reasoning, intelligence, and culture. Others filled the gap left by Darwin's neglect of man in *The Origin of Species.* Scientists such as Thomas Huxley and George Romanes ushered in the science of human development in the twentieth century. But Lamarckianism and recapitulation theory were still firmly entrenched; they shaped the notion of phylogenetic continuity of mental faculties that was developed in Darwin's later publications and in those of his supporters. In many theories, speculation continued to flourish.

According to Grinder (1967), George John Romanes deserves to be considered a pioneer of cognitive theorists, as he attempted to trace the history of mental evolution. In his volumes *Animal Intelligence, Mental Evolution in Animals,* and *Mental Evolution in Man,* published between 1883 and 1887, Romanes attempted to create a descriptive template of mental development. In the absence of evidence for his position, Romanes did not hesitate to insert anthropomorphic speculations based on animal behavior. Romanes' diagram of mental evolution is shown in Figure 1-4. For Romanes, this diagram described "in how striking quantitative, as well as qualitative, a manner the development of individual mind follows the order of mental evolution in the animal kingdom" (Grinder, 1967, pp. 171–172).

Such speculative humanizing of animal behavior began to draw criticism from other scientists. C. Lloyd Morgan (1909) presented strong arguments against these practices. He emphasized the need to separate facts from speculations on the origin and description of animal behavior. Morgan's (1909) principle of parsimony was a reaction against speculative and complex explanations of behavior: "In no case may we interpret an action as the outcome of the exercise of a higher psychical faculty, if it can be interpreted as the outcome of the

Figure 1-4
Romanè's (1884) Diagram of Mental Evolution.

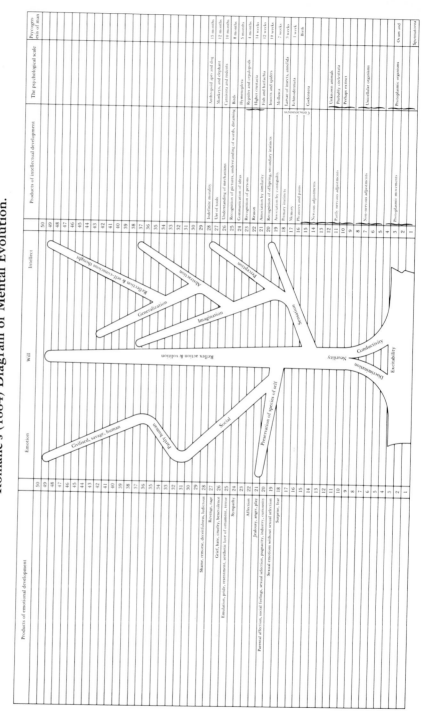

exercise of one which stands lower in the psychological scale" (p. 53). Undermined by such criticisms, the anecdotal, anthropomorphic descriptions of animal development, which had characterized much of the thinking and writing during this period, soon lost their popularity and acceptance.

G. Stanley Hall, considered to be the father of child psychology, was the last influential advocate of nineteenth century genetic psychology. An unrelentingly enthusiastic scholar, Hall became president and professor of Clark University where, in 1893, he introduced the first course ever offered in genetic psychology. Hall was a Neo-Lamarckian and a recapitulationist, extending and applying these concepts further than ever before. He initiated studies of child development, having published the first such American research in 1883. His publication, "The Content of Children's Minds," in 1891 marked the beginning of the child study movement in the United States (Grinder, 1967). Also in 1891, Hall founded the first journal dealing with child and adolescent studies, the *Pedagogical Seminary*. He went on to develop the questionnaire method for studying children, and in 1904 published a two-volume work, *Adolescence*.

Hall's fervent contributions and activities in genetic psychology were laced with an undisguised and admittedly unscientific commitment to, and acceptance of, recapitulation theory (Grinder, 1967). Hall firmly believed that cultural as well as phylogenetic stages of development are repeated in ontogenesis. Therefore, he used cultural recapitulation to explain the different stages of children's play activities, which presumably represented "rehearsals" of ancient activities. Grinder (1967) quotes a student of Hall as saying, years after genetic psychology had vanished, "There never would have been a recapitulation theory had as much attention been given to the dissimilarities as was given to the similarities" (p. 28).

The critics of genetic psychology grew as psychology developed in the twentieth century. Mendelism displaced Neo-Lamarckian views of evolution, and recapitulation theory was finally discredited. Edward L. Thorndike was among the foremost critics of G. S. Hall and genetic psychology. He severely attacked the nonscientific aspects of genetic psychology, while he contributed significantly to experimental and educational psychology as well as to developmental psychology.

Thorndike remains a substantial figure in the history of psychology. In 1913, Thorndike published *Educational Psychology* in which "he pronounced what amounts to the last rites for recapitulation theory and genetic psychology" (Grinder, 1967, p. 237). Armed with the knowledge of twentieth century science, Thorndike, in voicing his objections to recapitulation theory, concluded with the statement, "Consequently, one cannot help thinking that the influence which it has exerted upon students of human nature is due, not to rational claims, but to its rhetorical attractiveness" (Grinder, 1967, p. 244).

And here the history of developmental psychology begins, amidst the death throes of genetic psychology. As Grinder points out in his revealing treatise, there is little relationship between genetic psychology and contemporary developmental psychology, but the significance of genetic psychology lies in its agonizing struggle, against formidable obstacles, to focus on the study of human development.

REFERENCES

Barker, R. G., & Wright, H. F. Psychological ecology and the problem of psychosocial development. *Child Development,* 1949, *20,* 131–143.

Bell, R. Q. Convergence: An accelerated longitudinal approach. *Child Development,* 1953, *24,* 145–152.

Bell, R. Q. An experimental test of the accelerated longitudinal approach. *Child Development,* 1954, *25,* 281–286.

Bijou, S. W. Ages, stages, and the naturalization of human development. *American Psychologist,* 1968, *23,* 419–427.

Bitterman, M. E. The comparative analysis of learning. *Science,* 1975, *188,* 699–709.

Bower, T. G. R. *Human Development.* San Francisco: Freeman, 1979.

Campbell, D. T., & Stanley, J. C. *Experimental and quasi-experimental designs for research.* Chicago: McNally, 1963.

Carmichael, L. The onset and early development of behavior. In P. H. Mussen (Ed.), *Carmichael's handbook of child psychology* (Vol. 1). New York: Wiley, 1970.

Darwin, C. *On the origin of species by means of natural selection, or the the preservation of favored races in the struggle for life.* London: John Murray, 1859 (New York: Appleton, 1869).

Denenberg, V. H. *The development of behavior.* Stamford: Sinauer, 1972.

Endler, N. S., Boulter, L. R., & Osser, H. *Contemporary issues in developmental psychology* (2nd ed.). New York: Holt, 1976.

Friedrich, D. *A primer for developmental methodology.* Minneapolis: Burgess, 1972.

Grinder, R. *A history of genetic psychology.* New York: Wiley, 1967.

Haeckel, E. *The history of creation.* New York: Appleton, 1906.

Hall, C. A., & Lindzey, G. *Theories of personality.* New York: Wiley, 1975.

Hebb, D. O. *Organization of behavior.* New York: Wiley, 1949.

Kendler, H., & Kendler, T. S. Vertical and horizontal processes in problem solving. *Psychological Review,* 1962, *69,* 1–16.

Lamarck, J. B. P. A. *Zoological philosophy: an evaluation with regard to the natural history of animals,* 1809. Translated by H. Elliot. London: Macmillan, 1914.

Langer, J. *Theories of development.* New York: Holt, 1969.

Langer, J. Werner's comparative organismic theory. In P. H. Mussen (Ed.), *Carmichael's manual of child psychology* (Vol. 1). New York: Wiley, 1970.

Lewis M. Cross-cultural studies of mother-infant interaction: Description and consequence. *Human Development,* 1972, *15,* 75–92.

Meier, G. W. Understanding developmental trauma: New roads and new vistas. *Developmental Psychobiology,* 1975, *8,* 193–195.

Morgan, C. L. *Introduction to comparative psychology* (2nd ed.). London: Scott, 1909.

Munn, N. L. *The growth of human behavior* (3rd ed.). Boston: Houghton-Mifflin, 1974.

Piaget, J. *The psychology of intelligence.* New York: Harcourt, Brace, & World, 1950.

Planck, M. *Scientific autobiography.* New York: Philosophical Library, 1949.

Pratt, C. C. *The logic of modern psychology.* New York: Macmillan, 1939.

Reese, H. W., & Lipsitt, L. P. (Eds.). *Experimental child psychology.* New York: Academic Press, 1970.

Romanes, G. J. *Mental evolution in animals.* New York: Appleton, 1884.

Schaie, K. W. A general model for the study of developmental problems. *Psychological Bulletin,* 1965, *64,* 92–107.

Shontz, F. C. *Research methods in personality.* New York: Appleton Century, 1965.

Werner, H. The concept of development from a comparative and organismic point of view. In D. B. Harris (Ed.), *The concept of development*. Minneapolis: University of Minnesota Press, 1957.

Wohlwill, J. J. The age variable in psychological research. *Psychological Review,* 1970, *77,* 49–64.

Chapter

GENETIC FOUNDATIONS OF DEVELOPMENT

Two.

Few topics have been subject to more misunderstanding, confusion, distortion, and controversy than genetics and heredity. The science of genetics is the area of biology concerned with heredity and the processes by which hereditary characteristics are transmitted from parents to offspring. Our concern with the genetic foundations of development is a necessary one, as etiological factors in developmental phenomena dominate our approach to developmental psychology. Organic development originates with genetic transmission, which represents our starting point for developmental psychology. This fundamental biological foundation is indisputable. Biological structure and function underlie all behavior. Because structure and function are determined by the degree of integrity of genetic events interacting with internal and external environmental factors, all *basic* behavioral development is influenced by genetic components.

The genetic determinants of basic development should not be interpreted as strict determinants of behavioral development. As we shall see, genetic processes allow for a much wider range of alternatives in development than a beginning student might realize. Environmental factors, in continual interaction with genetic events, play no less a role in development, and in many cases are crucial in determining ultimate ontogenetic patterns of development. Because myths concerning genetic determinism and fatalism are still abundant, it is important to realize that genetic structure and function have evolved an amazing capacity for flexibility within the limits of organic specificity of the species. Not surprisingly, we find the greatest degree of such flexibility for structural and functional variability in humans.

The genetic phenomena and principles most relevant to developmental psychology are those that comprise the area of developmental and behavioral genetics. The major purpose of this chapter is to survey behavioral genetics and to review the major research findings demonstrating genetic influences on ontogenesis. However, an understanding of behavioral genetics requires some knowledge of basic genetic principles, molecular genetics, and transmission genetics, and so we will begin with a brief discussion of these topics.

HISTORICAL PERSPECTIVE

The systematic study of human genetics began in the mid-1800s with the work of Sir Francis Galton, English physician, anthropologist, mathematician, and meteorologist, and a cousin of Charles Darwin. Galton's early studies on inherited characteristics earned him the title of father of quantitative genetics and behavior genetics. However, the origins of contemporary genetics date to the rediscovery, in 1900, of Gregor Mendel's paper on inherited characteristics in several strains of peas, originally published in 1866 in an obscure Austrian journal. Mendel, an Augustinian monk of the Brünn Monastery in Austria, had read his paper on peas to the Brünn Society for Natural History in 1865, and it was published in their *Proceedings* the following year. Even though Mendel had sent copies of his paper to a few other scientists and the *Proceedings of the Brünn Society* were sent to more than 120 libraries, only four printed references to Mendel's paper before 1900 are known (Sturtevant, 1965). Perhaps one reason why Mendel's careful observations and conclusions went unnoticed for some 35 years was the lack of any other data to support a particulate theory of heredity. In addition, most scientists during the late nineteenth century were preoccupied with evolutional theory and theoretical speculation rather than research.

During the last quarter of the nineteenth century, however, biologists launched some significant research, which led to the rediscovery of Mendel's basic principles of heredity. In 1883, August Weismann, a zoologist, began to formulate his germ-plasm theory. In his embryological research with flies, Weismann discovered that germ cells (reproductive cells) become separated and isolated from somatic cells or somatoplasm (all body cells except reproductive cells) very early in embryonic development.* He suggested that this germ plasm was solely responsible for reproduction and heredity, emphasizing that the germ cells exert a continuous generational effect on organic structure rather than the reverse. Weismann also developed his ideas about chromosomes being the carriers of hereditary material. (Most of the basic details of chromosome behavior in cell division had already been described by W. Flemming, E. Strasburger, and E. van Benden.) Thus, Weismann was among the first to challenge Lamarck's theory of acquired characters and Darwin's hypothesis of pangenesis.

The second major event leading to modern genetics was the contribution of Hugo de Vries, a botanist. In 1889, de Vries published his theory of heredity, *Intracellular Pangenesis*. De Vries added to Weismann's theory by providing data indicating that hereditary units each govern a single characteristic, and these units become assembled in different ways in offspring. De Vries' discovery did much to clear the path for the rediscovery of Mendel and his particulate theory of heredity.

Traditionally, heredity had been viewed as a blending process in which offspring reflected a diluted mixture of parental characteristics. However, this view clashed with observations that offspring frequently possessed more characteristics from one parent than the other, while certain other characteristics appeared to remain unchanged in generation after generation. The phenomenon of variation in hereditary characteristics was a long puzzle, impeding the progress of evolutionary theory and general organic development. A big piece of the puzzle was solved when Hugo de Vries, Carl Correns, and Erich von Tschermak, all botanists, independently discovered the paper that Mendel had published in 1866. Mendel had demonstrated, using many generations of garden peas, that the appearance of different characteristics in offspring followed specific laws and could be predicted from parental characteristics.

Mendel's basic principles of heredity were quickly seized upon in light of the earlier discoveries in embryology, cytology,

---

*This separation of somatoplasm and germ plasm was deduced by Mendel on the basis of his own data, years before Weismann reached the same conclusion (Sturtevant, 1965).

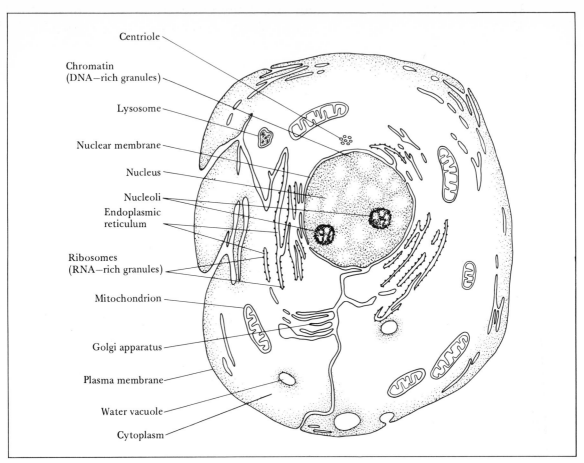

Figure 2-1
Diagram of a generalized cell, showing the principal organelles.

and botany, and his results were confirmed by de Vries, Correns, and Tschermak. Modern genetics was thus ushered into the twentieth century and began its accelerated development as a science. William Bateson introduced the term *genetics* to identify the field of study. In 1909, W. Johannsen, a Danish botanist, introduced the word *gene* to refer to the basic unit of heredity which Mendel had termed *character* and which Bateson had referred to as *factor*. Johannsen also proposed the distinction between *genotype,* the genetic composition of the individual, and *phenotype,* the expressed trait or characteristic of the individual which is observable and measurable.

THE PHYSICAL FOUNDATIONS OF GENETICS

Chromosomes and Genes

Cell theory states that all life forms are composed of cells, and that all cells derive from previously existing cells. Cellular structure consists of cytoplasm, which is the protoplasm contained within the cell membrane, and a nucleus, which is enclosed in its own membrane within the cytoplasm (see Figure 2-1). Cytoplasm contains several complex structures, known as cell organelles, which allow the cell to function. The most prominent structure in the cytoplasm, however, is the nucleus, the body that controls and directs cellular activity and inheritance.

The nucleus governs cellular reproduction, differentiation, and metabolism. It contains the hereditary information along with the genetic instructions that determine what part of a particular living organism the cell will become. This information is transmitted to daughter cells during cell division or reproduction. The nucleus contains elongated, threadlike structures, called chromosomes ("colored bodies") because of their staining properties with certain dyes. The biochemical composition of chromosomes consists of nucleic acid and protein. The chromosomes carry the basic units of heredity, the genes, in a linear organization along the chromosomes, with each gene occupying a specific locus on the chromosome. It has been estimated that each human chromosome carries approximately 20,000 genes. The genetic code for organic life and organization is contained within the genes, which regulate the biochemistry of life by directing the production of various enzymes. In addition to chromosomes, the nucleus also contains another major type of structure, the nucleolus, which organizes and controls intracellular interactions between the nucleus and the cytoplasm.

Chromosomes are clearly visible by microscopic observation only when a cell is in the process of division. When the cell is not dividing, chromosomal bodies appear as a dark structural network, called chromatin. Although chromosomes differ considerably from species to species, their number and structural configuration are constant for all normal members of a species. With some exceptions, every somatic (body) cell in a given organism contains the same number of chromosomes. Human somatic cells, for example, contain 46 chromosomes (see Figure 2-2).

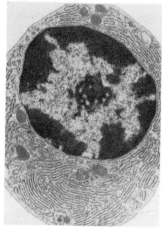

Plasma cell of a guinea pig (Cavia porcellus) showing the main cellular components: nucleus, nucleolus, chromatin (chromosomes during interphase), nuclear membrane, cytoplasm, mitochondria, and the cell membrane.

(Photo by D. W. Fawcett/Photo Researchers, Inc.)

Somatic chromosomes are found in homologous pairs, in which each member of the pair is alike in size and possesses the genes responsible for the same hereditary traits. The number of chromosomes characteristic of an organism is thus determined by the diploid number, which is the total number of chromosomes in all the homologous pairs (46 in the case of humans). While each somatic cell contains the diploid number of chromosomes, each gamete (germ cell) contains only half that number, or a haploid number of chromosomes. Thus a mature human sperm and a mature human egg each contain 23 chromosomes—only one member of each homologous pair. When a sperm cell fertilizes an egg cell, the resulting cell will contain a full complement (a diploid number) of chromosomes. Therefore, in each homologous pair of somatic chromosomes, one member of the pair is contributed by the mother and the other by the father.

There is no known relationship between level on the phylogenetic scale and the number of chromosomes characteristic of an organism. The number of chromosomes has no evolutional significance because it is the *nature* of the genes carried by the chromosomes that differentiates species of organisms. For example, the somatic cell diploid number ranges from two (certain roundworms) to 300 (protozoa) (see Table 2-1).

Figure 2-2
The chromosomes of the human male. Each pair of chromosomes has a characteristic size and proportion of the lengths of the arms on each side of the centromere, or central link between the paired chromosomes. This permits the trained microscopist to identify each chromosome and detect abnormalities in chromosome number in humans. The 23rd pair are the sex chromosomes.

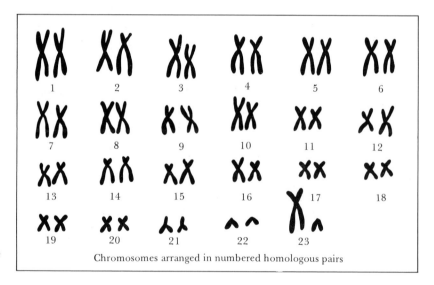

Chromosomes arranged in numbered homologous pairs

**Table 2-1
Chromosome Numbers
Found in Different
Species of Animals**

| | CHROMOSOMES | |
COMMON NAME	DIPLOID NUMBER	HAPLOID NUMBER
Man	46	23
Rhesus monkey	42	21
Dog	78	39
Cat	38	19
Horse	64	32
Rat	42	21
Pigeon	80	40
Frog	26	13
Carp	104	52
Silkworm	56	28
Red Ant	48	24
House Fly	12	6
Grasshopper	24	12
Honeybee	32	16
Freshwater Hydra	32	16

(Adapted from Strickberger, 1968, Copyright © 1968 by Monroe W. Strickberger.
Reprinted with permission of MacMillan Publishing Co., Inc.)

CELLULAR REPRODUCTION

Mitosis

All cells arise from previously existing cells. The capacity for physical growth is a prime requisite for survival of life forms. Perpetuation of a particular organism requires an evolved capacity for cellular division, a capacity that appeared very early in the evolution of multicellular organisms. One form of growth does involve simple enlargement of cells. But physical limitations inherent in cell properties and functioning impose severe restrictions on the extent to which cells can increase in size and volume and still survive. Primary physical growth, therefore, requires a mechanism for cell division, in which the hereditary material will be transmitted to subsequent cell generations, or daughter cells. That is, the parent cell must be capable of duplicating genetic information in the nucleus and distributing the genetic copies to each daughter cell.

The reproduction of somatic cells is a divisional process called mitosis. This form of cell division is quite different from

Mitotic cell division in the onion *(Allium cepa).* Each daughter cell will be an exact genetic duplicate of the parent.

(Photo by Manfred Kage/Peter Arnold, Inc.)

the type of division occurring in gametes or germ cells (ova and sperm). Mitotic cell division consists of two distinct processes that may or may not occur simultaneously. These two mitotic events are nuclear division and cytoplasmic division. Strictly speaking, mitosis is defined as the process in which the parent nucleus divides, producing two nuclei with identical sets of chromosomes and their genes. The second event in mitosis, usually occurring at the same time, is cytokinesis, which is marked by a cleavage of the cytoplasm and subsequent cell division. At this point in cellular reproduction, a daughter cell has received one duplicate nucleus and its complete (diploid) set of chromosomes. The exact replication process seen in mitosis does not occur in cytokinesis, as each daughter cell receives approximately half of the cytoplasmic organelles. However, the remaining complement of cell organelles is acquired through self-reproduction or synthesis by the new cells. At the completion of cell division, the two daughter cells are approximately comparable in size and cytoplasmic structure, and identical in genetic or hereditary material.

In summary, mitosis provides for the replication of parental cell chromosomes and their distribution to each daughter cell reproduced. Mitotic cell division is a continuous series of biochemical and biophysical events that are arbitrarily identified and described by four overlapping phases: prophase, metaphase, anaphase, and telophase. The term, interphase, describes the resting, nondividing cell. Mitosis and cytokinesis are depicted in Figure 2-3.

Meiosis   When we speak of heredity, we refer to both the similarity and the variability of organic life. In mitosis, cellular reproduction results in new cells that are genetic duplicates of the parental cell. Obviously, the characteristics of cells produced by mitosis will be identical to those of the parent cell. Therefore, mitotic cell division cannot produce genetic variation, because there is no mechanism for the recombination of genes between different individual cells. Mitosis represents the basic paradigm for asexual reproduction, which occurs only among simple life forms. Although mitotic asexual reproduction is a less complex mechanism than sexual reproduction, evolution has selected sexual reproduction for the great majority of life forms. The adaptive significance of this evolved capacity for sexual reproduction lies in its provision for continuous genetic variation and recombination. Despite the potential hazards and complications of sexual reproduction, natural selection has operated to maintain this form of reproduction in the higher invertebrates and all of the vertebrates. Sexual reproduction ensures and augments genetic variation, which in turn is the foundation for biological evolution, natural selection, and survival of the species under predator and environmental pressures. Sexuality thus may be viewed as the key to phylogenetic development.

We have described somatic cells as containing two of each type of chromosome, in homologous pairs. This chromosomal arrangement represents a diploid complement, and the cell is described as a diploid cell. Each human somatic cell normally has 46 chromosomes, arranged in 23 different chromosome pairs. A single pair of chromosomes is called a genome, with one chromosome of the pair being of paternal origin and the other of maternal origin. The primary function of mitosis is to increase the number of cells and to perpetuate the identity of chromosome endowment.

However, sexual reproduction requires a divisional process different from that of somatic cells, in order to preserve the

1. Interphase

Chromosomes not see as distinct
   structures.
Nucleolus visible.

2. Early prophase

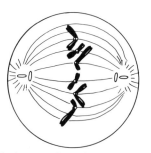

Centrioles moving apart.
Chromosomes appear as long thin
   threads.
Nucleolus becoming less distinct.

3. Middle prophase

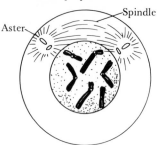

Centrioles farther apart,
   spindle beginning to form.
Each chromosome to be seen as
   composed of 2 chromatids held
   together by their centromeres.

4. Late prophase

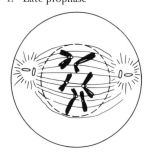

Centrioles nearly at opposite sides
   of nucleus.
Spindle nearly complete.
Nuclear membrane disappearing.
Chromosomes move toward equator.
Nucleolus no longer visible.

5. Metaphase

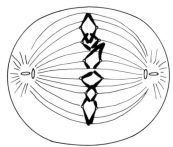

Nuclear membrane has disappeared.
Centromeres of each double-stranded
   chromosome attached to spindle
   microtubules at spindle equator.

6. Early anaphase

Centromeres have uncoupled and
   begun moving toward opposite
   poles of spindle.

7. Late anaphase

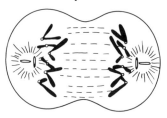

The 2 sets of new single-stranded
   chromosomes nearing respective
   poles.
Cytokinesis beginning.

8. Telophase

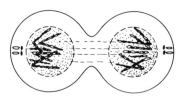

New nuclear membranes forming.
Chromosomes become longer, thinner,
   and less distinct.
Nucleolus reappearing.
Centrioles replicated.
Cytokinesis nearly complete

9. Interphase

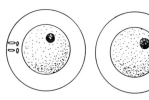

Nuclear membranes complete.
Chromosomes no longer visible.
Cytokinesis complete.

Figure 2-3
Mitosis and cytokinesis in an animal cell.

(Redrawn from *Biological Science*, 3rd ed., by William T. Keeton, with the permission of W.W. Norton &
Company, Inc. Copyright © 1980, 1979, 1978, 1972, 1967 by W.W. Norton & Company, Inc.)

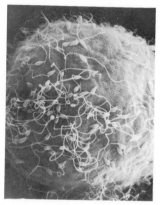

Spermatozoa swarming over the egg of a sea urchin *(Arbacia),* magnified 2400×. Even at this most rudimentary level, competition is keen. Literally thousands of sperm compete to fertilize a single egg, yet only one can be the victor.

(Photo by Mia Tegner and David Epel. From *Science,* 1973, *179,* 685–688, Fig. 2B. Copyright © 1973 by the American Association for the Advancement of Science.)

diploid number. If male and female gametes were formed by normal mitotic cell division, fertilization would produce a zygote with twice as many chromosomes as its parent cells, and chromosomal doubling would occur in each successive generation. Chromosome number soon would approach infinity, leading to large, diorganized cells, inefficient nuclei, and inadequate cytoplasm (Strickberger, 1968).

We know, however, that chromosome number remains invariant for all normal members of a species. Sexual reproduction employs a mechanism of cell division which reduces the usual chromosome number in each mature sex cell by one-half, to the haploid complement. Thus, when the egg and sperm unite in fertilization, the normal diploid number is restored (Figure 2-4). Each mature human germ cell, for example, will contribute 23 chromosomes to the fertilized egg, or zygote. The new individual will receive a total of 46 homologous chromosomes, or 23 pairs. Twenty-two of these pairs are autosomal (body) chromosomes, and there is one pair

Figure 2-4
The moment of fertilization in the sea urchin *(Arbacia).* The sperm consists of little more than a nucleus and a tail that enables it to move. Yet the amount of its hereditary material is nearly the same as that of the much larger egg.

(Photo courtesy of Everett Anderson, Harvard Medical School.)

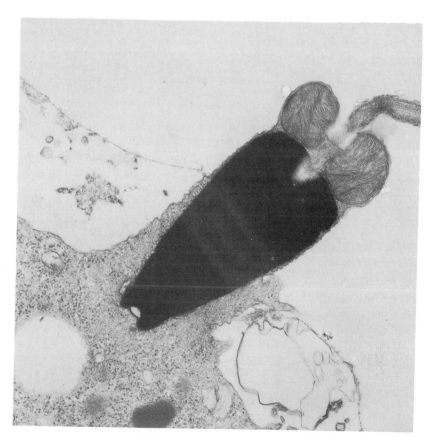

1. Early prophase I

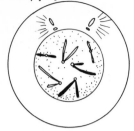

Chromosomes become visible as long,
well-separated filaments; they do
not appear double-stranded, though
other evidence indicates that
replication has already occurred.

2. Middle prophase I

Homologous chromosomes synapse
and become shorter and thicker.

3. Late prophase I

Chromosomes become clearly
double-stranded.
Nuclear membrane begins to
disappear.

4. Metaphase I

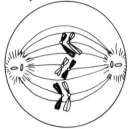

Each synaptic pair moves to the
equator of the spindle as a unit.

5. Anaphase I

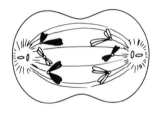

Centromeres do not uncouple.
Double-stranded chromosomes
move apart to opposite poles.

6. Telophase I

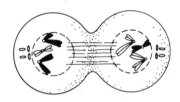

New haploid nuclei form.
Chromosomes are double-stranded
when they fade from view.

7. Interkinesis

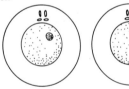

No replication of genetic material occurs.

8. Prophase II

9. Metaphase II

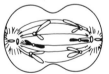

10. Anaphase II

11. Telophase II

12. Interphase

Figure 2-5
Meiosis in an animal cell.

(Redrawn from *Biological Science*, 3rd ed., by William T. Keeton, with the permission of W.W. Norton &
Company, Inc. Copyright © 1980, 1979, 1978, 1972, 1967 by W.W. Norton & Company, Inc.)

Conception! The joining of a human sperm and ovum. The products of meiotic cell division, the reproductive cells contain the haploid number of chromosomes. At conception, the two reproductive cells pair their chromosomes giving the resulting zygote a diploid complement, that is, the full number of chromosomes required for normal cellular development. It is interesting to note that there is no correlation between the diploid number of chromosomes in an organism and that organism's place in the natural order.

(Photo courtesy of the American Museum of Natural History.)

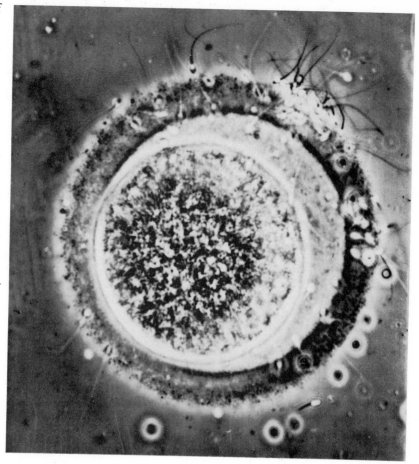

of sex chromosomes (Figure 2-2). This process of sex cell reduction is called meiosis; it is illustrated in Figure 2-5. We can view meiosis as the process by which chromosomes are separated and their number reduced from the diploid to the haploid complement. Once the zygote is formed, its growth and development proceed by means of mitotic cell division.

MOLECULAR GENETICS

Molecular genetics is concerned with the biochemistry of genetic material, its structure, and the biochemical mechanisms of genetic processes. We will briefly consider these topics in order to provide a basic understanding of the chemical nature of the gene and its action.

Chromosomes consist of protein in combination with a particular acid material, nucleic acid. Proteins in turn are

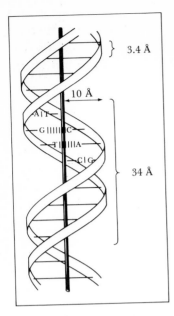

Figure 2-6
The Watson-Crick model of DNA. The molecule is composed of two polynucleotide chains held together by hydrogen bonds between their adjacent bases (S = sugar; P = phosphate; A, T, G, C = nitrogenous bases). The double-chained structure is coiled in a helix (shown here wound around a hypothetical rod). The width of the molecule is 20 angstroms (Å); the distance between adjacent nucleotides is 3.4 Å; and the length of one complete coil is 34 Å.

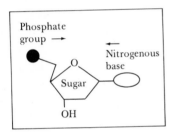

Figure 2-7
Diagram of nucleotide from DNA. A phosphate group and a nitrogenous base are attached to deoxyribose, a five-carbon sugar.

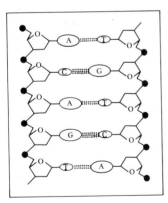

Figure 2-8
Diagram of a portion of a DNA molecule uncoiled. The molecule has a ladderlike structure, with the two uprights composed of alternating sugar and phosphate groups and the cross rungs composed of paired nitrogenous bases. Note that each cross rung has one purine base (large oval) and one pyrimidine base (small oval). When the purine is guanine (G), then pyrimidine with which it is paired is always cytosine (C); when the purine is adenine (A), then the pyrimidine is thymine (T).

composed of amino acids that are chemically bonded together by peptide linkages. There are 20 known amino acids, all different from one another. A protein may consist of hundreds or thousands of amino acids joined together, forming polypeptide chains. However, protein chains of the same length may differ considerably from each other because their amino acids are linked together in different sequences. Each type of protein has a particular function determined by its sequence of amino acids. Nucleic acid appears in the cell in two forms, ribonucleic acid (RNA) and deoxyribonucleic acid (DNA). RNA is found both in the cytoplasm and nucleus, whereas genetic DNA exists only in the nucleus of a cell.* The chemical composition and structure of the DNA molecule are "over-engineered" to provide the genetic information to produce all the biological products needed by an organism.

In 1953, Watson and Crick hypothesized that genetic material is composed of DNA, and presented a model of its molecular structure that would account for its biological properties. Their discovery has since been confirmed and accepted, opening a new era in molecular biology. DNA is composed of two complementary strands of nucleotide chains in the form of a double helix, resembling a circular staircase or ladder (see Figure 2-6). A nucleotide is a protein building block composed of three subunits: a simple five-carbon sugar (deoxyribose), a phosphate group, and a nitrogen base (Figure 2-7).

Each strand of DNA is composed of alternating sugar and phosphate groups. The two strands are bonded together at a fixed distance along the length of the molecule by pairs of hydrogen bonds between the nitrogen bases. DNA has four types of nitrogen bases: adenine, guanine, thymine, and cytosine. Adenine and guanine are structurally similar, as are thymine and cytosine; they are referred to as purine and pyrimidine bases, respectively. The result is two strands of alternating sugar and phosphate groups held together by the purine and pyrimidine bases, as shown in Figure 2-8. Adenine from one of the strands always attaches to thymine on the

---

*DNA also exists outside the cell nucleus, in the mitochondria, but mitochondrial DNA does not appear to play a role in the genetic transmission of traits in an organism.

opposite or complementary strand, and guanine from one strand always attaches to cytosine on the opposite strand. The order in which these four bases appear on the DNA molecule is different for different DNA molecules. The order determines DNA or gene specificity and therefore its biological function.

The DNA molecule is composed of a small variety of basic parts—a startling fact when you consider the astronomical number of different genes that must exist in order to account for all species of organic life. How can such a small variety of basic components make many different kinds of genes? A gene consists of a fixed number and sequence of nucleotides along a section of a DNA molecule. There may be up to 30,000 "rungs" on a DNA molecule, so a single molecule may contain hundreds of genes. A reversal in any single bond, from adenine–thymine to thymine–adenine, for example, alters the entire gene and its action. In mutations, more drastic changes occur such as the replacement of a cytosine–guanine bond for an adenine–thymine bond. Consider the number of combinations possible with four nucleotide bonds and 30,000 positions on a DNA molecule!

DNA Replication   The double-stranded structure and chemical characteristics of DNA enable it to replicate itself so that duplicates contain the same number of nucleotides, the same ratio of purines to pyrimidines, and the same sequences of adenine–thymine and guanine–cytosine bonds that occur in the parent molecule. In cell mitosis, the two chains, or helices, separate and unwind as the hydrogen bonds between the base pairs rupture (see Figure 2-9). Each single DNA chain (one-half of the original molecule) represents a template for completion of the complementary strand since it possesses all the information required for new DNA construction. Because adenine can only bond to thymine and guanine only to cytosine, the nucleotide sequence in one chain of the separated DNA molecule exactly determines the sequence of nucleotides in its new partner. Thus, the integrity of the DNA molecule is maintained. All the raw materials (phosphates, sugars, nitrogen bases) for the construction of new DNA are contained in the cell nucleus, and these nucleotides pair with the exposed nitrogen bases of the separated DNA chains. The result is a new double helix of DNA identical to the original.

Gene Action and the Genetic Code

Figure 2-9
A schematic representation of DNA replication. P = phosphate, S = sugar, A = adenine, T = thymine, G = guanine, C = cytosine. During cell division, DNA structure splits (bottom) and reforms as two new, identical structures by picking up appropriate P, S, A, T, G, and C elements from the surrounding cytoplasm.

We know that the nucleus controls and directs cellular metabolism and that most of this activity occurs in the cytoplasm. What is the mechanism by which the DNA molecule transmits its hereditary information for the organism from the nucleus to the cytoplasmic structures? Cells exert their effects on organic development through the production of enzymes, which are proteins capable of catalyzing, or triggering, a cellular reaction. Enzymatic reactions ultimately determine the physical characteristics of organisms, and it is now known that genes regulate the synthesis of these protein enzymes. The relationship between genes and specific enzymes takes the form of one gene–one polypeptide. That is, a protein polypeptide chain (recall that a protein is made of one or more polypeptide chains) is formed at the direction of its own single, specific gene. In short, DNA–gene information is expressed as specific enzymes. How, then, does the DNA get its information from the nucleus to the cytoplasm—the site of protein synthesis?

The genetic message is carried from the nucleus to the cytoplasm by another type of nucleic acid molecule mentioned earlier, RNA. This single-stranded molecule is similar to DNA, but differs in its sugar composition* and in its substitution of another base compound, uracil, for thymine. During DNA replication, a molecule of messenger RNA (mRNA) is synthesized by one of the DNA strands. A complementary strand of mRNA is formed against the DNA strand by a base-pairing process similar to that described for DNA replication. In this manner, the genetic message for protein synthesis is transcribed onto the mRNA molecule, which then leaves the nucleus and enters the cytoplasm.

In the cytoplasm are organelles called ribosomes, which serve as the sites for protein synthesis. As mRNA moves through the cytoplasm, several ribosomes attach to it and move along its

---

*The sugar component in RNA is ribose, whereas in DNA it is deoxyribose.

Figure 2-10
Synthesis of polypeptide chains by the ribosomes. As the ribosomes move along the messenger RNA, they "read" the coded information and synthesize a polypeptide chain according to that information.

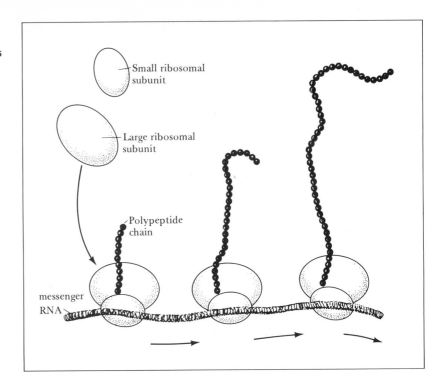

length, collecting, or "reading" the information coded on it (Figure 2-10). Another type of RNA, called transfer RNA (tRNA), is responsible for the actual production of the polypeptide chain. The tRNA molecules move through the cytoplasm, each picking up a molecule of amino acid specific to the particular tRNA (one for each of the 20 amino acids). The tRNA–amino acid complexes then line up along the mRNA according to its base-pairing genetic code. The tRNA molecules then attach to the mRNA and deposit their amino acids on the polypeptide chain. Finally, the now fully formed polypeptide (enzyme) falls away from the mRNA. The molecules of tRNA also detach to continue their function in the cytoplasm.

It is important to remember that actual protein synthesis begins only after tRNA deposits its specific amino acid on mRNA. The resulting protein peels off the ribosome and enters the cytoplasm, where it functions as a hormone, an enzyme, or a structural protein. The genetic code ordering any specific protein appears as a sequence of three bases which is carried by tRNA. Each of the 20 amino acids is coded by a particular series of three bases, as represented on a DNA strand, which becomes transcribed on mRNA. For example, the triplet TTT codes for the amino acid lysine. When attached to a ribosome, each base triplet on mRNA attracts a tRNA that has a complementary triplet sequence. In this case, therefore, the tRNA, which is carrying the amino acid, lysine, has a UUU code. The triplet code unit, called a codon, provides a system in which there are 64 possible combinations of triplet bases, more than enough to code for the 20 different amino acids. The mechanism of gene action is depicted in Figure 2-11, and

Figure 2-11
DNA, RNA, and protein synthesis.

(From Nirenberg, 1963.)

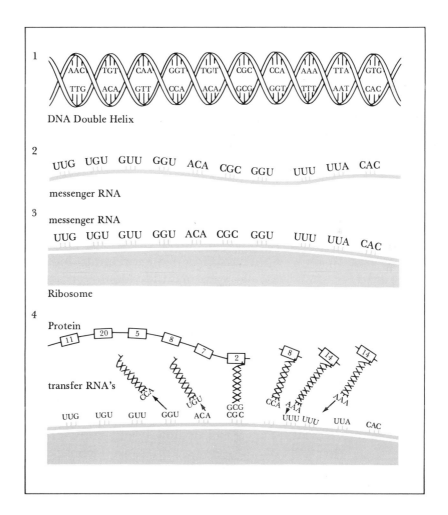

the genetic code is shown in Table 2-2. Most of the proteins produced in this way are functional enzymes, which control chemical reactions producing the characteristics displayed by an organism.

This simplified version of molecular genetics helps us to understand why some genes are dominant, recessive, co-dominant, or intermediate. Dominant genes, for example, direct the formation of a specific enzyme that will effect the expression of a specific trait, whereas a recessive gene either fails to do so or produces a defective enzyme. Very little is known about the thousands of genes and their enzyme relationships. But the developmental significance of gene mechanisms and protein synthesis can be better appreciated by viewing the gene as a DNA molecule coding for a particular polypeptide, with the average polypeptide of a protein consisting of a sequence of approximately 300 amino acids (Lerner, 1968). In humans, the number of genes is enough to code for hundreds of thousands of different proteins.

The difference between two proteins may be minor and yet vitally important. For instance, the etiology of sickle-cell anemia derives from the substitution of one amino acid for another on the human hemoglobin molecule. This occurs when one of the 861 base pairs in the two genes determining the hemoglobin molecule is altered. The result is a change in one amino acid out of 574 amino acids on the hemoglobin molecule (Winchester, 1971). The structural change in the hemoglobin molecule produces severe anemia and possibly early death. The difference between an individual with sickle-cell anemia and a normal individual is *one amino acid!*

In summary, a firm grasp of the physical foundation of genetics will greatly help you to comprehend the significance of developmental genetics and the etiology of genetically based alterations in ontogenetic development.

TRANSMISSION GENETICS

*L*et us now briefly consider the basic concepts and terminology of transmission genetics. Our goal is to describe the patterns of inheritance of genetic material, and to trace the transmission of biological similarities and variations from one generation to another. We will present and interpret the

Table 2-2
The Genetic Code

FIRST LETTER	SECOND LETTER A	G	T	C	THIRD LETTER
	Phe	Ser	Tyr	Cys	A
A	Phe	Ser	Tyr	Cys	G
	Leu	Ser	chain end	chain end	T
	Leu	Ser	chain end	Try	C
	Leu	Pro	His	Arg	A
G	Leu	Pro	His	Arg	G
	Leu	Pro	Gln	Arg	T
	Leu	Pro	Gln	Arg	C
	Ile	Thr	Asn	Ser	A
T	Ile	Thr	Asn	Ser	G
	Ile	Thr	Lys	Arg	T
	Met	Thr	Lys	Arg	C
	Val	Ala	Asp	Gly	A
C	Val	Ala	Asp	Gly	G
	Val	Ala	Glu	Gly	T
	Val	Ala	Glu	Gly	C

(Adapted from *The Genetics of Human Population* by L.L. Cavalli-Sforza and W.F. Bodmer. W.H. Freeman and Company. Copyright © 1971.)

Each amino acid is coded by a triplet of three bases, as shown in the table, which is a compact way of setting out the 64 possible triplets.

The four bases are denoted by the letters A, G, T, and C. In DNA the four bases are:

A = Adenine	T = Thymine
G = Guanine	C = Cytosine

The 20 amino acids are identified as follows:

Ala = Alanine	Lys = Lysine
Arg = Arginine	Met = Methionine
Asn = Asparagine	Phe = Phenylalanine
Asp = Aspartic acid	Pro = Proline
Cys = Cysteine	Ser = Serine
Glu = Glutamic acid	Thr = Threonine
Gln = Glutamine	Try = Tryptophan
Gly = Glycine	Tyr = Tyrosine
His = Histidine	Val = Valine
Ile = Isoleucine	Chain End.
Leu = Leucine	

concepts of classical Mendelian genetics in contemporary form, reflecting the fundamental Mendelian rules in light of current knowledge in genetics.

Gene Relationships and Expression

Earlier, we stated that chromosomes, and therefore genes, exist in diploid pairs in the body cells of sexually reproducing organisms. A gene is the hereditary material that determines some biological trait. Gene pairs that are located at a specific chromosomal locus point on homologous chromosomes are called alleles, an abbreviated form of allelomorph. Allele and gene are used interchangeably, but only when allele is used to identify the genes of a specific gene pair. Alleles may appear in identical or different forms. If the organism has identical alleles, it is homozygous for that particular gene pair. If the alleles exist in different forms, it is heterozygous. Homozygous individuals will display the trait determined by that gene pair, whereas heterozygous individuals will display the trait as a function of the relationship characteristics of the alleles. Dominant alleles express their effects over recessive alleles, meaning that the expression of a recessive gene cannot appear in a heterozygote possessing its dominant allele. Therefore, recessive traits appear only in individuals where both genes of an allelic pair are recessive (homozygous recessive).

Alleles do not always exist in a simple dominant–recessive relationship. They may also appear in the allelic form of codominance, in which case each allele fully expresses its qualitative trait in the heterozygote. A well-known example of codominance is the AB blood group, in which the individual receives one allele for type A blood and one for type B.* Both alleles will express themselves equally as the combination of type AB. There are other instances of allelic relationships where heterozygous individuals show a blending of the alleles. Such inheritance patterns, in which the heterozygote displays the effects of both alleles, are referred to as intermediate inheritance or incomplete dominance. For example, red-flow-

---

*There are actually four known alleles involved in the inheritance of blood type, and six possible blood types (O, A_1, A_2, B, A_1B, and A_2B).

ered four-o'clock plants crossed to white-flowered four-o'clocks product pink heterozygous flowers in the first generation.

In short, there may be no direct correspondence between the appearance of an organism and its genetic makeup. Thus it becomes necessary to differentiate the observable biological characteristics of an organism from its genetic characteristics. Phenotype refers to all forms of biological expressions, including behavioral, that the organism displays. Genotype describes only the inherited genetic combinations which the organism possesses.

Monohybrid Patterns of Inheritance

Our discussion to this point has been concerned with simple Mendelian laws of transmission genetics, involved in single phenotypic traits determined by a single gene pair. Such single trait-gene pair breeding crosses are known as monohybrid crosses. Mendel's first principle, the law of segregation, deals exclusively with monohybrid inheritance patterns. The law of segregation simply states that a hybrid organism from two different parental varieties possesses both types of parental genes (alleles), and that these separate or segregate in the gametes of the hybrid offspring. The phenotypic characteristics of the hybrid and subsequent hybrid crossings will be a function of the allelic relationships discussed in the previous section.

Mendelian Ratios

We can demonstrate Mendel's law of segregation by examining some simple examples of monohybrid inheritance patterns with and without dominance in the allelic relationships. Let us first consider monohybrid inheritance involving a dominant gene. Mendel used capital letters to represent dominant traits and small letters for recessive traits. In one of Mendel's original experiments, he crossed tall plants with dwarf plants. The tall plants are represented by the symbol TT (allelic pair), those for dwarf plants possessing pure recessive genes, as tt, and the hybrid of the cross as Tt. The hybrid offspring represents the first filial generation or F_1. In these simple Mendelian crosses, we can utilize the Punnett square to generate all the possible gamete combinations, or genotypes, produced in the second filial generation (F_2). First of all, crossing pure tall and pure dwarf plants will result in all F_1 individuals with the genotype of Tt, a hybrid tall plant. No other genotype combination is possible, since each parent contributes one of its homozygous alleles to the F_1 hybrid. Note that the hybrid is phenotypically tall, because tallness is dominant over the recessive allele for shortness, but that the genotype is Tt. Thus, the F_1 individuals are heterozygous and carriers of the recessive trait. If we now allow the F_1 generation to cross freely among themselves, the progeny they produce (F_2) can be shown in the Punnett square. (Remember that allelic pairs segregate in the gametes so that each sperm cell or egg cell will have only one allele, T or t.)

| | ♂ Male Gametes (sperm) | |
	T	t
T	TT Pure Tall	Tt Hybrid Tall
t	tT Hybrid Tall	tt Pure Dwarf

Female Gametes ♀ (eggs)

In monohybrid inheritance patterns involving dominance, the Mendelian ratio of genotypes in the F_2 generation is 1:2:1, ($TT:Tt:tt$), and the ratio of phenotypes is 3:1 (tall:short).

Using the Punnett square method, we can easily derive the monohybrid pattern of inheritance in cases of intermediate inheritance which, you recall, means an absence of dominance in the allelic relationship. Co-dominant alleles are each symbolized by a capital letter, but one is distinguished from the other by a prime or a subscript designating the particular trait. For our example, let us look at the inheritance pattern resulting from a cross of homozygous white and homozygous black Andalusian fowl. We can designate the homozygous black and white fowl with the symbols C^b and C^w, respectively. All the F_1

Figure 2-12
A visual summary of the results obtained in crossing black and white Andalusian fowls. The F_3 generation represents black-black, blue-blue, and white-white crosses.

(From Sinnott, Dunn, & Dobzhansky, 1958.)

Key:

■ = Black bird

▨ = Slate–blue bird

□ = White bird

hybrid offspring of this cross will be slate blue (C^bC^w), since the alleles involved do not have a dominant–recessive relationship. This is the only possible genotype combination in the F_1 generation. If we then permit the F_1 hybrids to cross freely, we can describe the plumage coloration of the F_2 progeny by looking at the Punnett square.

	C^b	C^w
C^b	C^bC^b Black	C^bC^w Slate Blue
C^w	C^wC^b Slate Blue	C^wC^w White

Observe that the Mendelian ratios for the phenotype and genotype are the same, 1:2:1. That is, large numbers of F_2 crossings will produce one black, two slate blue, and one white fowl in the ratio of 1:2:1. Mendelian ratios in the F_3 generation are shown in Figure 2-12. These principles hold for all mono-hybrid crosses of intermediate inheritance.

In reality, of course, all inheritance patterns or crosses involve many more than one trait and one gene pair. Mendel's second law, the law of independent assortment, deals with crosses of two or more pairs of different traits. This law states that whenever two or more pairs of contrasting characters are brought together in a hybrid, the genes for each character separate or segregate independently during meiosis. Crosses involving two pairs of genes and two traits are called dihybrid crosses. Trihybrid crosses involve three traits determined by three pairs of genes. Mendel's second law holds only when the genes for the different traits are located on different chromosome pairs. We need not concern ourselves with dihybrid and trihybrid crosses here, except to state that the Mendelian ratios become more complex. Our brief, simplified discussion of Mendelian genetics serves only to demonstrate some basics of transmission genetics.

Quantitative Inheritance
We have seen that simple combinations of independent genes produce progeny displaying discrete, qualitative phenotypic characteristics. The examples given above produce different classes of individuals with little overlap between groups. However, most traits reflect the action of many genes, multiple alleles, producing continuous, quantitative variations in phen-

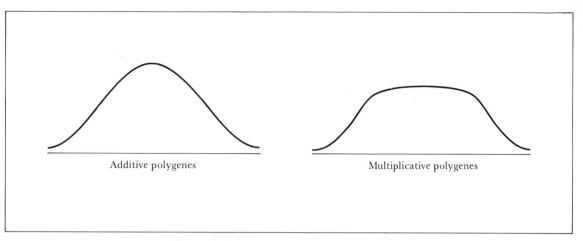

Additive polygenes

Multiplicative polygenes

Figure 2-13
Distribution of phenotypes as a function of additive and multiplicative polygene effects.

otypic expression. Polygene is the term currently used to define genes that exert a small effect on a particular trait, but which supplement each other, producing a joint, multiple, quantitative effect on that trait. Polygenetic effects can occur as an additive phenomenon, in which gene effects are added together in the development of a phenotype. In these cases, the phenotype would essentially represent the total of the positive and negative effects of all the individual polygenes involved. Polygenetic inheritance may also operate in a multiplicative fashion, with polygenes multiplying the effects of certain other genes. In both additive and multiplicative polygenetic action, we find phenotypes continuously displayed as quantitative changes. Additive polygene effects assume an approximate normal distribution in the phenotype, whereas multiplicative polygene influences produce greater variability in the phenotype. These differences are shown in Figure 2-13.

In polygenetic inheritance, then, we are dealing with continuous, quantitative development of the phenotype, quite a different phenomenon from the discrete classes of inheritance patterns found in Mendelian ratios. There are many inherited traits which are distributed as continuous expressions, such as skin pigmentation in humans, intelligence, height, general vigor, and so on. Such characteristics do not appear as discrete classes of events that can be qualitatively categorized. Instead, we find these traits existing in gradual transitions, for example, from very dark to very light skin, from very short to very tall, from very dull to very bright. Phenotypic variability of this sort may also be due to environmental factors, as we shall see later, but when they are due primarily to genetic events, they may be considered to be polygenetic or quantitative inheritance patterns.

ENVIRONMENTAL FACTORS, GENE EXPRESSION, AND GENE INTERACTIONS

To this point, we have been discussing genetic phenomena and ignoring environmental factors, both actual and potential, that may affect genetic expression. This does not mean that genetic material can be isolated from environmental factors, or that it is immune to environmental influences. In the introduction to this chapter, we stated that organic development proceeds as a function of the interaction between environmental factors and heredity. We have seen that genetic material provides the template for development. However, gene action and its ultimate phenotypic expression take place in an environmental vessel, whose many constituents can interact with gene activity at any point along the developmental process, altering, changing, and redirecting the relationship between genotype and phenotype.

It is inaccurate to draw a one-to-one correspondence between genes and a particular phenotype. The vast complexity of organic development reflects the evolved capacity for genetic plasticity, or modifiability, heightened by a lifelong interdependency between genetic material and its internal and external environment. This provides for great flexibility within the broad boundaries of the genetic template directing development. Therefore, we must dismiss any unidimensional conceptualization of gene determinism by understanding that genes in a given environment determine phenotypic expression. The relationship between genotype and phenotype cannot be understood or predicted outside of the context of the overall biological constitution of the individual and the individual's immediate environment during critical periods of development. Such factors can further alter gene activity and subsequent development. The notion that different genotypes react differently to the same environment, and that different environments may affect the same genotype differently, is referred to as the "norm of reaction."

When we refer to environmental factors contributing to genetic potential, we include the internal factors of intracellular and intercellular conditions along with external forces of the ambient, or immediate, environment surrounding the organism. Intracellular conditions include the activity of the cytoplasm and nuclear material surrounding the chromosomes. Differential structure in these cellular areas can influence ultimate gene action. Likewise, intercellular variations may also influence the behavior of any particular cell and its activity. Here, we are referring to the cells surrounding any reference cell. Mechanical pressure, bioelectric activity, and biochemical effects of cells or clusters of cells may influence one or any number of other cells in the immediate intercellular environment. The point to remember is that we deal with dynamic systems, any change in which produces changes throughout the system.

Penetrance and Expressivity

The most immediate evidence for environmental effects on gene expression can be seen in the phenomena of penetrance and expressivity. Penetrance is the frequency of phenotypic expression in an individual organism possessing the genetic combination for that expression. Penetrance reflects the ratio of expected phenotype to genotype. Expressivity is an index of the degree to which a particular trait is displayed—the qualitative aspects of the trait, such as its intensity or variability. In other words, penetrance denotes the number of individuals who express the genes they carry, regardless of degree of expression, whereas expressivity indicates to what extent that trait appears. It becomes increasingly apparent that the typical relationship between genes and their phenotypic expression is far from a simple and direct one. Variations in penetrance and expressivity are most commonly attributed to gene modifiers, although they can also occur as a function of external environmental factors.

Modifier Genes

Modifier genes are genes that alter or otherwise influence the phenotypic traits of other genes. The activity of one gene can quantitatively change or modify the activity of another gene or genes. A modifier gene can exert its influence by enhancing or inhibiting the action of another gene. The extent of such effects will be partly determined by the dominance or recessiveness of the modifier gene. Because modifier genes influence other genes and may also have a phenotypic expression of their own, they can produce multiple phenotypic alteration. This multiple modification is an example of pleiotropism, a general phenomenon in which one gene influences more than one phenotypic characteristic. Most genes appear to operate in a pleiotropic fashion. Many of the examples to be presented in our discussion of behavior genetics clearly demonstrate the phenomena of penetrance, expressivity, and pleiotropy.

External and Internal Environmental Effects

It is difficult to discern phenotypic changes produced by external environmental factors from those produced by internal factors. Strickberger (1968) defines external effects as those producing phenotypic alterations that appear to be directly correlated with obvious changes outside the organism. He identifies phenotypic changes correlated to intraorganism changes as being produced by internal effects. Temperature, light, nutrition, and maternal conditions during pregnancy are common examples of potential external factors. For example, certain mammals such as the Himalayan rabbit are susceptible to changes in fur coloration as a function of the external temperature. The expression of normally black fur areas on the feet, tail, ears, and nose is dependent upon the temperature during the time of fur growth. By placing young Himalayan rabbits in a warm ambient temperature, rather than the normal cooler one, the expected dark areas will develop white fur, as shown in Figure 2-14. There are numerous examples of gene–diet interactions in which the genotype will not be expressed as expected if dietary alterations occur. Diabetes is a hereditary defect of unknown etiology, but many genotypic diabetics will not demonstrate full expressivity if the diet is controlled.

Internal environmental conditions such as age and sex can also produce phenotypic changes in an organism. There are many examples of genes, present from conception, stimulated into action as a function of age. Apparently, internal biological

Figure 2-14
The effects of temperature on the expression of coat color genes in the Himalayan rabbit. (A) Normally black fur occurs only in the extremities where body temperature is lower. (B) White fur is plucked from an area on the back, and the temperature is artificially reduced by the application of an ice pack. (C) The new fur grown on the back is black. Although Himalayan rabbits are normally homozygous for the gene that controls synthesis of the black pigment, the gene is active only at temperatures below about 92°F (33.3° C).

conditions that develop in the aging process serve as catalysts for gene action and consequent phenotypic onset (e.g., pattern baldness, diabetes, muscular dystrophy). As we shall see in the following section, many phenotypic characteristics and differences appear as a function of the presence or absence of genes on the sex chromosomes. Many environmental influences also can alter gene effects. Further, certain environmental changes may so modify individual development as to produce a phenotype that mimics the effects of a particular gene, when in fact the individual does not possess the genotype for the trait. Such an individual is known as a phenocopy. A relatively rare condition of infants born with no arms and/or legs (phocomelia) has long been known to be caused by a recessive gene. In 1961, however, the incidence of phocomelia suddenly increased well beyond the point of expected frequency. This situation was subsequently traced to the use by pregnant women of a new drug, thalidomide, which had been prescribed to reduce nausea ("morning sickness") in early pregnancy. This drug disrupted the development of the embryo and young fetus, producing the same effect as the recessive gene. Drug-induced phocomelia represents a phenocopy of a genetic trait, in the absence of the recessive genes. As another example, the use of insulin by diabetics produces a phenocopy of a normal individual.

SEX AND INHERITANCE

Sex Determination

Like other traits, one's genetic sex is inherited. In diploid organisms, where sexuality exists in separated individuals, the chromosomal pattern is different for males and females. This difference is restricted to one pair of chromosomes, the sex

Figure 2-15
Metaphase chromosomes of mitosis in a human male and female arranged according to homologous pairs.

(Adapted from McKusick, 1964.)

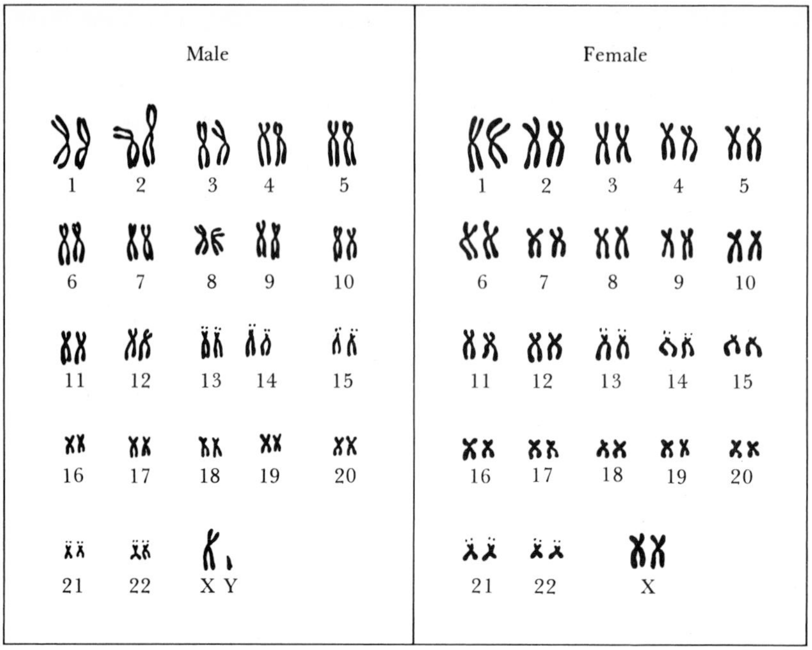

chromosomes, which are the primary material determining and affecting sexual development. Although we stated earlier that diploid organisms have two of each type of chromosome, homologous pairs identical in size and shape, the two sex chromosomes are very different from each other. Chromosome complements can be studied by the cytological technique of photographing cultured and stained blood cells, and then arranging them according to size and structural characteristics. This procedure results in a karyotype or chromosome complement of the individual (Figures 2-2, 2-15, and Table 2-3 all make use of this procedure). If we examine a karyotype of the chromosomes from human males and females, as shown in Figure 2-15, we can see that the chromosomes can be arranged into 23 pairs. The first 22 pairs are autosomal chromosomes, or autosomes. The sex chromosomes are the 23rd pair. Notice that for females, all 23 pairs are homologous, but that males have only 22 matched pairs—the autosomes. As you can see, the male sex chromosomes are markedly different, consisting of one long and one short chromosome.

Sex chromosomes are conventionally symbolized by X (female) and Y (male). Females have two X chromosomes and males one X and one Y chromosome. Of the 46 human chromosomes, then, 44 are autosomes and two are sex chromosomes. The X chromosome is much larger than the Y, and bears many more genes. It is the presence of the Y chromosome that determines maleness. We have learned that during male and female meiosis, all the chromosomes are separated and their numbers are reduced by one-half, to the haploid number. All egg cells receive one of each type of autosome plus one sex (X) chromosome. Since female egg cells have no Y chromosomes, all female gametes are alike in chromosomal content. In male meiosis, all sperm cells also receive one of each autosome, but one-half of the sperm cells will receive one *Y* and one-half will receive one *X* chromosome. When an egg is fertilized, the sex of the individual zygote will depend on which type of sperm cell fertilizes it. If an X chromosome bearing sperm fertilizes the egg, the zygote receives an XX sex

Table 2-3
Human Chromosome Designations According to the Denver System

GROUP DESIGNATION	CHROMOSOME NUMBERS	CHARACTERISTICS OF THE CHROMOSOMES
A	1–3	Very long with median centromeres
B	4–5	Long with submedian centromeres
C	6–12	Medium length with submedian centromeres
D	13–15	Medium length with near terminal centromeres
E	16–18	Short with median centromere in 16 and submedian in 17 and 18
F	19–20	Shorter than E group and with median centromeres
G	21–22	Very short with submedian centromeres
Sex Chromosomes	23	X similar to C group, Y similar to G group, but the chromatids tend to remain closer together

(From Winchester, 1971.)

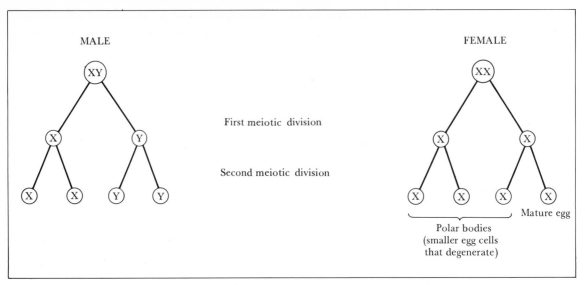

Figure 2-16
Simplified version of male and female meiosis (only sex chromosomes shown).

chromosome pair and develops into a female. A Y chromosome bearing sperm fertilizing an egg will result in an XY zygote, a male. Thus, the sex outcome of the new individual is a 50–50 chance occurrence, since one-half of all sperm cells contain a Y chromosome (Figure 2-16). It is the male parent, albeit indirectly and without controllable intent, who determines the sex of the offspring.

It appears that sex determination is triggered by interaction effects between the autosomes and sex chromosomes. The presence of the Y chromosome may switch total genetic action in the direction of male development. In early human embryonic development, for example, undifferentiated reproductive organs, appear, capable of producing either testes or ovaries. Then, at approximately seven weeks of embryonic age, these reproductive organs are stimulated to develop the organs of one sex, arresting any further development of the opposite sex organs, which remain dormant throughout life. The XY combination, interacting with the autosomes, produces the information for testicular development, simultaneously inhibiting ovarian development. The opposite takes place in XX combinations. Hormonal production from the resulting gonads then stimulates the genes to produce male or female characteristics. There are various sex-related phenomena that occur as a function of the sex chromosome combination. These phenotypic differences may arise from sex-linked genes, sex-limited genes, and sex-influenced genes.

Sex-Linked Inheritance

The X chromosome is larger than the Y and contains genes that are absent on the Y chromosome. In fact, the X chromosomes have no alleles on the Y chromosome (and vice versa—the Y chromosome contains genes not contained in the X chromosome). Genes on the X chromosome are known as sex-linked genes and produce sex-linked traits. Therefore, all males, who have only one of each sex-linked gene inherited from the mother, will express all the sex-linked genes they carry, whether dominant or recessive. There are also sex-linked traits that are more common in females than males, however. When a gene on the X chromosome is dominant, it will be displayed twice as often in females as in males. A father with such a gene can pass the trait on to his daughters but not to his sons.

Two of the best known examples of recessive, sex-linked traits in humans are color blindness and hemophilia. As expected in sex-linked traits, the frequency of color blindness is much higher in males than females (8% versus 1%). For a son to be color blind, the mother must be either homozygous or heterozygous (a carrier) for color blindness. For a daughter to inherit color blindness, however, she must receive both recessive alleles, meaning that the father must be color blind and the mother either a heterozygous carrier or color blind (homozygous). Hemophilia (bleeder's disease) is a condition of blood clotting deficiency that is caused by a recessive gene on the X chromosome. It is extremely rare in females (approximately one in 50 million births). In males, hemophilia has a frequency of about one in 10,000 births.

Not all sex-linked genes are X-linked. There are genes on the Y chromosome that have no X chromosome allele. Such Y-linked genes are called holandric. Hairy ears in males seems to be a trait that is Y-linked, always passed from a father to all his sons, which is what would be expected from a Y-linked gene (Winchester, 1971).

Sex-Limited Genes

Sex-limited genes are those whose expression occurs only in one sex, despite the fact that both X and Y chromosomes carry the same gene. Beards and pitch of the voice in males and breast development in females are examples of sex-limited traits. Their appearance is normally limited to males and females, respectively, but on rare occasion they appear in the wrong sex. Sex hormones may profoundly influence sex-limited traits.

Sex-Influenced Genes

Sex-influenced genes are neither sex-linked nor sex-limited, since they may appear in either sex, but are more common in one sex. Baldness results from a gene that is dominant in males and recessive in females and is a sex-influenced trait. The comparative lengths of the index finger and fourth finger is another example of a sex-influenced gene (Winchester, 1971). More males than females have an index finger shorter than the fourth finger, also apparently due to a gene that is dominant in males and recessive in females.

DEVELOPMENTAL BEHAVIORAL GENETICS

Most of our review of basic genetic principles and processes has focused on developmental genetics. The detailed presentation reflects the fact that developmental genetics is a primary precursor of abnormal patterns of behavioral development. An understanding of the etiology and implications of such deviations in ontogenesis, therefore, requires a basic familiarity with developmental genetics. Developmental genetics emphasizes the various genetic phenomena influencing developmental patterns of the individual organism along biochemical, gene–phenotype pathways.

We have seen that genes can exert their influence at any point along the developmental continuum, from the moment of conception to any time during the adult stage of life. We have also learned that the timing of gene activity and subsequent expression is different for different genes. Such genetic control of developmental events always occurs, as we have emphasized, in a given environmental complex of events. Gene effects are never isolated events separable from environmental, nongenetic factors. This interactional intimacy is constant, making it impossible to draw any conclusions about the relative significance of hereditary versus environmental contributions to development.

Despite this interaction system, we have seen that minute alterations in the biochemical structure of a single gene can initiate a chain of developmental events that may have serious, and sometimes lethal, consequences for the individual. In such cases, the genetic variation is so powerful in its direct effect that it disrupts the interaction balance, diminishing the relative contribution of environmental factors. The correspondence between genotype and phenotype then becomes much more obvious, making it easier to attribute a particular trait or traits to a genetic or hereditary factor. Remember, however, that environmental factors are only partially diluted in these instances, since every phenotype exhibits the phenomena of penetrance and expressivity. Relatively strict genetic determinism in certain genotypic patterns will surface in individual biobehavioral development because the genetic forces are so potent that developmental alternatives become significantly reduced. When this occurs, there is a very high probability of a one-to-one relationship between genotype and phenotype.

The restriction of alternate phenotypic outcomes to a single genetically determined path of development has been termed canalization by Waddington (1957). Waddington (1962) has provided a model of development that he calls the "epigenetic landscape" (Figure 2-17). The contour of the landscape represents the genotype, and the ball the developing phenotype. In development, represented by the forward rolling of the ball, environmental forces act on the ball and displace it from its original course into alternative developmental processes. Wide valley floors with low sloping sides permit significant phenotypic displacement by environmental factors. Narrow floors with steep walls represent a highly "buffered" or canalized developmental pathway. Prepotent genotypes may be hypothesized as engineering deep, narrow canalized paths, allowing for little deviation from gene expression in the developing organism. Although Waddington offers this model only as a suggestive representation of development, it does nicely illustrate the variable, flexible nature of gene–environment interaction.

Figure 2-17
Waddington's (1962) "epigenetic landscape."

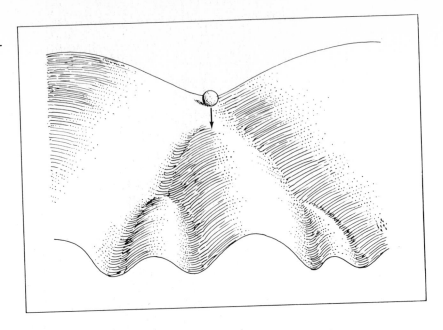

The field of developmental behavioral genetics comprises the study of the relationship between genotype and the developing behavioral phenotype. This definition implies that developmental behavioral genetics deals with the ontogenesis of behavioral differences as a function of genotypic variations. The goal of developmental behavior genetics, as far as developmental psychology is concerned, is to attain a better understanding of developmental patterns in ontogenesis. To what extent, for example, may certain individual differences be attributed to differential learning regimens (environmental conditions) rather than genetic differences? We know that within any given species, individuals differ from one another along a number of behavioral dimensions. Surely, some of these differences are due to differences in learned patterns of behavior. But it also seems reasonable to consider that certain individual behaviors may be strongly influenced by genotype. The genotype–phenotype pathway for behavioral traits is admittedly much more complex and harder to analyze than morphological and physiological traits. Nevertheless, it appears that our understanding of behavior can be greatly magnified by a knowledge of genetic contributions to behavior and its development. Developmental behavior genetics, then, is concerned with the genetic implications for individual differences in ontogenesis, and seeks genetic correlates of ontogenetic variations. As we shall see, the emphasis, direction, and goals of behavioral genetics have been a matter of concern for biologists and psychologists alike.

The Role of Behavioral Genetics in Developmental Psychology

Jack R. Vale (1973), a psychologist and behavioral geneticist, has raised some cogent questions about the role of behavioral genetics in psychology. He notes that the strategy of a strict environmental psychology has been shown to be incomplete at best. But the failure of behavioral genetics to clarify its scientific status and its potential contributions to the understanding of behavior has resulted in confusion over the relevance of behavioral genetics to general psychology. Vale emphasizes that the survival of behavioral genetics in the behavioral sciences depends on the fusion of genetics and psychology. Conceptually and operationally, behavioral genetics can assume two very different meanings and subsequently two different postures: genetic or psychological (see Figure 2-18). As Vale

Figure 2-18
The interdisciplinary nature of behavioral genetics is illustrated by these overlapping circles. Vale argues that behavioral genetics must be encompassed within the behavioral sciences if it is to be a useful science.

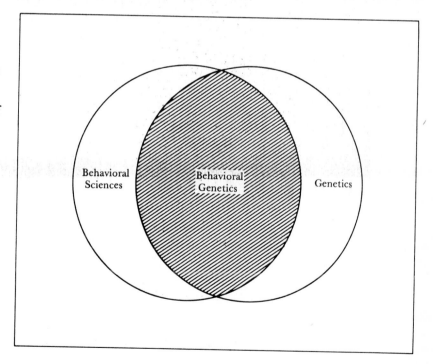

Behavioral Sciences

Behavioral Genetics

Genetics

points out, if behavioral genetics aligns itself primarily with genetics, it becomes a *genetics of behavior,* which investigates *gene* functioning by applying genetic tests to behavioral situations. This kind of behavioral genetics emphasizes the collection of genetic data, extending genotype–phenotype relationships from morphological and physiological traits to behavioral traits. Clearly, this genetic approach would have little implication for psychology, since the major goal is a genetic one.

Vale concludes his analysis of behavior genetics as a biological science by firmly stating that the genetic approach is neither feasible nor of any real value to genetics. Behaviors are not a good index for the study of genetics because acceptable behavioral phenotypes are rare. That is, in the absence of the assumption of trait equivalence, there are few behaviors that can be meaningfully analyzed because of their great variability, their poor reliability in identification, and their polygenetic origins. As a result, a genetics of behavior is not practical. Even if it were, Vale expresses grave doubts about its ability to generate new information about transmission genetics.

A very different sort of behavioral genetics emerges, however, when the emphasis is shifted to *the use of genotype in behavioral analysis.* Here, the goal is to increase our understanding of behavior. By employing the best use of genotype in behavioral analysis, we can maximize *behavioral* information. Vale describes this approach as "a genetically aware psychology," focusing on the independent-variable effects of genotype on behavioral processes. According to Vale, there is no alternative, with psychology having everything to gain and genetics little to lose. Vale (1973) concludes:

Behavior genetics has already participated at a crucial stage in one victory for reality by exposing the gratuitous assumptions and subterranean logic of radical behaviorism. But it is understood by all that success in the future demands a more positive role than that of a genetical gadfly about the head of a recalcitrant environmental psychology. It is thus not a question of whether to take the next step, but of whither. I believe the answer lies in that hoariest of all plagues and divisions, the nature–nurture controversy. Or rather, the answer lies in the lack *of a nature–nurture controversy. (p. 880)*

Vale's position may be clarified by some additional comments. The development of behavioral genetics as a science since the time of its formal introduction in 1960 (Fuller & Thompson, 1960) was very much influenced and accelerated by psychological research, particularly with animals. However, the initial impact of behavioral genetics on psychology was minimal because psychological thinking and research were dominated at that time by the learning or environmental school. This is the "environmental psychology" to which Vale refers with some heat.

The strictest form of environmentalism originates from John B. Watson, whose *Behaviorism,* published between 1914 and 1930, was quickly adopted by many American psychologists and forged into a formidable school of American psychology. Radical environmentalism was largely due to the tiresome nature–nurture controversy. These bipolar concepts of behavioral control and development, the biological–genetic and the environmental–learning, stirred an unrelenting debate in psychology for the first four decades of the twentieth century. Watson denounced the idea of inherited behavioral traits and dismissed the potential significance of genetics for development. Instead, he proclaimed the supreme importance of environment, learning, and child-rearing in molding behavioral traits. Thiessen (1972) pointed out that the nature–nurture controversy, and the predictably radical, extreme positions it generated, delayed the development of behavioral genetics by separating genetics and psychology. But over the past two decades, a growing body of evidence has clearly demonstrated the significance and influence of genotype on various behavioral patterns (Manosevitz, Lindzey, & Thiessen, 1969; McClearn & DeFries, 1973, Thiessen, 1972). The gene–environment interaction is now firmly established and their mutual, inseparable effects on developmental processes have been described by Moltz (1965) as an epigenetic approach to psychological development. This basically is Vale's "genetically aware psychology." Note that an epigenetic approach denies the doctrine of exclusive control of behavior by either genes or environment, a point we have made repeatedly.

Historical Perspective   Long before any formal knowledge of genetics existed, behavioral genetics was practiced in the form of animal husbandry, the breeding of animals for specific physical and behavioral characteristics. The belief that "like produces like" is a long-standing one that still prevails today, and notions of the heritability of such traits as criminality, pauperism, and mental deficiency were considered to be reflections of "bad blood" running in families. Dramatic, biased stories of hereditary control of those behaviors were presented as examples of the bad-blood thesis, ignoring the fact that like does not produce like in just as many cases. As we shall see, the appeal of this inborn traits notion eventually formed a primitive approach to human behavioral genetics that has more historical than scientific significance.

Early in the nineteenth century, Franz Joseph Gall revitalized phrenology, a system that associated various mental faculties and behaviors with skull protuberances—bumps on the head. Behavioral traits were assumed to be controlled by inherited amounts of brain tissue in specific regions of the brain. Relatively greater amounts of tissue in these regions produced pressure points on the interior skull, causing it to protrude slightly and form a bump. Thus, the degree of possession of such traits as criminality, dishonesty, and love could be "predicted" by assessing the size and location of the bumps. As amusing as this may sound now, phrenology became extremely popular in both Europe and America. Later in the nineteenth century, the Italian criminologist, Cesare Lombroso, formulated a system of identifying criminals or potential criminals on the basis of characteristics which Lombroso believed to be inherited physical stigmata (marks or signs). Lombroso listed a number of physiognomic features such as crooked noses, receding chins, and lobeless ears that supposedly signaled a genetic predisposition to criminal behavior.

Perhaps the most famous of the early family studies are those of the "Jukes" and the "Kallikaks" (both pseudonyms). In 1875, Richard Dugdale published his study, *The Jukes: A Study in Crime, Pauperism, Disease, and Heredity.* As a member of the Prison Association of New York, Dugdale had been assigned to inspect the county jails. Finding six related prisoners in one county, Dugdale traced the lineage of this family over a period of 130 years. Beginning with five sisters, the family increased to 2094 people, one-half of whom were found to have a sordid history of criminality, immorality, and mental deficiency. Although Dugdale was conservative in his conclusion about the effects of heredity, his study was widely accepted by the hereditarians as proof of "morbid inheritance" (McClearn & DeFries, 1973). In fact, Dugdale ignored environmental factors and made no attempt to estimate the effects of the Jukes' impoverished conditions, which fostered the behaviors he described. In addition, his method of data collection was unreliable, faulty, and often second-hand and anecdotal.

In 1912, Henry Goddard, psychologist and director of a New Jersey institution for the retarded, published his findings on the Kallikaks. Goddard believed he had found a family situation that controlled for the confounding of genetic and environmental effects. Goddard had discovered a "Martin Kallikak" who had originated two different branches of family descendants, one by his illicit affair with a mentally retarded woman while he was a soldier in the Revolutionary War, and the other by his marriage to a woman of "good family" after his discharge at the end of the War. The 480 descendants of the illicit affair resembled the Jukes in their behavioral characteristics, whereas those of his marriage were reportedly almost all normal, including a high proportion of individuals of accomplishment. Goddard interpreted his data as providing support for the inheritance of mental retardation, with little, if any, etiological significance given to environmental factors. Like Dugdale, Goddard failed to control for the effect of environment on the development of subnormal and normal intelligence. His methodology can also be criticized for the lack of precision and for the use of collateral information (data obtained from other individuals, such as friends, neighbors, and relatives, rather than the direct subject of interest). The impossibility of separating and controlling genetic and environmental factors in retrospective pedigree studies such as these make them useless, pointless efforts that have no scientific value. Nevertheless, these early efforts provided a crude behavioral genetics that attempted to establish a relationship between genotype and phenotype, and they were widely accepted as a solution to the nature–nurture controversy.

Francis Galton pioneered the use of twins and correlation techniques to study heredity. Between 1865 and 1869, he published two works, "Hereditary Talent and Character" and *Hereditary Genius,* in which he stressed the hereditary nature of intelligence, maximizing genetic effects and minimizing environmental contributions. He believed that genius tended to run in families, and that it was the obligation of man to improve his lot by controlling breeding. Galton coined the term, eugenics, and founded the eugenics movement in England. He was to become almost fanatically dedicated to eugenics, the improvement of humans by selective breeding or "good marriages." Although he stressed positive eugenics, Galton was also an advocate of negative eugenics, improving human stock by preventing individuals with certain defects from reproducing. So convinced was Galton of his data that he stated, "An enthusiasm to improve the race is so noble in its aim that it might well give rise to the sense of religious obligation" (Haller, cited in Thiessen, 1972, p. 134).

By the time of Galton's death in 1911, almost every civilized country had undertaken a eugenics movement of some sort (Thiessen, 1972). Inexorably, these early notions about behavioral genetics led to active programs of negative eugenics and the establishment of sterilization laws, directed primarily at the mentally deficient. American sterilization laws and programs preceded those of other countries by 20 years (Thiessen, 1972). The eugenics movement began fading in the late 1930s, with the final blow delivered by the murderously psychotic tactics of Adolph Hitler. Hitler's convictions of Aryan supremacy were not original, but were heavily based on the mid-ninteenth century writings of Count Gobineau and Houston Chamberlain and their distorted views of heredity (McClearn & DeFries, 1973). This should serve as a reminder that we are not engaged in irrelevant academic exercises in history. The intense scientific controversies that arise in the academic community often spill over into the public domain, to be seized and promoted by others who are capable of distorting scientific principles with disastrous results. By dint of emotional rhetoric and influence, it is tragically easy to convince people that action against certain groups designated as inferior or undesirable must be taken as a measure of national salvation.

Genetic Anomalies in Development

A primary goal of behavioral genetics is to discover genetic correlates of behavior, in order to further understand the bases of individual differences. Laboratory data have firmly established the fact that genes can affect or control certain behavior patterns in a variety of infrahuman organisms ranging from insects to mammals (McClearn & DeFries, 1973; Manosevitz et al., 1969; Strickberger, 1976; Thiessen, 1972). These laboratory studies demonstrate gene–ontogenesis relationships that contribute to our conceptual and empirical understanding of development and its variations. Since our major concern is human development, we will direct our discussion to human genotype–phenotype relationships.

Humans are subject to the same laws of biology as other animals, so it is reasonable to assume that similar genetic processes may contribute to behavioral development in humans, although in a much more complicated and subtle fashion. Remember, we are not speaking of genetic determinism but of genetic predisposition, or what Dobzhansky (1968) calls "genetic conditioning." This is especially true in normal development. The clearest examples of genetic influences on human development, both structural and behavioral, derive from abnormal genetic conditions, and these conditions provide the physical evidence for relating genotype and phenotype. However, even in these cases, the developmental pathways between gene activity and phenotype remain unknown, particularly for polygenetically determined behavioral traits. The major exception is the biochemistry related to some conditions of mental retardation caused by genetic anomalies or abnormalities.

For most people, the inheritance of the biochemical and morphological aspects of phenotype is a relatively easy notion to accept. However, the relationship between genes and behavior is much less obvious and much further removed from gene activity. Consequently, it is more difficult for some people, both intellectually and emotionally, to accept the idea that genes and heredity may affect the human behavioral variations that we observe daily. We have learned that the influence and effects of genes are not mysterious phenomena. Gene action begins with DNA and protein synthesis, enzyme formation, biochemical reactions, cellular activity, and the direction of tissue differentiation and development. It culminates in the development of the structure, organization, and function of each response system. The gene–phenotype pathway thus weaves through every organ system, with behavior, the most complex response system, being the most difficult to comprehend in terms of its genetic etiology and development. We will now discuss some instructive examples of human genetic anomalies, which should clarify developmental behavioral genetics and its role in revealing the etiology of certain patterns of ontogenesis.

Inherited Defects in Humans

V. A. McKusick (1971) has catalogued 1876 known inherited genetic defects in humans. Of these, 943 are autosomal dominant traits, 783 are autosomal recessive traits, and 150 are X-linked traits. Behavioral problems associated with genetic defects may be quite direct, as in some forms of mental retardation, such as Down's Syndrome. Other genetic defects may have indirect, subtle effects on the victims. For instance, the responses of other people may create a distorted social environment in which abnormal behavior patterns are learned, disrupting interpersonal relationships, attitudes, and perceptions (e.g., a child with hemophelia who is overprotected).

CLASSICAL PHENYLKETONURIA   Phenylketonuria (PKU) is the best-known example of genetic biochemistry related to the development of mental retardation. PKU was first described in 1934 by Folling, a Norwegian physician and biochemist. This hereditary metabolic disease is transmitted by an autosomal recessive gene, and therefore must be in a homozygous condition for its expression. The incidence of PKU (homozygotes) is approximately one in 10,000 births (.0014%) with about 50 in 10,000 births being heterozygous carriers. PKU is diagnosed by the presence of phenylpyruvic acid in the urine. PKU is a disorder of amino acid metabolism arising from the absence or inactivity of a specific liver enzyme, phenylalanine hydroxylase, which plays a critical role in catalyzing the conversion of phenylalanine to tyrosine. The recessive alleles prevent the formation or activity of this enzyme, thus blocking the amino acid conversion. Phenylalanine, an essential amino acid found particularly in meats and dairy products, subsequently begins to accumulate in the tissues, becoming transformed into phenylpyruvic acid and other toxic metabolites. The accumulation of these toxic metabolites soon reaches critical tissue levels and prevents normal development of the central nervous system (CNS).

Figure 2-19
Metabolic pathways of phenylalanine metabolism, showing blocks in phenylketonuria, alkaptonuria, and albinism. Intermediary steps are indicated by dashed arrows.

(After Lerner, 1968).

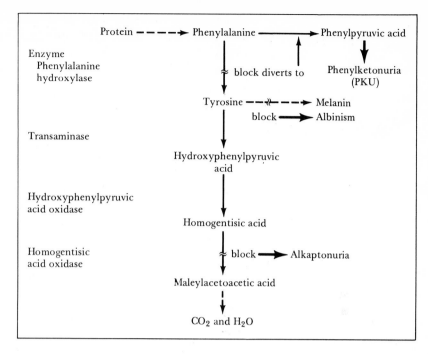

Within 6 months after birth, brain development is arrested or brain tissue damaged, resulting in mental retardation of moderate to severe proportions in more than 90% of the cases. Intelligence ranges from below 20 IQ to an IQ of approximately 85, although an occasional individual with PKU has been reported with a tested IQ of between 85 to above 100 (Matarazzo, 1972). Other symptoms that may accompany PKU are blond coloration, microcephaly, seizures, locomotor problems, and little or no language development. Generally, the child with PKU is hyperactive, irritable, and displays temper tantrums. Note that the morphological and behavioral symptoms have a considerable range of expressivity. The metabolic pathway in PKU is shown in Figure 2-19. Metabolic blocks other than the tyrosine block are also diagrammed. Alkaptonuria is a condition in which excreted urine turns black on exposure to the air, and may also appear in PKU. Another block in the same metabolic pathway results in albinism.

PKU is a particularly instructive genetic defect because it so clearly illustrates gene–environment interaction in its developmental etiology. Notice that the autosomal recessive genes and the subsequent disorder of phenylalanine metabolism are inherited, not PKU. The clinical symptoms of PKU develop when the infant begins to eat a normal diet. Normal diets contain large amounts of phenylalanine, which the child cannot metabolize. This triggers the chain of metabolic events depicted in Figure 2-19. PKU is also a signficant example in developmental behavioral genetics, because the discovery of its biochemistry has resulted in a therapeutic management program that prevents or significantly reduces symptom development. Treatment success depends on the very early placement of the infant with PKU on a low phenylalanine diet. This special diet, developed in 1953, results in biochemical normalization and thus normal CNS development. Prevention, however, is dependent upon early diagnosis and treatment. Treatment started after the age of 1 year may have little or no effect on clinical symptoms, since CNS damage will already have taken place. Reports of the efficacy of early diet management vary from prevention of mental retardation to partial amelioration of mental retardation and accompanying symptomatology (Berman, Waisman, & Graham, 1966; Hsia, 1970).

Treatment results no doubt depend on the potency of the allelic condition and its attending expressivity. Most states now require mandatory pediatric screening for PKU. The Guthrie test is used to assess phenylalanine in the blood, 24–48 hours following protein ingestion by the infant, within the first few days of life. A second urine test is conducted 4–6 weeks later. If the first test shows abnormally high phenylalanine levels, the infant is placed on the special diet of milk and meat substitutes. The child remains on the diet until maturation of the CNS is nearly complete and it is no longer susceptible to the toxic metabolites. Typically, the diet is maintained through middle childhood. The diet is a difficult one to maintain and requires constant monitoring. Reed (1975) describes some of the residual psychological problems that may arise in both children and parents under such a strict diet management, such as hostility, guilt, fear, and anxiety, which may generate behavioral problems not directly related to the genotypic condition.

The discovery of a treatment program for PKU may result in the development of a PKU genotype but normal phenotype—a phenocopy of a genetically normal individual—because the diet prevents the symptoms of PKU. PKU treatment programs are an example of euphenics (Lederberg, 1963), defined as the improvement of the phenotype by the environmental treatment of genetic defects. Here, the biochemical environment of PKU is altered to accomodate a defective phenotype. Euphenics is the opposite of eugenics, but such programs obviously increase the "genetic load," since a "cured" person with PKU still carries the homozygotic allelic condition. Consequently, all offspring will be carriers in cases where one parent has PKU. Clearly, genetic counseling is required to reduce genetic repetition in these instances. Phenalalanine loading (hyperphenylalanemia) tests to detect carriers are now available. Serious reproductive casualties are reportedly prevalent in pregnant PKU women because of the unfavorable intrauterine environment for the developing fetus (Howell & Stevenson, 1971). With such a high risk factor, pregnancy is not advisable.

LESCH–NYHAN SYNDROME   There are other types of heritable metabolic disorders that do not involve amino acid metabolism. Two examples of such genetic anomalies are the Lesch–Nyhan syndrome and Tay–Sachs disease. The Lesch–Nyhan syndrome is a lethal neurological condition transmitted by an X-linked recessive gene, affecting males only. This is a rare genetic defect with a frequency of one in 50,000 male births. The inheritance of this genotype produces a characteristic bizarre behavioral pattern in the affected individual. Neurological signs of mental retardation, cerebral palsy, and choreoathetosis (spasmodic, involuntary motor movements) typically develop before 1 year of age. By the age of 3, the child begins to display the behavioral syndrome of compulsive biting and self-mutilation of the lips and hands, head-banging, and aggressive behavior toward others. Most cases show severe levels of retardation, poor motor and locomotor development, and little language development. Patients rarely live beyond late adolescence. The etiology of the Lesch–Nyhan syndrome has been traced to the absence or inactivity of an enzyme controlling purine metabolism. Unmetabolized purine compounds are converted to uric acid and thus biochemical signs of this syndrome can be obtained from tests for uric acid in the urine and for enzyme levels in heterozygotic carriers. High risk pregnancies can be identified as fetal carriers or affected individuals with the procedure of amniocentesis, in which a sample of amniotic fluid is obtained by transabdominal puncture and analyzed. Positive identification of the genetic condition signals the need for genetic counseling, as there is no known cure for this condition.

TAY–SACHS DISEASE   Tay–Sachs disease is another lethal genetic defect transmitted by a recessive autosomal gene. This is a metabolic disorder of lipid (fat) metabolism caused by the absence of a specific enzyme component. This genetic disorder is much more common among Ashkenazi Jews, descendants of central and Eastern European Jews, than among non-Jewish populations.*

The Ashkenazim have an incidence of one in 5000 births versus one in 200,000 to 500,000 births for non-Jews. In Tay–Sachs victims, nystagmus (rapid, irregular eye movements) and paralysis develop during the first few months of life, with progressive and severe motor and neurological deterioration and blindness. Death occurs by 2 or 3 years of age. Autopsy has revealed an accumulation of lipids in CNS cells and neural degeneration. Carriers (1 in 39 among Ashkenazi Jews) can be identified by biochemical analysis and affected fetuses by amniocentesis.

HUNTINGTON'S CHOREA   We mentioned earlier in this chapter that genes may express themselves at any time along the developmental continuum. An example of this phenomenon of variable age of onset is Huntington's Chorea. It is inherited as a lethal dominant autosomal gene, so each of the children of an affected parent has a 50% chance of inheriting the disease. The incidence of Huntington's Chorea is approximately one in 24,000. It is characterized by progressive, insidious mental and CNS deterioration, and chorieform movement (disturbances in motor control). Behavioral symptoms of

---

*Dysautonomia is another genetic defect to which the Ashkenazi Jews are susceptible. Dysautonomia is also inherited as an autosomal recessive, resulting in inability to sense pain or temperature, absence of taste buds and tears, unstable blood pressure and body temperature, arrested growth, and retardation. Constant care is required for affected individuals and although the life span has been extended by medical improvements, the condition is lethal. Approximately one American Jew in 100 is a carrier. No screening tests are yet available to detect carriers or affected fetuses.

emotional disturbance frequently precede motoric disruption. Motor and intellectual deterioration become increasingly severe and death follows. Age of onset of Huntington's Chorea ranges from childhood to old age, but the mean age of onset is between 40 and 45 years. Diffuse cortical degeneration occurs in this genetic disorder, but the underlying biochemical events are not known. The characteristic variable age of onset demonstrates a genotypic condition, present at birth, but triggered at a later time by aging processes.

CHROMOSOMES AND BEHAVIOR

Up to this point, only examples of heritable *gene* defects and their developmental consequences have been presented. In this section, we will discuss some human chromosome configurations and their associated structural and behavioral anomalies. The correct number of human chromosomes has been known only since 1956, when Tijio and Levan demonstrated that the normal diploid number is 46 (cited in Hsia, 1968). Prior to that time, 48 chromosomes had been the recognized diploid number since 1923.

Abnormalities occurring in chromosomes involve much more DNA material than single gene defects do. Consequently, chromosomal problems can present serious developmental disruptions with a broad spectrum of symptoms. Chromosome anomalies may take the form of monosomy (one chromosome missing), trisomy (one extra chromosome), or partial loss of chromosome (chromosome deletion). Many spontaneous abortions are due to chromosome anomalies, and approximately one in 200 live births has one or another chromosome abnormality. Chromosomes function as the carriers of genes, as packaging units for transporting genes during cell division, and as bodies linking gene groups together within homologous chromosomes (Hsia, 1968). We can see, then, how alterations in chromosomal structure or function can profoundly affect ontogenesis by their effect on a large amount of DNA material and gene interactions. Although meiosis usually proceeds without incident, chromosomal rearrangements of either the autosomal or sex chromosomes sometimes occur. We will now briefly examine some of these anomalies and their etiological significance for development.

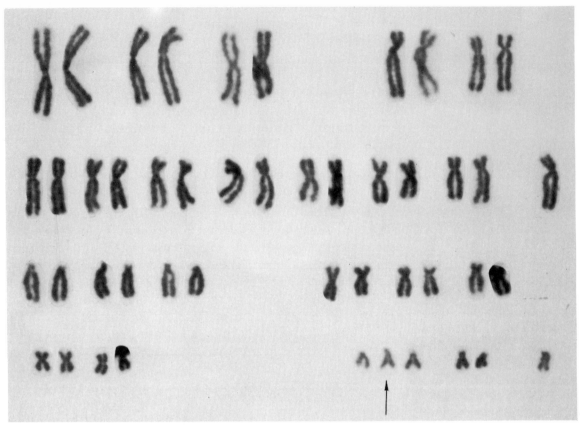

Figure 2-20
Karyotype of a male with primary G$_{21}$ trisomy.

(From Nadler & Borges, 1966. Copyright © 1966 by Year Book Medical
Publishers, Inc., Chicago. Reproduced by permission.)

Autosomal
Chromosome
Anomalies

DOWN'S SYNDROME   Down's syndrome was first described
in 1866 by Langdon Down and became known as "mongolism"
because the characteristic slanted skin folds over the eyes were
suggestive of the Mongol race. In 1959, Lejeune, Gauthier,
and Turpin (cited in Hsia, 1968), discovered that Down's
syndrome is the result of a chromosomal abnormality in which
one of the autosomal chromosomes, pair number 21, has three
chromosomes rather than two (trisomy-21). Thus, people with
trisomy-21 have 47 chromosomes instead of 46 as you can see
from the karyotype of an affected male patient shown in
Figure 2-20. This discovery was the first chromosomal anomaly

found in humans and therefore the first mental retardation syndrome for which a chromosome basis could be described. Down's syndrome is relatively common, occurring in one of each 500 to 600 births for a frequency rate of approximately .15% of all newborns.

Clinical symptoms of Down's syndrome include flattened facial features with protruding tongue, epicanthal eyefolds (small skin folds over the inner corners of the eyes), eye defects, cardiac defect, motor problems, unusual dermato-glyphic patterns (abnormal hand and finger prints), and mental retardation. The incidence of respiratory infections, cardiovascular problems, and leukemia is high and the mortality rate in these individuals is correspondingly high during the first 3 years of life. The degree of retardation is characteristically severe, ranging from 30 to 50 IQ, with diffuse neuropathological changes present. Patients are typically quiet but cheerful, with good dispositions.

Standard trisomy-21 has been traced to nondisjunction: the homologous pair fails to separate during meiosis (see Figure

A Down's syndrome (mongoloid) child playing. This genetic anomaly produces severe retardation and the characteristic physical features by which it is commonly known. Down's syndrome was the first chromosomal abnormality identified in human beings, and the first retardation syndrome for which a chromosomal basis could be determined. The incidence of mongolism in newborns increases with maternal age, and it has been determined that the average incidence in all births could be reduced by one-half if women completed childbearing before their mid-thirties.

(Photo by Sybil Shelton/ Monkmeyer Press Photo Service.)

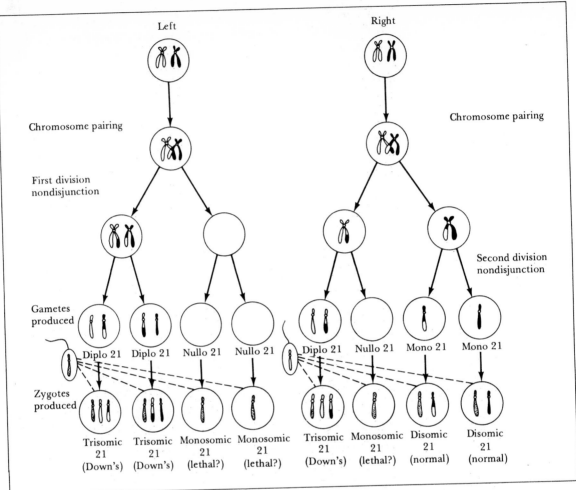

Figure 2-21
Schematic representation of nondisjunction occurring during *(left)* the first division and *(right)* the second division of meiosis in standard triosomy-21.

(From Penrose & Smith, 1966.)

2-21). The incidence of Down's syndrome has long been known to be related to maternal age. The distribution of Down's syndrome by maternal age is shown in Table 2-4. You can see that the ratio of trisomy-21 births to normal births is almost 40 times greater among women 45 years of age and above compared to 19-year-old women. More than 56% of infants with Down's syndrome are born to mothers 35 and older, whereas only 16% of normal infants are born to mothers of this age.

McClearn and Defries (1973) point out that the incidence of Down's syndrome could be reduced by one-half if women completed their childbearing before 35 years of age. There is no known relationship between paternal age and Down's syndrome.

The maternal age hypothesis in Down's syndrome is related to egg storage in females and the effects of long term exposure to internal biochemical changes on ovogenesis. Such internal environmental changes may produce nondisjunction in some of the eggs during the final stages of meiosis. In males, spermatogenesis involves the continuous production of gametes, with no cumulative effects of long term exposure to internal environmental factors. Approximately 90% of all cases of Down's syndrome are standard trisomy-21. The remainder involve other genetic phenomena such as translocation, in which an extra chromosome 21 becomes attached to a nonhomologous chromosome during meiosis. The offspring carrying the translocated chromosome have 46 chromosomes with pair 21 intact. The risk of producing an infant with Down's syndrome is much higher in a carrier of translocational Down's syndrome. Karyotyping siblings of translocational Down's syndrome and amniocentesis can be used for genetic counseling and informed decisions concerning childbearing and abortion.

CRI DU CHAT SYNDROME The cri du chat or "cat cry" syndrome is an autosomal chromosome anomaly that involves

Table 2-4 Distribution of Down's Syndrome by Mothers' Ages			

MOTHERS' AGE	% DOWN'S INFANTS BORN	% OF NORMAL BIRTHS	% DOWN'S BIRTHS / % NORMAL BIRTHS
−19	1.9	4.9	0.39
20–24	10.5	26.1	0.40
25–29	14.5	30.9	0.47
30–34	16.6	22.1	0.75
35–39	27.0	12.0	2.25
40–44	25.2	3.7	6.81
45–	4.3	0.3	14.33
Total	100.0	100.0	1.00
Mean Age	34.43	28.17	—

(From Smith & Berg, 1976.)

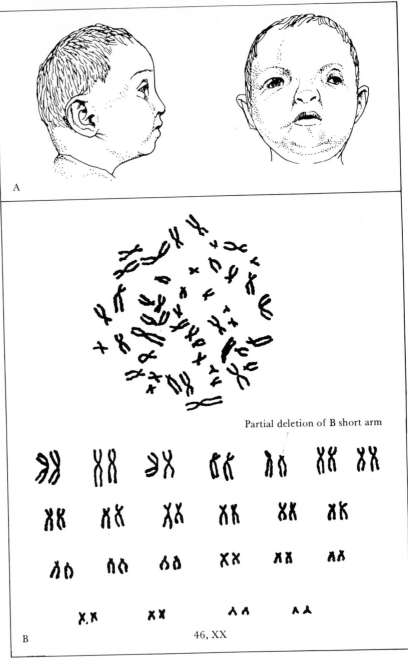

Partial deletion of B short arm

46, XX

Figure 2-22
A cri du chat patient (A) and the karyotype of such a patient (B),
showing partial deletion of the short arm of number 5.

(Adapted from *Introduction to Behavioral Genetics* by G. E. McClearn and J. C.
DeFries. W. H. Freeman and Company. Copyright © 1973.)

a deletion of about one-half of the short arm of chromosome 5 (Figure 2-22). The majority of infants with this syndrome have a strange, weak cry during infancy that is best described as sounding like the mewing of a cat. Other symptoms include microcephaly, cardiac defects, widely spaced eyes ("moon face"), arrested growth, and mental retardation. Incidence of cri du chat syndrome is lower than that of Down's syndrome, but exact figures are unknown. Hsia (1968) reports that maternal age has little effect on the incidence of cri du chat syndrome.

SEX CHROMOSOME ANOMALIES

Turner's Syndrome

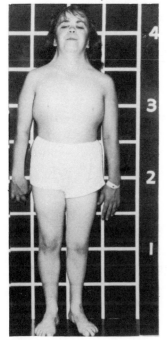

Figure 2-23
Patient with X0 Turner's syndrome.

(From Hsia, 1968. Copyright © 1968 by Yearbook Medical Publishers, Inc., Chicago. Reproduced by permission.)

We turn now to chromosome anomalies involving abnormal numbers of sex chromosomes and their ontogenetic effects. The severity of defects in individuals having autosomal anomalies is often, but not always, much more severe relative to those with sex chromosome aberrations. This is particularly true for individuals with extra X chromosomes. Apparently this is due to the inactivation of additional X chromosomes. While a number of sex chromosome complements can occur, we will review only a few of the better known ones.

Turner's syndrome was first clinically described in 1938. It is characterized by the sex chromosome complement of X0, with a total of only 45 chromosomes (karyotype 45, X). Phenotypically, the individual is female, but with only one X chromosome instead of the normal two. Approximately 80% of cases of Turner's syndrome are of the X0 type. The remaining cases involve other structural abnormalities of the sex chromosomes. Frequency of occurrence is estimated at one in 3000 female births, or about .03% of the population. Turner's syndrome is characterized by gonadal dysgenesis (lacking ovarian tissue), sterility, infantile sexual development, short stature, and webbed neck (Figure 2-23). Secondary sexual characteristics fail to develop at puberty because of the absence of sex hormones. Most females with Turner's syndrome are of normal intelligence and no neurological defects have been found. The etiology of this syndrome is meiotic nondisjunction of the sex chromosomes. There is no relationship of increased frequency with maternal age. Meiotic nondisjunction may occur in either male or female meiosis, resulting in a gamete having no sex chromosome. Figure 2-24 shows how combinations of egg and sperm cells can result in the X0 karyotype.

Current treatment of Turner's syndrome consists of estrogen administration to ameliorate some of the clinical symptoms of infantile sexual development. Affected females are susceptible to psychological problems of adjustment because of their appearance and parental attitudes. The behavioral effects of this genotype may, therefore, be much more subtle and indirect than in the previous examples we have considered.

Early Menopause Syndrome

The early menopause syndrome is another sex chromosome anomaly among phenotypic females. These individuals possess an XXX sex chromosome complement (karyotype 47, XXX). Triple-X females are typically retarded, but physically and sexually normal and fertile. Menstrual irregularities and early menopause are often reported, but Hsia (1968) indicates that there is little evidence to suggest that these symptoms are any more common among these patients than in the general population. The incidence of triple-X is reported to be approximately .14% among female newborns, but .39% among institutionalized retardates (McClearn & DeFries, 1973). There is no correlation between triple-X offspring and parental age. Mental retardation appears, then, to be the most outstanding feature of the early menopause syndrome, and the name of this syndrome may not reflect its defining characteristic.

Klinefelter's Syndrome

Klinefelter's syndrome was first described in 1942 as a condition of phenotypic males with clinical symptoms of sterility, little body and facial hair, gynecomastia (breast enlargement), and absence of secondary sex characteristics. Findings of mental retardation are inconsistent, with reports ranging from 25–50% retardation among individuals with Klinefelter's syndrome. No clear neurological defects have been found. The sex chromosome complement in these cases is typically XXY (karyotype 47, XXY), although variants occur as they do in all chromosome anomalies. The individual is a male because of the presence of the Y chromosome. Androgen treatment can be administered to stimulate development of secondary sex

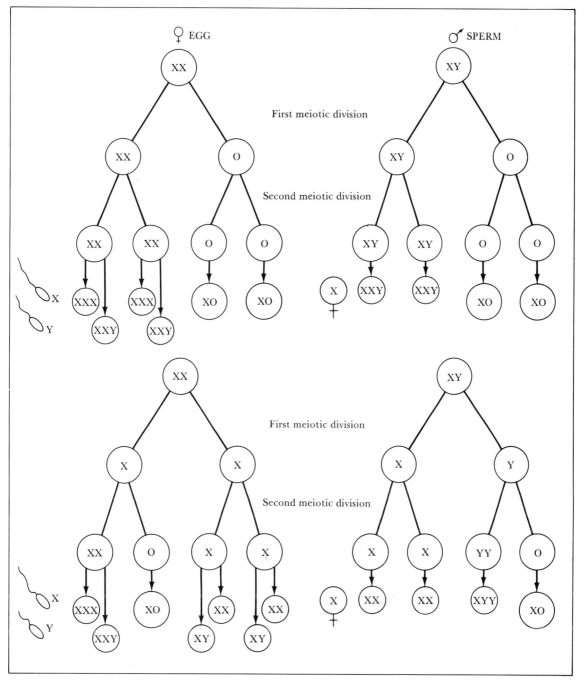

Figure 2-24
Diagrammatic representation of meiotic nondisjunction of sex chromosomes at first and second divisions and resulting karyotype.

characteristics. Klinefelter's syndrome can occur as a result of either male or female meiotic nondisjunction of the sex chromosomes (Figure 2-24), although there is an increased risk of this syndrome with increasing maternal age. The incidence of this syndrome is about two in 1000 male births. Reports of behavioral problems are much higher than those for Turner's syndrome (Reed, 1975). Such individuals appear to develop a variety of personality and emotional problems, but the etiology of these behavioral problems is obscured by the physical characteristics of individuals with Klinefelter's syndrome. Undoubtedly, the appearance of these males may present formidable adjustment problems throughout life, and it is not possible to relate these developmental difficulties to the genotype in any direct fashion. Reports of XXY males being genetically susceptible to homosexuality are not substantiated.

XYY Anomaly During the past 15 years, considerable interest has been aroused over the effects of an extra Y chromosome in males (karyotype 47, XYY). The first report of an XYY male appeared in 1961, describing an individual of normal intelligence, free from any physical or psychological defects. Between 1961 and 1968, scattered reports began to appear in which some investigators noted a possible relationship between XYY males and histories of violent, aggressive behavior. Some of these reports also noted that XYY males were taller than average (many were over six feet). Both the news media and various scientists quickly concluded that an extra Y chromosome genetically predisposed such males to antisocial and violent behavior. From this conclusion, it was a short step to claiming a biological basis for human aggression. Several cases of violent crimes committed by XYY males appeared in the literature. Some legal attempts were made by defense attorneys to dismiss the charges on grounds of insanity resulting from genetic disease. Most were not successful.

A great deal of research has since been conducted in an attempt to clarify the relationship between the XYY genotype and aggressive behavior. The data concerning the possible existence of an XYY syndrome and its potential relationship to aggressive behavior has been reviewed by Jarvik, Klodin, and Matsuyama (1973). The majority of clinical reports on the

XYY genotype seem to present a picture of tall physique, below average intelligence, and aggression. Jarvik et al. (1973) conclude, however, that none of these presumed attributes is necessary or sufficient for a diagnosis of XYY. These characteristics range from one end of the continuum to the other within XYY groups and can be found prominently in normal males. The conclusions of Jarvik et al., along with other investigators, are that no data at present clearly establish the existence of a behavioral syndrome associated with an XYY genotype, and thus it is premature and inaccurate to refer to this genotype as a syndrome. There is no symptom cluster to justify a syndrome classification.

The available data suggest an XYY incidence of .13% (approximately one per 1000) among newborn males. The incidence of XYY among institutionalized criminal populations is shown to be 1.9%, 15 times greater than that found in newborn males and normal adults. Jarvik et al. conclude that these data strongly suggest an association between criminal behavior and an extra Y chromosome. They point out that, even if these data are true, XYY males would comprise a negligible proportion of criminals. But despite their discussion of the many environmental factors contributing to criminal and antisocial behavior, Jarvik et al. do suggest that an extra Y chromosome predisposes one to aggressive behavior.

We must still deal with the fact that many XYY males are not aggressive or criminal, that many normal males are, and that females also are capable of aggression and violence. The environmental histories of convicted criminals are often so unfavorable as to provide an equally strong argument for an environmental etiology of the antisocial behavior. The data seem to suggest that the penetrance and expressivity of any assumed genetic predisposition to violent behavior, as expressed by the XYY genotype, would be extremely variable, plastic, and susceptible to major modification by environmental conditions from early childhood on.

In an impressive and ambitious multidisciplinary study of criminality in XYY and XXY men, Witkin, Mednick, Shulsinger, Bakkestrøm, Christiansen, Goodenough, Hirschhorn, Lundsteen, Owen, Philip, Rubin, and Stocking (1976) conducted a large-scale chromosomal survey of male Danish citizens born in Copenhagen between 1944 and 1947. Witkin et al. report prevalence rates of XYY and XXY as 2.9 and 3.9 per thousand, respectively. These incidence data are higher than those reported by other investigators (Jarvik et al., 1973). Witkin et al. found no evidence of heightened aggression among XYY and XXY men. Although the number of general criminal offenses was significantly higher among XYY men, there were no significant differences in the frequency of violent crimes among the XYY, XXY, and XY samples studied. Likewise, no evidence was found to support the aggression hypothesis among XYY men. Witkin et al. found that both their XYY and XXY cases performed significantly lower than normals on a Danish army selection intelligence test, and that both samples showed a much lower mean on an index of obtained educational level.

These data suggest that the elevated crime rate found among XYY men is not related to aggression but may be related to low intelligence. While their intellectual-dysfunction hypothesis seems to be an important mediating variable in the differential crime rate among XYY and XY males, Witkin et al. are very cautious in interpreting their findings. They point out that the similarities found between XYY and XXY individuals in intelligence, educational level, and height indicate that these characteristics may be the consequence of an extra X *or* Y chromosome, rather than being specific to an extra Y alone. Witkin et al. conclude with the statement that their findings do not justify the further identification of such men, since it appears that such efforts would not serve to reduce the social problem of aggressive crimes.

The XYY controversy still continues despite these findings. In some instances, researchers have been censured both by other scientists and the public because of the ethical and sociopolitical overtones of screening and identifying not only XYY males but also XXY males. Under heavy criticism and pressure, some of these research projects have been abandoned (Culliton, 1974, 1975). Such restraints on legitimate research delay scientific progress. Yet social mechanisms of some sort are needed to protect the rights of individuals and satisfy current ethical, legal, and political demands.

Objections are never raised and issues never develop in genetic research dealing with gross physical and behavioral abnormalities. However, when behavioral genetics ventures into more obscure areas such as human intelligence, aggression, and personality, controversy is inherent. Early identification of genotypes potentially related to certain undesirable behaviors may well lead to a self-fulfilling prophecy as a result of environmental pressures and distortions produced by such procedures. The resolution of these problems does not lie in social and academic tyranny and oppression of research inquiry. Rather, mechanisms and procedures must be developed that permit scientific investigation while simultaneously protecting the individual from discrimination and prejudice at all societal levels. We have seen in this chapter that genetics is a vital part of developmental psychology and that our understanding of developmental phenomena is greatly enhanced by some awareness of genetic processes. We have also learned that behavioral genetics as a tool for behavioral analysis can sensitize us to etiological considerations in developmental psychology. Although we are far from that goal, our discussion should keep potential genetic contributions to psychological development in the foreground.

REFERENCES

Berman, P. W., Waisman, H. A., & Graham, F. K. Intelligence in treated PKU children. *Child Development,* 1966, *37,* 731–747.

Cavalli-Sforza, L. L., & Bodmer, W. F. *The genetics of human populations.* San Francisco: Freeman, 1971.

Culliton, B. J. Patients' rights: Harvard is site of battle over X and Y chromosomes. *Science,* 1974, *186,* 715–717.

Culliton, B. J. XYY: Harvard researcher under fire to stop newborn screening. *Science,* 1975, *188,* 1284–1285.

Dobzhansky, T. Genetic differences between people. *Scientific Research,* 1968, *22,* 32–34.

Dugdale, R. L. *The Jukes: a study in crime, pauperism, disease, and heredity.* New York: G. P. Putnam's Sons, 1877.

Fuller, J. L., & Thompson, W. R. *Behavior Genetics.* New York: Wiley, 1960.

Galton, F. Hereditary talent and character. *Macmillan's Magazine,* 1865, *12,* 157–166; 318–327.

Galton, F. *Hereditary Genius.* London: Macmillan, 1869.

Goddard, H. H. *The Kallikak Family.* New York: Macmillan, 1912.

Howell, R. R., & Stevenson, R. E. The offspring of phenylketonuric women. *Social Biology Supplement,* 1971, *18,* 19–29.

Hsia, D. Y. Y. *Human developmental genetics.* Chicago: Yearbook Medical Publishers, 1968.

Hsia, D. Y. Y. Phenylketonuria and its variants. In A. G. Steinberg & A. G. Bearn (Eds.), *Progress in medical genetics* (Vol. 7). New York: Grune & Stratton, 1970, 29–68.

Jarvik, L. F., Klodin, V., & Matsuyama, S. S. Human agression and the extra Y chromosome. *American Psychologist, 1973, 28,* 674–682.

Keeton, W. T. *Elements of biological science.* New York: Norton, 1969.

Keeton, W. T. *Biological Science* (3rd ed.). New York: Norton, 1980.

Lederberg, J. Biological future of man. In G. Wolstenholme (Ed.), *Man and his future.* Boston: Little, Brown, 1963, 263–273.

Lerner, I. M. *Heredity, evolution, and society.* San Francisco: Freeman, 1968.

Manosevitz, M., Lindzey, G., & Thiessen, D. D. (Eds.). *Behavior genetics: method and research.* New York: Appleton-Century Crofts, 1969.

Matarazzo, J. D. *Wechsler's measurement and appraisal of adult intelligence.* Baltimore: Williams & Wilkins, 1972.

McClearn, G. E., & DeFries, J. C. *Introduction to behavioral genetics.* San Francisco: Freeman, 1973.

McKusick, V. A. *Mendelian inheritance in man.* Baltimore: Johns Hopkins Press, 1971.

Moltz, H. Contemporary instinct theory and the fixed action pattern. *Psychological Review,* 1965, *72,* 27–47.

Nadler, C. F., & Borges, W. H. Chromosomal structure and behavior. In D. Y. Y. Hsia (Ed.), *Lectures in medical genetics.* Chicago: Yearbook Medical Publishers, Inc., 1966.

Nirenberg, M. W. The genetic code: II. *Scientific American,* 1963, *208,* 80–94.

Penrose, L. S., & Smith, G. F. *Down's Anomaly.* London: J. & A. Churchill, 1966.

Reed, E. W. Genetic anomalies in development. In F. D. Horowitz (Ed.), *Review of child development research* (Vol. 4). Chicago: University of Chicago Press, 1975, 59–99.

Sinnott, E. W., Dunn, C. L., & Dobzhansky, Th. *Principles of genetics* (5th ed.). New York: McGraw-Hill, 1958.

Smith, G. E., & Berg, J. M. *Down's Anomaly* (2nd ed.). London: Churchill, 1976.

Strickberger, M. W. *Genetics.* New York: Macmillan, 1976.

Sturtevant, A. H. *A history of genetics.* New York: Harper & Row, 1965.

Theissen, D. D. *Gene organization and behavior.* New York: Random House, 1972.

Vale, J. R. Role of behavior genetics in psychology. *American Psychologist,* 1973, *28,* 871–882.

Vries, H. De. *Intracellular Pangenesis.* Chicago: Open Court, 1889.

Waddington, C. H. *The strategy of the genes.* New York: Macmillan, 1957.

Waddington, C. H. *New patterns in genetics and development.* New York: Columbia University Press, 1962.

Watson, J. D., & Crick, F. H. C. Molecular structure of nucleic acids. A structure for deoxyribonucleic acids. *Nature,* 1953, *171,* 737–738.

Weismann, A. *Essays on heredity.* New York: Oxford University Press, 1891.

Winchester, A. M. *Human Genetics,* Columbus: Merrill, 1971.

Witkin, H. A., Mednick, S. A., Schulsinger, F., Bakkestrøm, E., Christiansen, K. O., Goodenough, D. R., Hirschhorn, K., Lundsteen, C., Owen, D. R., Philip, J., Rubin, D. B., & Stocking, M. Criminality in XYY and XXY men. *Science,* 1976, *193,* 547–555.

Chapter

PRENATAL FACTORS IN DEVELOPMENT

Three

In this chapter, we will discuss human prenatal development, both normal and abnormal, in order to describe how prenatal factors and experiences can affect the development of postnatal behavior and ontogenesis. As we describe various patterns of prenatal development, we will draw upon data from the science of embryology, which deals with the origin and development of the individual organism, and its subdisciplines such as developmental anatomy, developmental physiology, chemical embryology, and experimental embryology.

Especially important to developmental psychology is the field of behavioral embryology. Behavioral embryology is the study of the origin and development of the nervous system and behavior; it explores the relationships between the embryogenesis of neurobehavioral development and later psychological development. Behavioral embryology is steeped in the developmental method and focuses on etiology of structure and function. It is now well known that behavior does not begin at birth. Many behavioral and biological scientists believe that an understanding of prenatal determinants of behavior will enhance our knowledge of general psychological development and eventually will help to prevent developmental casualties. As we discuss prenatal factors in development, we will consider some basic normative data describing general prenatal growth and development. We will examine the role of intrauterine environmental factors and maternal states in reproductive casualties and their developmental consequences and explore some perinatal conditions that endanger infants.

In Chapter Two, the basic mechanisms of genetics and genetic transmission and some of the ontogenetic consequences of various genetic anomalies were presented. The transmission and operations of hereditary material, therefore, represent the first critical stage in the conception and formation of the organism during prenatal development. Following fertilization of the egg, cellular proliferation and differentiation, and the subsequent formation of all the major organs (organogenesis) constitute the second critical stage in prenatal development. This second stage is also a critical one because during this period of rapid development, the individual is extremely susceptible to changes, deficiencies, and disruptions in the intrauterine environment. Since all morphological development of the individual occurs during the early weeks of prenatal life, the majority of fetal and neonatal abnormalities derive from adverse intrauterine conditions existing at this time. It is commonly believed that the uterine environment is an ideally protective one for the prenatal organism, and to a large extent it is. Although the maternal–fetal complex is a marvelously designed support system for the developing individual, it is far from perfect in isolating and protecting it from potentially hazardous maternal states and intrauterine conditions. The developing human in the uterus is better protected from the external environment than it will ever be again. Simultaneously, however, in no other developmental period will the individual be so critically sensitive and vulnerable to alterations in its immediate environment (Joffe, 1969).

PRENATAL DEVELOPMENT

Embryonic Growth

From a single fertilized egg cell or zygote of about .14 millimeters in diameter weighing less than one milligram, the human embryo grows to a size of approximately 500 millimeters and a birth weight of 3000 grams. Growth, the increase in size and mass, occurs primarily as a function of cellular reproduction and the increase in cellular size. Growth velocity is most rapid during the early stages of prenatal development, gradually decreasing with advancing term of pregnancy. As the zygote grows from an undifferentiated sphere of a few cells, it undergoes a series of changes in cellular organization and morphology. These developmental changes are a result of cellular differentiation in which the structural and functional characteristics of cells change, leading in turn to the formation of new cells and new organ tissues. Embryonic form also changes because various structures develop at differential growth rates, resulting in the relatively disproportionate appearance of the embryo at different periods of prenatal development. The final size that the fetus attains depends upon cellular growth rate, intrauterine nutritional factors, and duration of pregnancy. Although growth rate and ultimate fetal size are largely under genetic control, environmental factors such as malnutrition, maternal disease states, and prolonged pregnancy can alter fetal growth patterns.

General growth of the fetus is roughly correlated to the enlargement of the uterus and placenta. Due to the increasing fetal requirements for nutrients, respiration, excretion, and endocrine exchange, the placenta steadily increases in area as the uterus expands. Placental weight increases most during the first half of pregnancy, after which the rate of growth slows markedly. The ratio of placental to fetal weight, therefore, decreases dramatically over the second half of pregnancy. Since the placenta serves as a digestive system, lung, kidney, and endocrine system for the fetus, the ability of the placenta to adequately supply fetal needs is markedly lowered as the term of pregnancy approaches.

The fetal–placental complex appears to function, in part, as an interactive feedback system so that these critical ratio levels may play some role in fetal growth and pregnancy termination. Data from experimental embryology, in which embryos of one animal species are transplanted to a maternal host of another species, suggest a dynamic feedback system between the fetus and placenta in regulating fetal growth (Dickinson, 1960; McLaren, 1965). Such studies show, for example, that when an embryo of a Shetland pony is transplanted into a full size mare, the Shetland fetus grows larger than normal. At birth, the Shetland pony is much larger than one born to a Shetland mother. Opposite effects are found when the embryo of a horse is transplanted into a Shetland mare. There is evidence implicating fetal genetic factors and both fetal and maternal hormonal factors in the control of gestation periods in various organisms (Asdell, 1946). But the factors that determine length of pregnancy, or gestation period, are still poorly understood.

Prenatal Periods of Development

Human prenatal development is commonly divided into three main periods:

1 *The Pre-Embryonic Period or Period of the Ovum.* This period of prenatal development occupies approximately the first 3 weeks of life. During the first 2 weeks of this period, the ovum is fertilized, becomes implanted to the uterine wall, and begins to form into the embryonic disc, a flattened, disc-shaped hollow mass of cells. Subsequent differentiation of the three germ layers of the embryonic disc takes place. These germinal layers, the entoderm, ectoderm, and mesoderm, are the origin of human tissues (Figure 3-1). The entoderm gives rise to mouth and throat structures, the digestive system, respiratory system, the glandular system, and the genitourinary tract. The ecto-

Figure 3-1
Origins of human tissue.

(From Tuchmann-Duplessis, David, & Haegel, 1972.)

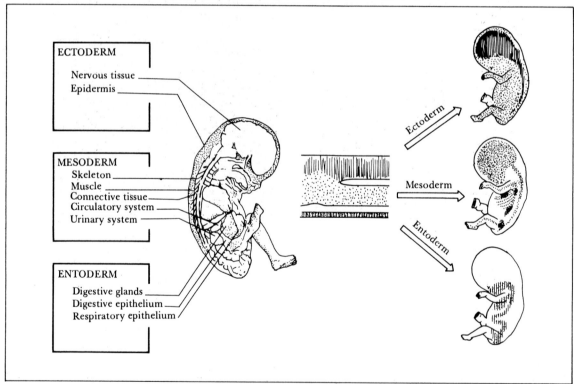

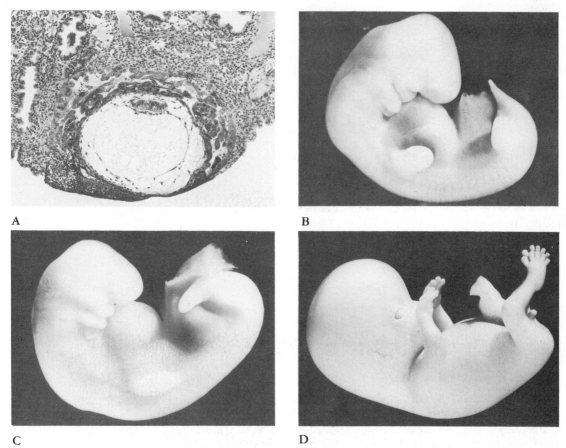

A human embryo (A–D) at 11, 28, 33, and 57 postovulatory days, respectively. During the first trimester of pregnancy, prenatal development is marked by cellular differentiation and the formation of all the major organs. This time period is critical as the developing embryo is especially vulnerable to disruptions in its intrauterine environment. Despite this vulnerability, the womb offers the developing human more protection now than it will ever have at any time after birth.

(Photo courtesy of the Carnegie Institute of Washington, Department of Embryology, Davis Division.)

derm evolves into the skin, sense organs, and the nervous system. The mesoderm, lying between the entoderm and ectoderm, develops into the musculoskeletal system, cardiovascular system, excretory system, and the reproductive system. **2** *Period of the Embryo.* The period of the embryo extends from the beginning of the fourth week to the end of the eighth

Figure 3-2
A graded series of human embryos at natural size.

(From Arey, 1974.)

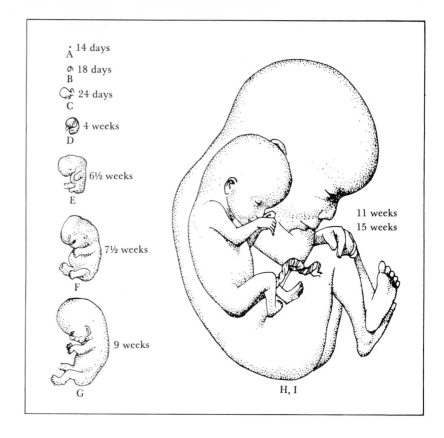

week. This is a period of rapid growth and differentiation in which all the major systems, organs, and external body features are formed (Figure 3-2).

3 *Period of the Fetus.* The fetal period extends from the beginning of the ninth week to birth at 40 weeks. The fetal period is characterized by growth and further development of those organs and systems now established during the period of the embryo.

For clinical purposes, human gestation is more often, and less precisely, divided into 9 calendar months called the first, second, and third trimesters, with each trimester representing a period of 3 months (Table 3-1). The first trimester of pregnancy includes both the pre-embryonic and embryonic

Table 3-1
A Reference Table of Correlated Human Development

AGE IN WEEKS	SIZE (CR) IN MM	BODY FORM	RESPIRATORY SYSTEM	SKELETAL SYSTEM	MUSCULAR SYSTEM	NERVOUS SYSTEM	SENSE ORGANS	AGE IN WEEKS
2.5	1.5	Embryonic disc flat. Primitive streak prominent. Neural groove indicated.		Head process (or notochordal plate) present.		Neural groove indicated.		2.5
3.5	2.5	Neural groove deepens and closes (except ends). Somites 1–16± present. Cylindrical body constricting from yolk sac. Branchial arches 1 and 2 indicated.	Respiratory primordium appearing as a groove on floor of pharynx.	Mesodermal segments appearing (1–16±). Older somites begin to show sclerotomes. Notochord a cellular rod.	Mesodermal segments appearing (1–16±). Older somites show myotome plates.	Neural groove prominent; rapidly closing. Neural crest a continuous band.	Optic vesicle and auditory placode present. Acoustic ganglia appearing.	3.5
4	5.0	Branchial arches completed. Flexed heart prominent. Yolk stalk slender. All somites present (40). Limb buds indicated. Eye and otocyst present. Body flexed; C-shape.	Trachea and paired lung buds become prominent. Laryngeal opening a simple slit.	All somites present (40). Sclerotomes massed as primitive vertebrae about notochord.	All somites present (40).	Neural tube closed. Three primary vesicles of brain represented. Nerves and ganglia forming. Ependymal mantle and marginal layers present.	Optic cup and lens pit forming. Auditory pit becomes closed, detached otocyst. Olfactory placodes arise and differentiate nerve cells.	4
5	8.0	Nasal pits present. Tail prominent. Heart, liver and mesonephros protuberant. Umbilical cord organizes.	Bronchial buds presage future lung lobes. Arytenoid swellings and epiglottis indicated.	Condensations of mesenchyme presage many future bones.	Premuscle masses in head, trunk and limbs.	Five brain vesicles. Cerebral hemispheres bulging. Nerves and ganglia better represented. [Suprarenal cortex accumulating.]	Chorioid fissure prominent. Lens vesicle free. Vitreous anlage appearing. Octocyst elongates and buds endolymph duct. Olfactory pits deepen.	5

AGE IN WEEKS	SIZE (CR) IN MM	BODY FORM	RESPIRATORY SYSTEM	SKELETAL SYSTEM	MUSCULAR SYSTEM	NERVOUS SYSTEM	SENSE ORGANS	AGE IN WEEKS
6	12.0	Upper jaw components prominent but separate. Lower jaw-halves fused. Head becomes dominant in size. Cervical flexure marked. External ear appearing. Limbs recognizable as such.	Definitive pulmonary lobes indicated. Bronchi sub-branching. Laryngeal cavity temporarily obliterated.	First appearance of chondrification centers. Desmocranium.	Myotomes, fused into a continuous column, spread ventrad. Muscle segmentation largely lost.	Three primary flexures of brain represented. Diencephalon large. Nerve plexuses present. Epiphysis recognizable. Sympathetic ganglia forming segmental masses. Meninges indicated.	Optic cup shows nervous and pigment layers. Lens vesicle thickens. Eyes set at 160°. Naso-lacrimal duct. Modeling of ext., mid. and int. ear under way. Vomero-nasal organ.	6
7	17.0	Branchial arches lost. Cervical sinus obliterates. Face and neck forming. Digits indicated. Back straightens. Heart and liver determine shape of body ventrally. Tail regressing.	Larynx and epiglottis well outlined; orifice T-shaped. Laryngeal and tracheal cartilages foreshadowed. Conchae appearing. Primary choanae rupturing.	Chondrification more general. Chondrocranium.	Muscles differentiating rapidly throughout body and assuming final shapes and relations.	Cerebral hemispheres becoming large. Corpus striatum and thalamus prominent. Infundibulum and Rathke's pouch in contact. Chorioid plexuses appearing. Suprarenal medulla begins invading cortex.	Chorioid fissure closes, enclosing central artery. Nerve fibers invade optic stalk. Lens loses cavity by elongating lens fibers. Eyelids forming. Fibrous and vascular coats of eye indicated. Olfactory sacs open into mouth cavity.	7
8	23.0	Nose flat; eyes far apart. Digits well formed. Growth of gut makes body evenly rotund. Head elevating. Fetal state attained.	Lung becoming gland-like by branching of bronchioles. Nostrils closed by epithelial plugs.	First indications of ossification.	Definitive muscles of trunk, limbs and head well represented and fetus capable of some movement.	Cerebral cortex begins to acquire typical cells. Olfactory lobes visible. Dura and pia-arachnoid distinct. Chromaffin bodies appearing.	Eyes converging rapidly. Ext., mid. and int. ear assuming final form. Taste buds indicated. External nares plugged.	8
10	40.0	Head erect. Limbs nicely modeled. Nail folds indicated. Umbilical hernia reduced.	Nasal passages partitioned by fusion of septum and palate. Nose cartilaginous.	Ossification centers more common. Chondrocranium at its height.	Perineal muscles developing tardily.	Spinal cord attains definitive internal structure.	Iris and ciliary body organizing. Eyelids fused. Lacrimal glands budding. Spiral organ begins differentiating.	10

12	56.0	Head still dominant. Nose gains bridge. Sex readily determined by external inspection.	Conchae prominent. Nasal glands forming. Lungs acquire definitive shape.	Smooth muscle layers indicated in hollow viscera.	Notochord degenerating rapidly. Ossification spreading. Some bones well outlined.	Brain attains its general structural features. Cord shows cervical and lumbar enlargements. Cauda equina and filum terminale appearing. Neuroglial types begin to differentiate.	Characteristic organization of eye attained. Retina becoming layered. Nasal septum and palate fusions completed.	12
16	112.0	Face looks 'human.' Hair of head appearing. Muscles become spontaneously active. Body outgrowing head.	Accessory nasal sinuses developing. Tracheal glands appear. Mesoderm still abundant between pulmonary alveoli. Elastic fibers appearing in lungs.	Cardiac muscle appearing in earlier weeks, now much condensed. Muscular movements *in utero* can be detected.	Most bones distinctly indicated throughout body. Joint cavities appear.	Hemispheres conceal much of brain. Cerebral lobes delimited. Corpora quadrigemina appear. Cerebellum assumes some prominence.	Eye, ear and nose grossly approach typical appearance. General sense organs differentiating.	16
20-40 (5–10 mo.)	160.0–350.0	Lanugo hair appears (5). Vernix caseosa collects (5). Body lean but better proportioned (6). Fetus lean, wrinkled and red; eyelids reopen (7). Testes invading scrotum (8). Fat collecting, wrinkles smoothing, body rounding (8–10).	Nose begins ossifying (5). Nostrils reopen (6). Cuboidal pulmonary epithelium disappearing from alveoli (6). Pulmonary branching only two-thirds completed (10). Frontal and sphenoidal sinuses still very incomplete (10).	Perineal muscles finish development (6).	Carpal, tarsal and sternal bones ossify late; some after birth. Most epiphyseal centers appear after birth; many during adolescence.	Commissures completed (5). Myelinization of cord begins (5). Cerebral cortex layered typically (6). Cerebral fissures and convolutions appearing rapidly (7). Myelinization of brain begins (10).	Nose and ear ossify (5). Vascular tunic of lens at height (7). Retinal layers completed and light perceptive (7). Taste sense present (8). Eyelids reopen (7–8). Mastoid cells unformed (10). Ear deaf at birth.	20-40 (5–10 mo.)

(Adapted from Arey, 1974.)

periods. The second trimester of prenatal development includes the final stages of organogenesis and growth, while the third trimester of pregnancy is devoted almost exclusively to growth.

The Determination of Embryonic Age

One major task for embryologists is to describe in detail the development of structures and functions in the prenatal organism. Such observations require the recording of embryonic processes and events as they occur over species-specific biological timetables. That is, the biological mechanisms controlling embryonic development of form and function in each species is an invariant, progressive series of events. These epigenetic events—events involving the creation of new structures—occur sequentially over the course of prenatal development.

Because the embryonic emergence of structure and function is related to time-controlled biological processes, the use of embryonic age is the only way to establish normative patterns of prenatal development. The relationships established between prenatal development and age contribute greatly to our understanding of both normal and abnormal embryogenesis, and such age determinations become an important factor in discussing prenatal growth and development.

For all practical purposes, it is impossible to exactly determine the age of a human embryo or fetus. To do so would require precise information on the coital and menstrual history of the mother. Embryogenesis begins with fertilization, but reliable data on the hour, day, or week of conception is extremely difficult to obtain. Most pregnant women do not have an obstetric examination until their pregnancies are well advanced, and by this time reports of coitus or menstrual cycles are typically too vague for accurate determination of conception date. In humans, length of gestation is calculated at 10 lunar months or 280 days, with a range of 250–310 days, measured from the onset of the last menstrual period. Two-thirds of all births occur between 266 and 294 days.

Prenatal age can be estimated by three basic methods: (1) estimated conception date, (2) size of the embryo, and (3) degree of embryonic development. In obstetric practice, prenatal age is almost always dated from the beginning of the last menstrual period (10 lunar months), but menstrual irregularity and early post-conception bleeding can easily mask the actual time of the last menstrual period. Nevertheless, menstrual age remains the most common clinical method for age estimation.

Ovulation age is another method for arriving at some idea of conception date. The first day of the last menstrual period is approximately 2 weeks before ovulation, the liberation of an ovum from the ovary and its capture by the fallopian tube. Therefore, menstrual age is usually 14 ± 2 days longer than ovulation age. The actual time for human gestation is 38 weeks or 266 days, when determined from the time of ovulation. When the exact time of ovulation is unknown, 2 weeks are added to the last onset of normal menstruation, resulting in 10 lunar months (28-day months) in the estimation of menstrual age. Ovulation age is commonly determined by recording body temperature fluctuations and the level of blood progesterone at the approximate midpoint of the 28-day menstrual cycle.

When feasible, coital age becomes another method for estimating prenatal age. Coital age can be calculated to be within 2 or 3 days from ovulation age. The reason for this is the known viability for human ova and sperm cells. The ovum remains receptive to fertilization for a period of only approximately 24 hours before it begins to degenerate. Sperm cells lose their fertilizing power within 24–48 hours after entering the female genital tract (Cary, 1936; Crowley, 1974). However, one must add additional time to the period of sperm viability because sperm cells require several hours in the female genital tract before they acquire the ability to fertilize. This developmental period of fertilization capacity is called capacitation, an unknown process of sperm activation and physiological change.

In the absence of the data required to determine the date of conception, estimations of prenatal age can also be made on the basis of the size of the embryo or fetus. Tables of normative data on embryonic size–age relationships have been carefully compiled from selected clinical examinations of recovered embryos and fetuses (abortuses). These normative data provide guidelines for estimating prenatal age by comparing physical measurements. Like all normative data, they are variable and approximate, and the differential effects of intrauterine conditions, health, and rates of maturation must be considered when using this method of age determination. The most commonly used measurement is the head-to-tail length or sitting-height length, which is called the crown–rump (CR) length. Age measures of prenatal maturity may also be estimated as a function of weight and degree of anatomical development. Concise tables of such data have been available for many years.

Because of the variability in prenatal growth and development and the absence of any single method of accurate age determination, all three criteria of estimated conception date, size, and anatomical development need to be included for the closest approximation of prenatal age.

HUMAN BEHAVIORAL EMBRYOLOGY

Historical Perspective

The field of behavioral embryology began with the publication in 1885 of William Preyer's work, *Spezielle Physiologie des Embryos.* Preyer was an English physiologist who compiled the first thorough and empirical description of behavioral development in a variety of prenatal infrahuman organisms. It was Preyer's views of "psychogenesis" (origins of the mind) that initiated his research on prenatal development. His subsequent publication of a 3-year behavioral biography of his son in 1888 and 1889, *The Mind of the Child,* also had a great impact on the development of child psychology.

On the basis of his research with embryos and fetuses, Preyer developed his theory of motor primacy in prenatal behavioral development. Preyer's observations led him to conclude that chick embryos are active before they are reactive; that is, that the sequence of prenatal motor behavior is first autogenous (independent of external stimulation and arising from spontaneous neural activity) and then later reactive (i.e., reflexive). Preyer's motor primacy theory of 1885 has subsequently been verified (Gottlieb, 1973, 1976), and may have implications for mammalian prenatal development as well.

Although Preyer launched behavioral embryology as a science, G.E. Coghill (1929) is considered to be the father of behavioral embryology. Coghill's contributions firmly established behavioral embryology in the twentieth century. Embryological research was at its peak of activity during the first half of the century, with most of the research efforts directed toward establishing general, descriptive data on prenatal development. Theoretical activity was lively, as the leading embryologists searched for some principle of prenatal development that would provide basic generalizations or laws about the prenatal course of behavioral development. A good deal of research activity, debate, and controversy followed, diminishing in the 1940s and 1950s with the growing inactivity of the major contributors, followed by a resurgence of new interests, issues, and activity since 1960 (Gottlieb, 1976).

Although some early reports of human fetal development appeared in the early nineteenth century, credit for the first systematic observations of human prenatal development is given to Minkowski (cited in Carmichael, 1970), a German psychiatrist, who began his investigations in 1920. During the more than 50 years following Minkowski's reports, a number of other investigators in the United States, Europe, and the Soviet Union have reported their findings on human fetal development and activity. The difficulties in obtaining and studying recovered fetuses are complex, and the total number of fetuses investigated since 1920 is probably less than 300. The human fetus *in utero* cannot be studied adequately for accurate description of its behavior. Consequently, our data on the prenatal development of behavior is based on spontaneous or therapeutically planned abortions of nonviable fetuses and on fetuses delivered prematurely. Research on human fetuses probably will not accelerate in the United States inasmuch as legislation passed by Congress in 1979 has rigidly proscribed the types of such research that can be done and the permission required to do it.

Conceptions of Prenatal Development

Interpretations of various phenomena play an important role in the development of a scientific discipline because they provide the investigator with a set of general assumptions, views, and approaches to a field of inquiry. These conceptual frameworks quickly lead to hypotheses that in turn determine the nature and method of experimental designs calculated to verify and extend original ideas. Therefore, the most promising, prevailing, or, at times, fashionable concepts are seized upon by many investigators. The result may be to establish a major pool of selected knowledge at the expense of other less "acceptable," but potentially fruitful approaches. We have discussed some examples of such occurrences in Chapter One.

Gottlieb (1970, 1973, 1976) reviewed and clarified both historical and contemporary conceptions of prenatal development, seeking to establish new directions of research and thinking in behavioral embryology. Gottlieb points out that epigenesis is now the dominant assumption shared by all contemporary behavioral embryologists, displacing the nineteenth century concept of preformationism. In prenatal development, epigenesis refers to the emergence of structure and function (behavior, activity, or sensitivity) through a patterned series of transformations and reorganizations. In this view, new structures and behavioral systems come into existence as a gradual consequence of embryonic development. These new structural and functional developments are considered to represent new properties and totalities that cannot be directly derived from preexisting levels or elements found at earlier stages of prenatal development. Carmichael (1970) has also discussed this conceptual view of prenatal development. He cites F. A. Lange's (1925) reference to the insistence on reductionism to simpler levels or elements to explain higher organizational events as the "error of potentiality." The error of potentiality refers to the idea that although simpler elements may make up a new totality of higher and more complex organization, the function and characteristics of that later-formed totality cannot be found in the elements that originally preceded it. Therefore, it is incorrect to assume that the simpler elements or structures contain the potential characteristics of the higher, more complex structure. The example of the water molecule, H_2O, is often used to clarify this concept. Hydrogen and oxygen together form a new totality, water. But the characteristics of water cannot be found in the simpler components of hydrogen and oxygen alone.

While the epigenetic character of prenatal development is the basic doctrine among behavioral embryologists, thoughts about the essential nature of epigenesis are divided between theories of predetermined and probabilistic epigenesis. Proponents of predetermined epigenesis view prenatal development strictly in terms of genetically controlled maturation of the organism, and believe that the developmental course of prenatal behavior can be understood by an adequate explanation of embryonic maturation. Maturation refers to the structural development, both anatomical and physiological, of organs and organ systems. Note that the concept of predetermined epigenesis revolves around the idea that structure determines function, and that environmental factors play little more than a passive role in prenatal development. The structure–function relationship is seen as a unidirectional one which establishes discontinuities between early and late stages of prenatal development.

Those who approach behavioral embryology in terms of probabilistic epigenesis are diametrically opposed to the predeterministic perspective. Advocates of probabilistic epigenesis are convinced that prenatal environmental factors such as physical, sensory, thermal, and general neurophysiological stimulation actively facilitate and determine maturational and behavioral development of the prenatal organism.

According to Gottlieb's analysis (1970, 1973, 1976) probabilistic theories implicitly assume that functional and environmental factors actively contribute to prenatal neurobehavioral development. These theories argue for a reciprocal relationship between structure and function in which structural maturation affects function, and function, in turn, modulates maturation. Gottlieb (1976) describes the facilitative effect of function (general neural activity, muscular and sensory activity, and global embryonic behavior) as possibly affecting the rate at which structural maturation or behavioral development proceeds. The determinative or inductive nature of functional effects might conceivably alter the direction of general development (i.e., sex determination, changes in species-specific behavior), according to Gottlieb. A bidirectional or reciprocal interpretation of the relationship between structure and function implies continuity between early and later developmental stages of prenatal behavior. To summarize, the traditional and contemporary views of prenatal epigenetic development may be depicted as follows (Gottlieb, 1976):

PREDETERMINISTIC: GENES→STRUCTURAL MATURATION→-
FUNCTION

PROBABILISTIC: GENES⇌STRUCTURAL MATURATION⇌FUNCTION

It should be clear that the term, probabilistic, derives from the variability of events which can occur in a hypothesized relationship among genes, structure, and function. Such organic relationships in prenatal development generate a large number of possible event and process outcomes, and subsequent variable terminal states of neural and behavioral development. Even the possibility of gene activation and deactivation by maturational events is recognized as probable. Hence, since we are talking about probabilities of events and outcomes, the term probabilistic is apt. Predeterministic epigenesis, on the other hand, seems clearly to assume an invariant series of prenatal events and developmental outcomes. Within this perspective of a genetically regulated, predictable organic process, the term deterministic is accurately descriptive.

Gottlieb admits that predetermined epigenesis may describe the very earliest stages of embryonic development when the organism is essentially inert. Nevertheless, he favors the probabilistic approach to behavioral embryology, marshalling some cogent, if sparse, evidence from experimental embryology in his 1976 paper to support his position as well as his notions of facilitation and induction in prenatal and postnatal organisms. Although the evidence is meager at this time, the case for organic developmental plasticity is compelling, particularly for the higher forms of life. (The notion of organic and developmental plasticity was briefly discussed in Chapter Two.) If the empirical basis for embryonic plasticity is still tenuous, various inferences from organic evolution seem likely to verify probabilistic phenomena and their implications for human development.

Methodological Considerations in the Study of Human Prenatal Behavior

We noted earlier that the primary methods of investigating human fetal behavior include observations of surgically removed fetuses and of surviving prematurely born fetuses. The lower limit of gestation age for viability or survival for the prematurely born fetus is approximately 28 weeks menstrual age. Fetuses delivered earlier than 28 weeks lack the ability for postnatal independent respiration. Consequently, most fetuses asphyxiate if born much earlier than 28 weeks. Viable premature fetuses of 28–38 weeks appear to display behavioral capacities very similar to those of the full-term infant, although some differences in sensory development and functioning have been reported (Windle, 1940; Hooker, 1952). Therefore, the data describing the developmental sequence of human prenatal behavior are based mainly on studies of operatively removed fetuses.

Live human fetuses that have been available for study are those whose surgical removals by cesarean section were necessary for medical reasons. The usual procedure is to remove both the fetus and the placenta at cesarean section, with the operation performed under local anesthesia. General anesthetics administered to the mother cross the placental barrier and anesthetize the fetus, suppressing or diminishing fetal behavior. The surgical separation of the placenta from the mother deprives the fetus of its sole source of oxygenation. In fetuses less than 26–28 weeks menstrual age, asphyxia probably begins immediately, and metabolites rapidly accumulate in the fetus, resulting first in hyperactivity and then hypoactivity. This factor, along with the general effects of physical, thermal, and physiological insult to the fetus following surgical removal, produce complications in the evaluation of observed fetal behavior. We are no longer dealing with a normal fetus and normal movements, so there is always the question of to what extent do the experimental procedures confound the data. These methodological problems, and the differential interpretations attending them, led to some debate and controversy over the sequential development of fetal behavior during the period between 1930 and 1950.

Because fetal reactivity is of short temporal duration, rapidly executed, and sometimes complex in the number of components involved, the most accurate observation procedure is the use of motion picture photography of fetal activity. This technique permits detailed analyses of fetal behavior in terms of reaction time, duration, and complexity through slow motion procedures and single frame analysis. Visual observation alone as a basis for the description of fetal behavior is difficult indeed, owing to the nature of the responses and the size of the fetus.

Another consideration in the evaluation of fetal behavior is the type of stimulus used to elicit responses. Tactile stimulation is most often used. For this purpose, instruments of graded human or animal hair with known pressure values have most commonly been used to stimulate human fetuses, with other forms of stimulation used less often (Humphrey, 1970). Related to the types of stimulus used is the problem of the locus of stimulation. Different kinds of responses will occur as a function of direct stimulation of muscle neurons or motor neurons. Such strong, localized responses are called myogenic or neurogenic responses, respectively. These may be erroneously interpreted as true reflexes, but in fact are not since they do not involve a reflex arc (Carmichael, 1970; Hooker, 1952; Humphrey, 1970).

Clearly, the methodological problems in recording fetal behavior are formidable and technically complex. Variations in procedures from surgical removal to type and locus of stimulation have produced inconsistent findings and subsequent controversy over the stages and sequence of fetal behavior. We will discuss some of these issues later in this chapter.

The Ontogeny of Human Fetal Behavior

The following outline of the appearance of human fetal behavior describes only the highlights of behavioral events during the course of prenatal development. The prenatal growth of human behavior is briefly summarized from the work of Fitzgerald and Windle (1942), Hooker (1952, 1960), and Windle (1940). More detailed reviews of prenatal development may also be found in Carmichael (1970) and Humphrey (1970). The reported observations of fetal behavior are

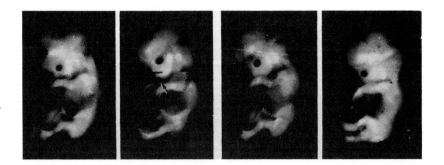

Figure 3-3
Contralateral head, trunk, and rump flexion to perioral stimulation in an 8½-week-old fetus.

(From Hooker, 1952.)

A human fetus at (A) 8
weeks and (B) 12 weeks of
estimated menstrual age.
During this period of de-
velopment, the fetus begins
to register reflex responses
to outside stimuli, such as
light pressure applied to
the mother's abdomen.
Note (A) the amniotic sac,
the umbilical cord, and the
placenta—all of which contribute to the fetal support
system. Despite increasing
cellular development and
differentiation during this
period, the fetus is still
many weeks away from
being able to survive outside the mother's womb.

(Photos by Donald Yeager)

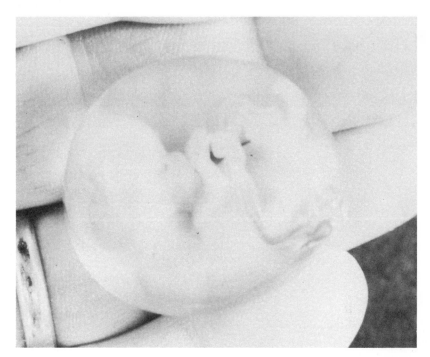

A

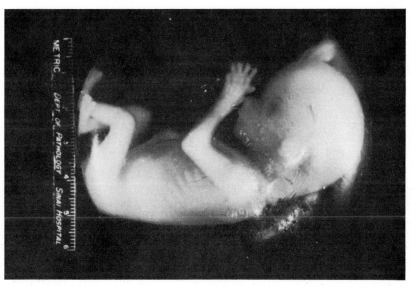

B

Figure 3-4
Partial grasp reflex in an
11-week-old fetus.

(From Hooker, 1952.)

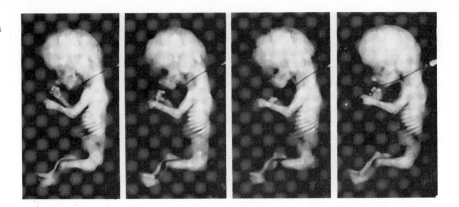

given in relationship to estimated menstrual age. Following Carmichael (1970), true behavior is considered to begin with the appearance of neuromuscular activity. This reflects a degree of maturation of the central nervous system that permits either spontaneous fetal behavior or the ability of the sense organs to respond to external stimulation, leading to CNS activity and subsequent activation of muscles or glands. This point in development may be what Gesell (1929) refers to as the ontogenetic zero of behavior.

With the establishment of this reference point, our discussion of fetal behavior begins with approximately the period demarcating the end of the embryonic and the beginning of the fetal stage. The only movement observed in fetuses less than 8 weeks old is the embryonic heart beat, which begins at about 3 weeks of age. This is not a neuromuscular response, but rather an independent muscle contraction that has no behavioral significance.

THE THIRD MONTH   Hooker's observations indicate that the earliest reliable reflex movements in human fetuses occur at about 8½ weeks. This is a fetal response to light tactual stimulation of a 10 milligram hair applied to the perioral region of the face (mouth–nose area). The response consists of a neck, head, and trunk contraction usually in the direction opposite to the side stimulated—a contralateral response—accompanied by a backward extension of the shoulders and a

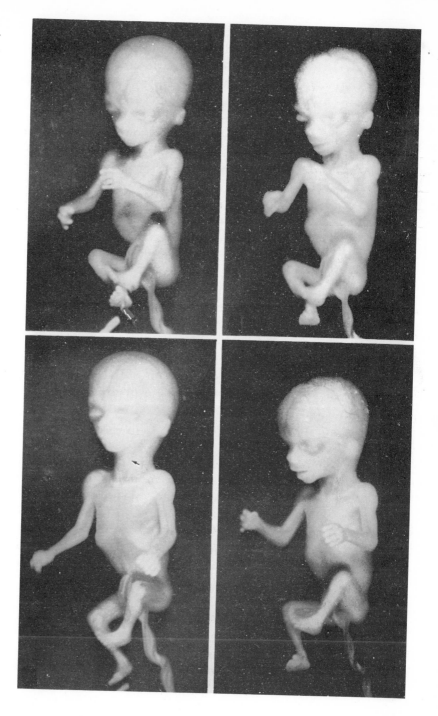

Figure 3-5
Withdrawal reflex to stimulation of sole of left foot in
a 14-week-old fetus.

(From Hooker, 1952.)

slight rump rotation (Figure 3-3). The reflex appears as an avoidance reaction, and is a stereotyped, integrated movement that might be described as widespread or generalized movement of the entire fetus. Hooker was unable to elicit any other reflex activity in fetuses this age when stimulated in other body regions.

At 9½ weeks, spontaneous fetal movements may be observed. Whether such movements are in fact autogenous or the result of unknown external stimuli is not clear. Between 10 and 11 weeks, the fetus exhibits trunk and neck extension as additional components, or replacements, of the reflex pattern to perioral stimulation. Also at about 10½ weeks of age, tactual stimulation of the palm results in a rapid, partial closure of the fingers—the palmar or grasp reflex—occurring either alone or with some wrist and arm movements (Figure 3-4).

Between 11 and 11½ weeks, a complete plantar reflex (foot withdrawal) can be observed in response to tactual stimulation to the sole of the foot (Figure 3-5). From this period onward, perioral stimulation produces little activity from the lower extremities, and some reduction in upper extremity movements. Between 8½ and 10½ weeks, fetal reflexes appear as integrated, widespread reactions, after which a transition period of more localized reflex activity begins to develop, as seen in movement reduction and in the palmar and plantar reflexes.

THE FOURTH MONTH   At 13–14 weeks, the human fetus possesses the basic elements of neonatal reflexes, although in an incomplete form. Only the top and the back of the head remain insensitive to stimulation, and the mechanical, stereotyped nature of both spontaneous and reflexive behavior is replaced by more coordinated, flowing movements. By 16 weeks, all the discrete reflexes that can be elicited from the newborn infant, with the exception of respiration, vocalization, and the true grasping reflex, are present in the fetus, but they are comparatively sluggish. During the 15th and 16th weeks, there is a notable increase in the vigor of fetal movements as muscles develop and strengthen. In a period of 8 weeks, human fetal behavior develops from generalized, stereotyped, and nonspecific motor movements to those of fundamental, discrete reflexes that represent localized and specific responses (Table 3-2).

Table 3-2
Fetal Reflexes to Perioral Stimulation (14 to 20 Weeks)

AREA STIMULATED	ORAL REFLEX ELICITED	ACCOMPANYING HEAD, TRUNK, OR EXTREMITY MOVEMENTS	MENSTRUAL AGE IN WEEKS
Palm of hand	Wide mouth opening. Tongue elevation and mouth closure.	Tight flexion of fingers with forearm flexion and hand extension ipsilaterally.	14
Upper lip	Mouth closure and swallowing.	Ventral head flexion.	14
Across both eyelids	Ipsilateral squint and sneer-like reflexes.	Contralateral head flexion and extension.	14
Back (lumbar area to neck)	Mouth opening, closing, and inspiratory gasp.	Head flexion and head and trunk extension, and extremity movements.	14
Upper and lower eyelids	Mouth opening, squint reflex, tongue elevation.	Only flexion of fingers at metacarpophalangeal joints and extension at interphalangeal joints ipsilaterally.	15.5
Lips and tongue	Lower lip lowered and lifted. Tongue grooved.	None	15.5
Lower lip, lateral to medial	Lower lip lowered and protruded. Tongue visible.	None	15.5
Ala nasae to upper lip	Lips protrude slightly, then jaw lowers.	Extension of fingers of ipsilateral hand as lips protrude.	16
Medial canthus to upper lip	Scowl, squint and lip closure.	None	16
Inside of mouth and back of tongue	Gag reflex.	None that are unrelated.	18.5
Lower lip	Puckering of upper lip, protrusion of lower lip with mouth closing and tongue movements.	None	20

(From Humphrey, 1968.)

THE FIFTH MONTH TO BIRTH   By 25 weeks of menstrual age, the fetus displays a greatly increased behavioral repertoire. True grasping and sucking reflexes can be elicited, and respiration accompanied by a weak, high-pitched cry can be observed. We can see that although the fetus is basically equipped for postnatal existence, the life sustaining response systems require further maturation. The respiratory reflex is inadequate for survival because of muscular weakness and insufficient lung capacity. Similarly, the sucking reflex can be elicited by perioral stimulation, but the 25-week fetus does not have the muscular strength to obtain food by sustained sucking. The fetus is still a "spinal organism" with regard to its behavior—that is, there is little evidence of any cerebral involvement or control in its activity.

The view that reflex activity is under subcortical control is corroborated by clinical reports of anacephalic infants (infants born without a cerebral cortex) who possess normal reflexes at birth, as well as electroencephalogram (EEG) studies of fetal cortical activity (Ellingson, 1967). Fetal EEG patterns similar to those of newborns do not appear until 28–32 weeks. As mentioned earlier, the fetal age of 27–28 weeks is an important developmental period, since it is the lower limit of viability in the event of premature birth. With stringent pediatric care, the fetal infant of this age often survives. Between 32 and 40 weeks, fetal maturation of structural and functional systems continues, and movements become more active, sustained, and positive. At 36 weeks, the fetus exhibits the Moro reflex (startle reaction), a firm response to light and sound, a strong hunger cry, and periods of being awake. The fetus at 36–40 weeks has good muscle tone, a strong Moro reflex, and definite periods of alertness.

Our summary review of fetal development reveals a clear pattern of sequential behavioral development (Table 3-3). Postnatal development continues this pattern, elaborating on basic behavioral elements laid down during prenatal development via maturation of existing fetal characteristics and their interaction with environmental factors. It also seems clear that prenatal development takes place with little or no energy exchange between the fetus and its environment. The unfolding of structure and function appears as sequential phenomena under endogenous control of genetic and epigenetic events.

Table 3-3 Human Prenatal Ontogeny	AGE IN WEEKS	NERVOUS SYSTEM ELICITED RESPONSES	SPONTANEOUS FUNCTION
	7½–8	First spinal reflex at seven and one-half weeks: contralateral flexion of neck when area near mouth touched lightly. Quick arm, leg, trunk movements when amniotic sac tapped. Characteristic reflex is stereotyped and mechanical.	
	9–9½	At nine and one-half weeks, limb flexes when it is stretched: means end-organs in muscles, tendons, joints are capable of function.	Slow, uncoordinated general movements appear.
	10–11	Localized movement in any part of whole extremity when part touched. Reflexes often complex. Trunk extension. Muscular twitch of foot when sole touched lightly (plantar reflex); also grasp reflex when palm touched lightly.	Brain-wave pattern (bipolar, frontal occipital) irregular and slow from higher levels, with superimposed fast waves at greater depth (24).
	12–13	Slight movement of eyelid when it is touched, also eye movements underneath lid. Movement at every joint. Withdrawal of head from point stimulated. Sectioning of spinal cord indicates elicited reflexes are mediated by it.	
	13	Contralateral reaction of limb on opposite side of body stimulated. Entire skin area except back of head sensitive to stimulation.	First respiratory (rhythmic chest movements: the "law of anticipatory function."
	14	Dorsal flexion of toes when sole of foot touched lightly. Reflexes and movements more flexible and fluid. Has most of the behavioral repertoire of the neonate.	First spontaneous movement of the whole fetus: cerebellar involvement.

(table continued)

AGE IN WEEKS	NERVOUS SYSTEM ELICITED RESPONSES	SPONTANEOUS FUNCTION
15	Fingers close and stay closed when touched with a hair.	Fetal activity was affected by removal of cerebral cortex.
16–20	Sluggishness of previously lively responses.	Muscular movements detected.
20–24	Big toe extends and other toes flex (Babinski reflex) when sole touched. Respiratory movements when medulla stimulated. Grasp and "trot" reflex readily elicited.	Generalized body activity. Hiccups fifteen to thirty times a minute (medullar involvement).
24–28	Knee-jerk, Achilles-tendon, and sucking reflexes all elicitable.	
28–32	Reflexes more pronounced and intense.	Crying occurs during seventh through ninth months. (Fetus' own internal environment may afford it vague pressure sensations as it moves; it may also receive sensory stimulation from contact pressures (14)).
32–36	Toe reflex more variable. Spreading of toes occurs.	
36–40	Still no neocortical control.	The birth-cry is essentially a respiratory reflex.

(Adapted from Milner, 1967.)

Environmental events external to the fetus do not seem to affect the development of fetal activity, as long as they permit a minimally adequate intrauterine environment. Minimally adequate prenatal care is a known requirement for normal prenatal development in a normal fetus, even though we may have difficulty in defining "minimally adequate." However, there is no evidence that "excellent" prenatal care, extending well beyond minimal requirements for fetal survival, produces a superior fetus in terms of facilitating fetal development.

Theoretical Issues in Behavioral Embryology

During the formative years of behavioral embryology, the principal researchers struggled to formulate a general theory of prenatal development. The problem revolved around the degree of generality that could be attributed to the findings of different investigators studying different organisms under different experimental conditions and methods. The pressing need to establish a single, general principle that would explain the course of prenatal development for all species, behavioral systems, and neural systems resulted in a major controversy over the basic sequence of development in human fetal behavior. Does fetal behavior begin as a generalized pattern of nonspecific activity from which localized, specific reflexes eventually emerge and become differentiated? Or do the earliest fetal responses to stimuli originate as localized and specific reflexes, which subsequently combine to form general, total patterns of activity? In the first view, the initial total behavioral patterns of the fetus lead to the capacity for discrete movements. The second position holds that local reflexes are the building blocks for the development of general, coordinated behavioral patterns.

The Coghill–Windle Controversy

G.E. Coghill (1929) was the first to offer a general principle of prenatal behavioral development. He described this development as progressing from an integrated, total pattern to partial, localized patterns of reflex activity. Coghill's conclusions were based on his extensive research with salamander embryos (*Amblystoma*). Coghill found that when embryonic salamanders were lightly stimulated with a graded hair, the earliest responses observed were total response patterns involving the entire organism. The activity pattern began in the neck region and spread downward through the trunk and tail (cephalocaudal direction). Early embryos displayed a coil reaction to the stimulus, whereas older embryos responded with a body configuration in the shape of an "S"—the basic swimming movement of the salamander. When the limbs of the organism appeared, they moved passively with trunk movements, with the forelimbs moving earlier than the hindlimbs. Coghill also noted that when limb movements occurred independently in a later embryonic stage, the limb activity, along with other discrete movements, appeared as a proximodistal sequence. That is, they progressed from the body axis outward to the more distant areas such as the forearms, feet, and digits. In short, functional development appeared first in structures closest to the body and last in those most distant from the body.

Coghill then analyzed the early observations of Minkowski (1928, cited in Carmichael, 1970) on human fetal behavior, in an attempt to correlate his findings and impressions with the available data on human fetal development. In 1940, Coghill concluded that the mammalian prenatal sequence fitted his original observations: Prenatal behavioral development occurs as a process of individuation or differentiation in which discrete, local reflex activity originates and develops from an integrated overall pattern of activity. Davenport Hooker (1936, 1944, 1952) reached the same conclusion as a result of his laborious work with human fetuses.

Over this same period of time, Windle and associates (Fitzgerald & Windle, 1942; Windle, 1934, 1940; Windle & Orr,

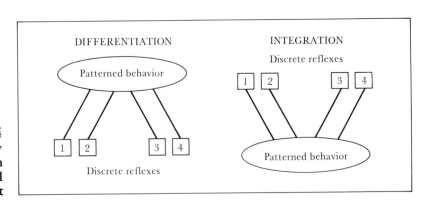

Table 3-4
Differentiation Theory versus Integration Theory of Prenatal Development

1934) were reporting their observations of embryonic development in a number of other organisms, including human fetuses. Windle concluded that specific reflexes are the first basic units of behavior to appear in the higher vertebrates, and that later coordinated patterns of behavior result from the integration of various earlier reflexes. This is Windle's theory of integration, which he offered as a general principle of prenatal development in opposition to Coghill (Table 3-4).

Windle and co-workers were the leading critics of both Coghill and Hooker. Windle's major criticism was that conclusions leading to the theory of individuation were based on observations of abnormally responding fetuses. According to Windle, the fetuses studied by Minkowski and Hooker were slowly asphyxiating because of the diminishing supply of fetal oxygen. Windle believed that the integrated behavior pattern observed by Hooker was an abnormal mass movement of a fetus responding to asphyxia or anoxia, and not the beginning normal fetal activity. A lively series of disputes and controversies, accompanied by a renewed surge of research activity, raged into the 1940s, with additional empirical challenges of both positions also appearing in the literature.

One significant effect of the Coghill–Windle controversy was to stimulate more research in fetal development. Recent research has undermined both views of fetal development; the claimed generality of individuation or integration as a basic principle of prenatal behavioral development has been seriously weakened by contradictory evidence (Gottlieb, 1973). Some research results support Coghill's sequence and some results support Windle's concept of integration. But other evidence suggests that both localized and general patterns exist and occur simultaneously during the embryonic development of many species. Gottlieb (1973, 1976) has pointed out that the search for a single, general principle is futile and fruitless as an approach to understanding fetal behavioral development.

The contemporary view of this problem is that both patterned and partial responses can be observed in embryonic organisms, depending on the type and intensity of stimulation used, the species of organism, the interpretation of the response observed, the age of the organism, and the methodological procedures employed. Carmichael (1970) cautions against the acceptance of "easy generalizations" about the course of fetal development and their indiscriminate application across species and developmental stages. He goes on to say:

Before generalizations can be made with assurance, there must be a large amount of accurate measurement and . . . statistical norms in regard to the development of each of the specific developmental stages in each form considered. . . . Certain essential relationships between diffuseness and specificity and between individuation and integration of behavior will become clearer after the parts played by the specific senses in fetal life have been considered. (p. 515)

Similar warnings apply to Coghill's generalizations about the cephalocaudal and proximodistal character of embryonic development. It now appears that these sequential patterns of development may be more characteristic of postnatal than prenatal development (Milner, 1967).

INTRAUTERINE INFLUENCES ON PRENATAL DEVELOPMENT

As we have seen, the field of behavioral embryology focuses on the normal development and growth of the embryonic organism and the immediate consequences of morphological and functional ontogenesis. It is less concerned with postnatal effects or the implications of hazardous prenatal environments for postnatal life. During the course of prenatal development, various environmental factors and maternal conditions may threaten the survival or normal development of the organism. In Chapter Two, we discussed the developmental consequences of some genetic anomalies occurring under normal environmental conditions. Here, we will explore some abnormal environmental factors that can affect a genetically "normal" prenatal organism. We have seen how the etiology of many abnormal developmental patterns can be traced to abnormal genetic conditions. Now we will see how abnormal or deleterious environmental conditions also may have etiological significance for both prenatal and postnatal development.

Earlier, we mentioned the critical nature of the maternal–fetal relationship, and the susceptibility of the human prenatal organism to changes in its intrauterine environment. Typically, environmental factors and maternal conditions affect prenatal development by disrupting or impairing the intrauterine environment in terms of its protective, nutritive, and biochemical maintenance systems. Only in rare cases, such as exposure to high dosage levels of X-irradiation or to chemicals capable of producing genetic mutations, is there a direct effect on the embryo or fetus.

Each year, approximately 250,000 babies are born with a developmental defect. Some 500,000 fetuses a year are aborted, either spontaneously or operatively, because of abnormal development. Congenital birth defects account for the death of another 18,000 infants per year under the age of 1. Those who live beyond 1 year of age succumb at a mortality rate of 60,000 per year. These statistics are indeed alarming, particularly since 75% of the morbidity (developmental defects) and mortality rates are attributed to environmental factors or agents.

Although there is a long history of myths and superstitions about the effect of environmental influences and maternal experiences on the unborn child, the scientific evidence demonstrating adverse effects of environmental factors on developing organisms dates back less than 50 years. Between 1940 and 1960, researchers established that environmental influences such as maternal nutritional deficiencies, infectious diseases, and drugs could produce predictable malformations in mammalian embryos, including humans. There is now a voluminous body of evidence that the prenatal organism is at risk, and that the maternal organism cannot protect it against all of the many environmental factors that are potentially hazardous to the developing organism. We can define the environment as everything outside the prenatal organism, including the amniotic fluid, uterus, the maternal body, and the environment external to the mother. The scientific study of the deleterious effects of the environment on developing organisms is called teratology. Teratology is the branch of embryology that deals with the etiology and manifestation of abnormal structural and functional development in prenatal and postnatal organisms. Developmental defects that involve structural abnormality are often referred to as terata or malformations. But for our purposes, anomalies, birth defects, and congenital defects may be used as broad descriptive terms for both structural and functional developmental defects.

An environmental factor that produces a developmental

defect is called a teratogen. Teratogens often produce characteristic and predictable patterns of defects. Wilson (1957) refers to such teratogenic phenomena as "agent specificity." Agent specificity occurs because particular teratogens disrupt only particular phases of metabolism and enzymatic processes, thus producing characteristic patterns of abnormal embryogenesis. Since enzymatic and metabolic events are rather strictly related to cell differentiation and tissue formation, we can understand the specificity relationship between certain teratogenic agents and symptom manifestation. In describing the mechanisms leading to a sequence of abnormal developmental events (pathogenesis), Wilson (1973) states:

An initial action followed by a chain reaction seems to be the course of events in teratogenesis: not the cause alone, but the cause together with the particular sequences of responses it elicits in cells and tissues determines how development will be diverted. These early reactions in response to the environmental cause are here called mechanisms. *(pp. 5–6)*

Principles of Teratology and the Concept of Critical Periods

The major categories of teratogens known in mammals include radiation, chemicals, nutrition, infection, anoxia, metabolic imbalance, and physical injury. Of these, only four categories contain agents of known teratogenicity in humans. These are ionizing radiation, chemicals or drugs, infectious conditions, and metabolic–endocrine imbalances (see Table 3-5). We will briefly discuss some examples from these teratogen groups later in this chapter. More detailed discussion and general reviews may be found in Burrow and Ferris (1975), Joffe (1969), Warkany (1971), and Wilson (1973). Wilson (1973) lists six general principles of teratology that describe typical teratogenic phenomena:

1 *Susceptibility to teratogenesis depends on the genotype of the conceptus and the manner in which this interacts with adverse environmental conditions.*
2 *Susceptibility to teratogenesis varies with the developmental stage at the time of exposure to an adverse influence.*
3 *Teratogenic agents act in specific ways (mechanisms) on developing cells and tissues to initiate sequences of abnormal developmental events (pathogenesis).*

**Table 3-5
Known Causes of
Developmental Defects
in Humans**

Known genetic transmission	20%
Chromosomal aberration	3–5%
Environmental causes	
Radiations	<1%
Therapeutic	
Nuclear	
Infections	2–3%
Rubella virus	
Cytomegalovirus	
Herpesvirus hominis	
Toxoplasma	
Syphilis	
Maternal metabolic imbalance	1–2%
Endemic cretinism	
Diabetes	
Phenylketonuria	
Virilizing tumors	
Drugs and environmental chemicals	2–3%
Androgenic hormone	
Folic antagonists	
Thalidomide	
Organic mercury	
Some hypoglycemics (?)	
Some anticonvulsants (?)	
Potentiative interactions	?
Unknown	65–70%

(From Wilson, 1972.)

4 *The access of adverse influences to developing tissues depends on the nature of the influence (agent).*
5 *The four manifestations of deviant development are death, malformation, growth retardation, and functional deficit.*
6 *Manifestations of deviant development increase in frequency and degree as dosage increases, from the no-effect to the totally lethal level. (pp. 12–34)*

For some time, it has been known that developing organic systems are most vulnerable to adverse influences and subsequent damage during particular stages of development. Teratogenic susceptibility is greatest during the embryonic and early fetal stages of prenatal development. It is during these stages that cell differentiation, tissue specialization, and organ-

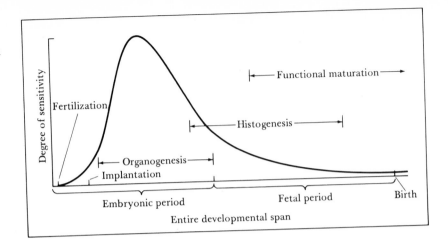

Figure 3-6
Curve approximating the susceptibility of the human embryo to teratogenesis.

(From Wilson, 1972.)

ogenesis take place. In humans, the degree of sensitivity to structural damage peaks between about 20 and 60 days of embryonic age. Before and after this period, there is less susceptibility to teratogenesis (see Figure 3-6).

After 60 days, progressive cell differentiation and organ development provide increased resistance to teratogenic agents. Larger doses of teratogens are necessary to produce effects more easily induced during the embryonic period. This differential sensitivity to teratogens is related to gene activation and the onset of genetic coding for the production of specific enzymes and proteins involved in cellular differentiation and organogenesis. Teratogenic insult during these periods of embryonic activity can result in cellular death, agenesis (failure of tissues to develop), and dysgenesis (incomplete or excessive tissue development). This is sometimes called the classical theory of developmental arrest, in which the etiology of developmental defects is attributed to the interruption of developmental processes prior to, or during, the critical period of their completion.

The theory of critical periods in embryology was first stated in 1921 by C.R. Stockard. Stockard discovered that he could experimentally induce similar malformations in fish embryos by exposing them to different teratogens, providing that the teratogenic agents were introduced during the same period of organogenesis. Stockard referred to this phenomenon as "critical moments" of embryonic development, a concept that led to a basic rule in embryology. This rule stated that the most rapidly growing tissues and organs in an embryonic organism are most vulnerable to any adverse environmental influences.

Stockard's view that critical periods represent a one-to-one correlation between embryonic development and defect specificity is no longer accepted. Wilson (1973) advises that the concept of critical periods should be considered a rule-of-thumb notion rather than a scientific principle. He cites ample evidence refuting the concept of defect specificity and developmental period, stating that it is more reasonable to invoke the critical period concept in estimating the approximate time of onset of developmental defects in the embryonic organism.

Ionizing Radiation Effects

Ionizing radiation can take a number of forms. Different sources of radiation may generate alpha, beta, gamma, and X rays, or a combination of these. Ionizing radiation affects the nuclear material of cells, changing the atomic structure of chromosomes and genes, and thus seriously altering development. Exposure to such radiation also accelerates the frequency of genetic mutations, most of which are deleterious. Both laboratory data from experimental teratology and data from clinical cases in the medical literature indicate that early prenatal exposure to ionizing radiation may result in CNS defects, intellectual impairment, structural and behavioral anomalies, and cancer (Dekaban, 1968; Furchtgott, 1956; Joffe, 1969; Sternberg, 1970; Yamazaki, 1966). Thus, the need for therapeutic radiation treatment in pregnant women, particularly of the pelvic area, raises crucial questions. Such a decision must weigh the health needs of the mother, the stage of pregnancy, and the degree of accumulated radiation exposure.

Therapeutic abortion may be the wisest decision when radiation dosage and gestation age exceed the minimal safe threshold levels for high risk (8.8 rads during the first 12 weeks of gestation). Studies of pregnant women who were exposed to heavy radiation from the nuclear explosions at Hiroshima and Nagasaki reveal that their infants exhibited an unusually high number of birth defects such as microcephaly, leukemia, mental retardation, retarded growth, and a number of other physical anomalies.

Drug Effects   Drugs can affect the fetus only if they are able to cross the placental barrier. Although the maternal and fetal circulatory systems are totally separate, they become closely aligned within the placenta, permitting the transfer of some drug substances to the fetal circulatory system. A number of survey studies over the past 10 years indicate that more than 90% of all pregnant women take one or more drugs during the course of their pregnancies. These medically prescribed and self-administered drugs range from aspirin to barbiturates, and some reports suggest that the typical pregnant woman takes an average of five different drugs.

These are worrisome statistics, particularly in light of the thalidomide catastrophe two decades ago. The effects of drugs on embryogenesis have been intensively investigated, and to date only three have been positively identified as teratogenic for humans: thalidomide, steroid hormones, and folic acid antagonists (Wilson, 1973). However, difficulties in methodology and experimental control have prevented more definitive conclusions concerning a number of other drugs that are suspected of having teratogenic potential. Given this state of affairs, a sensible mother will not take any drug or medication during the first trimester of pregnancy without obstetric approval.

The fact that a pregnant woman may not experience any ill effects from a drug is absolutely no indication of its potential effect on an unborn child, as the thalidomide incident painfully points out. One insidious aspect of teratogenic drugs is that the mother may experience no physical sign of its toxicity to the fetus. This emphasizes the differential sensitivity to pharmacological substances in the maternal–fetal complex.

In Chapter Two, the prenatal consequences of taking thalidomide during the first trimester of pregnancy were discussed. This sedative produces a number of musculoskeletal deformities, including agenesis of the extremities and facial malformations. CNS involvement is rare, and intelligence is normally distributed among thalidomide infants reared in normal home environments. There have been reports of mild intellectual impairment in thalidomide infants (Decarie, 1969). But such observations are confounded by the secondary effects of structural deformity, abnormal maternal-infant relationships, lowered levels of stimulation, and decreased opportun-

Thalidomide children at the Orthopedic Clinic of the University of Heidelburg, Germany. Thalidomide is one of three substances known to be teratogenic for humans. Used extensively in Europe during the early 1960s to combat "morning sickness," the drug tragically illustrates one characteristic of most teratogens: the mother may have no indication of the drug's effect on the developing being within her.

(Photo copyright © 1978 by Doring Stern/Black Star Photos.)

ities for learning among peers of equal intellect.

Steroid hormones such as androgen and estrogen have also been implicated, as teratogenic drugs. Their administration during the first 12 weeks of pregnancy may result in organ and structural malformations and, in the case of androgen treatment, the masculinization of female fetuses (pseudohermaphroditism).

Folic acid is one of the B-group vitamins required for the formation of blood in the body. Folic acid antagonists are compounds that neutralize the action of folic acid, producing folic acid deficiency. Folic acid antagonists are used to treat such diseases as leukemia and Hodgkin's disease. However, with pregnant women these should be used only in extreme cases. Such treatment during the early months of pregnancy usually results in abortion, but congenital malformations of multiple and varied symptomology have been reported.

A number of other drugs have been implicated as possible or potential teratogens, but research efforts have not yet clearly identified them as definitely involved in embryogenesis. Among these suspected drugs are anticonvulsants for the treatment of epileptic disorders, amphetamines, oral drugs used to control diabetes such as tolbutamide, certain drugs used in the chemotherapy of cancer, aspirin, several antibiotics, quinine, insulin, and antidepressants (Wilson, 1973). Scattered reports of the possible teratogenicity of these drugs in either animals or humans place them on the suspect list, but research has not yet clarified their effects on the human embryo and fetus. It should be noted that a finding of susceptibility or resistance to any particular teratogen in a variety of experimental animals has no necessary implication for humans, and vice versa. For example, low dosage exposure to thalidomide is almost invariably toxic to the human embryo, while most laboratory animals are relatively insensitive to this drug, requiring much heavier doses to produce comparable effects. Many species of animals show no toxic effect at all to thalidomide exposure. Therefore, results from experimental teratology, while important, must be taken cautiously with regard to their implications for humans.

Smoking and Alcohol During the past 20 years, the relationship between maternal smoking and prenatal development has attracted much attention. Cigarette smoke contains a number of toxic substances that are absorbed by the maternal body and possibly transferred to the fetus. Therefore, concern about the potential teratogenicity of smoking has aroused a great deal of research activity and a large body of literature on the prenatal effects of smoking.

Simpson (1957) was among the first to report higher rates of premature births among smoking mothers compared to nonsmokers. Since then, an impressive number of studies have confirmed this general finding (Joffe, 1969; Yerushalmy, 1972, 1973). Recently, maternal smoking has been implicated as a potential teratogen (Fedrick, Alberman, & Goldstein, 1971). However, the correlational nature of these studies, their serious methodological flaws, and the confounding of socioeconomic class, nutritional status, race, and genetic background of the parents with the independent variable of smoking provides only a preliminary basis for cause-and-effect statements about the effects of maternal smoking.

Although the most consistent finding is that maternal smoking is related to low birth weight and prematurity, Yerushalmy (1962, 1972, 1973) has reported significant correlations between birth weight and the *father's* smoking, no differential perinatal mortality rate in infants of smoking and nonsmoking mothers, and a *lower* infant mortality rate among smoking mothers. These data complicate the case for a direct causal role of smoking, and demonstrate the complex nature of this problem. Yerushalmy believes that it may be the general characteristics of the smoker that produce differences in prenatal development, not smoking itself. In summary, the literature related to the teratogenic effects of smoking is far from complete. It is not known whether the common observation of low birth weight and prematurity among maternal smokers is a function of the smoker (including perhaps the father) or of smoking. Nevertheless, we must remain cautious about maternal smoking and its potential effects on the fetus.

The literature dealing with the prenatal effects of alcohol is also equivocal. Although it is known that alcohol quickly crosses the placental barrier, very little is known about its teratogenicity. A recent review of the literature (Green, 1974) does suggest that chronic and excessive drinking of alcohol can have deleterious prenatal effects. There have been reports of higher mortality rates, reduced birth size and weight, malformations, altered enzyme activity, and metabolic disorders in infants of heavy drinkers. As Green points out, however, these studies are complicated by poor methodology and uncontrolled variables. Since most of the studies reviewed by Green involved chronic alcoholics, it is not known to what extent other factors related to alcoholism may have contributed to the observations. Three recent studies have reported the discovery of a so-called "alcohol syndrome" in infants of alcoholic mothers (Jones, Smith, Ulleland, & Streissguth, 1973; Jones & Smith, 1973; Palmer, Warner, & Leichtman, 1974). This syndrome, first observed by Jones et al. (1973), has been described as a consistent pattern of craniofacial, limb, and cardiovascular defects associated with growth deficiencies and developmental delay. Palmer et al. (1974) also observed similar patterns of malformations.

In the three studies cited above, the alcohol syndrome had been observed in only 13 infants; most were either black or Indian, and all were born to mothers of low socioeconomic status. These findings were further confounded by maternal complications including anemia, malnutrition, and venereal disease. But more recent studies continue to suggest that alcohol may have teratogenic effects on the human prenatal organism (Clarren & Smith, 1978; Clarren, Alvord, Sumi, Streissguth, & Smith, 1978; Ouellette, Rosett, Rosman, & Weiner, 1977). Although more recent findings of a fetal alcohol syndrome are based on larger, more representative samples (Streissguth, 1977), problems of control still prevent the clear identification of alcohol as a human teratogen. Inconsistent findings are still reported (Clarren et al., 1978), and other factors may be contributing to, or potentiating, observed fetal abnormalities. In short, the term, fetal alcoholic syndrome, may be more descriptive at this time (Palmisano, Sneed, & Cassady, 1969; Sneed, 1977).

Maternal Diseases and Conditions

The major considerations in the teratogenic characteristics of maternal diseases and conditions are infectious diseases and maternal conditions involving metabolic disturbances.

Infectious diseases, particularly viral diseases, can be transmitted to the prenatal organism either by placental diffusion or infection of the female genital tract, resulting in viral invasion of the embryo or fetus and subsequent cell destruction (see Table 3-6). Metabolic disturbances such as diabetes and hypothyroidism affect the embryo or fetus secondarily by interrupting or impairing fetal requirements of biochemicals, nutrients, or oxygen that are vital for normal development. That is, the altered physiological state of the maternal body results in an inadequate support system for the developing organism.

Maternal contraction of rubella (German measles) during the first trimester of pregnancy produces a now familiar

Table 3-6
Viral Infections in Pregnancy

VIRUSES	MATERNAL AND/OR FETAL EFFECTS
Agents causing common respiratory illnesses	None
Influenza	Usually none; increased maternal morbidity and mortality in certain epidemics; ? fetal anomalies
Mumps	Abortion; ? fetal anomalies
Poliomyelitis	Increased maternal morbidity and mortality; congenital and neonatal paralytic poliomyelitis
Coxsackie B	Neonatal myocarditis and encephalitis; ? congenital heart disease
Echovirus 6 and 9	None
Hepatitis	Abortion, stillbirth; prematurity, neonatal hepatitis; persistent postnatal infection (hepatitis B)
Measles	Abortion
Smallpox	Abortion; congenital disease
Vaccinia	Congenital disease
Varicella-zoster	Congenital disease; disseminated neonatal infection; ? congenital anomalies
Herpes simplex	Prematurity, neonatal disease, localized or disseminated
Cytomegaloviruses	Prematurity; intrauterine growth retardation; congenital disease; congenital anomalies; persistent postnatal infection
Rubella	Abortion, stillbirth; intrauterine growth retardation; congenital disease; congenital anomalies; persistent postnatal infection

(From Burrow & Ferris, 1975.)

syndrome of congenital cardiac defect, blindness, deafness, microcephaly, and mental retardation. If contracted during the first month of pregnancy, rubella causes developmental defects in approximately 50% of the newborns. If the mother is infected during the second or third month of pregnancy, 22% and 10% of the infants, respectively, will show defects (Sever, 1970). Gumple, Hayes and Dudgeon (1971) report that rubella infection during the second trimester may result in functional defects such as retardation without the number of structural defects observed when infection occurs in the first trimester of pregnancy.

Maternal conditions such as diabetes and thyroid disorders are examples of metabolic disturbances that can have teratogenic effects on the embryo or fetus. Maternal hypothyroidism results in a deficiency of iodine supply to the fetus. The consequence may be congenital cretinism, a condition involving brain damage, mental retardation, and structural defects in the infant. Among diabetic women, the frequency of birth defects approaches 80%. Fetal exposure to high levels of unmetabolized sugar results in the abnormal enlargement of the pancreas, excessive weight and size dimensions, and musculoskeletal abnormalities. Some 50% of the fetuses of diabetic mothers will abort or be stillborn because of the toxic intrauterine environment.

Perinatal Factors in Development

Perinatal factors are those conditions or states that arise between the 30th week of pregnancy and the second week after birth. Such conditions may give rise to various pregnancy and birth complications, that in turn may influence subsequent ontogenesis. Perinatal factors include nutritional deficits, anoxia, low birth weight and prematurity, and maternal emotional states. These perinatal considerations have generated much research activity and controversy about their implications for postnatal psychological development.

NUTRITION   There is considerable evidence demonstrating the teratogenicity of specific dietary deficiencies in laboratory animals. Controlled restriction of various nutrients such as vitamins, minerals, and proteins, along with reduction of general caloric intake, may produce malformations, growth retardation, or death in laboratory embryonic organisms (Joffe, 1969; Wilson, 1973). The laboratory data reveal that to demonstrate a clear teratogenic effect for any nutritional factor, it must be restricted from the prenatal organism during the period of organogenesis. A nutritional deficiency produced during the perinatal period may result in higher rates of mortality, prematurity, and growth retardation, but not malformations or developmental defects.

At this time, no nutritional deficiencies have been positively identified as teratogenic in humans, except for those involving folic acid antagonists (Wilson, 1973). A number of studies have implicated maternal nutritional deficiency in the impairment of CNS development, resulting in smaller brain cells, reduced brain weights, and subsequent functional impairment (Montagu, 1962; Parekh, Pherwani, Udani, & Mukherjie, 1970; Ramalingaswami, 1973; Winick, 1969, 1970; Zamenof, van Marthens, & Granel, 1971). Clear evidence relating malnutrition to impaired CNS development and subsequent intellectual development is lacking, however. A recent study by Stein, Susser, Saenger, and Morolla (1972) indicates no relationship between mental performance at age 19 and exposure to severe prenatal malnutrition. These investigators studied the effect of maternal starvation during pregnancy that occurred in the Dutch famine of 1944–1945 in Nazi-occupied Holland. Despite the severe nutritional and caloric deprivation imposed on women in various stages of pregnancy (450 calories per day), no differences could be found in adult mental performance of their children as a function of prenatal malnutrition compared to matched controls. Also, mental performance was not found to be associated with birth weight, but was related to social class.

The contradictory data available on the developmental effects of nutritional factors force us to recognize the complex nature of these phenomena. It is extremely difficult to isolate maternal dietary factors and deficiencies from the many other complicating conditions associated with, and arising from, malnutrition. Disease states, hormonal and metabolic disruption, and physical trauma may all accompany malnutrition. Factors known to be associated with socioeconomic status can also differentially contribute to prenatal conditions attributed to malnutrition. It is also known that prepregnancy nutritional history and status can play a role in prenatal and birth complications (Drillien, 1964).

There is little question that nutritional deficiencies may affect general prenatal development, and that these states can contribute to complications of pregnancy that threaten the fetus. However, whether malnutrition as a single, causative factor produces structural and/or functional defects in the pre- and postnatal stages of human development remains an unanswered question at this time.

ANOXIA   Anoxia is a condition in which the oxygen supply to body tissues is reduced below the physiological requirements of the organism. Anoxia, asphyxia, and hypoxia are often used interchangeably to refer to this condition. As a potential influence on subsequent psychological development, perinatal anoxia has been a subject of considerable concern to both medical and behavioral scientists. Some perinatal anoxia is inherent in the birth process; all newborn infants experience at least mild oxygen deprivation during labor and delivery. Birth complications such as prolonged labor, or abbreviated labor of less than 7 hours, may result in more serious fetal levels of anoxia, but improved obstetric techniques can substantially reduce this danger. Abnormal intrauterine conditions during the late stages of pregnancy may result in diminished fetal oxygen supplies. Such conditions, which are often undetected, increase the risk of postnatal mortality and morbidity. Anoxic conditions may result in CNS dysfunction or structural damage, with a number of attendant behavioral symptoms occurring as a function of anoxic severity. Developmental consequences reportedly range from learning disabilities to motor disruption to brain damage and mental retardation. There does not appear to be any specific pattern of deficit involved.

A relationship between perinatal anoxia and subsequent developmental defect has been suspected for more than 100 years. In 1861, W. J. Little, a physician, described what he observed to be the clinical sequelae of prolonged, difficult labor and neonatal anoxia. He was the first to document clinical cases of cerebral palsy, mental retardation, and related problems in children, and hypothesized that these conditions were caused by perinatal anoxia.

More than 70 years passed before other researchers pursued the relationship between perinatal anoxia and behavioral development. During the past 50 years, research by a growing number of investigators has strengthened the belief that perinatal anoxia can lead to many kinds of behavioral and neurological impairments. Most of these studies have dealt with the phase of the perinatal period that extends from the onset of labor to birth. Recent reviews of the human clinical data (Gottfried, 1973; Meier, 1971; Sameroff & Chandler, 1975) and the experimental data with infrahuman organisms (Meier, 1971) point out the methodological complexities in this research area. They also reveal the controversial and inconclusive nature of the relationship between perinatal anoxia and its developmental consequences.

The human clinical studies are necessarily correlational in design and are beset with a number of control problems that obscure the findings. There are methodological obstacles to the precise assessment of perinatal anoxia, the independent variable, as well as in the accurate assessment of the dependent variables such as intelligence, learning disabilities, and various motor and emotional behaviors. The identification and assessment of anoxia is by no means a simple procedure. The use of any single measure has not been fruitful or precise in specifying the amount and duration of perinatal anoxia.

Without precise measurements and a way to isolate anoxic states, it is difficult to draw any conclusions about the etiologic role of anoxia in abnormal development. Likewise, it is hard to clearly assess the various dependent measures implicated for anoxia, and to separate those behavioral dysfunctions attributed to anoxia from those possibly related to postnatal environmental factors. All of these difficulties prevent us from observing any certain cause-and-effect relationship. Despite the potent face validity of Little's hypothesis, the empirical supporting data have been elusive indeed. Both the human clinical data and the experimental data have been inconclusive and inconsistent, a situation that led Meier (1971) to sum up the current status of the research in this area as "ragged." In short, there is still no convincing body of replicable evidence that describes the effects of anoxia on human intellectual, motor, and emotional development.

Gottfried (1973) has written a critical review of the human research dealing with the intellectual consequences of perinatal anoxia. He offers some tentative conclusions that he has deduced from the literature:

1 *The intellectual consequences of perinatal anoxia—lower IQ scores—are more prevalent in infants and preschoolers than in older children and adolescents.*
2 *Anoxic subjects as a group are not mentally retarded.*

3 *Experiencing anoxia may increase the probability of retardation.*
4 *There is no evidence at this time that anoxic subjects are deficient in specific intellectual abilities. (p. 240)*

Similarly, neurological and behavioral dysfunctions cannot be directly traced to perinatal anoxia. The diagnosis of perinatal anoxia in the fetus and newborn is often a consequence of some other abnormal intrauterine condition that existed *before* the anoxia states. In these situations, some other prenatal condition may cause *both* anoxia and subsequent abnormal development. For example, a structural defect would occur first, followed by anoxia. Undetected, this state of affairs would likely be seen as an anoxia-defect sequence. One must also be sensitive to the postnatal environment of the infant and child, with its known potential for producing intellectual and emotional defects. Thus, until researchers control for race, social class, sex, genetics, age, birth weight, and prenatal and postnatal factors, and solve the methodological problems already mentioned, we cannot spell out the role of perinatal anoxic trauma in development.

Low Birth Weight and Prematurity

Since 1935, in the United States a prematurely born infant has been defined as a liveborn infant weighing 2500 grams (5½ pounds) or less at birth. In 1950, this definition was adopted by the World Health Organization. The WHO Committee on Maternal and Child Health recommended in 1961 that the term "premature" be replaced by "low birth weight," restricting the former designation to infants born at less than 37 weeks of menstrual age. The American Academy of Pediatrics also adopted these recommendations in 1964. Infants who weigh less than 2500 grams but are born after 37 weeks of gestation age are now described as "infants of low birth weight." Prematurity and low birth weight can occur together, particularly when the infant weighs less than 1500 grams at birth, and both perinatal conditions are associated with increased neonatal mortality and morbidity rates.

Because of the recent changes in defining prematurity and

A premature infant in intensive care. This "premie" is protected from the outside environment by a closed incubator with special machinery to condition the air to a preestablished degree of temperature and humidity. Sleeve apertures, which close around the forearms of the person attending the baby, serve to maintain the controlled environment. The premature or low-birth-weight infant is usually kept in the incubator until it weighs 2500 grams (5½ pounds) and certainly until it is able to regulate its own body temperature.

(Photo by Julie O'Neil. Copyright © 1977 by Stock, Boston, Inc.)

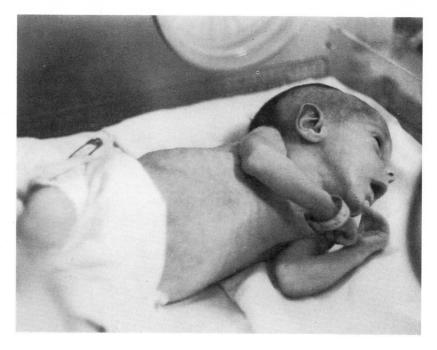

low birth weight, exact statistical data have not yet been determined. But the available information suggests that the incidence of low birth weight in the United States is approximately 7.2% in white liveborn infants and 14% among nonwhite populations. Prematurity (short gestation) has an approximate incidence of 5% among white liveborn infants, and 10% among nonwhite groups. Generally, premature birth occurs because of uterine inability to retain the fetus, interference with the course of pregnancy, placental separation, or some stimulus producing early uterine contractions. Conditions that result in placental insufficiency, retarded fetal growth, or poor maternal nutrition and health are associated with low birth weight.

There is an extensive literature describing the developmental consequences of low birth weight and prematurity. However, an analysis of the reports reveals problems like those described in the anoxia research, complicating our understanding of the developmental significance of these perinatal conditions (Caputo & Mandell, 1970; Sameroff & Chandler, 1975). Shortcomings in the earlier investigations include the failure to distinguish between low birth weight and prematurity, the use of a single criterion (weight) to identify prematurity, and the assumption that all premature or low birth weight infants are homogeneous in terms of etiology and outcome.

Drillien (1964) has addressed these inadequacies by noting that low birth weight infants fall into three categories, each of which may have differential ontogenetic consequences. Low birth weight may be seen in infants born of physically small mothers. Infants in this category have very low morbidity rates and are essentially normal in their general development. Drillien's second category of low birth weight infants comprises those born between 37 and 40 weeks gestation, but significantly underweight because of some abnormal intrauterine condition such as malnutrition or placental insufficiency. His third category of low birth weight infants includes those with short gestation ages.

Each of these three groups may have different etiologies and different outcomes. Clearly, the indiscriminate inclusion of infants from these three different groups may neutralize, exaggerate, or otherwise confound one's data and conceal the actual relation between these perinatal factors and subsequent development. Additional methodological considerations involve controlling for race, socioeconomic status (SES), abnormal prenatal conditions, and pregnancy complications, all of which are known to be associated with the incidence of low birth weight and prematurity. Again, on the dependent variable side, we have the validity problem in behavioral and intellectual assessment, and the extent to which observed behavioral dysfunctions might be due to postnatal environmental factors, rather than the coincidence of low birth weight or prematurity.

In their careful and critical review of the literature dealing with the consequences of low birth weight, Caputo and Mandell (1970) offer the following conclusions:

1 *The strongest evidence for intellectual impairment in children of low birth weight is found only among very low birth weight individuals (less than 2000 grams). In the heavier groups of low birth weight infants, there is little, if any, evidence of intellectual impairment.*

2 *Low birth weight individuals are over-represented in institutionalized populations of mental retardates and in special classes, in groups institutionalized for a variety of disabilities, and in high school dropouts.*
3 *Emotional disorders, hyperkinesis, and autism are more often characteristic of prematures than of maturely born children.*
4 *Deficits in language development and reading are often associated with prematurity.*
5 *Deficits in physical growth, motor behavior, and neurological functioning, along with physical anomalies, are strongly correlated with prematurity. (p. 380)*

It should be clear that other independent variables such as SES, race, history of pregnancy, and the postnatal environment may interact significantly with prematurity and low birth weight, to the point of obviating any definitive statements about cause and effect relationships between these perinatal conditions and ontogenesis. The number of variables potentially influencing developmental outcomes in perinatal research requires the use of multivariate designs in order to determine the differential contributions of each specific independent variable and their etiological signficance, if any.

Maternal Emotional States

Armed with increasing knowledge about prenatal factors in human development, investigators have begun to study maternal emotional states during pregnancy and their relationship to reproductive problems and postnatal development. Laboratory research with animals suggests that maternal stress may produce increased emotional reactivity in offspring (Joffe, 1969) and disruptions in maternal-infant relations (Smith, Heseltine, & Corson, 1971). But such effects appear to be species specific or strain specific and are not always consistent in their direction. While it is plausible that chronic, high-level emotional states in humans may contribute to pregnancy and perinatal complications, the evidence remains obscure and by no means compelling (Carlson & LaBarba, 1979). Numerous reports have related maternal emotional disturbances such as anxiety, neurosis, and psychosis to increased incidence of prematurity, spontaneous abortion, stillbirths, delivery problems, and a variety of behavioral disturbances during infancy and early childhood (Bahna & Bjerkedal, 1974; Gorsuch &

Key, 1974; Harper & Williams, 1974; Joffe, 1969; Sameroff & Chandler, 1975; Woerner, Pollack, & Klein, 1973). There are many hypotheses about the mechanisms underlying these associations between maternal emotional states and reproductive problems. These hypotheses include neuroendocrine (hormonal, metabolic) effects on the fetus, fetal anoxia caused by contraction of uterine arteries, increased maternal susceptibility to disease, general health problems, and labor and delivery difficulties.

While it is intriguing to consider the etiological significance of maternal emotional states for prenatal and postnatal development, we cannot attach any cause–effect status to the reported relationships. The methodological deficiencies in this area of research are the same as those characterizing most of the work in perinatal anoxia and low birth weight. Failure to control the large number of variables that are known to influence the general course of pregnancy, labor and delivery, and postnatal behavior is serious enough to prevent any conclusive statements about the contributions of these maternal conditions (Copans, 1974; Joffe, 1969; Sameroff & Chandler, 1975).

Problems in assessing maternal emotional conditions and infant disturbances further compound this situation. High levels of maternal emotional disturbances are often accompanied by alcohol and drug abuse, nutritional neglect, and other forms of potentially harmful behavior that present hazards to the fetus and mother. It is also possible that abnormal intrauterine conditions and their effects on the maternal body may precipitate emotional states in the mother, in which case fetal damage would be independent of her emotional condition. Serious maternal emotional states require obstetric and psychological management. If they are controlled with no secondary effects on the mother, and if there are no biological implications, there is no clear evidence of any fetal hazard. When a mother suffers continued postpartum emotional disruption, then disturbances in infant feeding, behavior, and general development may just as easily be attributed to the environment provided by the mother as to the emotional state during pregnancy. In summary, although maternal emotional states may disrupt the physical environment for the fetus and infant, there is little evidence that such states are a direct cause of abnormal prenatal and postnatal development.

OBSTETRIC MEDICATION

*T*he first attempt to relieve the pain of childbirth with medication has been credited to James Simpson, who administered ether to a woman in labor in 1847 (Macfarlane, 1977). The use of obstetric medication to relieve the pain of labor and delivery has steadily increased ever since. Today, the use of medication of some type is routine practice in most Western maternity wards. Perhaps as many as 90% of American mothers have received obstetric medication during labor and delivery (Conway & Brackbill, 1970). The drugs commonly used in obstetrics are general anesthetics, local anesthetics, analgesics and narcotics, sedatives, and tranquilizers. All these drugs can cross the placental barrier. Bowers (1970) has described three ways in which such obstetric medication may influence the fetus. First, the drug may cross the placenta unchanged, as in the case of barbiturates and volatile anesthetics. Second, a metabolite of the drug may cross the placenta. Third, a drug may alter maternal physiology, resulting in labor difficulties or cardiovascular problems that can adversely affect the fetus.

Effects of Obstetric Medication on Infants

Virtually all of the research on the effects of obstetric medication has focused on short-term effects observed in infants during the first few weeks or months of life. A number of investigators have reported temporary disruptions of infant functioning in feeding and sucking behavior, brain activity (EEG), motor development, auditory and visual responses, reflexes, muscle tone, cardiovascular activity, alertness, and activity level, along with poorer test performance on standardized infant scales of development (Brackbill, 1979). These various effects of obstetric medication have typically been found to be short-lived, ranging from a few hours to 4 or 5 months in duration.

Much of the research on the effects of obstetric medication has focused on neonatal and infant habituation, the ability to cease responding to a repetitive stimulus. In general, studies of auditory and visual habituation have shown that infants whose mothers were heavily medicated during labor and delivery took longer to habituate than infants of mothers who had received less medication or none (Brackbill, Kane, Manniello, & Abramson, 1974; Conway & Brackbill, 1970; Friedman, Brackbill, Caron, & Caron, 1978). Studies on the effects of obstetric medication have been plagued by methodological problems (Mirkin & Singh, 1976). Still, the consensus has been that moderate to heavy medication during labor and delivery may produce transient effects on the postnatal behavior and development of the infant, sometimes placing the infant at greater risk. Differences observed between infants of heavily medicated mothers and nonmedicated controls typically disappear, and no further developmental consequences have been reported.

The Brackbill and Broman Study

Until recently, no longitudinal studies on the developmental effects of obstetric medication existed. But the preliminary reports of Yvonne Brackbill and Sarah Broman (Brackbill, 1979; Broman, 1979; Kolata, 1978) have challenged the long-standing belief that the common practice of obstetric medication holds no serious or permanent developmental risk to the infant. The first evidence that obstetric medications may affect children's later behavior comes from a comprehensive prospective study, the National Collaborative Perinatal Project (NCPP), conducted by the National Institute of Neurological and Communicative Disorders and Stroke (NINCDS).

The Brackbill and Broman study is still in preparation. Nonetheless, in 1978, Brackbill announced to the press, a Senate subcommittee on Health and Scientific Research, and on a national television program that obstetric medication during labor and delivery may have permanent, detrimental effects on a child's intellectual and behavioral development. In the spring of 1979, Brackbill again reported their preliminary findings before the Anesthetic and Life Support Drug Advisory Committee of the Food and Drug Administration.

Using the data obtained from the NCPP on over 50,000 babies born between 1959 and 1966, Brackbill and Broman selected 3400 of the healthiest full-term, white infants born to healthy mothers with low-risk pregnancies and uncomplicated deliveries. Infants were given a variety of pediatric, neurological, and behavioral examinations at birth, 4 months, 8 months, 12 months, 4 years, and 7 years. Brackbill reported that infants of heavily medicated mothers lagged in general motor development during the first year of life. They also were deficient in habituation and in the ability to stop crying when comforted. At older ages, these children also showed impairment of language and cognitive skills. Brackbill stated that obstetrical medication may cause an average loss of four IQ points in a child (Kolata, 1979). Brackbill found the effects to be dose related. The greatest effects are observed among children whose mothers received the strongest drugs or the highest dosages.

The implications of the Brackbill and Broman study, and the manner in which the preliminary findings were released, quickly stirred intense, angry reactions within the scientific community. With the study still unpublished, a careful evaluation of its methodology and conclusions is not possible. However, the study has already been seriously attacked by a number of physicians and statisticians (Kolata, 1979). A major concern of critics is that publicity about Brackbill and Broman's conclusions may cause women to refuse all medications, possibly endangering their infants, or they may feel guilty about accepting them (Kolata, 1979). In her report, Kolata (1979) concludes, "What should have been a dispassionate study of important data has become an adversary proceeding with the familiar protagonists—the obstetricians and anesthesiologists against the natural childbirth advocates—reaching an impasse once again" (p. 392). Clearly the possible long-term effects of obstetric medication require further evaluation and research before this controversy can be resolved.

Although many developmental abnormalities may arise from reproductive or prenatal complications, their maintenance, disappearance, decrease, or increase may become a function of the postnatal environment and the general family complex. Just as there is a continuum of reproductive casualty from mild to severe (Pasamanick & Knoblock, 1966), Sameroff and Chandler (1975) have proposed a continuum of caretaking casualty ranging from mild environmental deprivation or disruption to multiple, severe adverse conditions. The prediction of developmental outcome thus requires an analysis of where a particular child falls on the two continua of reproductive casualty and caretaking casualty.

Sameroff and Chandler (1975) point out that the broad range of observed developmental problems does not appear to be related to pregnancy or perinatal complications, and that many infants who experience such complications do not suffer from later difficulties. This lack of difficulties may be due to such environmental factors as family constellation and socio-economic status, according to Sameroff and Chandler. That is, the ontogenetic effects of reproductive complications may be modulated by the postnatal environment. The caretaking, in short, may lead to increases or decreases, appearance or disappearance, in a variety of developmental dimensions such as intelligence, emotional behavior, and language. This provocative model of development may help to clarify many puzzling questions about the prenatal determinants of behavior.

REFERENCES

Arey, L. B. *Developmental Anatomy* (7th ed.). Philadelphia: Saunders, 1974.

Asdell, S. A. *Patterns of mammalian reproduction.* New York: Comstock, 1946.

Bahna, S. L., & Bjerkedal, T. The course and outcome of pregnancy in women with neuroses. *Acta Obstetrics and Gynecology of Scandinavia,* 1974, *53,* 129–133.

Bowers, W. A. Obstetrical Medication and infant outcome: A Review of the literature. *Monograph of the Society for Research in Child Development,* 1970, *35,* 3–23.

Brackbill, Y. Obstetrical medication study. *Science,* 1979, *205,* 447–448.

Brackbill, Y., Kane, J., Manniello, R., & Abramson, D. Obstetric meperidine usage and assessment of neonatal status. *Anesthesiology,* 1974, *40,* 116–120.

Burrow, G. W., & Ferris, T. F. (Eds.). *Medical complications during pregnancy.* Philadelphia: Saunders, 1975.

Caputo, D. V., & Mandell, W. Consequences of low birth weight. *Developmental Psychology,* 1970, *3,* 363–383.

Carlson, D. B., & LaBarba, R. C. Maternal emotionality and reproductive outcomes: A review of the literature. *International Journal of Behavioral Development,* 1979, *2,* 343–376.

Carmichael, L. The onset and early development of behavior. In P. H. Mussen (Ed.), *Carmichael's manual of child psychology* (Vol. 1) (3rd ed.). New York: Wiley, 1970.

Cary, W. H. Duration of sperm cell migration and uterine secretions. *Journal of the American Medical Association*, 1936, *106*, 2221–2223.

Clarren, S. K., & Smith, D. W. The fetal alcohol syndrome. *New England Jounal of Medicine*, 1978, *298*, 1063–1067.

Clarren, S. K., Alvord, E. C., Sumi, S. M., Streissguth, A. P., & Smith, D. W. Brain malformations related to prenatal exposure to ethanol. *The Journal of Pediatrics*, 1978, *92*, 64–67.

Coghill, G. E. *Anatomy and the problem of behavior*. Cambridge, England: Cambridge University Press, 1929.

Coghill, G. E. Early embryonic somatic movements in birds and in mammals other than man. *Monographs of the Society for Research in Child Development*, 1940, *5*, 1–48.

Conway, E., & Brackbill, Y. Delivery medication and infant outcome: An empirical study. *Monographs of the Society for Research in Child Development*, 1970, *35*, 24–34.

Copans, S. A. Human prenatal effects: Methodological problems and some suggested solutions. *Merrill-Palmer Quarterly*, 1974, *20*, 43–52.

Crowley, L. V. *An introduction to clinical embryology*. Chicago: Year Book Medical Publishers, 1974.

Decarie, T. G. A study of the mental and emotional development of the thalidomide child. In B. M. Foss (Ed.), *Determinants of infant behavior* (Vol. 4). London: Metheun & Co., 1969.

Dekaban, A. Abnormalities in children exposed to x-irradiation during various stages of gestation: Tentative timetable of radiation injury to the human fetus. Part I. *Journal of Nuclear Medicine*, 1968, *9*, 471–485.

Dickinson, A. G. Some genetic implications of maternal effects—an hypothesis of mammalian growth. *Journal of Agricultural Science*, 1960, *54*, 379–390.

Drillien, C. M. *The growth and development of the prematurely born infant*. Baltimore: Williams & Wilkins, 1964.

Ellingson, R. J. The study of brain electrical activity in infants. In L. P. Lipsitt & C. C. Spiker (Eds.), *Advances in child development and behavior* (Vol. 3). New York: Academic Press, 1967.

Fedrick, J., Alberman, E. D., & Goldstein, H. Possible teratogenic effect of cigarette smoking. *Nature*, 1971, *231*, 529–530.

Fitzgerald, J. E., & Windle, W. F. Some observations on early human fetal movements. *Journal of Comparative Neurology*, 1942, *76*, 159–167.

Friedman, S. L., Brackbill, Y., Caron, A., & Caron, R. Obstetric medication and visual processing in 4- and 5-month-old infants. *Merrill-Palmer Quarterly,* 1978, *24,* 111–128.

Furchtgott, E. Behavioral effects of ionizing radiations. *Psychological Bulletin,* 1956, *53,* 321–334.

Gesell, A. Maturation and infant behavior. *Psychological Review,* 1929, *36,* 307–319.

Gorsuch, R. L., & Key, M. A. Abnormalities of pregnancy as a function of anxiety and life stress. *Psychosomatic Medicine,* 1974, *36,* 352–362.

Gottfried, A. W. Intellectual consequences of perinatal anoxia. *Psychological Bulletin,* 1973, *80,* 231–242.

Gottlieb, G. Conceptions of prenatal behavior. In L. R. Aronson, E. Tobach, D. S. Lehrman, & J. S. Rosenblatt (Eds.). *Development and evolution of behavior. Essays in memory of T. C. Schneirla.* San Francisco: Freeman, 1970.

Gottlieb. G. Introduction to Behavioral Embryology. In G. Gottlieb (Ed.), *Studies on the development of behavior and the nervous system* (Vol. 1: *Behavioral embryology*). New York: Academic Press, 1973.

Gottlieb, G. Conceptions of prenatal development: Behavioral Embryology. *Psychological Review,* 1976, *83,* 215–234.

Green, H. G. Infants of alcoholic mothers. *American Journal of Obstetrics and Gynecology,* 1974, *118,* 713–716.

Gumpel, S. M., Hayes, K., & Dudgeon, J. A. Congenital perceptive deafness: Role of intrauterine rubella. *British Medical Journal,* 1971, *2,* 300–304.

Harper, J., & Williams, S. Early environmental stress and infantile autism. *Medical Journal of Australia,* 1974, *1,* 341–346.

Hooker, D. Early fetal behavior in mammals. *Yale Journal of Biology and Medicine,* 1936, *8,* 579–602.

Hooker, D. *The origin of overt behavior.* Ann Arbor: University of Michigan Press, 1944.

Hooker, D. *The prenatal origin of behavior.* Lawrence, Kansas: University of Kansas Press, 1952.

Hooker, D. Developmental reaction to environment. *Yale Journal of Biology and Medicine,* 1960, *32,* 431–440.

Humphrey, T. The development of mouth opening and related reflexes involving the oral area of human fetuses. *Alabama Journal of Medical Sciences,* 1968, *5,* 126–157.

Humphrey, T. The development of human fetal activity and its relation to postnatal behavior. In H. W. Reese and L. P. Lipsitt (Eds.), *Advances in child development and behavior* (Vol. 5). New York: Academic Press, 1970.

Joffe, J. M. *Prenatal determinants of behavior.* London: Oxford Press, 1969.

Jones, K. L., Smith, D. W., Ulleland, C. N., & Streissguth, A. P. Pattern of malformation in offspring of chronic alcoholic mothers. *Lancet,* 1973, *3,* 1267–1271.

Jones, K. L., & Smith, D. W. Recognition of the fetal alcohol syndrome early in infancy. *Lancet,* 1973, *2,* 999–1001.

Kolata, G. B. Scientists attack report that obstetrical medications endanger children. *Science,* 1979, *204,* 391–392.

Macfarlane, A. *The psychology of childbirth.* Cambridge: Harvard, 1977.

McLaren, A. Genetic and environmental effects on foetal and placental growth in mice. *Journal of Reproduction and Fertilization,* 1965, *9,* 79–98.

Meier, G. W. Hypoxia. In E. Furchtgott (Ed.). *Pharmacological and biophysical agents and behavior.* New York: Academic Press, 1971.

Milner, E. *Human neural and behavioral development.* Springfield: Thomas, 1967.

Mirkin, B. L., & Singh S. Placental transfer. In B. L. Mirkin (Ed.), *Perinatal pharmacology and therapeutics.* New York: Academic Press, 1976.

Montagu, M. F. A. *Prenatal influences.* Springfield: Thomas, 1962.

Ouellette, E. M., Rosett, H. L., Rosman, N. P., & Weiner, L. Adverse effects on offspring of maternal alcohol abuse during pregnancy. *New England Journal of Medicine,* 1977, *297,* 528–530.

Palmer, R. H., Warner, L., & Leightman, S. R. Congenital malformations in the offspring of a chronic alcoholic mother. *Pediatrics,* 1974, *53,* 490–494.

Palmisano, P. A., Sneed, R. C., & Cassady, G. Untaxed whiskey and fetal lead exposure. *Journal of Pediatrics,* 1969, *75,* 869.

Parekh, V. C., Pherwani, A., Udani, P. M., & Mukherjie, S. Brain weight and head circumference in fetus, infant and children of different nutritional and socio-economic groups. *Indian Pediatrics,* 1970, *7,* 347–358.

Pasamanick, B., & Knoblock, H. Retrospective studies on the epidemiology of reproductive casualty: Old and new. *Merrill-Palmer Quarterly,* 1966, *12,* 7–26.

Ramalingaswami, V. The effect of malnutrition on the individual: Cellular growth and development. In A. Berg, N. S. Schrimshaw, and (Eds.), *Nutrition, national development, and planning.* Cambridge: MIT Press, 1973.

Sameroff, A. J., & Chandler, M. J. Reproductive risk and the continuum of caretaking casualty. In F. D. Horowitz (Ed.), *Review of child development research* (Vol 4). Chicago: University of Chicago Press, 1975.

Sever, J. Viruses and embryos. In F. C. Fraser and V. A. McKusick

(Eds.), *Congenital malformations.* Amsterdam: Excerpta Medica, 1970.

Simpson, W. J. A preliminary report on cigarette smoking and the incidence of prematurity. *American Journal of Obstetrics and Gynecology,* 1957, *73,* 808–815.

Smith, D. J., Heseltine, G. F. D., & Corson, J. A. Pre-pregnancy and prenatal stress in five consecutive pregnancies: Effects on female rats and their offspring. *Life Science,* 1971, *10,* 233–242.

Sneed, R. C. Editorial correspondence. *Journal of Pediatrics,* 1977, 374.

Stein, Z., Susser, M., Saenger, G., & Marolla, F. Nutrition and performance. *Science,* 1972, *178,* 708–713.

Sternberg, J. Irradiation and radiocontamination during pregnancy. *American Journal of Obstetrics and Gynecology,* 1970, *108,* 490–495.

Streissguth, A. P. Maternal alcoholism and the outcome of pregnancy. In M. Greenwealth (Ed.), *Alcohol problems in women and children.* New York: Grune & Stratton, 1977.

Tuchmann-Duplessis, H., David, G., & Haegel, P. *Illustrated human embryology* (Vol. 1: *Embryogenesis*). New York: Springer-Verlag; Paris: Masson, 1972.

Warkany, J. *Congenital malformations, notes and comments.* Chicago: Yearbook, 1971.

Wilson, J. G. Is there specificity of action in experimental teratogenesis? *Pediatrics,* 1957, *19,* 755–763.

Wilson, J. G. Environmental effects on development—teratology. In N. S. Assali (Ed.), *Pathophysiology of gestation.* New York: Academic Press, 1972.

Wilson, J. G. *Environment and birth defects.* New York: Academic Press, 1973.

Windle, W. F. Correlation between the development of local reflexes and reflex arcs in the spinal cord of cat embryos. *Journal of Comparative Neurology,* 1934, *59,* 487–505.

Windle, W. F., & Orr, D. W. The development of behavior in chick embryos: Spinal cord structure correlated with early somatic motility. *Journal of Comparative Neurology,* 1934, *60,* 287–307.

Windle, W. G. *Physiology of the fetus.* Philadelphia: Saunders, 1940.

Winick, M. Malnutrition and brain development. *Journal of Pediatrics,* 1969, *74,* 667–679.

Winick, M. Nutrition and nerve cell growth. *Federation Proceedings,* 1970, *29,* 1510–1515.

Woerner, M. G., Pollack, M., & Klein, D. F. Pregnancy and birth complications in psychiatric patients: A comparison of schizophrenic and personality disorder patients with their siblings. *Acta Psychiatry of Scandinavia,* 1973, *49,* 712–721.

Yamazaki, J. N. A review of the literature on the radiation dosage required to cause manifest central nervous system disturbances from in utero and postnatal exposure. *Pediatrics,* 1966, *27,* 877–903.

Yerushalmy, J. Statistical considerations and evaluation of epidemiological evidence. In G. James and T. Rosenthal (Eds.), *Tobacco and health.* Springfield: Thomas, 1962.

Yerushalmy, J. Infants with low birth weight from before their mothers started to smoke cigarettes. *American Journal of Obstetrics and Gynecology,* 1972, *112,* 277.

Yerushalmy, J. Smoking in pregnancy. *Developmental Medicine and Child Neurology,* 1973, *15,* 691–692.

Zamenof, S., van Marthes, E., & Granel, L. Prenatal cerebral development: Effect of restricted diet, reversal by growth hormone. *Science,* 1971, *174,* 954–955.

Chapter

MATURATION, GROWTH, AND LEARNING

Four

INTRODUCTION

In our discussion of prenatal development, we noted that the concept of maturation is central to the classical view of predetermined epigenesis. Maturation was defined as the anatomical and physiological development of organs and organ systems. This structural development of the organism was also seen as the mechanism underlying function and behavior. Without structural maturation and subsequent neural functioning, there is no true behavior. The process of maturation is typically attributed to hereditary or genetic factors that determine the nature and rate of neurostructural development. Such intrinsic control permits the development of species-specific structure and function that determine the characteristics and limits of an organism's behavior. We saw in Chapter Three that prenatal development assumes a pattern of inherent growth and maturation with little, if any, energy exchange between the fetus and its environment. In other words, maturation appears to proceed with no requirements of exercise, learning, or overt interaction between the prenatal organism and its external environment.

The question remains, however, as to whether functional activity of a fetal organ, such as muscle contraction or neuronal activity, contributes to structural maturation during the prenatal period. Such reciprocal interaction between structure and function is the basis for the probabilistic epigenesis theory described in Chapter Three. Although there is no evidence that maturational development requires functional activity, there are data suggesting that maturation may be accelerated by functional activity (Gottlieb, 1976). Also, certain functional experiences during embryonic life may determine the presence or absence of a particular behavioral pattern. Gottlieb (1976) refers to these phenomena as inductive influences of function or experience. Acceleration and induction may be signs of the plasticity of maturation. Such plasticity would allow for the potential modulation of maturation by spontaneous or evoked functional experience during prenatal development. We will discuss this topic in more detail later in this chapter.

The terms mature and immature are often used to describe the quality or appropriateness of a person's social or emotional behavior. In this context, maturity means the degree to which a person's psychological functioning meets some norm of expectation relative to chronological age and experience. Such psychological maturation, or observed behavior, should not be confused with biological maturation. Psychological maturation at any point in development reflects the acquisition of social skills through experience, training, insight, and the like. Our concerns in this chapter are with the biological notion of maturation and its significance for development. We will also deal with the related, but separate, phenomena of growth during infancy, how human development is influenced by maturation and learning, and environmental influences on maturational processes.

MATURATION AND GROWTH

Historically, maturation, growth, and development were used interchangeably to refer to the intrinsic "ripening" or growing older of an organism. Although growth and development are inseparable aspects of maturation, they are not the same, and most developmentalists differentiate between these concepts. Growth is viewed as quantitative changes in the dimensional or volumetric characteristics of tissues, organs, and structures (Baer, 1973). Baer (1973) describes three aspects of growth that help clarify the distinction between growth and maturation. Growth may involve size increases, size decreases, and differential growth patterns. While many aspects of physical growth involve the addition of cells and tissues leading to structural increases in size, there are organs and structures that decrease in size or volume after adolescence, such as lymphoid tissue (thymus, lymph nodes, and tonsils) and subcutaneous fat in boys. The development of normal adult body proportions is the result of differential growth rates. Compar-

Figure 4-1
Growth curves of different parts and tissues of the human body, showing the four chief types. All the curves are of size attained and are plotted as percents of total gain from birth to 20 years of age, so that size at age 20 is 100 on the vertical scale.

(Adapted from Tanner, 1962.)

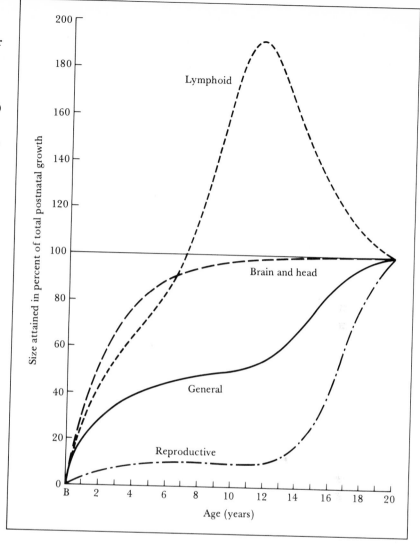

isons of body proportions at birth, infancy, and adulthood reflect this aspect of growth, as you can see in Figures 4-1 and 4-2.

While maturation may imply growth, it is not limited to physical or structural growth. Maturation describes the neurophysiological and neuroanatomical development of the organism (Gottlieb, 1976). It is the process by which the structural

Figure 4-2
Changes in body form and
proportion as a function of
differential growth rates
during pre- and postnatal
periods.

(Adapted from Patten, 1933.)

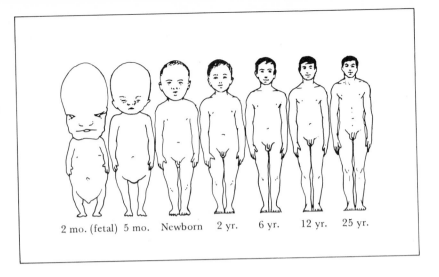

and functional characteristics of an organ or organ system, or some part of it, become operational. Growth contributes to maturation insofar as it provides the cellular and tissue prerequisites for it. Thus, growth is a necessary but not a sufficient condition for maturation.

In behavioral embryology, maturation describes both the emergence of new tissue, organs, and structures *and* their neurophysiological functioning. Maturation is not simply a ripening effect because it involves more than quantitative changes in the organism. Many developmentalists describe maturation as a process of qualitative changes, involving structural–functional differentiation and neurophysiological organization and reorganization of the central nervous system (CNS). Since every behavioral activity has its structural basis in the nervous system and skeletomuscular system, no behavior can emerge without some maturation of the structures underlying that behavioral act. The biological apparatus must be structurally and functionally operational in order for the organism to perceive, respond, process information, and learn.

In humans, the degree of maturation is related to the ability to engage in increasingly complex behavior from infancy to early adolescence. That is, maturational changes permit the emergence of new behaviors, and of new mechanisms for organizing and coordinating those behaviors. Maturation also enables the individual to explore the environment more effectively. In this way, the individual learns new information that interacts with maturational phenomena. This reciprocal relationship is quickly established as a continuous one, beginning shortly after birth. At the very least, experience and learning serve a maintenance function for maturation and development. Recent evidence, to be discussed later, suggests that certain kinds of stimulation may speed up maturation in the immature organism. Development, in short, is the product of growth, maturation, and learning. And these developmental components are inseparable because of their dynamic, reciprocal relationship.

Because of continual gene–environmental interaction, we cannot describe maturation solely as a product of genetic determinism. To be sure, no *specific* environmental influences are necessary parts of the maturational process. But the external environment must provide minimal levels of general,

An infant lifting her head from the prone position. This action represents a part of the normal sequence in the infant's physiological development and is one of many actions that helps build future motor capacity. Since this action literally gives the infant a new angle on the world, it may also assist in the development of cognitive processes.

(Photo by Erika Stone/Peter Arnold, Inc.)

nonspecific stimulation, which serve to maintain the organism and that may accelerate its maturation as well. Stimulus or experiential deprivation below species-specific minimal requirements will prevent normal maturation, thereby disrupting behavioral ontogenesis.

MATURATION AND LEARNING

Maturation provides for the development of structural and functional competence within the species-specific limits genetically established along the phylogenetic scale. Throughout the period of life from birth to maturity, maturational level sets ever-expanding limits of biopsychological competence and general development. When these maturational levels permit, an infant or child becomes able to display some new behavior, profit from training for a specific skill, understand and generate more complex language patterns, or develop a richer emotional life. Immature organisms go through a series of maturational periods during which they are prepared to interact with their environment at a level of complexity proportionate to their level of maturation. Thus, both the biological and the psychological components of behavior mature in a series of stages. In short, learning capacity, rate of learning, and meaningful interaction with, and understanding of, the environment are similarly limited by maturational levels at any developmental point during immaturity.

Educators and psychologists describe this pattern as maturation-dependent behavior and have shaped these observations into the concept of readiness to learn. While this concept may be useful in the training and education of children, it is subject to abuse, distortion, and misunderstanding. It requires a knowledge of developmental schedules—age-related, normative data describing the average age of appearance of motor, social, personal, and intellectual skills in children. However, these data represent only rough guidelines, and certainly they are not solely dependent on age. Not only are there individual differences in rate of maturation (i.e., fast and slow maturers), but also, different response systems mature at different rates. And as we shall see, experience and learning play an equally important role in behavioral development.

Early work on infant development suggested that behavior "unfolded" in an invariant, universal pattern, uninfluenced by learning, training, or experience. Thus, behavioral development thought to be a consequence of heredity (maturation) was differentiated from development thought to be primarily a product of learning. Predictably, a dichotomy of maturation versus learning was contrived, leading to endless controversy over which was responsible or more important for the appearance of a particular behavior. Like the heredity–environment argument, the maturation versus learning controversy was pointless. Both interact and contribute to development. Maturation without the opportunity for learning will not result in normal ontogenesis. Similarly, opportunities for learning and environmental stimulation are ineffectual until the individual reaches the appropriate level of maturation.

Maturational processes, although biological in nature, are no more immune to environmental factors than are genes and gene functioning. Learning effects begin with the initial appearance of a new behavior, and learning effects established earlier undoubtedly contribute to that behavior. For example, we might argue that the first locomotor act involved in the emergence of walking in the infant may appear in the absence of any direct, overt learning. But learning effects on walking begin almost instantly, contributing substantially to the further maturation and skill development of locomotion. And what is the contribution to learning of motor responses developed prior to locomotion? How have learning effects on crawling, sitting, and standing contributed to the maturation and emergence of locomotion? Surely trial-and-error learning plays some role in all behavioral maturation phenomena, from one developmental period to the next. Maturation and learning are not dichotomous, isolated phenomena. They are different but inseparable components of, and contributors to, development, equally important and indispensable. Maturational processes in normal organisms assure behavioral potentials. But learning, experience, and external stimulation precipitate that potential, producing differential levels of skills and efficiency, whether they are terminal developmental levels or individual differences.

It appears unlikely that learning phenomena play any role in embryonic development and maturation. However, we cannot preclude the possibility that neural function and spontaneous or evoked neural stimulation of the embryonic organism may influence maturation. It has been argued that such neural activity influences maturation in terms of altering, directing, or facilitating maturation and development (Gottlieb, 1976; Humphrey, 1970; Woolf, Bixby, & Capranica, 1976). Although the question of such maturational plasticity remains speculative, there is some evidence that human fetal activity results in the strengthening of muscles during prenatal development (Humphrey, 1970).

HISTORICAL PERSPECTIVE

The term maturation was first used by biologists to describe the period when male and female gametes (sperm and egg cells) are capable of meiotic division—the maturation of germ cells. Later, maturation was the concept employed by behavioral embryologists to account for the embryogenesis of organisms. Clearly, the concept of maturation was, and remains, a biological one. The major difference between classical and contemporary views of maturation revolves around the question of plasticity. Maturational plasticity refers to the degree to which maturational phenomena are influenced by experience, function, and learning.

With the increasing use of maturation to describe organic development as an "unfolding" or "ripening," psychologists and physicians studying infant growth and behavior began to apply the term to behavioral development. To these early observers, the emergence of behavior was analogous to the emergence of structure—a matter of maturation. The term maturation of behavior appeared equally appropriate because the behavioral development of infants occurred in the absence of any known learning experiences. Nor could behavioral development be explained in terms of learning theory. Indeed, most child developmentalists of the early twentieth century were unwilling to attribute early human development to mere conditioning. The need for a theoretical concept of behavioral growth made it easier to borrow the concept of maturation from biology, and for some it became a refuge, as we shall see.

Arnold Gesell, a pediatrician, psychologist, and student of G. Stanley Hall, was undoubtedly the major and most unrelenting advocate of maturation theory. Gesell's view of maturation was greatly influenced by Hall and his biological perspective of development. In fact, much of Gesell's fervor is reminiscent of that of his teacher, Hall, as was his influence on developmental thinking in the twentieth century. Gesell viewed maturation as *the* developmental principle of growth and behavior. He saw maturation as a hereditary process in which the CNS ripens or matures, causing predictable patterns of behavior changes. Growth and development were processes regulated by maturation, providing for "stability and balance" in children. Gesell (1928) referred to maturation as "the inherent progressive alteration which tends to bring a growing organism to a state of completeness. It is a more restrictive term than growth and is intended to designate those changes which are primarily dependent upon nutrition and duration, rather than extraneous factors" (p. 359). Although Gesell did not totally deny the role of environmental factors in development and interactions with heredity, he clearly relegated such extrinsic factors to a minor role as determining factors in basic development. He believed that "growth potency" is fundamentally dependent upon original equipment (heredity). In one of his earliest works, Gesell (1928) stated his position with eloquent conviction:

All things considered, the inevitableness and surety of maturation are the most impressive characteristic of early development. It is the hereditary ballast which conserves and stabilizes the growth of each individual infant. It is indigenous in its impulsion; but we may well be grateful for this degree of determinism. If it did not exist, the infant would be a victim of flaccid malleability which is sometimes romantically ascribed to him. His mind, his spirit, his personality would fall a ready prey to disease, to starvation, to malnutrition, and worst of all to misguided management. As it is, the inborn tendency toward optimum development is so inveterate that he benefits liberally from what is good in our practice, and suffers less than he logically should from our unenlightment. Only if we give respect to this inner core of inheritance can we respect the important individual differences which distinguish infants as well as men. (p. 378)

Gesell (1929) never relinquished his conviction that maturation is the "impulse" for development, or his view that limitations on learning are established by the intrinsic, organic resistance to the possibly disruptive influence of conditioning. During this period, Gesell and Catherine Amatruda embarked on several decades of a longitudinal normative research program at the Yale Clinic of Child Development, in which detailed developmental schedules of infant and child behavior were formulated. Specific behavior sequences were analyzed and meticulously described. The result was Gesell's new discipline of developmental diagnosis or infant neuropsychiatry, designed to provide early diagnosis of developmental defects and deviations. *Developmental Diagnosis* first appeared in 1941, and was revised and enlarged by Knoblock and Pasamanick (1974), physicians and students of Gesell and Amatruda.

In 1943, Gesell and one of his collaborators, Frances L. Ilg, published *Infant and Child in the Culture of Today*. This work, the culmination of Gesell's research and thinking, was directed to professional and lay workers in the field of early child welfare and education. It presented a developmental framework for child guidance in the home and nursery school, and reflected Gesell's intense interest in children as a clinician and scientist. It described a method of individualized child guidance, based on Gesell's developmental philosophy of providing guidance and training in keeping with his notions of the "growth career" of a child. The idea was to take maximal advantage of the child's developmental status at any point in time.

This was one of Gesell's last attempts to express his convictions on the importance of maturation and heredity for development. He sought to put the child's guidance "in league with nature," and to utilize the "ancient wisdom in the natural mechanisms of growth" (Gesell, 1943, p. 256). His theme was "nature through maturation and culture through guidance." With messianic overtones and picturesque but vague language, Gesell sought to apply his theories and interests to social and moral issues in child development. Gesell's work fell out of favor at Yale University and he eventually lost his financial support. He was ignored and isolated by his medical colleagues long before his retirement from the Yale Child Development Clinic (Knoblock & Pasamanick, 1974).

The development of Gesell's maturational theory was heavily influenced by the findings of the early behavioral embryologists. His thinking about the maturational process and its significance for development can be traced directly to the observations of Carmichael (1926, 1927, 1928) and Coghill (1926, 1929) on the maturation of the nervous system in frog and salamander embryos. Gesell was particularly impressed with Coghill's findings and theories of human development, stating that "there is no suggestion that the growing complex of infant behavior can be accounted for by a combination of smaller units" (1928, p. 361). However, the classic series of experiments by Carmichael provided the basis for many of Gesell's ideas about the role of maturation in human development.

Using salamander and frog embryos, Carmichael (1926, 1927, 1928) demonstrated that the development and emergence of swimming movements in these organisms occur as a function of maturation and in the absence of any external stimulation, exercise, or practice. Carmichael selected young embryonic salamanders and frogs at a stage of development in which they were still inert and without motor movements. In order to eliminate the influences of external stimulation, exercise, or practice, Carmichael placed experimental groups of embryos in a solution of chloretone, an anesthetic that immobilizes these organisms without affecting cellular growth. Control groups of salamander and frog embryos were placed simultaneously in ordinary tap water to develop under relatively normal conditions. Within 5 days, the control animals began to swim normally, and at this time the experimental animals were removed from the chloretone solution and placed in tap water. In 30 minutes, the previously anesthetized animals began swimming normally and could not be distinguished from the controls that had been swimming for almost 5 days.

To determine whether the 30-minute delay before the anesthetized group began swimming was a practice period required for these animals to learn to swim, Carmichael (1927) placed normally reared and swimming salamanders in a chloretone solution until they were completely immobilized. Then he placed them in tap water. These animals also required up to 30 minutes before they began swimming again, demonstrating that the anesthetizing effects of the chloretone took this long to wear off. In a third study, Carmichael (1928) replicated his findings under different environmental conditions. He concluded that swimming develops in salamanders (*Amblystoma*) and frogs without the requirement of external stimulation, exercise, practice, or learning—that maturation is sufficient for species-specific behavioral development. It is easy to understand the impact of Carmichael's work on someone searching for a single, guiding principle of human development.

During this same time, Mary M. Shirley began a 2-year longitudinal study on motor, intellectual, and personality development in 25 infants (1931a, 1933). She described the normative patterns of motor development in infants (1931a, 1931b) and concluded that the nature and consistency of the pattern of motor development could be explained only by the theory of maturation. Her observations led her to doubt that learning or exercise played any significant role in motor development. Maturation enabled the infant to engage in motor behavior, then practice resulted in proficiency. The maturation-learning controversy was well under way. Gesell and Thompson (1929) had already performed one of the first human infant studies on the effects of practice on motor development. They concluded that "there is no . . . evidence that practice and exercise even hasten the actual appearance of types of reactions like climbing and tower building. The time of appearance is fundamentally determined by the ripeness of the neural structures" (p. 75).

Between 1939 and 1941, Myrtle McGraw published 13 research reports on the neuromuscular development of children, which are summarized in her book (1943), *The Neuromuscular Maturation of the Human Infant*. On the basis of her research and that from the field of neurophysiology, McGraw offered a theoretical framework of infant maturation based on the traditional view and interpretation of maturation. For McGraw, neuromuscular development and function were controlled by two major divisions of the central nervous system: the cerebral cortex and subcortical centers in the brain.

At birth, the behavior of the infant is controlled by the subcortical centers because the cortex is still immature and essentially nonfunctional. Some of these behaviors remain dominated by the subcortical centers throughout life, including such basic reflexes as the eye blink, breathing, and heart beat. With increasing maturation, the cortex assumes dominance over the subcortical centers, inhibiting their previous influence over many of the infant's activities. For instance, many of the neonatal reflexes disappear within a few months as new behaviors emerge and become integrated into efficient, coordinated movements. These developmental trends in neuromuscular development are related to cortical maturation. They proceed in a cephalocaudal direction, which means that motor activities associated with the head develop earlier than those associated with the lower extremities. Building on her observations and theoretical notions, McGraw (1943) offered the following "educational hints":

1 *Training in any particular activity before the neural mechanisms have reached a certain state of readiness is futile.*

2 *Exercise of a newly developing function is inherent in the process of growth, and if ample opportunity is afforded at the proper time, specific achievements can be advanced beyond the stage normally expected.*

3 *Periods of transition from one type of neuromuscular organization to another are an inherent part of development and are often characterized by disorganization and confusion.*

4 *Spurts, regressions, frustrations, and inhibitions are integral parts of organic growth, and there is reason to believe that they also function in the development of complex behavior activities.*

5 *Maturation and learning are not different processes, merely different facets of the fundamental process of growth.*

6 *Evidence that a child is ready for a particular educational subject is to be found in certain behavior "signals," or behavior "syndromes," which reflect the maturity of neural mechanisms. (pp. 130–131)*

Clearly, McGraw was a maturationist, but her views about the relationship between maturation and learning were more moderate and insightful than those of her predecessors, and her work was the first statement of an alternative to Gesell's extreme maturational hypothesis. McGraw (1946) noted that the structure-function relationship may not be a unidirectional sequence of events, as was generally assumed at the time. She commented:

It seems fairly evident that certain structural changes take place prior to the onset of overt function; it seems equally evident that cessation of neurostructural development does not coincide with the onset of function. There is every reason to believe that when conditions are favorable function makes some contribution to further advancement in structural development of the nervous system. An influential factor in determining the structural development of one component may be the functioning of other structures which are interrelated. (p. 363)

How similar this statement is to the contemporary notion of probable epigenesis described in Chapter Three. But despite the theoretical significance of McGraw's reinterpretation, her concepts drew little scientific attention from other developmentalists.

Between 1921 and 1967, the developmentalist Z. Y. Kuo performed a series of studies of embryonic behavior in chicks, and became an outspoken critic of the maturational hypothesis and of the role of unlearned behavior in development (Kuo, 1967). Kuo strongly disagreed with Coghill's generalizations and the notion of predetermined development. His classical work on behavioral development in chicken embryos led to his epigenetic principles of development, which stressed organism–environment interaction and the role of embryonic activity for subsequent posthatching behavior.

Kuo argued that much of what appears to be a strict function of maturation and unlearned behavior in the chick is directly related to observable functional activity during the embryonic stage of development. Kuo observed chick embryos by cutting away a portion of the eggshell and the underlying membrane, and then applying melted vaseline to the inner membrane. In this manner, he could repeatedly observe and photograph embryonic activity. Through this procedure, Kuo reported that posthatching pecking in the chick had behavioral components in embryonic form, as did other postembryonic behaviors. Kuo emphasized the inadequacy of a strict maturational or predeterministic approach to development and elevated environmental factors to an active role in development. His central theme was that neonatal behaviors depend upon their prenatal component precursors, which become reorganized into new behaviors as a function of environmental changes occurring during both prenatal and postnatal development.

The maturation–learning (nature versus nurture) controversy began declining in intensity and divisiveness during the 1950s. With the growing strength of learning theory, the growing number of reports of experiential effects on maturation, and new laboratory data on animal development, an interaction approach to development gained general acceptance. Anastasi (1958) rejected the additive model of the contributions of heredity and environment, urging investigations of *how* these factors interact to arrive at predictable relationships. Fowler (1962), in his review of the literature on learning in infancy and childhood, concluded that early studies supporting the maturation hypothesis were designed to maximize maturation efforts and minimize learning contributions. He listed a number of methodological deficiencies that produced these results, including lack of adequate controls, emphasis on simple sensorimotor and social–emotional development to the exclusion of cognitive development, the omission of antecedent or experiential data on the subjects observed, and the application of superficial training or practice procedures, with little or no regard for motivational variables.

ENVIRONMENTAL INFLUENCES ON MATURATIONAL PHENOMENA

We have described some of the classical research that sustained the maturation hypothesis of development. Our historical survey paid little attention to the data that demonstrated the influences of environmental and experiential factors on maturational phenomena and development. We now will turn to such an analysis and show how experiential–environmental variations may produce ontogenetic alterations in immature organisms. Such alterations in development involve not only basic maturational processes but also the sequencing and form of behavioral development. For example, early experiential–environmental conditions may alter the expected age-related emergence of behavior by apparently affecting maturation rate or velocity. Also, the manipulation of experiential and environmental variables can alter the sequence of events that characterize motor development, for example, or the manner in which certain motor behaviors are displayed. The intimate relationship between maturation and experiential opportunity reveals much about the plasticity of organic development. We may study environmental influences on maturation and development by manipulating environmental variables in one direction or the other. That is, we can restrict opportunities for experience, practice, or learning, or we can increase them.

The Effects of Environmental Restriction

Studies dealing with the effects of environmental restriction have employed three basic methodologies: the actual prevention of activity; isolation; or depriving the organism of normal levels of stimulation input (a technique known as sensory deprivation). These procedures may overlap; isolating an organism may also result in sensory and social deprivation, for example. In the two sections to follow, we will explore some of the animal and human studies dealing with the developmental effects of environmental restriction.

ANIMAL STUDIES We have already reviewed a classical example of the method of prevention of activity—Carmichael's work with frog and salamander embryos. This research strategy dates back even further to the studies of Spalding (1873). Spalding prevented a group of immature swallows from making characteristic flight movements and observed that these birds developed impaired flying ability as adults. Using similar restriction procedures, Cruze (1935) and Padilla (1935) reared newly hatched chicks in the dark for 2 to 3 weeks, feeding them by hand and thereby preventing them from pecking. These chicks failed to develop the pecking pattern. They never learned to peck and eventually starved. Other groups of chicks were reared in darkness for shorter periods of time or given brief, intermittent exposure to light, and their pecking abilities developed normally.

Recall Carmichael's (1926, 1927, 1928) conclusions that swimming in frogs and salamanders develops as a function of maturation and does not depend on environmental or experiential influences. Prevention of activity was effected by the chloretone solution for a period of about 1 week. Carmichael's investigations were replicated and extended by Mathews and Detwiler (1926) and Fromme (1941). When these investigators increased the duration of chloretone immobilization in salamander and frog tadpoles to periods of up to 2 weeks, they found that later swimming speed and coordination were permanently impaired.

Many other studies indicate that exposing immature animals to different forms of environmental–experiential restriction and deprivation produces abnormal, debilitating alterations in ontogenesis. These effects appear to be related to the disruption of maturational processes, and have been found in animal species ranging from the rat to the chimpanzee. Independent variable manipulations have included visual and perceptual deprivation (Riesen, 1947; Riesen, Chow, Semmes, & Nissen,

1951), somesthetic (touch, temperature, pressure, and sensation of movement) deprivation (Nissen, Chow, & Semmes, 1951), social isolation (Melzack & Thompson, 1956; Harlow & Harlow, 1962), and auditory deprivation (Thorpe, 1961).

Withholding these and other kinds of experiential opportunities from young animals may disrupt or alter development by failing to provide a minimally adequate environment and the necessary component to maturation—experience and stimulation input. The laboratory data strongly support Hebb's (1949) theory that stimulation is vital for the development and maturation of the central nervous system. In their selective review of the literature, Horn, Rose, and Bateson (1973) conclude that the morphological and functional organization of parts of the CNS can be modified by changes in the internal and external environments. For additional reviews of the literature, see Hunt (1979), Newton and Levine (1968), and Thompson and Grusec (1970). A sample of studies of the effects of environmental restriction on animals is summarized in Table 4-1.

Our brief summary of the effects of restriction on maturational phenomena requires a reevaluation of simple cause-and-effect relationships purporting to show the contributions of heredity and environment. The demonstration of independent-variable effects rests on consideration of the parameters involved. A parameter is a level, characteristic, or attribute of a variable, a dimension of the independent or dependent variable. Thus, we find that the duration and intensity of the independent variable, along with the period of development (maturation) at which the manipulation occurs, affect the outcome. Duration, intensity, and developmental stage are parameters of independent variables. The choice of response parameters may also determine whether we will observe effects or not. For these reasons, the failure to freely explore variable parameters may result in misleading, incomplete data, and incorrect conclusions.

HUMAN STUDIES   In analyzing the consequences of environmental restriction on maturation in human infants, we cannot, of course, impose or manipulate the experimental conditions employed in animal studies. Severe restrictions of experiential opportunity or reduction in environmental stim-

Table 4-1
Effects of Restriction on Animal Development

INVESTIGATOR	ORGANISM	INDEPENDENT VARIABLE	RESULTS
Spalding (1902)	Chicken	Reared in darkness; isolation (10 days)	Failed to respond to mother's call
Hebb (1937)	Rat	Reared in darkness (60 days)	Impairment of discrimination learning
Riesen (1947)	Chimpanzee	Reared in darkness; maternal separation (16 months)	Visual/perceptual abnormalities
Nissen et al. (1951)	Chimpanzee	Restriction of tactual, kinesthetic, and manipulative experience (30 months)	Abnormal locomotor behavior and response to stimulation
Thompson & Heron (1954)	Dog	Isolation (9 months)	Deficiencies in problem-solving capacity
Melzack & Thompson (1956)	Dog	Isolation (9–12 months)	Abnormal social behavior and disorganized emotional behavior; lack of avoidance response to painful stimulus
Thorpe (1961)	Bird	Auditory isolation (3–4 days)	Disruption of bird song
Harlow & Harlow (1962)	Monkey	Maternal separation/ isolation (6 months)	Abnormal behavior patterns and postures; motivational, emotional, and social disturbances. Disruption of later maternal behavior
Held & Hein (1963)	Cat	Dark-reared, perceptual deprivation, prevention of activity (8–12 weeks)	Visual–motor impairment, discrimination deficits
Moltz (1968)	Ducks, geese, chicks	Visual deprivation, prevention of activity, isolation (0–24 hours)	Disruption or redirection of imprinting response

ulation would place the infant at risk. Therefore, researchers seek these conditions as they exist in much milder forms in certain cultures or special environments (see the discussion of quasi-experiments in Chapter One) or attempt to experimentally create very limited, innocuous conditions of short duration. A series of studies by Dennis and Dennis (1935, 1938, 1940, 1941) provides examples of both methods and also some insights concerning the relationship between maturation and experience.

During the summers of 1937 and 1938, Dennis and Dennis (1940) ran a cross-cultural study of the care and behavioral development of Hopi Indian children in northern Arizona. Among their many observations, the Dennises analyzed the effects of Hopi cradling practices on the age of onset of walking. By comparing the records of 63 Hopi children who had been reared on the cradleboard with 42 children who had not, Dennis and Dennis were able to obtain data on the effects of this type of restriction on a specific locomotor response. Shortly after birth, the Hopi infant is wrapped securely in a blanket and bound to a cradleboard so that very little movement is possible. The infant is removed from the cradleboard only for daily changing and bathing, activities that take approximately 1 hour. All feeding, sleeping, and transportation occurs while the infant is on the board. Infants receive a good amount of fondling and carrying and are never left alone. The duration of cradling is from 6 to 12 months. Despite this degree of restraint and restriction of activity, Hopi infants do not cry or struggle in response to cradling. In fact, Dennis and Dennis report that these infants become agitated, cry, and do not sleep when kept off the board for periods longer than usual. They often must be slowly weaned from the board; the Dennises observed some children dragging their cradles behind them after they had learned to walk. The average age of walking among the cradled children was 14.98 months, compared to 15.05 months for those who were not reared on the cradle—a difference of less than 2 days.

Dennis and Dennis concluded that walking develops autogenously, with little or no requirement of learning, practice, or exercise. While appearing to support a strict maturation hypothesis at first glance, the report of Dennis and Dennis clearly reveals that cradled Hopi infants received large amounts of stimulation and social interaction. Between 3 and 6 months of age, these infants were permitted increasing amounts of daily freedom off the board to engage in various motor activities. Although the Hopi rearing practices are certainly restrictive relative to non-Indian practices, their general pattern of development is comparable to white infants. These findings do not establish that learning or experiential factors play no role in the development of walking. They do demonstrate that this form of partial restriction, in the presence of high levels of social and sensory stimulation, does not retard the onset of walking.

At approximately the same time, Dennis and Dennis (1935, 1938, 1941) were observing the development of a pair of fraternal twins, Del and Rey, under the experimental condition of restricted practice and minimal social stimulation. The Dennises obtained their subjects from a mother who was unable to provide for them and whose father had deserted the family. Dennis and Dennis reared Del and Rey in their home from the age of 36 days to 14 months. Confined to a nursery, the infants saw no other children and few other adults, receiving the minimal attention required to keep them physically healthy. They were kept in individual cribs separated by a screen so they could not see each other except when removed for feeding and bathing. Dennis and Dennis refrained from any social or verbal interactions with the infants and never encouraged or reinforced behavioral activities. Opportunity for practice or learning was minimized by withholding toys or other objects and by placing the infants in a horizontal position as much as possible.

Dennis and Dennis then compared the pattern of development of Del and Rey with normative schedules of infant development (Figure 4-3). In general, the behavioral development of Del and Rey during the first 7 months fell within the age range of children reared in normal environments, with a few exceptions. Dennis and Dennis concluded that these

Figure 4-3
The median age and age range for the appearance of 50 items of infant behavior, as recorded in 40 biographical investigations, and the age at which these behavior items appeared in infants reared under experimental conditions of restricted activity and social stimulation.

(Adapted from Dennis & Dennis, 1941.)

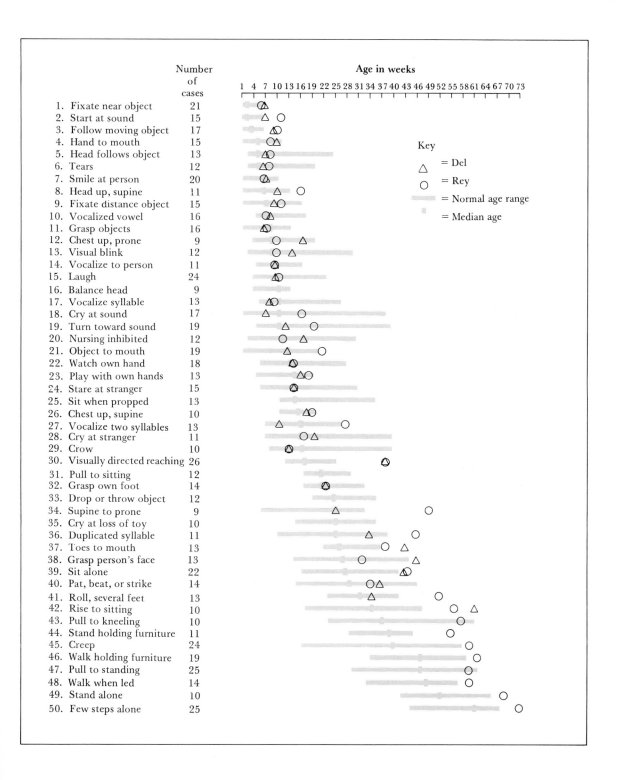

exceptions were due to the poor nutritional condition of the infants when they received them. At approximately 9 months of age, however, some retardation in the appearance of visually directed grasping (prehension) and various locomotor responses was observed. These effects were only temporary and normal skill levels were quickly attained and established with training.

It was subsequently discovered that Del suffered from left hemiplegia attributed to cortical injury at birth, and her locomotor development was seriously impaired and retarded in age of appearance. Despite this injury, Del's development during the first 9 months was normal. Dennis and Dennis were very cautious about the degree to which these infants displayed genuine developmental retardation, and they doubted that their conditions of restriction had any developmental effects at all. They had serious questions concerning the validity of the available normative data, which were derived from a small number of children. Insightfully, Dennis and Dennis commented that the appearance and establishment of an apparently autogenous or "instinctive" behavior may depend on the previous learning of elemental acts that have no obvious relationship to the final behavior. For example, in discussing the appearance of laughter in an infant who has never laughed before, Dennis and Dennis point out that the child first engages in smiling, vocalizations, and different forms of breathing. Each of these learned components now contributes to laughter, so laughter no longer can be considered a solely instinctive or autogenous behavior (see also Dennis, 1943).

Dennis and Dennis concluded that retardation was due to lack of normal learning situations and that maturation alone was insufficient to account for their observations. Curiously, they nevertheless maintained their earlier position (Dennis & Dennis, 1940) that most of the responses during the first year of life develop autogenously without special training or encouragement. Yet their later conclusion stresses the importance of learning in the development of autogenous behaviors. They go on to say that "while maturation is a major factor in infant development its importance lies chiefly in making learning possible. Maturation in and of itself seldom produces new developmental items, but maturation of structures when accompanied by self-directed activity leads to new infant responses" (Dennis & Dennis, 1941, p. 154).

It appears that Dennis and Dennis became aware of the interaction between learning and maturation, which undermined the role of maturation as uniquely important for development. Yet, they seemed unable or unwilling to relinquish the traditional notions despite their data. The restrictive conditions imposed upon Del and Rey were mild, and certainly gave them opportunities for much more stimulation and learning than seems obvious. They could not be isolated from all environmental sources of experience, learning, and exercise. Again we must raise the question, from what were they isolated? Clearly, Dennis and Dennis knew they had not demonstrated that learning does not contribute to development, nor that maturation alone guides development.

Dennis continued his research on the effects of restricting activity and social stimulation by observing the development of children reared in orphanages (Dennis & Najarian, 1957; Dennis, 1960). The results of both these studies seriously weakened the maturation hypothesis, clearly demonstrating the importance of experience and learning in postnatal development. In 1957, Dennis and Najarian compared the behavioral and social development of children placed in Creche, an orphanage in Beirut, Lebanon, with that of normally reared children from the same community. The infants at Creche received adequate medical and health care but were exposed to conditions of general environmental deprivation. Opportunities for activity, learning, and sensory and social stimulation were minimal.

The ratio of caretakers to infants was 1:10, and infants received adult attention only when necessary for feeding and changing. Infants remained on their backs in cribs whose sides were draped with sheets, restricting their view to a white ceiling. Feeding consisted of getting a bottle propped up on a pillow, since the low number of caretakers did not allow for individual holding and feeding. An infant scale of development was administered to both the experimental and the control groups at different ages. Dennis and Najarian found that the Creche children between the ages of 3 and 12 months scored significantly lower on general measures of motor and social development compared to controls. However, when a group of Creche children between 4 and 6 years of age were given a number of motor and intelligence tests, they scored as well as controls. The retardation effects observed during the first year of life were found to be temporary ones. Increasing opportunities for learning, experience, and stimulation in the subsequent years neutralized the earlier deprivation effects, indicating that adequate performance on infant scales of development, which are based on normative data, requires opportunities for learning in addition to maturation.

In a similar investigation of children reared in orphanages in Iran (Dennis, 1960), Dennis obtained similar results, strengthening his earlier findings (1957) that motor development is more than a maturation-controlled sequence of events.

The results of the present study challenge the widely held view that motor development consists in the emergence of a behavior sequence based primarily upon maturation. . . . The present study shows that . . . norms are met only under favorable environmental conditions. Among the children of Institution I (for children up to three years of age), not only was sitting alone greatly retarded but in many cases creeping did not occur. Instead, an alternate form of locomotion (scooting) was employed. These facts seem to indicate clearly that experience affects not only the ages at which motor items appear but also their very form. No doubt the maturation of certain structures . . . is necessary before certain responses can be learned, but learning is also necessary. Maturation alone is insufficient to bring about most postnatal developments in behavior. (Dennis, 1960, p. 57)

Dennis concluded that the retardation observed in institutionalized children was specific to the task required and dependent upon specific skills acquired by experience and learning. Thus, the greatest degree of retardation was found in locomotor behaviors. Here, adequate performance is dependent upon skill developed through opportunity for practice. In tasks less dependent upon specific skill acquisition and more dependent upon reflexive behavior, Dennis found no retardation. Therefore, the effects of deprivation observed in Dennis' research were not a generalized disruption in development. Rather, the effects were specific, temporary ones that were experience dependent; i.e., skill specific. It is unlikely that there are any purely autogenous responses free from any environmental influence, for the progressive maturation of such a response immediately and simultaneously facilitates learning and/or experiential feedback of one sort or another.

The Effects of Environmental Stimulation

Another approach to the study of maturation versus learning is to examine the effects of increased training or experience on early behavioral development. If development is indeed controlled by maturational phenomena, then stimulation by direct training and learning opportunities should have little effect on the emergence and patterns of infant behavior. But if such increased stimulation facilitates or accelerates development, this would further weaken the maturation hypothesis by demonstrating the interactive influences of maturation and environment on behavioral development.

ANIMAL STUDIES   Investigation of the behavioral and biological effects of neonatal stimulation in animals is currently a major enterprise in developmental psychology. Some of the earliest laboratory studies dealing with the ontogenetic effects of neonatal stimulation were done by Bernstein (1952) and Weininger (1953). These two investigators reported that rats that had been handled from birth to weaning (21 days of age) were less emotional, healthier, and superior in maze tasks compared to controls. These reports generated a line of research that has grown at an exponential rate during the past 20 years. Numerous forms of stimulation have been employed (e.g., handling, cooling, shock, noise), and many dependent variables examined (maze learning, exploratory behavior, resistance to disease, brain growth). Reviews of this literature, although not entirely consistent (Daly, 1973), generally suggest that neonatal stimulation may result in beneficial alterations in the ontogenesis of such behavioral systems as learning, emotionality, and stress responses to noxious and pathogenic stimuli (Denenberg, 1964; Hunt, 1961, 1979; LaBarba, 1970; Newton & Levine, 1968; Russell, 1971; Thompson & Grusec, 1970). The research literature also contains reports of accelerated maturation as a function of neonatal stimulation in rats (Levine, 1960), in cats (Meier, 1960), and in birds exposed to auditory stimulation during the incubation period (Gottlieb, 1976; Woolf, Bixby, & Capranica, 1976).

Findings contradicting the earlier research with rodents have recently been reported, however (Greenough, 1975; King, 1969; Cross & LaBarba, 1978; Stein & LaBarba, 1977). Thus, the question of neonatal stimulation and the acceleration of maturation remains obscure at this time. Nonetheless, it appears there is now cogent evidence for the active contribution of experience and environmental stimulation to the subsequent behavioral development of animals. Research activities designed to determine the question of maturational plasticity are currently receiving attention, and there are signs that the time course of species-specific, ontogenetic development may be alterable. Let us now turn to some of the human studies dealing with the effects of environmental stimulation on maturation.

HUMAN STUDIES   In 1929, Gesell and Thompson reported their findings on the effects of direct training on a number of locomotor activities. Identical twins were used as subjects, with one of the twins receiving daily training in stair climbing, creeping, pulling up to standing position, and walking. This training period extended from 46 weeks of age to 52 weeks of age. The control twin received no training. Comparisons of locomotor skills were made prior to the training period and at various points during the 6-week training session. Additionally, at 53 weeks of age, the control twin was given a similar 2-week training session to determine the effects of practice at a later age. The control twin quickly reached the skill levels of the trained twin with much less practice. Gesell and Thompson concluded that maturation is of "preponderant importance" in the development of infant behavior patterns. They also stated that there was no evidence that exercise or practice hastens the appearance of these locomotor activities. Even earlier, Gesell (1928) stated that "There is no convincing evidence that acceleration of development can be readily induced by either pernicious or enlightened methods of stimulation" (p. 364).

In 1932, Myrtle McGraw began her now classic study of Johnny and Jimmy (1935). This intensive analysis of behavioral development attracted a great deal of interest because of reports of a baby swimming under water and climbing steep inclines when less than a year old and roller skating by the age of 16 months. McGraw launched this study for two reasons. First, she was challenged by the pronouncement by Gesell and Thompson (1929) that the infant's nervous system does not respond to practice effects and that infant development proceeds as a function of neural maturation. Second, McGraw questioned the then-current pediatric and psychiatric idea that infant overstimulation was harmful and should be avoided. McGraw wanted to analyze the normal sequence of changes through which an infant acquires a given performance skill and then determine whether such sequential stages in development can be altered by stimulation or restriction. McGraw's basic assumption was that there must be some time in the course of development when the child responds to, and profits from, experience and training.

Johnny and Jimmy, fraternal twins, were selected as subjects for this experiment at 21 days of age. A group of 57 infants, examined at weekly or biweekly intervals, served as a control group. During the next 22 months, both infants were observed in the laboratory 5 days a week from 9 A.M. to 5 P.M. Over this experimental period, Johnny was given daily, direct practice designed to improve his skills in such activities as tricycling, roller skating, climbing, manipulation, and swimming. Jimmy was kept in a crib with a few toys and received no special training whatever. At 22 months of age, Jimmy was given intensive practice in the same activities that Johnny had been given earlier. Both infants were tested periodically for skill levels in these behaviors until they were 6 years old. The control group was also observed for assessment in the same activities.

In her conclusions about the effects of increased and restricted exercise on the development of the various activities under investigation, McGraw grouped the activities into two categories according to their susceptibility to practice effects. Phylogenetic activities, or those behaviors acquired by, and common to, all normal children (grasping, sitting up, crawling, standing, walking, etc.), were considered to be more "fixed" and much less susceptible to modification or improvement through practice. Ontogenetic activities, or those behaviors that a child may or may not acquire as a function of individualized learning, opportunity, or advantage (swimming, riding a bike, skating) were found to be significantly accelerated by practice.

With regard to the appearance of phylogenetic activities, then, McGraw found no differences between the twins or between their performance and that of the control group. However, the time of appearance and attained skill levels of ontogenetic activities were quite a different matter. Johnny was swimming before he was a year old, skillfully roller skating before 16 months of age, and riding a tricycle at 19 months of age. After the 22-month experimental period was over, Jimmy received practice in these activities and learned them much more rapidly than Johnny had.

The answer to McGraw's inquiry about when the infant can profit from experience or repetition of performance is clear. McGraw concluded that facilitation can occur at any time, once the maturational level of the infant is sufficient to support the activity. Given sufficient maturation, there is no developmental stage before which the infant is incapable of improving through exercise and after which improvement is possible. McGraw noted that different activities are more or less susceptible to exercise effects because the nervous system does not mature uniformly. This differential maturation results in differential emergence of behavior capacities, and successful modification of these behaviors is dependent on their emergence. Exercise or practice of an activity prior to an infant's ability to engage in that behavior has no effect, as McGraw observed. Thus, level of maturation is a critical factor in attempts to speed up behavioral development. The contributions of experience and learning to behavioral development were now clearly evident, as was the interactive nature of maturation and experience.

In her longitudinal followup of Johnny and Jimmy, McGraw (1939) reported that some of the skills attained earlier were lost, while others remained, depending on the amount of practice the twins engaged in during the subsequent years. At 6 years of age, McGraw described both twins as being of average intelligence. Johnny was reported to have superior general muscular coordination compared to Jimmy. In personality and attitudes, Johnny was considered "more complex," but there was no way of relating any such differences to the experiment. In general, the two boys were found to be normal 6-year-old children.

McGraw's conclusion that the efficacy of practice is a function of maturation of the underlying structures and mechanisms was later supported in her study of the effect of training on the achievement of bladder control (1940). McGraw used two pairs of 1-month-old identical twin boys as subjects. The twins were in the laboratory 5 days a week between 9 A.M. and 5 P.M. One boy from each set of twins was placed on a training potty for voiding at hourly intervals. This went on until they were 17 and 26 months of age, respectively. Their brothers were not given any toilet training until they were 14 and 24 months old, respectively. The results of McGraw's study are shown in Figure 4-4. The achievement curves of the four children reveal that the experimental twins did not profit from the early toilet

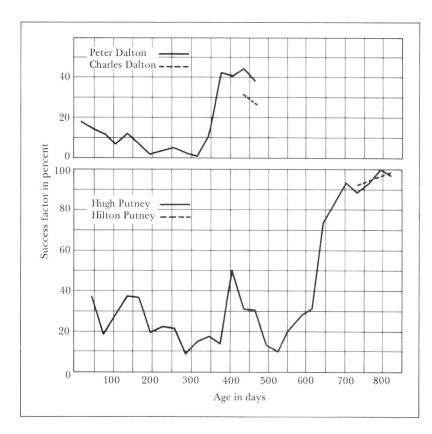

Figure 4-4
Curves obtained from the records of two sets of identical twin boys showing their achievement of bladder control.

(From McGraw, 1940.)

training. Note how rapidly the control twins attained similar levels of bladder control. McGraw attributed the rapid rise in bladder control to the maturation of cortical centers in the brain and of the neuromuscular control of the sphincter muscle in the bladder. She concluded that toilet training can be delayed until the last quarter of the second year of life for the average child. Earlier attempts at toilet training will be unsuccessful, for the most part, because of the absence of voluntary bladder control.

As mentioned earlier, McGraw completely abandoned the maturation versus learning hypothesis a few years later, calling it a cumbersome conceptual framework (McGraw, 1946). Even her thinking about the maturation → structure → function relationship seems to have changed. We should note also that McGraw forecast some of the key elements of probabilistic epigenesis, but with regard to postnatal, rather than prenatal, development.

McGraw's conclusions concerning the ineffectiveness of exercise on phylogenetic or species-specific activities have recently been challenged by the findings of Zelazo, Zelazo, and Kolb (1972). Zelazo et al. found that brief, daily exercise of the neonatal walking reflex leads to a high rate of responding at 8 weeks of age, the time at which this reflex normally disappears. In addition, these investigators found that infants receiving this exercise walked significantly earlier than controls. Since walking is considered a phylogenetic response, these data clash with McGraw's conclusions, and suggest that maturation of those structures subserving walking can be accelerated by exercise. Zelazo et al. hypothesize that the function of the neonatal walking reflex may be to assist the infant in the development of walking, and that it should be stimulated. They add that the widespread belief in the invariance of the motor sequence as reflected in normative data and developmental schedules may be more a reflection of our child-rearing practices than of the capacities of infants. Curiously, McGraw (1943), though aware of the neonatal walking reflex and its similarities to later independent walking, concluded that exercising this reflex would not facilitate later walking. This reflex was never considered for exercise in her 1935 study.

The implication that maturation rates in human infants may be accelerated and general development facilitated has re-

Learning to stand . . . with a little help! The adult taking this photograph is probably encouraging the little fellow to take that first step. Recent research suggests that the age at which children normally begin to walk can be reduced by exercising the walking reflex in newborns. This is an excellent example of the plasticity of maturation: the external environment acting to accelerate the development of the physical structures necessary for locomotion. Such research findings also suggest that much of the normative data on child development may be out of date, the products of habit and tradition rather than a true reflection of neonatal developmental capacities.

(Photo copyright © 1973 by Suzanne Szasz/Photo Researchers, Inc.)

ceived some further empirical support. These studies have concentrated on increasing the stimulation input via various modalities in premature, low birth weight, and term infants (Ambrose, 1969; Rice, 1977; White & LaBarba, 1976). The findings suggest that at least temporary facilitation of development and possible, temporary acceleration of maturational rates occur in neonatal infants exposed to tactile, kinesthetic, vestibular (inner ear), and visual stimulation. Although preliminary, these data have exciting implications. The possibility of maturational and organizational plasticity may open new horizons for human development. It may be possible to alter not only the temporal aspects of ontogenesis, but also the nature and content of the elements comprising behavioral systems. Such facilitation could result in changes in the pattern of human development and a fuller realization of human capacities. We must emphasize, however, that there has yet been no clear demonstration that maturational velocity in either human or nonhuman organisms can be experimentally accelerated. While certain developmental patterns may be altered or facilitated by early stimulation input to immature organisms, it remains to be shown that maturational phenomena are as plastic as behavioral phenomena.

LEARNING

It is no secret that infants learn, and that learning becomes increasingly obvious with age. The intimate relationship between learning and development is a continuous one, providing the ingredients for the development of both phylogenetic, or species-specific, events and individual differences, or ontogenetic events. The significance of experiential or learning phenomena for general development is no longer a contested or controversial topic. Theoretical and empirical efforts in developmental psychology are now directed toward questions of what kind of learning processes occur, when, how, and under what conditions during different periods of development. From this perspective, the emphasis is on learning as a developmental process. The attempt is to discover the details of how learning phenomena account for various patterns of development and the conditions under which learning processes may differentially influence developmental events. These are etiological considerations of some significance to developmental psychology. If there is any single innate human capacity that gives special evolutionary advantage, it is the capacity for learning and modification by learning. We shall see that this capacity is revealed shortly after birth.

Definition and Distinction of Learning Processes

No definition of learning is acceptable to all learning theorists. However, according to the most general definition (which should meet the least resistance), learning is reflected in changes of behavior that result from training, practice, or experience (Brackbill & Koltsova, 1967). This definition is meant to exclude behavior changes determined by maturation and genetic or biological factors. It also excludes those resulting from transitory psychological or physiological states, such as depression, sensory adaptation, or intoxication. An alternative general definition describes learning as behavior acquired by associations of stimuli that occur through practice (McGeoch & Irion, 1952). We may say that a conditioned response is acquired when, after paired associations of stimuli, (1) a response is elicited or intensified by a stimulus that did not previously elicit it, or did not elicit it as strongly, or (2) a response is emitted under the control of environmental circumstances that did not previously control it. These two requirements generally establish learning. They also distinguish Pavlovian or classical conditioning from operant or instrumental conditioning (Lipsitt, 1963). It should be noted that learning phenomena can no longer be easily dichotomized and categorized into classical or operant conditioning (see Mackintosh, 1974 for a thorough discussion of contemporary learning theory).

Classical conditioning describes learning processes and effects due to the temporal pairing of an originally neutral or "conditional" stimulus (CS) with an already effective or unconditioned stimulus (US) that evokes a reliable response. A US will reflexively evoke an unconditioned response (UR) when presented alone. After temporal pairing of the CS and US, a functional connection is formed between the UR and the CS. That is, the CS, presented alone, now evokes a conditioned version of the UR. This response elicited by the CS is called the conditioned response (CR).

In operant conditioning, the response rate of a specific behavior is modified by the consequences of the response. The organism first emits a response that operates or acts on the environment. The modification in responding that occurs is based upon the contingency between the response and its consequence, usually referred to as the response–consequence or reinforcement. The response and its various components become associated with the reinforcement stimulus, and the response frequency is either increased or decreased depending on whether the consequence is rewarding or punishing.

In classical conditioning, the reinforcement is not contingent on the occurrence of the CR, whereas in instrumental conditioning the response must precede the reinforcement in order for it to be delivered. Skinner (1938) identified classical conditioning with respondent behavior elicited by an explicit stimulus and instrumental conditioning with emitted behavior (operants) that occurs in the absence of an identifiable eliciting stimulus. Although Kimmel (1973) raises some questions about the differentiation between classical and instrumental conditioning, we may accept the traditional distinction for our purposes. Presumably, you are familiar with basic learning principles, so we will present only these schematic illustrations of classical and instrumental conditioning as a reminder:

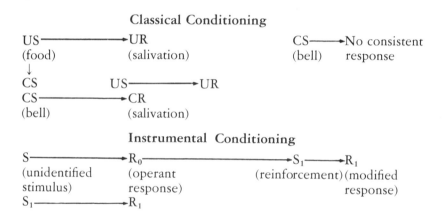

Classical Conditioning

US————————►UR   CS————►No consistent
(food)   (salivation)   (bell)   response
↓
CS   US————————►UR
CS————————►CR
(bell)   (salivation)

Instrumental Conditioning

S————————►R_0————————————————►S_1————►R_1
(unidentified   (operant   (reinforcement) (modified
stimulus)   response)   response)
S_1————————►R_1

Contemporary Status of Infant Conditioning Research

Relatively few empirical studies of infant conditioning appeared in the literature prior to 1960. Lipsitt (1966) mentioned three factors that contributed to this neglect: (1) the scarcity of infants as subjects, (2) the traditional biological–maturational conception of development, and (3) the belief that the infant was incapable of complex behavior. As Kessen (1963) points out, American psychologists preferred to construct theoretical babies rather than observe real ones. Now these obstacles and preconceptions have been removed, and Fitzgerald and Porges (1971) describe the "explosion" of infant research in conditioning that has occurred since 1960. The current surge of interest in infant conditioning and learning is documented by the many reviews and volumes of collected papers that now appear in the psychological literature (Fitzgerald & Porges, 1971; Fitzgerald & Brackbill, 1976; Hulsebus, 1973; Reese, 1971, 1974; Samaroff, 1971).

The advantages of studying infant behavior and its subsequent conditioning are that they are at their simplest level of form and complexity. Insights into simple learning phenomena may provide us with information about the development of other processes and how more complex responses are learned. In addition, such information may provide for the more efficient application of learning principles as we are able to specify learning capacities during childhood. Recognition of the importance of studying infant learning, along with the realization that the young infant is a competent learning organism, have significantly advanced our knowledge of the learning capacities of the human infant.

Basic Processes in Learning

The infant is born with a large number of reflexes, some of which disappear within a few months, and some of which are retained and modified to serve as foundations for the development of more complex behaviors. Two such reflexes (respondents) are of critical importance because many of the infant's other reflexes are dependent upon their operation. Thus, they serve to determine the general nature of the infant's responses to the environment. Second, these two reflexes constitute basic, elemental processes in learning. These two reflexes are the orienting reflex—OR—(Lynn, 1966; Pavlov, 1927; Sokolov, 1960) and the attending reflex (Cohen, 1973).

If an organism is presented with a new stimulus, the observed response pattern to that stimulus serves to maximize reception, with full attention directed to the novel stimulus. Evidently, the OR optimizes the ability of the organism to perceive, process, and evaluate the significance of the stimulus event. The OR consists of a number of discrete reflexive components such as orientation of the receptors toward the stimulus source, arrest of ongoing activity, and a number of physiological changes that facilitate stimulus reception. Once alerted and oriented to the stimulus event, the attending reflex

Orienting and attending reflexes. These two reflexes are fundamental to all learning. The orienting reflex focuses the infant's senses on specific stimulus (in this instance, a small doll) while ignoring other stimuli (such as the photographer) that may also be present. The attending reflex keeps the infant's attention on the stimulus, which allows the infant to process information about it. The same stimulus will continue to elicit both reflexes until habituation occurs. The intent expression on this toddler's face is characteristic of the orienting and attending reflexes in action.

(Photo by George Roos/Peter Arnold, Inc.)

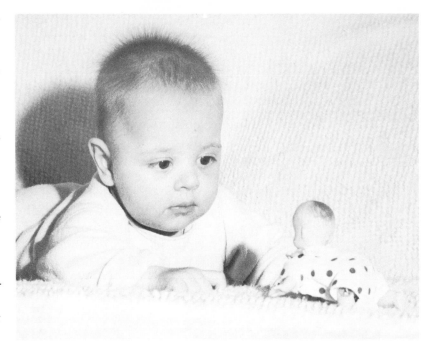

enables the maintenance of fixation and subsequent processing of the stimulus as a function of its complexity, novelty, and significance.

Clearly, these reflexes are indispensible for learning and adaptation, for without them learning cannot begin. These are the origins of attentional control, operants that subsequently arise and develop from originally unlearned, reflexive responses. Thus, even the newly developing infant is equipped to give priority to changing events in the environment. But given the infinite variety of stimulation potential for the infant, relevant and irrelevant, this capacity to respond to change would have little survival value in and of itself. It must be accompanied by a mechanism that will selectively terminate the attentional reflexes in the face of irrelevant or insignificant stimuli. Such a mechanism is habituation, another basic learning phenomenon that also has considerable significance for development.

Habituation   What is the effect on the OR and attending reflex if the eliciting stimulus is presented repeatedly? They habituate, gradually fade, with diminishing probability of subsequent responding to the same stimulus presentations. From the earliest reports of the infant habituation phenomenon (Jeffrey & Cohen, 1971; Razran, 1971), there has been some dispute over whether habituation is a learning phenomenon or merely the result of sensory adaptation or muscle and receptor fatigue. The argument for the latter has been weakened by demonstrations of the recovery of the attentional reflexes when a new stimulus is presented after habituation occurs. This recovery, dishabituation, readily appears with stimulus change. But if habituation and conventional learning phenomena share some fundamental similarities, there are also differences between them. They both involve behavioral changes, but whereas learning usually involves response acquisition or a change in the control of a response, habituation is characterized by response decrement. A number of leading developmentalists and learning theorists view habituation as a simple learning process—learning not to respond (Jeffrey & Cohen, 1971; Razran, 1971). We may consider habituation as one of the most primitive mechanisms for, and the simplest process of, learning.

Infant habituation has been extensively studied across a variety of stimulus and response modalities (Jeffrey & Cohen, 1971; Kessen, Haith, & Salapatek, 1970; Razran, 1971). Habituation in neonates and infants has been investigated using auditory, visual, tactile, olfactory (smell), and temperature stimuli. Response habituation of heartrate, respiration, galvanic skin response (GSR), startle reaction, fixation time, vocalization, activity, and sucking are among the most frequently examined responses to repeated stimulus presentations. The literature generally supports the habituation phenomenon in infants between 2 and 3 months of age. The data are inconsistent about the generality of habituation and its strength or rate in younger infants and neonates. Friedman, Bruno, and Vietze (1974), for example, report visual habituation in newborn infants 1 to 3 days of age. Friedman et al. state that the failure of other studies to demonstrate habituation in neonates may be due to the use of short duration times of stimulus exposure to the neonate. Sex differences in habituation have been reported, but these data are also inconsistent and contradictory. They do not yield any consistent findings of differential sensitivity to habituation (Kessen et al., 1970). Methodological problems of control and response interpretation increase with decreasing age levels, and it becomes more difficult to demonstrate habituation consistently in neonates and young infants. The physiological and behavioral instability of such young infants presents formidable problems to the researcher.

Implications of Infant Habituation

In his discussion of habituation, Razran (1971) states that "it offers a closer look into the underlying neurophysiological, indeed biophysical, foundations of the learning process—into its very birth" (p. 57). Razran (1971) describes the fundamental properties of habituation as being those of learning: memory, generalization, and discrimination. Thus, infant habituation may have significant implications for basic developmental studies of attention, memory, and learning. Additionally, the rate at which habituation develops may aid diagnostic evaluation of normal and abnormal neurological development.

If habituation occurs in an infant, it must mean that the infant has remembered, in some form, the first presentation of the repeated stimulus. The memory of that stimulus has been stored and then retrieved just before habituation occurs. Thus, such events may lead to the discovery of basic information about the mechanisms of memory storage, retrieval of information from memory storage, and how these capacities develop. Sokolov (1960) has proposed a "neuronal model" to explain the orienting reflex and its habituation. His theory proposes that cortical cells preserve information about the intensity, quality, duration, and order of presentation of stimuli. This information is formed into a neuronal model and stored away. Continued stimulus repetition now is analyzed and compared to the stored neuronal model previously formed. If the new information input matches the model, the stimulus is recognized, the OR blocked, and the habituation response initiated. If the incoming stimulus information does not match the neuronal model, the OR is elicited.

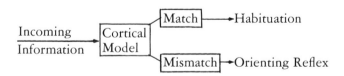

There is now a strong resurgence of interest in infant habituation, and this phenomenon is assuming a position of greater importance in psychology. Future research in this area undoubtedly will reveal the fundamental processes of a number of developmental phenomena and contribute significantly to general psychological theory.

Neonatal and Infant Conditioning
We have seen that the young human infant is capable of simple learning in terms of discrimination and differential responding. Some of the habituation data also indicate that these fundamental processes may be present shortly after birth. Since the attentional reflexes and the habituation response comprise the fundamental elements and prerequisites of more complex, associative learning, we will look at the question of conditionability in the human infant. Our discussion deals with the contingencies to which infants can respond and show learning, and the earliest age at which infants can be classically and instrumentally conditioned.

Stimulated by Pavlov's (1927) pioneering research on classical conditioning in dogs, both Soviet and Western psychologists have pursued the question of whether conditioned responses can be established in the newborn infant. The answer has not always been easy to determine. In the case of classical conditioning, the answer seems to be no—or maybe. On the other hand, instrumental conditioning in neonates has been clearly established as a reliable learning process. This discrepancy has aroused some dispute for both theoretical and empirical reasons. In his review of the literature, Sameroff (1971) observes that one clear generalization can be drawn from the outcomes of neonatal conditioning research. The unsuccessful studies have typically been attempts to classically condition newborn infants, whereas instrumental conditioning attempts have been successful. Sameroff's analysis of the data suggests that classical conditioning has not been reliably demonstrated in infants younger than 3 weeks of age, while instrumental conditioning has been reported in neonates less than 5 days old.

Sameroff hypothesizes that the newborn infant is unable to respond differentially to the specific stimuli employed in classical conditioning, and consequently cannot associate two previously unrelated stimuli (CS and US) in different sensory modalities. Inexperience with the CS means that it is not related to any of the activity of the newborn, and thus there is no place for the CS in the newborn's cognitive structure or "schema." Response integration via different sensory modalities does not occur and classical conditioning fails to become established until the necessary cognitive structures or schemas are acquired through experience. Sameroff points out that in instrumental conditioning, cross-conditioning of sensory and response systems is not present. All that is required in neonatal instrumental conditioning is the ability to detect general changes in the environment and to utilize existing reflexes, whose cognitive schema are well represented and easily associated with stimulus elicitation. For example, sucking and head turning can be operantly conditioned to a number of reinforcing stimuli involving food getting. Sameroff's position represents an interesting blend of learning theory and the cognitve theory of Jean Piaget.

Sameroff's conclusions notwithstanding, there are a number of investigators who report classical conditioning in neonates. In 17 studies of neonatal classical conditioning reported between 1931 and 1974, 8 describe positive results, four have equivocal outcomes, and 5 yield no conditioning (Fitzgerald & Brackbill, 1976). These outcomes contrast with the much more frequent positive reports of instrumental conditioning in neonates (Hulsebus, 1974; Lipsitt, 1969; Sameroff, 1971). As Fitzgerald and Brackbill (1976) point out, the evidence for neonatal classical conditioning is certainly not clear. Moreover, their review of classical conditioning in infancy also reveals that it is no easier to demonstrate classical conditioning in infants between the ages of 12 days and 9 months. In 22 studies of classical conditioning conducted between 1928 and 1974, 10 report positive results, 5 have negative outcomes, and 7 report equivocal findings (Fitzgerald & Brackbill, 1976). Unlike the data from instrumental conditioning, there appears to be no evidence that classical conditioning occurs more readily in older infants than in younger infants. Fitzgerald and Brackbill conclude that infant conditionability is (1) a function of CS–CR specificity, (2) more easily demonstrated in simple conditioning procedures than in more complex ones, (3) not related to chronological age except for the length of the interstimulus interval (younger infants require longer intervals), (4) is related to the orienting response, and (5) is related to biobehavioral state, ranging from deep sleep to awake, alert, and active. Obviously, the circumstances involving classical conditioning are much more complex than those related to instrumental conditioning. As Fitzgerald and Brackbill point out, there is a need to focus attention on the ontogenetic factors that constrain learning. They go on to question the notions of equivalence of conditionability from one situation to another and the generality of the laws of learning (Seligman, 1970).

From the number of empirical demonstrations of successful instrumental conditioning in infants, it appears that the human infant is "prepared to learn" (Seligman, 1970) under such conditions. Operant responding in infants is readily obtained in sucking, head turning, looking, vocalization, smiling, and arm and leg movements (Hulsebus, 1974). The status of infant classical conditioning, however, suggests that the human infant is "unprepared" or "contraprepared" to learn (Seligman, 1970) via this process. Perhaps the difficulties in establishing classical conditioning in infants reflect its evolutional status. Is the process of classical conditioning a phylogenetically older one, from which the capacity for instrumental conditioning has evolved (Razran, 1971)? It also appears that the instrumental process is more efficient, although we must remember that the traditional dichotomy between classical and instrumental conditioning as separate processes has been questioned (Mackintosh, 1974; Razran, 1971).

It seems clear that the most significant and obvious aspects of learning occur under instrumental conditions, and that such processes are of paramount importance to developmental phenomena. The significance of classical conditioning is not denied in this context, as we shall see in later chapters. It is probably true that we are constantly being classically conditioned. However, even autonomic processes such as heart rate, GSR, and blood pressure, long thought to be susceptible only to classical conditioning, have now been demonstrated to be modifiable by instrumental conditioning procedures (Kimmel, 1974). These findings are of enormous basic and applied significance to development and to the treatment of various

Infant in a Skinner box. Instrumental or operant conditioning seeks to modify the subject's initial response to a stimulus by reinforcement (reward or guidance) to achieve a desired or secondary response. The Skinner box creates a controlled environment in which external stimuli can be closely monitored and responses noted, reinforced, and modified accordingly. Note the objects on top of the box, which include a rattle, a music box, and a stuffed animal. Each of these objects (as well as those in the box itself) provides sensory stimulation that can be used to encourage desired responses from the infant. While classical conditionability of infants remains a point of uncertainty among developmentalists, most studies suggest that babies do respond to operant conditioning at a very early age.

(Photo by Falk/Monkmeyer Press Photo Service)

psychological and psychosomatic disorders. They are also testimony to the plasticity of behavior and the potency and pervasiveness of learning phenomena.

The Question of Fetal Conditioning

Interest in the conditionability of the human fetus is related to Pavlov's (1927) suggestion that the cerebral cortex is required for conditioning. Reports of fetal reactivity to loud sounds during the last month of pregnancy (Forbes & Forbes, 1927) suggested to Ray (1932) and Sontag and Wallace (1934) that the startlelike movements of the late fetus to loud sounds might be classically conditioned. Such attempts using vibration of the abdominal wall as the CS and a loud sound as the US were unsuccessful. Spelt (1948) again attempted to demonstrate fetal classical conditioning using more refined techniques and methodology. Employing the same CS–US paradigm of Ray and Sontag and Wallace, Spelt reported evidence of conditioning, extinction, and spontaneous recovery of the CR. But there are serious methodological and control problems in Spelt's study, and there is, therefore, no convincing data at this time to suggest that human fetuses *in utero* can be conditioned. These findings have no necessary implications for the conditionability of late fetuses, however. There is data suggesting that prematurely delivered fetuses can be conditioned (Hulsebus, 1974). There is no reason to believe that late fetuses are any less conditionable than term infants, barring any physical problems attending early delivery. In short, attempts to condition late fetuses *in utero* appear to be more of a technological challenge than an empirical or theoretical one.

REFERENCES

Ambrose, A. *Stimulation in early infancy.* New York: Academic Press, 1969.

Anastasi, A. Heredity, environment, and the question "How?" *Psychological Review*, 1958, 65, 197–208.

Baer, M. J. *Growth and maturation.* Cambridge, Massachusetts: Doyle Publishing Co., 1973.

Bernstein, L. A note on Christie's "Experimental naivete and experiential naivete." *Psychological Bulletin*, 1952, 49, 38–40.

Brackbill, Y., & Koltsova, M. M. Conditioning and learning. In Y. Brackbill (Ed.), *Infancy and early childhood*. New York: Freepress, 1967.

Carmichael, L. The development of behavior in vertebrates experimentally removed from the influence of external stimulation. *Psychological Review*, 1926, *33*, 51–58.

Carmichael, L. A further study of the development of behavior or in vertebrates removed from the influence of external stimulation. *Psychological Review*, 1927, *34*, 34–37.

Carmichael, L. A further experimental study of the development of behavior. *Psychological Review*, 1928, *35*, 253–260.

Coghill, G. E. Correlated anatomical and physiological studies of the growth of the nervous system of *Amphibia*. VI. The mechanism of integration in *Amblystoma punctatum*. *Journal of Comparative Neurology*, 1926, *41*, 95–152.

Coghill, G. E. *Anatomy and the problem of behavior*. Cambridge: University Press. New York: Macmillan, 1929.

Cohen, L. B. A two-process model of infant visual attention. *Merrill-Palmer Quarterly*, 1973, *19*, 157–180.

Cross, M. S., & LaBarba, R. C. Neonatal stimulation, maternal behavior, and accelerated maturation in BALB/c mice. *Developmental Psychobiology*, 1978, *11*, 83–92.

Cruze, W. W. Maturation and learning in chicks. *Journal of Comparative Psychology*, 1935, *19*, 371–409.

Daley, M. Early stimulation of rodents: A critical review of present interpretations. *British Journal of Psychology*, 1973, *64*, 435–460.

Denenberg, V. H. Critical periods, stimulus input, and emotional reactivity: A theory of infantile stimulation. *Psychological Review*, 1964, *71*, 335–351.

Dennis, W. On the possibility of advancing and retarding the motor development of infants. *Psychological Review*, 1943, *50*, 203–218.

Dennis, W. Causes of retardation among institutional children. *Journal of Genetic Psychology*, 1960, *96*, 47–59.

Dennis, W., & Dennis, M. G. The effect of restricted practice upon the reaching, sitting, and standing of two infants. *Journal of Genetic Psychology*, 1935, *47*, 21–29.

Dennis, W., & Dennis, M. G. Infant development under conditions of restricted practice and minimum social stimulation: A preliminary report. *Journal of Genetic Psychology*, 1938, *53*, 151–156.

Dennis, W., & Dennis, M. G. The effect of cradling upon the onset of walking in Hopi children. *Journal of Genetic Psychology*, 1940, *56*, 77–86.

Dennis, W., & Dennis, M. G. Infant development under conditions of restricted practice and minimum social stimulation. *Genetic Psychology Monographs*, 1941, *23*, 149–155.

Dennis, W., & Najarian, P. Infant development under environmental handicap. *Psychological Monographs*, 1957, *71*, No. 7.

Fitzgerald, H. E., & Brackbill, Y. Classical conditioning in infancy: Development and constraints. *Psychological Bulletin*, 1976, *83*, 353–376.

Fitzgerald, H. E., & Porges, S. W. A decade of infant conditioning and learning research. *Merrill-Palmer Quarterly*, 1971, *17*, 79–117.

Forbes, H. S., & Forbes, H. B. Fetal sense reactions: Hearing. *Journal of Comparative Psychology*, 1927, *7*, 353–355.

Fowler, W. Cognitive learning in infancy and early childhood. *Psychological Review*, 1962, *59*, 116–152.

Friedman, S., Bruno, L. A., & Vietze, P. Newborn habituation to visual stimuli: A sex difference in novelty detection. *Journal of Experimental Child Psychology*, 1974, *18*, 242–251.

Fromme, A. An experimental study of factors of maturation and practice in the behavioral development of the embryo of the frog *Rana pipiens*. *Genetic Psychology Monographs*, 1941, *24*, 219–256.

Gesell, A. *Infancy and human growth*. New York: Macmillan, 1928.

Gesell, A. Maturation and infant behavior patterns. *Psychological Review*, 1929, *36*, 307–319.

Gesell, A. *Infant and child in the culture of today*. New York: Harper, 1943.

Gesell, A. The ontogenesis of infant behavior. In L. Carmichael (Ed.), *Manual of child psychology* (2nd ed.). New York: Wiley, 1954.

Gesell, A., & Thompson, H. Learning and maturation in identical infant twins: an experimental study by the method of co-twin control. *Genetic Psychology Monograph*, 1929, *6*, 1–124.

Gottlieb, G. Conceptions of prenatal development: Behavioral embryology. *Psychological Review*, 1976, *83*, 215–234.

Greenough, W. T. Experiential modification of the developing brain. *American Scientist*, 1975, *63*, 37–46.

Harlow, H. F., & Harlow, M. K. Social deprivation in monkeys. *Scientific American*, 1962, *207*, 136–144.

Hebb, D. O. The innate organization of visual activity: I. Perception of figures by rats reared in total darkness. *Journal of Genetic Psychology*, 1937, *51*, 101–126.

Hebb, D. O. *The organization of behavior*. New York: Wiley, 1949.

Held, R., & Hein, A. Movement-produced stimulation in the development of visually guided behavior. *Journal of Physiological and Comparative Psychology*, 1963, *56*, 872–876.

Horn, G. Rose, S. P. R., & Bateson, P. P. G. Experience and plasticity in the central nervous system. *Science,* 1973, *181,* 506–515.

Hulsebus, R. C. Operant conditioning of infant behavior: A review. In H. W. Reese (Ed.), *Advances in child development and behavior.* New York: Academic Press, 1973.

Humphrey, T. The development of human fetal activity and its relation to postnatal behavior. In H. W. Reese & L. P. Lipsitt (Eds.), *Advances in child development.* New York: Academic Press, 1970.

Hunt, J. McV. *Intelligence and experience.* New York: Ronald, 1961.

Hunt, J. McV. Psychological development: Early experience. *Annual Review of Psychology,* 1979, *30,* 103–143.

Jeffrey, W. E., & Cohen, L. B. Habituation in the human infant. In H. W. Reese (Ed.), *Advances in child development and behavior.* New York: Academic Press, 1971.

Kessen, W. Research in the psychological development of infants: An overview. *Merrill-Palmer Quarterly,* 1963, *9,* 83–94.

Kessen, W., Haith, M. M., & Salapatek, P. H. Human infancy: A bibliography and guide. In P. H. Mussen (Ed.), *Carmichael's manual of child psychology.* New York: Wiley, 1970.

Kimmel, H. D. Reflex "habituability" as a basis for differentiating between classical and instrumental conditioning. *Conditional Reflex,* 1973, *8,* 10–27.

Kimmel, H. D. Instrumental conditioning of autonomically mediated responses in human beings. *American Psychologist,* 1974, *29,* 325–335.

King, D. L. The effect of early experience and litter size on some weight and maturational variables. *Developmental Psychology,* 1969, *1,* 576–584.

Knobloch, H., & Pasamanick, B. (Eds.). *Gesell and Amatruda's developmental diagnosis.* New York: Harper & Row, 1974.

Kuo, Z. Y. *The dynamics of behavioral development.* New York: Random House, 1967.

LaBarba, R. C. Experiential and environmental factors in cancer: A review of the research with animals. *Psychosomatic Medicine,* 1970, *32,* 259–276.

Lagerspetz, K. Nygard, M., & Strandvick, C. The effects of training in crawling on the motor and mental development of infants. *Scandinavian Journal of Psychology,* 1971, *12,* 192–197.

Levine, S. Stimulation in infancy. *Scientific American,* 1960, *202,* 80–86.

Lipsitt, L. P. Learning in the first year of life. In L. P. Lipsitt & C. C. Spiker (Eds.), *Advances in child development and behavior.* New York: Academic Press, 1963.

Lipsitt, L. P. Learning processes of newborns. *Merrill-Palmer Quarterly,* 1966, *12,* 45–71.

Lipsitt, L. P. Learning capacities of the human infant. In R. J. Robinson (Ed.), *Brain and early behavior.* New York: Academic Press, 1969.

Lynn, R. *Attention, arousal, and the orienting reaction.* Oxford: Pergamon, 1966.

Mackintosh, N. J. *The psychology of animal learning.* New York: Academic Press, 1974.

Mathews, S. A., & Detwiler, S. R. The reaction of *Amblystoma* embryos following prolonged treatment with chloretone. *Journal of Experimental Zoology,* 1926, *45,* 279–292.

McGeoch, J. A., & Irion, A. L. *The psychology of human learning.* New York: Longmans, Green, & Company, 1952.

McGraw, M. B. *Growth: A study of Johnny and Jimmy.* New York: Appleton-Century, 1935.

McGraw, M. B. Later development of children specially trained during infancy: Johnny and Jimmy at school age. *Child Development,* 1939, *10,* 1–19.

McGraw, M. B. Neural maturation as exemplified in achievement of bladder control. *Journal of Pediatrics,* 1940, *16,* 584.

McGraw, M. B. Maturation of behavior. In L. Carmichael (Ed.), *Manual of child psychology.* New York: Wiley, 1946.

McGraw, M. B. *The neuromuscular maturation of the human infant.* New York: Columbia University Press, 1943; New York: Hafner, 1963.

Meier, G. W. Infantile handling and development in Siamese kittens. *Journal of Comparative and Physiological Psychology,* 1960, *62,* 433–436.

Melzack, R., & Thompson, W. R. Effects of early experience on the response to pain. *Canadian Journal of Psychology,* 1956, *10,* 82–90.

Moltz, H. An epigenetic interpretation of the imprinting phenomenon. In G. Newton & S. Levine (Eds.), *Early experience and behavior.* Springfield: Thomas, 1968.

Newton, G., & Levine, S. (Eds.). *Early experience and behavior.* Springfield, Illinois: Thomas, 1968.

Nissen, H. W., Chow, K. L., & Semmes, J. Effects of restricted opportunity for tactual, kinesthetic, and manipulative experience on the behavior of a chimpanzee. *American Journal of Psychology,* 1951, *64,* 485–507.

Padilla, S. G. Further studies on the delayed pecking of chicks. *Journal of Comparative Psychology,* 1935, *20,* 413–443.

Patten, C. M. (Ed.). *Human Anatomy* (9th ed.). New York: McGraw-Hill, 1933.

Pavlov, I. P. *Conditioned reflexes.* London: Oxford University Press, 1927.

Ray, W. S. A preliminary report on a study of fetal conditioning. *Child Development,* 1932, *3,* 175–177.

Razran, G. *Mind in evolution.* Boston: Houghton-Mifflin, 1971.

Reese, H. W. (Ed.). *Advances in child development and behavior.* New York: Academic Press, 1971.

Reese, H. W. (Ed.). *Advances in child development and behavior.* New York: Academic Press, 1974.

Rice, R. D. Neurophysiological development in premature infants following stimulation. *Developmental Psychology,* 1977, *13,* 69–76.

Riesen, A. H. The development of visual perception in man and chimpanzee. *Science,* 1947, *106,* 107–108.

Riesen, A. H., Chow, K. L., Semmes, J., & Nissen, H. W. Chimpanzee vision after four conditions of light deprivation. *American Psychologist,* 1951, *6,* 282.

Russell, P. A. "Infantile Stimulation" in rodents: A consideration of possible mechanisms. *Psychological Bulletin,* 1971, *75,* 192–202.

Sameroff, A. J. Can conditioned responses be established in newborn infants: 1971? *Developmental Psychology,* 1971, *5,* 1–12.

Seligman, M. E. P. On the generality of the laws of learning. *Psychological Review,* 1970, *77,* 406–418.

Shirley, M. M. *The first two years: A study of 25 babies* (Vol. 1). Minneapolis: University of Minnesota Press, 1931.(a)

Shirley, M. M. A motor sequence favors the maturation theory. *Psychological Bulletin,* 1931, *28,* 203–204.(b)

Shirley, M. M. *The first two years: a study of 25 babies* (Vol. 2). Minneapolis: University of Minnesota Press, 1933.

Skinner, B. F. *The behavior of organisms.* New York: Appleton-Century, 1938.

Sokolov, E. N. *Perception and the conditioned reflex.* New York: Macmillan, 1960.

Sontag, L. W., & Wallace, R. F. Study of fetal reactivity. *American Journal of Disturbed Children,* 1934, *48,* 1050–1057.

Spalding, D. A. Instinct. *Macmillan's,* 1873, *27,* 282–293.

Spalding, D. A. Instinct: With original observations on young animals. *Popular Science Monographs,* 1902, *61,* 126–142.

Spelt, D. K. The conditioning of the human fetus *in utero. Journal of Experimental Psychology,* 1948, *38,* 338–346.

Stein, C. K., & LaBarba, R. C. Neonatal stimulation and accelerated maturation in BALB/c mice. *Developmental Psychology,* 1977, *13,* 423–424.

Tanner, J. M. *Growth at adolescence* (2nd ed.). Oxford: Blackwell Scientific Publications; Philadelphia: Davis, 1962.

Thompson, W. R., & Grusec, J. E. Studies of early experience. In P. H. Mussen (Ed.), *Carmichael's manual of child psychology.* New York: Wiley, 1970.

Thompson, W. R., & Heron, W. The effects of restricting early experience on the problem-solving capacity of dogs. *Canadian Journal of Psychology,* 1954, *8,* 17–31.

Thorpe, W. H. *Learning and instinct in animals.* Methuen, 1961.

Weininger, O. Mortality of albino rats under stress as a function of early handling. *Canadian Journal of Psychology,* 1953, *7,* 111–114.

White, J. L., & LaBarba, R. C. The effects of tactile and kinesthetic stimulation on neonatal development in the premature infant. *Developmental Psychobiology,* 1976, *9,* 569–577.

Woolf, N. K., Bixby, J. L., & Capranica, R. R. Prenatal experience and avian development: Brief auditory stimulation accelerates the hatching of Japanese quail. *Science,* 1976, *194,* 959–960.

Zelazo, P. R., Zelazo, N. A., & Kolb, S. "Walking" in the newborn. *Science,* 1972, *176,* 314–315.

Chapter

MOTOR AND PERCEPTUAL DEVELOPMENT

Five

INTRODUCTION

Motor and perceptual development are the gateways to infant behavioral competence. They are the tools that enable infants to explore and adapt to the external environment. Research in sensorimotor and perceptual development in infants is currently receiving much more attention than motor development alone. Much of this differential concern reflects the impact of the early developmentalists and their widespread belief in the invariance of motor development. As we saw in Chapter Four, these early findings virtually silenced further research.

We can identify at least two more reasons for the current emphasis on perceptual–motor development relative to motor development. Compared to the perceptual capacities of infants, motor capacities are relatively undeveloped. They lag well behind the perceptual competence of the infant and, therefore, are difficult to use as an index of learning and sensitivity. The perceptual responsivity of the young infant and its obvious susceptibility to learning phenomena are also factors that have come to command more attention from psychologists. Therefore we may conclude that the current research emphasis on perceptual development arises from historical, biological, empirical, and theoretical reasons. In later infancy and early childhood, these difficulties largely disappear as motor skills increase and become integrated with perceptual abilities.

Early recorded descriptions of infant motor development took the form of baby biographies, beginning as early as the eighteenth century. As we have seen in previous chapters, these anecdotal reports gave way to G.S. Hall's questionnaire method and eventually to longitudinal studies of the age-related emergence of motor activities in infants and children. The essence of a historical perspective on human motor development has been presented in Chapter Four. That perspective revolved around the maturation-learning controversy. The systematic studies of motor development that have emerged in the literature may be classified into three major categories:

1 Normative studies, which were the major preoccupation during much of the first half of the twentieth century. These studies focused on the average age at which various motor behaviors appear and the sequence of their emergence.

2 Analytical studies, a natural sequel to the normative research, were exemplified by the work of Gesell, McGraw, and Shirley. In many respects, such observations are extensions of the normative data, involving detailed recording of the nature and mechanics of motor acts. The goal was to analyze the components of motor behavior into its phasic, sequential, anatomical, and neuromuscular aspects. No detail was overlooked in the search for how the infant assumed control over its movements. With the use of motion pictures, one could document, in exquisite detail, every body movement involved in the progression of some motor act.

3 The third category of research on motor development is represented by experimental studies in which an independent variable is manipulated. Although such studies date back to Arnold Gesell, Wayne Dennis, and Myrtle McGraw, they were to disappear with the waning of the maturation controversy in the mid-1940s. Any significant experimental research in motor development was not to appear again until some 30 years later with the publication of the Zelazo, Zelazo, and Kolb study in 1972. With increasing evidence of plasticity in motor development, experimental research in this area is being revived.

Current research no longer involves normative or analytical studies, although some researchers suggest that contemporary normative data need to be established since existing data are out of date and perhaps no longer applicable to today's infants.

Although the philosophical roots of human perception date back more than 300 years, few developmental psychologists in the first half of the twentieth century were concerned with perceptual capacities and development in infants. Such behavior was incorporated into sensorimotor development, the integration of sensory and motor functioning so that sensory information becomes coordinated with motor acts. Gesell, Ilg, and Bullis (1949) were among the first to describe such sensorimotor development. They studied visual and motor development in infants and related increasing motor complexity to the expanding visual world of the infant. As we shall see, interest in infant perceptual development is relatively recent, but has produced a great deal of information during the past 20 years.

NEONATAL REFLEXES: THE ORIGINS OF MOTOR DEVELOPMENT

We have already learned that motor movements begin in the human fetus *in utero*. These movements take the form of spontaneous or reflexive movements. For our purposes, however, we will begin our discussion with neonatal capacities for movement and motor reflexes. As we assess neonatal motor abilities, we must exercise some caution in differentiating motor capacities from the general, diffuse movements associated with nonspecific activation. For example, the motor activity accompanying the newborn's alert waking state and crying may include more or less vigorous movements that have no significance for motoric capacities (Wolff, 1966). Typically, the term "state" is employed as an index of level of arousal along the continuum between sleep and crying. Clearly, infant states are critical variables in behavioral studies of the newborn. Fluctuations in infant states present problems of stimulus sensitivity and infant responsivity. As infant states change, a number of neurophysiological and biological aspects of functioning also change (Prechtl, 1965).

At birth, the newborn infant is limp and relatively inert, but shortly after respiration begins, spontaneous movements occur. The infant assumes definite postural positions when placed in either the prone or supine stations (lying on the stomach or back). Head-turning and brief, weak head-lifting also appear shortly after birth, becoming stronger with each passing day. These responses seem initially to be spontaneous movements insofar as they occur in the absence of any known external stimulus. Nevertheless, they appear related to the neonatal rooting reflex, involved in sucking, which can be elicited by oral tactile stimulation.

There are large individual differences in infant state, temperament (responsivity, irritability), and general activity levels (Bridger & Birns, 1968), but the motor activity associated with these events cannot all be described as nonspecific motor activity. The human infant is born with a large repertoire of reflexes. A reflex is an unlearned response that involves a partial reaction of an organism to a specific, eliciting stimulus. It is an involuntary, automatic response that is localized and

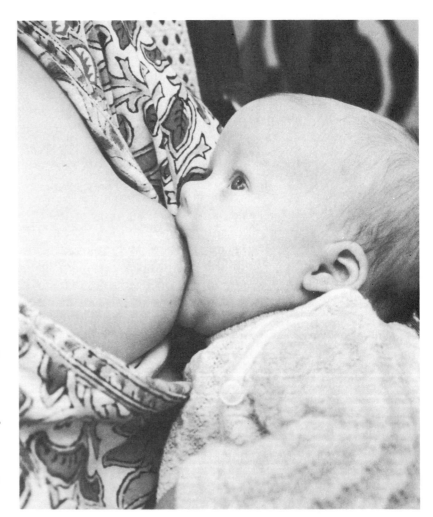

Newborn nursing. The sucking reflex is one of the few neonatal reflexes that has an immediate survival value for the infant. Beyond providing the means for obtaining nourishment, this reflex establishes the first of many bonds between infant and mother.

(Photo copyright © 1979 by Erika Stone/Peter Arnold, Inc.)

discrete in nature. Under ordinary circumstances, specific reflexes are elicited only by stimulation of a specific sensory surface and will not occur in the absence of such stimulation. A partial list of neonatal reflexes is presented in Table 5-1.

Some neonatal reflexes, such as rooting and sucking, clearly have immediate survival value for the infant. These reflexes and others disappear as reflexive responses gradually come under voluntary control and become operant behaviors. The survival value of many neonatal reflexes is less obvious because the usefulness of their selection has become obscured among the vestigial remains of evolution. Neonatal reflexes such as the Moro (Figure 5-1), tonic neck (Figure 5-2), palmar, and plantar reflexes, which have lost their original function in humans, can be seen as phylogenetically old reflexes of high survival value in infrahuman organisms.

Most neonatal reflexes have voluntary, learned counterparts whose components become integrated and organized in the ontogenesis of motor behavior. The developmental trend of motor behavior is a continuous phenomenon whose origins can be traced to the neonatal reflexes, the building blocks of later motor behavior. The expression of increasing motor efficiency and skill proceeds as a function of increasing neuromuscular maturation, experience, and learning. But first, the neonatal motor movements must be released from the restrictions of reflexive responses. Under these conditions, nonspecific learning and experience are maximally effective. The normal disappearance of neonatal reflexes is an approximate index of maturational velocity. The persistence of reflexes beyond the normal range of expectancy may be a pathological sign of CNS defects or neurological dysfunction (Pieper, 1963).

To identify the antecedents of a behavioral system is a difficult task. Although one cannot state with certainty that a particular neonatal response represents the precursor to a later one because it is similar or precedes it in time, we can make empirical and logical arguments for its etiological significance. Neonatal reflexes and their operant motor equivalents are separated by time, maturation, and environmental influences, all of which serve to obscure the question of response equivalence or independence. We learned in Chapter Four that early studies failed to demonstrate any effects of practice or restriction on motor development. This failure was largely due to

Table 5-1
Neonatal Reflexes

REFLEX	ELICITING STIMULUS	RESPONSE	APPROXIMATE COURSE OF DEVELOPMENT
Moro	Loud sound, loss of support, sudden movement	Extension of forearms and fingers followed by return to chest	Disappears within 3 months
Tonic neck reflex	Stretching of neck muscles	Ipsilateral extension of limbs, contralateral limb flexion	Disappears within 6 months
Palmar	Pressure against palm	Grasping	Disappears within 4–6 months
Plantar	Pressure to balls of feet	Flexion of toes (toe grasping)	Disappears within 10 months
Walking	Upright position and feet touching level surface	Walking movements	Disappears within 2 months
Righting of head and body	Head or leg turning	Trunk or head movement in the same direction	Disappears within 1 year
Withdrawal	Painful stimulus	Limb withdrawal	Permanent
Rooting	Perioral stimulation	Head movement toward stimulus	Disappears within 4–6 months
Sucking	Object inserted into mouth	Sucking	Disappears within 4–6 months
Tendon	Tendon taps	Tendon jerks or limb extension	Permanent
Crawling	Prone position and pressure applied alternately to soles of feet	Crawling pattern	Disappears within 4 months
Swimming	Placed in water with head supported	Swimming movements	Disappears within 5 months
Climbing	Held in horizontal position	Climbing movements	Disappears within 6 months

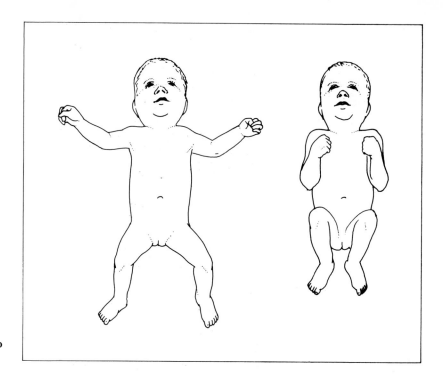

Figure 5-1
The two stages of the Moro
reflex.

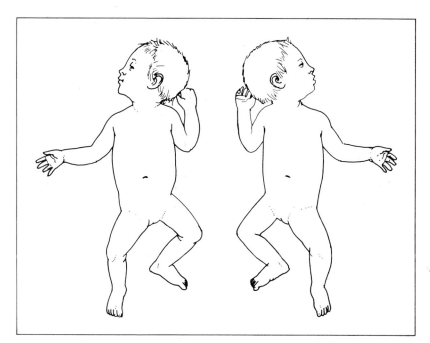

Figure 5-2
The tonic neck reflex
(TNR) in infants.

A hospital pediatrician examining a newborn and grading his reflexes (Apgar score). Since *in utero* checks of reflexes are impracticable, testing reflexes at birth provides some immediate knowledge of the course of the infant's development in the womb. If the child registers the expected reflexes, the probability is that normal development has occurred. Missing reflexes may signal abnormalities or deficiencies in development. In either case, these tests provide useful data for determining the sort of environment that can maximize the infant's potential.

(Photo by Jim Harrison/ Stock, Boston.)

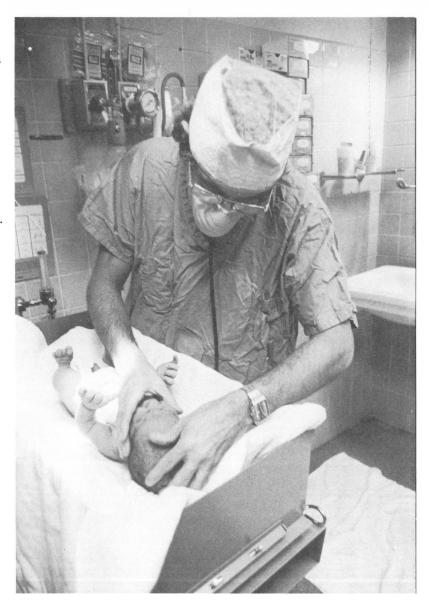

the use of nonspecific procedures and the indiscriminate selection of behaviors, including early behaviors possibly not critically related to later target behaviors. More recent studies of accelerated motor development, relying on specific manipulations of specific response systems, indicate an antecedent relationship between neonatal reflexes and subsequent motor development. Aside from these findings, we may question the evolution of motor reflexes in such large numbers and diversity if they do not play some role in later development, even a diminished one at the human level. The continuity seems apparent. It is the mechanisms and the laws of organization and control which are elusive.

THE DEVELOPMENT OF MOTOR COMPETENCE

The description of motor development in infants and children is well documented in a number of normative and analytical studies and reviews (Ames, 1937; Appleton, Clifton, & Goldberg, 1975; Cratty, 1970; Dennis, 1934; Kessen, Haith, & Salapatek, 1970; McGraw, 1943; Shirley, 1931; Stoddard & Wellman, 1934). Therefore, our discussion of the development of motor competence will cover only the general principles that seem to describe the ontogenesis of gross motor activities and skills.

Developmental Trends in Gross Motor Development

In the past, the study of motor development commanded considerable interest, and a vast amount of normative data was collected. This led to the construction of schedules of development, with which we can assess the pattern of infant growth and progress. Items from infant developmental schedules have also been utilized in scales of infant intelligence, which attempt to assess the current status of an infant's sensorimotor development and abilities. Developmental schedules, and their clinical application, derive from common observations suggesting that motor development follows characteristic and predictable patterns. From repeated observations of the apparently invariant nature of motor development, certain principles of motor development were formulated (Gesell, 1954; Irwin, 1930; McGraw, 1943; Shirley, 1931, 1932). Several of these principles were based on the embryological findings of Coghill described in Chapter Three. The patterns of motor development were then defined as developmental trends, which are claimed by many as being universal characteristics, independent of cultural or child-rearing practices. Five such trends are now widely cited in textbooks and generally accepted as descriptions of gross motor development in normal infants:

1 *The sequential nature of motor development.* Infants display differential rates of maturation and learning, and there may be considerable variance in the ages at which motor abilities appear, but the serial phases in motor development appear to be predictable. Motor development seems to follow a sequence of events related to neuromuscular maturation, general CNS maturation, and the organization of control functions by the brain. Thus, we see gross motor development progress from the inert prone position, to limb movements, rolling, sitting, crawling, creeping, standing, and walking (Figures 5-3). Although once a matter of contention, it now seems relatively clear that these sequential characteristics are a continuous, gradual series of events rather than discrete, discontinuous phenomena.

2 *The cephalocaudal progression.* The principle of a cephalocaudal trend in motor development states that the organization and control of motor activities appear first in the head region and spread downwards toward the feet. Control of head and eye movements precedes arm and hand control, which in turn precede leg and foot control.

3 *The proximodistal progression.* Related to the cephalocaudal trend is the principle that motor abilities emerge and develop first in structures nearest to the axis of the body, spreading outward to the extremities. Control of upper arm and leg movements develops earlier than that of lower arm and leg movements (Figure 5-4).

4 *Mass to specific activity.* The observation that infant motor development proceeds from a general, diffuse motor activity pattern to specific, discrete movements is often described as a generalization or principle of gross motor development. There are, however, some difficulties with the mass-to-specific trend and its generality. This principle is an active remnant of the Coghillian sequence described in Chapter Three. Its utility as a principle of prenatal development has already been critically discussed and evaluated. For the same reasons, this notion has serious weaknesses when applied to the postnatal organism (McGraw, 1935). We have seen that the newborn infant has a large number of discrete reflexes, some quite specific and localized in nature, which cannot be considered mass activity. Both mass and specific activity are present concurrently, and

Figure 5-3
Fourteen development stages in prone progression. The median age of attainment of each stage by 20 infants is given in parentheses. *A.* One knee and thigh forward beside the body (28 weeks). *B.* Knee and thigh forward, inner side of foot contacting the floor (28 weeks). *C.* Pivoting (29 weeks). *D.* Inferior low creep position (30 weeks). *E.* Low creep position (32 weeks). *F.* Crawling (34 weeks). *G.* High creep position (36 weeks). *H.* Retrogression (36 weeks). *I.* Rocking (36 weeks). *J.* Creep-crawling (36 weeks). *K.* Creeping on hands and knees (40 weeks). *L.* Creeping near step with one foot (42 weeks). *M.* Creeping step with one foot (45 weeks). *N.* Quadrupedal progression: creeping on hands and feet (49 weeks).

(From Ames, 1937.)

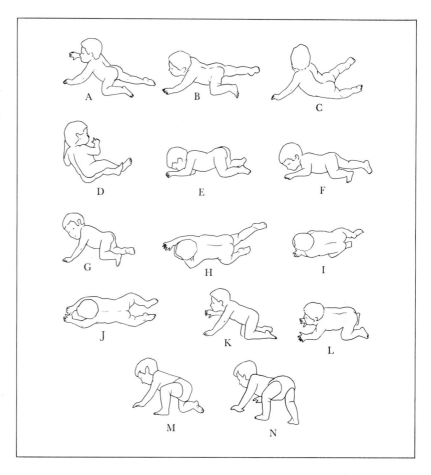

motor progression may be seen to develop from mass to specific and/or vice versa, depending on the response system. **5** *Large to small muscle progression.* This principle is related to the notion of mass to specific activity and describes motor development as progressing from control of large muscles to control of small muscles. That is, fine motor movements develop only after gross motor control. While this generalization seems reasonable, there may be exceptions to the order of appearance in some motor items such as visual-motor responses and hand and finger movements.

In summary, some "principles" of motor development may

be loose generalities that do not withstand close scrutiny. The cephalocaudal progression is seen by some to be the strongest principle of motor development (Cratty, 1970). Cratty (1970) offers empirical challenges to some of the most often cited principles of motor development, stating that under certain conditions they may be true some of the time and for certain response systems. We may invoke the same argument about the sequential nature of motor development.

It is difficult to deny the serial nature of motor development and the inherent aspects of its emergence. Sequentiality, however, does not necessarily make a case for invariance or preprogramming of the motor sequence. Commonality of motor phenomena may also result from commonality in child-rearing practices. Expectations of infant capabilities are so firmly embedded in every culture that deviations from cultural norms and practices are rare. The degree to which infants are given common experiences and opportunities may contribute to the similarities seen in infant motor development.

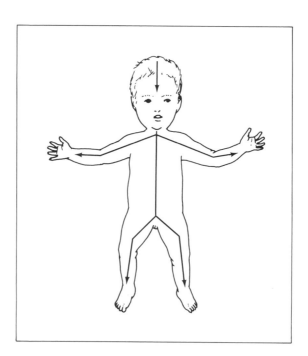

Figure 5-4
Cephalocaudal and proximodistal directions of development.

Learning theory has not yet provided an adequate account of motor development. On the other hand, it has not yet been demonstrated that motor development, as we know it, can occur in the absence of environmental events. Current research continues to be contradictory. For example, Pikler (1968, 1972) has reported that direct help with, and encouragement of, motor activity is not required for basic motor development through the first 2 years of life. Pikler's observations of large numbers of "taught" versus "untaught" infants have led her to believe that uninstructed children are more skilled, courageous, and less accident-prone than those who have been subjected to training experiences. These findings are inconsistent with those of Freedman and Cannady (1971), who studied delayed emergence of prone locomotion in seven infants. Although Freedman and Cannady found the expected pattern of crawling behavior, they reported that environmentally deprived children tended to begin forward locomotion before they were able to lift their abdomens. These investigators suggest that the emergence of typical patterns of prone progression is partially dependent upon adequate levels of early stimulation. The importance of visual experience and feedback for motor development is reported by Adelson and Fraiberg (1974). Gross motor activity and locomotion were delayed in congenitally blind infants despite normal maturation rates and the appearance of initial postural behaviors.

The task of clarifying the sequential aspects of motor development is formidable. Factors that clearly play a complex role in such development include environmental influences, experience, and motivation. All of these factors interact with motor development capable of emerging under extreme ranges of environmental conditions.

THE QUESTION OF DIFFERENTIAL MOTOR DEVELOPMENT

Most differential motor development falls within the age ranges described by normative tables of development. When such differences are within normal variability limits, they are not considered significant. Variations from the median age of appearance on motor items can be accounted for by

Table 5-2
Frankenburg & Dodds Norms for Gross Motor Behavior. The Ages are Presented by Percent of Population Passing the Item.

GROS MOTOR ITEM	PERCENT OF POPULATION PASSING BY AGE			
	25%	50%	75%	90%
Prone, lifts head				0.7 mo.
Prone, head up 45 degrees			1.9 mo.	2.6 mo.
Prone, head up 90 degrees	1.3 mo.	2.2 mo.	2.6 mo.	3.2 mo.
Prone, chest up, arm support	2.0 mo.	3.0 mo.	3.5 mo.	4.3 mo.
Sits—head steady	1.5 mo.	2.9 mo.	3.6 mo.	4.2 mo.
Rolls over	2.3 mo.	2.8 mo.	3.8 mo.	4.7 mo.
Bears some weight on legs	3.4 mo.	4.2 mo.	5.0 mo.	6.3 mo.
Pulls to sit, no head lag	3.0 mo.	4.2 mo.	5.2 mo.	7.7 mo.
Sits without support	4.8 mo.	5.5 mo.	6.5 mo.	7.8 mo.
Stands holding on	5.0 mo.	5.8 mo.	8.5 mo.	10.0 mo.
Pulls self to stand	6.0 mo.	7.6 mo.	9.5 mo.	10.0 mo.
Gets to sitting	6.1 mo.	7.6 mo.	9.3 mo.	11.0 mo.
Stands momentarily	9.1 mo.	9.8 mo.	12.1 mo.	13.0 mo.
Walks holding on furniture	7.3 mo.	9.2 mo.	10.2 mo.	12.7 mo.
Stands alone well	9.8 mo.	11.5 mo.	13.3 mo.	13.9 mo.
Stoops and recovers	10.4 mo.	11.6 mo.	13.2 mo.	14.3 mo.
Walks well	11.3 mo.	12.1 mo.	13.5 mo.	14.3 mo.
Walks backwards	12.4 mo.	14.3 mo.	18.2 mo.	21.5 mo.
Walks up steps	14.0 mo.	17.0 mo.	21.0 mo.	22.0 mo.
Kicks ball forward	15.0 mo.	20.0 mo.	22.3 mo.	2.0 yr.
Throws ball overhand	14.9 mo.	19.8 mo.	22.8 mo.	2.6 yr.
Balances on 1 foot 1 second	21.7 mo.	2.5 yr.	3.0 yr.	3.2 yr.
Jumps in place	20.5 mo.	22.3 mo.	2.5 yr.	3.0 yr.
Pedals trike	21.0 mo.	23.9 mo.	2.8 yr.	3.0 yr.
Broad jump	2.0 yr.	2.8 yr.	3.0 yr.	3.2 yr.
Balances on 1 foot 5 seconds	2.6 yr.	3.2 yr.	3.9 yr.	4.3 yr.
Balances on 1 foot 10 seconds	3.0 yr.	4.5 yr.	5.0 yr.	5.9 yr.
Hops on 1 foot	3.0 yr.	3.4 yr.	4.0 yr.	4.9 yr.
Catches bounced ball	3.5 yr.	3.9 yr.	4.9 yr.	5.5 yr.
Heel-to-toe walk	3.3 yr.	3.6 yr.	4.2 yr.	5.0 yr.
Backward heel-toe	3.9 yr.	4.7 yr.	5.6 yr.	6.3 yr.

(From Frankenburg & Dodds, 1967.)

differences in maturation rates, experience, environmental stimulation, and sociocultural factors. Occasionally we find examples of infant precocity in which motor development, or development in general, appears much earlier than would be predicted by developmental schedules. Such accelerated rates are observed in less than 25% of infants within a particular age-group. An infant who begins walking independently at 9 months of age is certainly well beyond the expected lower age limits for locomotion, displaying a motor ability seen in probably less than 5% of all 9-month-old infants. Precocious development of this degree of magnitude is difficult to explain.

To a degree, all infants today show some degree of precocity relative to the normative data of 40 years ago. If one compares the norms published by Frankenburg and Dodds (1967) with those of McGraw and Shirley, it can be seen that infants today show more rapid gross motor development (Table 5-2). This superiority in terms of age of appearance is doubtless due to nutritional, experiential, and child-rearing factors rather than any changes in basic maturational phenomena.

If we consider differential gross motor development among groups of infants distinguished by sex, race, social class, and intelligence, we find that a great deal of research has been conducted in the search for group differences. To establish group differences and the relative characteristics of groups, we must demonstrate that there are differences in the mean or median age of appearance in behavior and also show that the group distributions do not overlap to any significant extent. It may be common to find both statistically significant mean differences between groups and extensive overlapping of scores, such that within-group variability is greater than between-group variability (Figure 5-5). The significant difference between the groups shown in Figure 5-5 does not demonstrate a *group* differential in motor development, since most members of Group 2 reach or exceed the mean of Group 1. Nearly all of the individuals in both groups fall within the same range of scores. The individual differences within each of the groups are so large, compared to the between-group means, that group membership does not really provide much information about any given individual's motor development.

Sex Differences

By definition, sex differences in behavior are those that stem

Figure 5-5
Fictitious data on motor development in two groups of
infants.

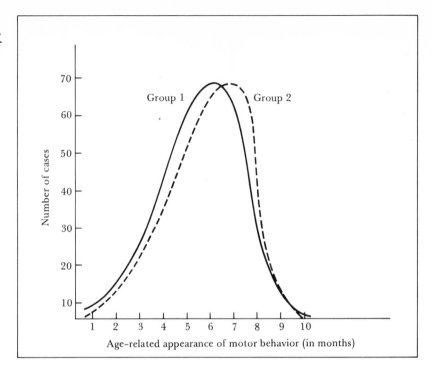

from hereditary and biological factors. If we can show that differential patterns of behavior result from biological differences between the sexes and are not a function of sexual stereotypes, sex roles, cultural expectations and pressures, motivation, or differential opportunities for learning, then we have identified true sex differences. When these differential patterns of behavior are controlled for, no significant sex differences are reported in gross motor development during the first few years of life (Maccoby & Jacklin, 1974).

Sex differences in gross body coordination and in motor activities involving strength and endurance begin to appear at approximately 5 years of age (Cratty, 1970). At 5, boys start to surpass girls in such activities as running, throwing, and jumping, partly due to a true sex difference in muscular development, strength, and body size. At this same age, girls begin to excel in rhythmic jumping, catching, and manual dexterity (Cratty, 1970). Such differences continue to be confounded with sociocultural expectations and pressures. Maccoby and Jacklin (1974), for example, report that parents consistently encourage gross motor behavior more often in sons than in daughters, a differential treatment pattern that probably persists through childhood.

Female infants show accelerated physical and skeletal development, dentition, and onset of puberty compared to males, but these sex differences do not result in acceleration of gross motor development. The normative data are the same for boys and girls. Also, the sex difference in accelerated maturation,

Young children in an exercise class. Sex differences do not seem to have any significant effect on motor development in infants. After about 5 years of age, however, some motor differences do appear: boys tend to excel in gross motor activities, such as running, while girls tend to excel in activities requiring pedal and manual dexterity, such as dancing. It is difficult to determine whether or not these differences are genuinely related to sex differences: they may simply reflect the prevailing culturally reinforced behaviors in children.

(Photo copyright © 1975 by Michael Philip Manheim/Photo Researchers, Inc.)

present at birth, is unlikely to proceed at uniform rates throughout the early years of development or to exert any observable, significant influence on early motor development. Kagan (1971) reports no major sex differences in activity or postures at 4, 8, or 13 months of age. Kagan also cites evidence of differential CNS maturation favoring girls, but goes on to state that these data are only suggestive and that "they do not even come close to proving that there are sex differences in CNS organization" (p. 182–183). Maccoby and Jacklin (1974) come to the same conclusion in their review of the literature on infant activity. In short, it appears that the relationship between physical and behavioral development is very complex and indirect, and sex differences are not a predominant influence.

Race Differences

Accelerated gross motor development in American black infants has been reported by Knobloch and Pasamanick (1953) and Williams and Scott (1953). Both studies concluded that observed motor superiority in black infants was attributable to greater permissiveness in infant rearing practices among blacks relative to white families. Black infants reared under strict conditions scored significantly lower than those reared in permissive homes, and closer to white norms (Williams & Scott, 1953). When such environmental factors are controlled, there is no convincing evidence of racial differences between black and white infants.

The question of motor precocity in African infants has been thoroughly reviewed by Warren (1972). In his critical analysis of the research on African infant motor development, Warren concludes that there is no convincing data for motor precocity in the newborn African infant. Further, Warren states that a pattern of developmental precocity or acceleration in motor development among African infants has not been scientifically demonstrated under controlled conditions. Thus, there is no reliable basis for a racial–genetic hypothesis about any observed differences in motor development among African infants. Instead, differences appear to be a function of cultural practices and rearing patterns. African infants reared under "Western" practices have been found to be less motorically advanced than those reared under African patterns. Warren did find that motor differences tend to appear in African infants as a function of social class. Infants from homes of low social level generally show initially advanced motor development compared to infants from higher social classes. Warren points out that in the absence of more stringent research designs, it is not possible to identify or explain differences in motor development among African infants.

Social Class, Intelligence, and Motor Development

Differences in motor development can be affected by social factors, as well as any number of other environmental factors. However, group differentials in gross motor development have not consistently been reported. Instead, one finds motor precocity or retardation occurring across social classes as a function of specific rearing practices or common stimulation procedures (Williams & Scott, 1953; Warren, 1972). As we learned in Chapter One, social class is a carrier variable and not a specifiable independent variable. Therefore, social class membership has no clear antecedent significance. There is no evidence of differences in gross motor development among infants of normal intelligence. Precocity or mild retardation in motor development has little implication for intelligence and is a poor predictor for later intelligence (McCall, Hogarty, & Hurlburt, 1972). Although Terman (1925) has reported some acceleration of motor development in gifted children, this is not a consistent finding. Parental recognition of intellectual precocity may result in an increase in general stimulation, training, and opportunity. At this time, there is little evidence of a direct, parallel relationship between intellectual status and motor development.

THE DEVELOPMENT OF PREHENSION

Prehension is a sensorimotor response that involves reaching for and grasping an object. It is a sensorimotor act because it requires the infant to coordinate visual perception, arm movement, and grasping in an integrated, controlled response pattern. Prehension, or prehensile behavior, is more than the simple combination of reaching and grasping abilities seen in the neonate. Reaching and spontaneous arm movements in the neonate and young infant are uncontrolled motor

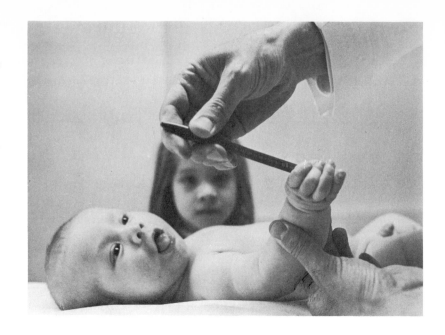

Prehension: A pediatrician tests a baby's grasping reflex. The ability to grasp objects voluntarily requires sensory, cognitive, and motor development and integration. As such, a baby's prehensile ability gives the physician significant feedback on the infant's overall development.

(Photo copyright © 1975 by Herb Levart/Photo Researchers, Inc.)

acts with little or no sensory or cognitive components. In addition, such movements are not accompanied by grasping, so reaching and grasping may occur quite independently of each other. The grasping reflex is an isolated, involuntary response that occurs when pressure is applied to the palm of the hand. Like initial arm movements and reaching, there are no sensory or cognitive functions or events that are necessary for the grasping reflex or that become integrated with it.

Prehension, on the other hand, is visually controlled and directed reaching to grasp an object. Note that we are now describing an act that is under voluntary control. Prehension is an intentional, purposeful response that requires the organization of such sensory–cognitive events as depth perception, an awareness of arm and hand location in space (kinesthesis), tactile stimulation, and voluntary grasping of the object, all under sustained attentional control. Although sucking and visual following are among the first acts that infants bring under voluntary control, the development of prehension is the first voluntary behavior that enables the infant to interact actively and meaningfully with its environment.

Prior to the emergence of prehension, the infant is largely restricted to passively experiencing the environment. It has little or no ability to manipulate the environment directly. The emergence of prehensile ability has major developmental implications for subsequent sensorimotor and cognitive development (Bruner, 1973). A great deal of significance has been attached to human prehensile skills. For instance, prehension has been described as the evolutionary development that enabled humans to invent and use tools (Fishbein, 1976). Because it is one of the earliest sensorimotor functions to emerge in the infant, prehension is of considerable significance in general sensorimotor development (Appleton et al., 1975; Fishbein, 1976; Bower, 1974). Piaget (1952) has described prehension and other early sensorimotor functions as the origins of intelligence and cognitive development. Prehensile behavior is viewed by Bower (1974) as a convenient response for analyzing various models and theories of development. In short, behavioral competence depends on sensorimotor development in general and, to a large extent, on prehension specifically. Therefore, many researchers have carried out extensive investigations of these behaviors (Appleton et al., 1975).

The Normative Sequence in Prehension

The classical research on prehensile development is represented by the normative work of Gesell (Knobloch & Pasamanick, 1974), Halverson (1931, 1932), and McGraw (1943). These studies provide detailed analyses of the ontogeny of prehension within the prevailing framework of the maturation hypothesis. For a contemporary description of the normative sequence in prehension, see the studies of White and collaborators (White, 1971) and of Bower (1974). These recent studies are much more rigorous and controlled in their design and also provide data more characteristic of infants today. White's goal was to obtain current information on prehension that would allow for sensitive and accurate measurement scales. Such information would then provide a basis for studying the role of environmental factors on prehensile development. White used 34 physically normal infants born and reared in an institution. Infants were observed and tested for reaching and prehension at weekly intervals. The stimulus object was a brightly colored paper party toy that was presented to each infant at different positions (left side, right side, and midline to the face), and at a distance of 5 inches from the infant's eyes. Observations were conducted over the first 6 months of life and are summarized in 2-week intervals (White, 1971).

4–6 weeks: The infant lies in the tonic neck reflex (TNR) position, engaging only in minimal visual pursuit. The infant cannot focus on visual stimuli closer than 7 inches, and the target stimulus fails to elicit attention.

6–8 weeks: TNR usually present, and sustained visual fixation of 5–10 seconds occurs only on the side of the favored TNR.

8–10 weeks: TNR present but the head only half turned to the side. Visual pursuit of stimulus target can be elicited and swiping at the target occurs with the near hand on the favored TNR position. The hand remains fisted.

10–12 weeks: TNR less frequent, with the head near the midline position. Sustained hand regard is observed. The stimulus elicits immediate fixation accompanied by a decrease in activity. Swiping or unilateral hand raising to within 1 inch of the stimulus is observed.

12–14 weeks: TNR is rarely observed. Frequent bilateral arm activity and hand regard are seen. Side presentations of stimulus result in one or both hands raised toward stimulus and alternating glances from the stimulus to the hand.

14–16 weeks: TNR is absent. Hand clasping over the midline with visual pursuit of hands is common. Response to stimulus is similar to that of 12–14 weeks, but combined with turning of the torso toward the stimulus.

16–18 weeks: Sustained hand regard decreases in frequency while general activity increases. Bilateral arm and hand movements are the common responses to the stimulus, along with torso orientation. Fumbling and incomplete grasping are seen when the stimulus is touched. Hand opening may be seen.

18–20 weeks: Top level reaching to stimulus occurs as one hand is lifted out of the visual field to the stimulus. The hand opens as the infant anticipates contact with the stimulus, culminating in successful grasping. Prehension skills rapidly improve over the next few weeks.

White (1971) has recorded an orderly, invariant sequence in

prehensile development and has described these events as a gradual integration of various independent sensorimotor systems into a coordinated response system. The pattern of ontogeny is similar to that described by Piaget (1952). White's analysis of prehensile development places great importance on the emergence of swiping as a key factor in successful prehension, along with other environmental–experiential events. Bower (1974), in his analysis of White's model of development, has summarized White's sequence (p. 152).

Discovery of the hand ⟶ Hand regard
Object in the visual field ⟶ Swiping
Object contact ⟵ ⟶ Tactually elicited hand opening and closing
Prehension

White's description of prehensile development is one of neuromuscular and sensorimotor maturation with strong components of learning. For the first time, the infant is able to explore and understand its immediate environment, and this new ability enables it to learn by intentionally manipulating and modifying that environment. The information now available to the infant is dramatically increased and will play a significant role in the development of general behavioral competence.

Environmental Influences on Prehensile Development

Having constructed a model of prehensile development based on his normative sequence, White (1971) attempted to accelerate the appearance of prehension in his subjects. An experimental group of infants was given 20 minutes of extra daily handling between the ages of 6 days and 30 days. Handling consisted of holding the infant upright and rocking continuously in a rocking chair. A second experimental group was given "massive enrichment" involving 20 minutes of extra daily handling from 6 to 36 days of age, placing in the prone position 45 minutes a day from 37 to 124 days of age, and enriched visual stimulation via a multicolored stabile suspended over the crib from 37 to 124 days of age. A third experimental group received modified enrichment. In this condition, two pacifiers were attached to red and white discs mounted on the crib rails 6 to 7 inches away from the infants' eyes. This modification was introduced between 37 and 68 days of age. The control group received only the minimal handling and care characteristic of normal hospital and institutional procedures.

No differences in prehensile development were found between the controls and handled infants. On the other hand, the massive enrichment group developed prehension 45 days earlier than controls (98 days versus 143 days). However, the onset of hand regard in the massive enrichment group was delayed by approximately 12 days and did not appear until after the onset of swiping. Under modified enrichment, infants showed the most rapid acceleration in prehensile development at 89 days. In both of these experimental groups, top level reaching occurred before tactually elicited hand closing. These sequential descriptions do not agree with White's model of the normative sequence in prehensile development. Nevertheless, he has provided clear evidence of the plasticity of prehensile development and of the importance of environmental stimulation in the development of prehension.

Bower (1974) has critically reviewed the data on prehensile development and disagrees with the normative sequence described by White. Bower believes that hand regard originally results from increasing attentional capacity, and that it disappears when the infant becomes able to attend simultaneously to both hand and object. Rather than being a precursor to swiping, Bower views hand regard as an epiphenomenon—an accidental residual of other events and processes. Bower states that growing attention span, extinction of visually elicited grasping, and reinforcement of tactually elicited grasping can account for prehensile development.

PERCEPTUAL DEVELOPMENT

Human infants are not born with the information and capacities they need to immediately extract and process complex stimulus events and meaning from the environment. Infants must learn to use their sensory abilities to receive, recognize, and selectively respond to stimuli. They do so by refining these skills through exposure to, and experience with, incoming stimuli. These processes lead to perceptual development. Perception becomes more selective as the infant learns to discriminate among various stimuli and its responses to them.

For Gibson (1969), perception is the ability to extract information selectively from the environment. Thus, developmental changes in this ability amount to increasing efficiency in obtaining useful information from the environment. Gibson describes perceptual development and learning as "adaptive modification of perception," an active process of exploring and searching. The infant does not merely experience its world passively. It seeks stimulation and information in the absence of external reinforcement and is prepared to respond to stimuli, as we saw in our discussion of the orienting reflex and habituation. Despite its motoric helplessness, the newborn infant is able to receive and process some sensory experiences. If we view perception as the acquisition of knowledge from a structured environment, then the neonate's basic capacities for orienting and attending to stimulus events become the foundations for the ontogeny of perception and perceptual learning. As we shall see, newborn infants are able to perceive and discriminate certain stimuli. This has led Fantz (1967) to comment that "the acquisition of knowledge about the environment begins at the first look" (p. 218).

Developmental psychologists have been particularly interested in visual perception in infants and young children, and visual development has been investigated more than any other sensory system. There are several reasons for this preoccupation with visual perceptual development. Vision is the dominant sensory system in humans and the major modality for interacting with the environment. The infant's initial exploration of the environment is through vision. Early visual perceptual development plays a major role in sensorimotor development and in the later development of complex cognitive, emotional, and social behavior patterns. Visual perceptual development also provides a pathway for understanding cognitive development and CNS maturation. Finally, vision is the easiest sensory system to study. As a result, most of what we know about perception derives from visual research. Our discussion of perceptual development will, therefore, be restricted to events and processes in visual perception. We will emphasize the ontogeny of visual perception in neonates and infants.

Historical Perspective The question of perception and perceptual development has its roots in classical philosophical thought. Attempts to explain perception can be traced to the seventeenth century, when the British empiricists struggled with the problem of the origins of human knowledge. That is, how do we come to know the world and its structure? How are we able to recognize and understand space, objects, and their properties and relationships? Clearly these are problems of perception, perceptual learning, and perceptual development, but they originated as philosophical, not psychological, concerns. British empiricists such as Locke, Hobbes, and Berkeley argued that the source of human knowledge (perception) is experience, and that we experience the world only through our senses. Knowledge and understanding arise as separate sensory experiences and become associated with each other.

John Locke, the founder of systematic empiricism, proposed that the mind at birth is a *tabula rasa,* or blank slate, and that all knowledge is furnished through experience alone. Perceptions are conveyed to the mind by our senses and then we perceive the operation of our minds in associating ideas from the various senses. William Molyneux, a seventeenth century Irish philosopher, presented the following problem to Locke: Suppose a person, blind from birth, is taught to discriminate a sphere from a cube by touch. If vision is suddenly given to this person, will he be able to identify the cube and the sphere by sight alone, without touching them? In his *Essay Concerning Human Understanding,* written in 1690, Locke answered that the blind person would be unable to identify the objects because he lacked the necessary visual experience. Modern laboratory and clinical data support Locke's conclusions.

The doctrine of psychological empiricism was challenged early in the eighteenth century by the nativists, led by the German philosopher Immanuel Kant. Nativism held that our knowledge and ideas of the world and space were innate, divinely endowed, and inherent in our original biological constitution as humans. Therefore it is the nature of human structure that provides for immediate knowledge and perception of the world. While experience was recognized as producing alterations in knowledge, the "essence" of human nature prevailed.

The nativism–empiricism controversy regarding the origin of knowledge became a major epistemological issue between the seventeenth and nineteenth centuries, before giving way to the nature–nurture controversy in the twentieth century. By this time, the problem had been assumed and perpetuated by psychologists. The controversy continues today, less heated perhaps, but no less elusive in its solution nor less questionable in utility or meaningfulness. Boring (1942) identifies modern nativists and empiricists as gestalt psychologists and behaviorists, respectively. More detailed discussion of classical theories in perception can be found in Allport (1955), Boring (1942), Gibson (1969), and Lowry (1971).

A contemporary variation of the nativism–empiricism controversy may be seen in the Gibson and Gibson (1955a, 1955b) and Postman (1955) perceptual learning controversy, although the participants may not agree with this comparison. The Gibsons' view of perceptual learning has been described as differentiation and that of Postman as enrichment. According to Gibson and Gibson, we may innately possess all the perceptual capacities and skills necessary for perceptual competence, but we must learn to differentiate stimuli in order to attain some level of required competence. Postman, on the other hand, views perceptual learning as beginning with John Locke's blank slate; through experience and learning of S–R associations we enrich our perceptual competence. The differentiation approach to perceptual learning is based on learning specific responses to specific stimuli; the enrichment approach involves learning to associate stimuli and responses. Clement (1978) refers to this perceptual learning controversy as "prospecting versus Croesian riches." For Clement, the enrichment procedure is analogous to a prospector gradually finding more and more perceptual "valuables," while the differentiation approach sees the newborn infant as inheriting all possible wealth and having to "sort out the embarassing largess into meaningful and coherent chunks."

Perceptual development and perceptual learning attracted little interest among developmental psychologists in the early decades of the twentieth centruy. Perception was considered to be a component of general sensorimotor development and was predominantly viewed within the empiricist framework of experience and association of sensory and motor systems. The major exception to the empiricist trend was Arnold Gesell. As we might predict from our previous discussion of Gesell, he emphasized maturational processes in the visual development of children. Included in his longitudinal observations and descriptions of infant and child development at Yale University were his normative reports of visual (actually visual–motor) behavior and development (Gesell et al., 1949). Gesell did not become involved in the polemics of perceptual theories and controversies since he was a committed maturationist interested in the normative stages of development. The following statement from Gesell (1950) summarizes his position on visual development:

The development of vision in the individual child is extremely complex, because this development compresses into a short time the countless stages of evolution which brought vision to its present advanced state in the human species. The child's patterns of visual behavior go through progressive stages of maturity correlated with his changing postural control, his manual coordinations, his intelligence, and even his personality. Indeed, vision is so completely identified with the whole child that we cannot understand the phenomenon without investigating the whole child. (p. 3)

Intensified interest and activity in human perceptual development began in the 1950s, followed by the appearance of a number of cognitive and S–R theories of perception. Gibson (1969) describes both cognitive and learning theories generally an enrichment theories, but with different assumptions about the supplemental processes contributing to perceptual development.

Cognitive theories emphasize various cognitive processes such as inferences, hypotheses, or problem-solving as models of perceptual development. Learning theories, on the other hand, emphasize associative responses as the basic process in perceptual development. In contrast is Gibson's (1969) differentiation theory. Gibson views perceptual development as learning to differentiate stimulus structure by selectively filtering and abstracting available information. The proliferation of theories of perceptual development during the past 25 years has produced many overlapping concepts. Many perceptual theories move into the area of cognitive development, and others resemble information processing, with its blend of perceptual and cognitive activities.

Much of the early research in perceptual development sought to identify and describe the perceptual abilities of infants and children. Piaget's views on perceptual and cognitive development did much to renew interest in perceptual development. In addition, the work of several experimental psychologists and ethologists on the modification of perception in animals began to draw attention. These experimental and ethological investigations on the phylogenesis of perception revealed that the "innate" perceptual characteristics of various animal species could be significantly altered by environmental factors, both physical and social, to which the young organism was exposed (Denenberg, 1972; Gibson, 1969; Newton & Levine, 1968). Strict adherence to either a nativist or empiricist position gave way to the growing recognition that innate and learned factors interact in perceptual development.

With the marked increase in empirical research in this area, the emphasis has shifted. Many researchers now are attempting to discover which ontogenetic processes and events are characteristic of human perceptual development. We will consider some of the classical research describing the perceptual capacities of infants. Then we will look at more recent research efforts, which have revealed some of the ontogenetic events in early perceptual activities. Much of this data does not fit neatly into any particular theoretical framework. Therefore, in our treatment of perceptual development, we will be more concerned with ontogenetic phenomena than with theoretical issues.

THE DEVELOPMENT OF VISUAL PERCEPTION

Perceptual Prerequisites in the Human Infant

What perceptual capacities and abilities does the human infant possess at birth? Is the visual world of the newborn infant similar to that perceived by older children and adults, or is it the "great blooming, buzzing confusion" described by William James (1890)? An absence of perceptual form and organization in the human infant would suggest the absence of visual structures and/or functions required for perception, and the inability to respond differentially to visual stimuli. Hershenson(1967) has reviewed the research on the visual system of the newborn infant to assess the presence of the prerequisites for perception.

Anatomical and functional studies have revealed the structural differentiation of rods and cones in the retinas of 7-month-old human fetuses. Additional neurophysiological studies have demonstrated that both visual systems (photopic and scotopic) are functional at birth. Hershenson also concludes that the functional integrity of some neural pathways between the eye and the cortex suggests some degree of organization of the CNS in the newborn infant. Several studies during the past 20 years have demonstrated that newborn infants have the muscular control and visual apparatus minimally necessary to maintain a retinal image of an object, at least for short durations. Acuity in the newborn visual system is sharp enough for a fair amount of resolution (20/200 in infants under 1 month of age). Hershenson concludes that the evidence indicates the presence of sufficient sensory capacity in the newborn to synthesize a perceptual world, along with the possible potential to perceive form.

Form Perception

When we speak of the perception of form, we are referring to responses to stimuli such as shape, pattern, size, or solidity. One requirement for the demonstration of form perception in infants is that they must respond to an entire stimulus rather than to a stimulus dimension or some simple feature of the stimulus. That is, do infants discriminate between a circle and a square, or do they respond to some dimension or feature of these stimuli, such as curved versus straight lines or angles versus no angles?

Hershenson (1967) describes two procedures that may help solve the problem of isolating the effective stimulus eliciting observed responses in infants. The first procedure is the developmental study of the scansion of forms. This involves the analysis of visual scanning patterns by means of precise measurements of infant ocular behavior. The infant's direction of eye fixations is used to track features of the stimulus that are eliciting and maintaining attention. The second procedure involves the infant's response to pattern characteristics of a stimulus. In this approach, stimuli are presented either singly or in pairs and responses reflecting discrimination, preference, or equivalence of visual patterns are obtained. Analysis of the nature of responses recorded under visual scanning and pattern preference procedures may reveal the extent to which infants perceive form.

Using the visual scanning procedure, Salapatek and Kessen (1966) studied the organization of looking behavior in 10 newborn infants 4 to 7 days of age. Each infant was shown an 8-inch equilateral black triangle at a distance of 9 inches. The ocular orientation of one eye was photographed by using infrared lights placed behind the triangle. This procedure permitted the precise measurement of pupil orientation and an analysis of which parts of the triangle were being scanned. The visual scanning patterns of the infants are shown in Figure 5-6. As you can see, the infants' visual orientation was localized toward the vertices of the triangle. In addition, the scanning pattern is primarily horizontal across this feature of the triangle. Salapatek and Kessen concluded that newborn infants do not respond to or perceive total form, but rather respond to some feature of a stimulus; in this case, an angle.

Subsequent studies by Nelson and Kessen (1969) and Salapatek (1968, 1969) with newborn infants confirm the feature-selection characteristic of newborn looking. Although there appears to be some organization in the visual perception of newborn infants, the response is not to total form but to simple stimulus features. It also seems apparent from these studies that visual scanning in the newborn infant is dispersed more in the horizontal than the vertical dimension of the visual field. This characterizes newborn visual scanning even in the absence of a stimulus in the visual field (Salapatek & Kessen, 1966; Kessen, Salapatek, & Haith, 1972). Bond (1972) suggests that the essentially horizontal nature of newborn scanning may be due to the presence of neurophysiological coding mechanisms specifically "tuned" to such stimuli as contours and angles. Appelle (1972) has made a compelling argument for such neurophysiological mechanisms underlying visual preferences for vertical or horizontal orientations throughout the animal kingdom, from man to octopus.

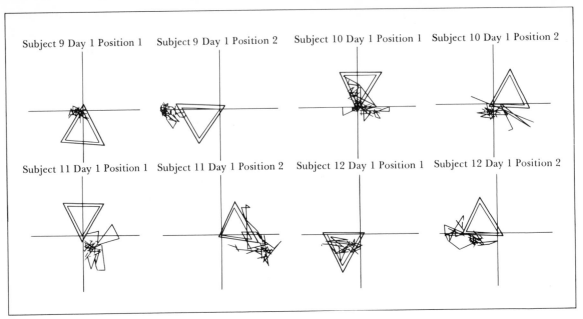

Figure 5-6
Records of ocular orientation for infants in Salapatek and Kessen's experiment. The outer triangle on each record represents the outline of the solid black equilateral triangle, 8 inches to a side, presented to the subject.

(Adapted from Salapatek & Kessen, 1966.)

When older infants between the ages of 4 and 10 weeks are presented with more complex geometric patterns that contain both internal and external contours and angles, they fixate more on the internal features and for longer durations relative to newborns (Salapatek, 1969). Older infants also scan larger portions of the stimulus. Bond (1972) questions whether the apparent shift in attention from external to internal features among older infants is a real one, or simply a function of the maturational capacity to converge both eyes on a single stimulus. Bond points out that the only clear change with age is an increase in the portion of stimulus scanned by infants. Although the data from the visual scanning experiments suggest only partial form perception in newborns, total form perception cannot yet be ruled out. It is possible that total forms may be perceived through passive looking with little eye movement (Bond, 1972).

Pattern Perception

One of the major figures in perceptual research with infants is Robert Fantz. Fantz has concentrated on the infant's response to pattern characteristics in his research on the development of form perception. In one of his early studies with infants, Fantz (1958) examined preferential looking behavior in 30 infants aged 1 to 15 weeks. With the use of a "looking chamber" (Figure 5-7), Fantz randomly presented four pairs of test

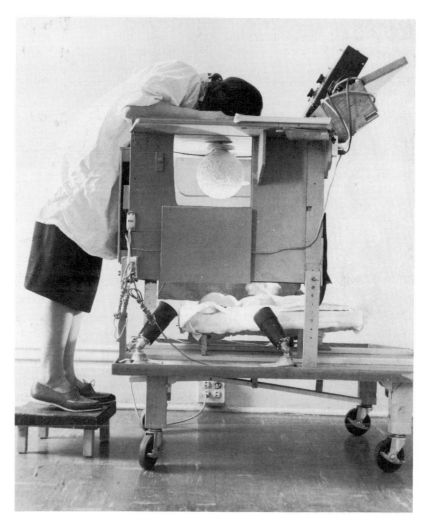

Figure 5-7
Fantz developed this "looking chamber" to test the visual interests of chimpanzee and human infants. Here a human infant lies on a crib in the chamber, looking at objects hung from the ceiling. The observer, watching through a peephole, records the attention given each object.

(From *The Origins of Form Perception* by R. L. Fantz. Copyright © May 1961 by Scientific American, Inc. All rights reserved. Photo courtesy of David Litton.)

Figure 5-8
Interest in form was proven by infant's reactions to various pairs of patterns *(left)* presented together. (The small and large plain squares were used alternately.) The more complex pairs received the most attention, and within each of these pairs differential interest was based on pattern differences. These results are for 22 infants in 10 weekly tests.

(From *The Origins of Form Perception* by R. L. Fantz. Copyright © May 1961 by Scientific American, Inc. All rights reserved.)

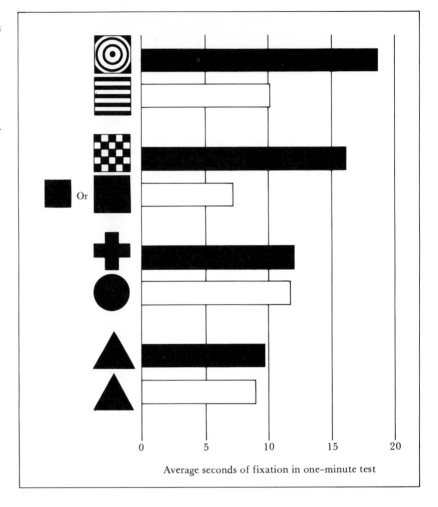

patterns to each infant at weekly intervals. Fantz found significant differences between the total time spent looking at the various pairs, with the more complex pairs receiving preference (Figure 5-8). Differential responding to the patterns appeared at all ages tested, suggesting that visual preferences were not a function of learning. Stirnimann (cited by Fantz, 1961), a Swiss pediatrician, had obtained similar results with newborn infants 1 to 14 days of age. Stirnimann concluded that very young infants prefer to look at patterned stimuli rather than plain ones, and that this represents an elemental

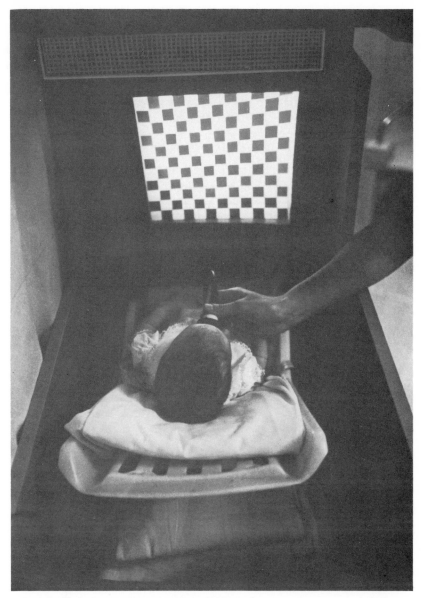

Testing a baby's visual perception. Because humans process more information about the world through their eyes than through any of their other senses, vision is an important key to normal development. From a very early age, babies show a preference for shaded and patterned surfaces over plain ones. This tendency seems to highlight the role of the visual environment in the maturation of the child.

(Photo by Jason Laure, reproduction courtesy of Dr. Sequeland, Boston University.)

capacity for form perception. These data lead to the same conclusion that Fantz derived from visual scanning studies. A number of studies by Fantz and others have verified these original observations that infants prefer to look at patterned stimuli (Bond, 1972).

There are several studies dealing with infants' responses to human faces (Gibson, 1969; Bond, 1972). Young infants respond to human faces as they do to other stimuli on the basis of feature characteristics. There is no evidence that infants under the age of 2 months are able to discriminate the feature arrangement of faces. That is, they show no preferences for looking at organized or scrambled faces (Haber & Hershenson, 1973). Between the ages of 2 and 4 months, some inconclusive data suggest preferences for a normal face (Bond, 1972). At 4 months of age, infants show consistent preferences for faces and are able to discriminate arrangement of facial features.

The pattern of development in infants' responses to faces seems to follow the same trend we have seen for other stimuli. Visual attention is initially directed at relatively simple stimulus characteristics such as contours, angles, and complexity. With increasing maturation and learning capacity, the infant becomes less stimulus bound and more selective in its visual perceptual experiences.

Depth Perception   Spatial perception—the perception of the relative location, size, and distance of objects—is a fundamental process in all visual organisms. A major component of spatial perception is the ability to perceive depth. Depth perception is a form of distance perception, and its development is complexly determined by the development of other perceptual skills. Information about distance and depth is specified by such stimulus information as binocular disparity, motion parallax, motion perspective, and texture gradients (Table 5-3). Information from these stimuli becomes related to the perceived distance of objects and then it is used to determine distance and depth. At least one of these stimuli must be available in order to determine distance.

Table 5-3
Developmental Characteristics of Stimulus Cues for Distance Perception

1.	Binocular disparity	Difference in visual array which occurs between each eye.	Present in some degree in 1-week-old neonates (Bower, Broughton, & Moore, 1970).
2.	Motion Parallax	Apparent movement of objects which occurs when the head or eyes move. Amount of apparent movement is inversely proportional to the distance between observer and object.	Present at approximately 60 days of age (Bower, 1965).
3.	Motion Perspective	General changes in object movement which accompany observer movement.	Present in newborns (Bower, Broughton, & Moore, 1971).
4.	Texture Gradients	Changes in object texture which occur as a function of distance.	Earliest appearance unknown.

The first studies of infant depth perception were conducted by Gibson and Walk (1960), using the visual cliff apparatus shown in Figure 5-9. In a classic series of studies (Walk & Gibson, 1961; Walk, 1966, 1969), they demonstrated that infants are capable of depth perception by the time they reach the crawling stage of development. Gibson and Walk (1960) used the visual cliff in order to determine the extent to which infants could distinguish the shallow and deep sides of the cliff. The visual cliff consisted of a large glass-topped table under which a textured surface could be placed at various distances from the table top. On the shallow side, the patterned surface was placed directly under the glass top. Under the other half of the table top, the patterned surface was placed on the floor which was 40 inches below the table. Thirty-six infants, 5 to 14 months of age, were tested on the visual cliff.

Each child was placed on the centerboard separating the shallow and deep sides. Then the infant's mother, standing alternately at the shallow and cliff sides of the apparatus, tried to coax the infant to crawl to her. Of the 27 infants who crawled off the centerboard when called, all crawled over the shallow side, but only 3 crawled over the cliff side. The observation that only 11% of the infants could be coaxed into

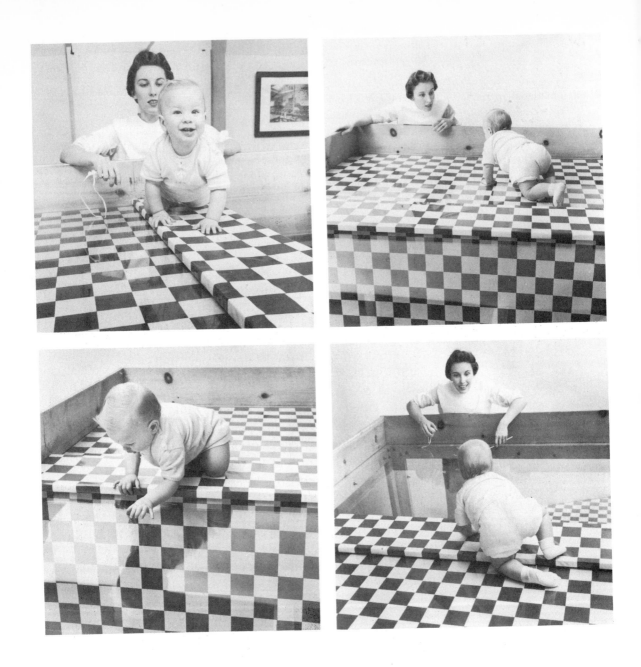

crawling over the visual cliff demonstrated that infants can perceive a depth of at least 40 inches.

In subsequent studies with the visual cliff, Walk (1966) found that infants between 6½ and 15 months of age could discrim-

Figure 5-9
A child's depth perception is tested on the visual cliff. The apparatus consists of a board laid across a sheet of heavy glass, with a patterned material directly beneath the glass on one side and several feet below it on the other. Placed on the center board (top left), the child crawls to its mother across the "shallow" side (top right). Called from the deep side, he pats the glass (bottom left), but despite this tactual evidence that the "cliff" is in fact a solid surface, he refuses to cross over to the mother (bottom right).

(From Gibson & Walk, 1960. Photos courtesy of William Vandivert and *Scientific American.*)

inate depths of less than 5 inches. Walk later demonstrated that texture was an important variable that affected the infants' performance on the visual cliff (Walk, 1969). When the checkered surface of the visual cliff was replaced with a homogeneous gray surface, 50% of the infants tested crawled over the deep side. Evidently, texture gradient is an important cue for depth perception in infants of this age-group, but it is not the only cue available to them. It appears that motion parallax is also important information for infant depth perception.

Although we know now that infants of crawling age possess depth perception, these data do not reveal much about its development or its earliest time of appearance in the human infant. In its traditional use, the visual cliff apparatus requires locomotion (crawling) as the index variable of depth perception and cannot be used with prelocomotor infants. There are alternatives to this procedure that tell us more about the development of depth perception in younger infants. Bower (1965) used a learning paradigm to determine depth perception in 70- to 85-day-old infants. These infants were conditioned by a reinforcement procedure to turn their heads in the presence of a 12-inch cube placed 3 feet away. After they learned this response, the infants were tested under different stimulus conditions in which the distance and size of the cube were varied. With this procedure, Bower was able to control for size, distance, and retinal projection of the stimulus object. The infants clearly responded more to the original reinforced stimulus condition, indicating distance perception in prelocomotor infants. Bower also concluded that the size and distance of the stimulus control distance perception at this age, not the retinal size of the image.

The looming avoidance phenomenon (Schiff, 1965) has also been used as an index variable of distance perception in prelocomotor infants. Looming refers to the rapidly increasing change in the optical size of an approaching object that occurs before collision with that object. This leads to defensive, avoidance behavior such as eye widening, head retraction, and raising the arms and hands to shield the face from the object. Studies by Bower, Broughton, and Moore (1971) and Ball and Tronick (1971) tested young infants in the looming avoidance situation. Neonates were found to display the looming avoidance response as early as 1 week of age, indicating the ability to perceive distance and the change of distance. The looming response in very young infants is apparently a reflexive response pattern, which comes under voluntary control later in childhood.

Another method of studying depth perception in prelocomotor children was developed by Campos, Langer, and Krowitz (1970). Campos et al. used the cardiac response as an index measure of depth perception on the visual cliff. Since heart rate is a sensitive index of attention and discrimination in prelocomotor infants, this response may serve to detect the perception of depth on the visual cliff. Campos et al. studied visual cliff discrimination in two prelocomotor age samples by measuring cardiac changes—heart acceleration and deceleration—when infants were placed on the deep and shallow sides of a visual cliff. The median ages of the two groups of infants were 106 and 55 days. When the infants were placed on the shallow side, they showed a small, nonsignificant change in cardiac response. On the cliff side, large, highly significant cardiac deceleration occurred in both groups of infants. Infants spent an average of 22.3 seconds per trial looking down on the deep side, but only 15.7 seconds on the shallow side. Similarly, infants cried an average of only 2.1 seconds on the deep side and 7.7 seconds on the shallow side. All of these responses suggest an orienting response to, and a discrimination of, depth. Note that prelocomotor infants show little or no distress or fear on the deep side of the visual cliff, even though they perceive depth and an apparent loss of optical support. Recall that in the original studies of Gibson and Walk (1960), observation of fear and distress were reported in postlocomotor infants on the deep side of the visual cliff. Emotional responses to depth develop independently and some time after the development of depth perception, but before 6 months of age.

THE PERCEPTUAL ENVIRONMENT

We have seen that the human infant is able to use visual information and display perceptual skills as early as 1 week of age. Such perceptual skills have been shown to have more fundamental bases that appear to be innate. However, we also know that perception is a function of the complex interaction between maturation and learning. Moreover, perceptual systems interact with the perceptual environment to bring about normal perceptual development. If either the perceptual environment or the biological components of perception are disrupted, perceptual systems and behavior deteriorate, fail to develop, or become distorted. We have already discussed how environmental factors may facilitate the development of visually guided reaching. The importance of perceptual experience, stimulation, and learning is not the issue here. Rather, the degree of perceptual plasticity that exists and the nature of the interaction between maturation and learning remain critical questions in development.

A large number of studies describe the perceptual impairments that occur when the perceptual environment of young organisms is restricted, removed, or impoverished. Such deprivation experiments clearly demonstrate the importance of a minimally adequate environment for normal perceptual development. For example, Riesen (1947, 1961) reported that chimpanzees reared in total darkness or in diffuse light continued to suffer from serious visual perceptual impairments. A general finding in laboratory research with animals is that the degree of perceptual deficit is a function of the length and severity of perceptual deprivation. Fantz (1965) varied the amount of visual deprivation in infant rhesus monkeys from 3 days to 20 weeks. The animals showed different degrees of perceptual impairment on the visual cliff, locomotion, and visual localization as a function of duration of perceptual restriction. Further, the amount of impairment was different for various perceptual systems, as was the reversibility of the impairment following placement in a normal perceptual environment.

The importance of motor interaction with the environment for some aspects of perceptual development has been described by Held and Hein (1963). They reared kittens in darkness and prevented them from walking and self-produced movement and visual experiences. These kittens were unable to discriminate depth on the visual cliff. In addition, these animals showed deficits in perceptual–motor behavior. Clearly, both active and passive feedback from interaction with the perceptual environment are required for normal functional development of the perceptual systems. It is not simply a matter of having the perceptual equipment. Although visual experience is not required for the initial development and organization of the perceptual system, its subsequent biological integrity and functioning depend on some minimal level of visual stimulation and experience. Hubel and Wiesel (1963), for example, found that cellular degeneration can occur in the visual system of cats reared under prolonged light restriction.

The sensory deprivation studies reveal the importance of environmental experience for perceptual development, but little about developmental processes. Clearly, the message is that normal development depends upon the interaction between maturation and environment. Impoverished perceptual environments during early developmental stages may result in impaired development of selective attention and perceptual motivation (Gibson, 1969).

REFERENCES

Adelson, E., & Frailberg, S. Gross motor development in infants blind from birth. *Child Development,* 1974, *45,* 114–126.

Allport, F. H. *Theories of perception and the concept of structure.* New York: Wiley, 1955.

Ames, L. B. The sequential patterning of prone progression in the human infant. *Genetic Psychology Monographs,* 1937, *19,* 409–460.

Appelle, S. Perception and discrimination as a function of stimulus orientation: The "oblique effect in man and animals." *Psychological Bulletin,* 1972, *78,* 266–278.

Appleton, T., Clifton, R., & Goldberg, S. The development of behavioral competence in infancy. In F. D. Horowitz (Ed.), *Review of child development research* (Vol 4). Chicago: University of Chicago Press, 1975.

Ball, W., & Tronick, E. Infant responses to impending collision. *Science,* 1971, *171,* 818–820.

Bond, E. K. Perception of form by the human infant. *Psychological Bulletin,* 1972, *77,* 225–245.

Boring, E. G. *Sensation and perception in the history of experimental psychology.* New York: Appleton, Century-Crofts, 1942.

Bower, T. G. R. Stimulus variables determining space perception in infants. *Science,* 1965, *149,* 88–89.

Bower, T. G. R. *Development in infancy.* San Francisco: Freeman, 1974.

Bower, T. G. R., Broughton, J. M., & Moore, M. K. The coordination of visual and tactual input in infants. *Perception and Psychophysics,* 1970, *8,* 51–53.

Bower, T. G. R., Broughton, J. M., & Moore, M. K. Infants' responses to approaching objects: An indicator of response to distal variables. *Perception and Psychophysics,* 1971, *9,* 193–196.

Bridger, W. H., & Birns, B. Experience and temperament in human neonates. In G. Newton & S. Levine (Eds.), *Early experience and behavior.* Springfield, Illinois: Thomas, 1968.

Bruner, J. S. Organization of early skilled action. *Child Development,* 1973, *44,* 1–11.

Campos, J. J., Langer, A., & Krowitz, A. Cardiac responses on the visual cliff in prelocomotor infants. *Science,* 1970, *170,* 196–197.

Clement, D. E., Perceptual structure and selection. In E. C. Carterette & M. P. Friedman (Eds.), *Handbook of perception* (Vol. 9). New York: Academic Press, 1978.

Cratty, B. J. *Perceptual and motor development in infants and children.* New York: Macmillian, 1970.

Denenberg, V. H. *The development of behavior.* Stamford: Sinauer, 1972.

Dennis, W. A description and classification of the responses of the newborn infant. *Psychological Bulletin,* 1934, *31,* 5–22.

Fantz, R. L. Pattern vision in young infants. *Psychological Record,* 1958, *8,* 43–47.

Fantz, R. L. The origin of form perception. *Scientific American,* 1961, *204,* 66–72.

Fantz, R. L. Ontogeny of perception. In A. M. Schrier, H. F. Harlow, & F. Stollnitz (Eds.), *Behavior of nonhuman primates.* New York: Academic Press, 1965.

Fantz, R. L. Visual perception and experience in early infancy: A look at the hidden side of behavior development. In H. W. Stevenson, E. H. Hess, & H. L. Rheingold (Eds.) *Early behavior: Comparative and developmental approaches.* New York: Wiley, 1967.

Fishbein, H. D. *Evolution, development and children's learning.* Pacific Pallisades, California: Goodyear, 1976.

Frankenburg, W. K., & Dodds, J. B. The Denver developmental screening test. *Journal of Pediatrics,* 1967, *71,* 181–191.

Freedman, D., & Cannady, C. Delayed emergence of prone locomotion. *The Journal of Nervous and Mental Disease,* 1971, *153,* 108–117.

Gesell, A. Infant vision. *Scientific American,* February 1950.

Gesell, A. The ontogenesis of infant behavior. In L. Carmichael (Ed.), *Manual of child psychology.* New York: Wiley, 1954.

Gesell, A, Ilg, F. I., & Bullis, G. E. *Vision: Its development in infant and child.* New York: Hoeber, 1949.

Gibson, E. J. *Principles of perceptual learning and development.* New York: Appleton Century, 1969.

Gibson, E. J., & Walk, R. D. The "visual cliff." *Scientific American,* 1960, *202,* 64–71.

Gibson, J. J., & Gibson, E. J. Perceptual learning: Differentiation or enrichment? *Psychological Review,* 1955, *62,* 32–41. (a)

Gibson, J. J., & Gibson, E. J. What is learned in perceptual learning? A reply Professor Postman. *Psychological Review,* 1955, *62,* 447–450. (b)

Haber, R. N., & Hershenson, M. *The psychology of visual perception.* New York: Hall, 1973.

Halverson, H. M. An experimental study of prehension in infants by means of systematic cinema records. *Genetic Psychology Monographs,* 1931, *10,* 107–286.

Halverson, H. M. A further study of grasping. *Journal of Genetic Psychology,* 1932, *43,* 3–48.

Held, R., & Hein, A. Movement-produced stimulation in the development of visually guided behavior. *Journal of Comparative and Physiological Psychology,* 1963, *56,* 872–876.

Hershenson, M. Development of the perception of form. *Psychological Bulletin*, 1967, *67*, 327–336.

Hubel, D. H., & Wiesel, T. N. Receptive fields of cells in striate cortex of very young, visually inexperienced kittens. *Journal of Neurophysiology*, 1963, *26*, 994–1002.

Irwin, O. C. The amount and nature of activities of newborn infants under constant external stimulating conditions during the first ten days of life. *Genetic Psychology Monographs*, 1930, *8*.

James, W. *The principles of psychology.* New York: Holt, 1890.

Kagen, J. *Change and continuity in infancy.* New York: Wiley, 1971.

Kessen, W., Haith, M. M., & Salapatek, P. H. Human infancy:A bibliography and guide. In P. H. Mussen (Ed.), *Carmichael's manual of child psychology.* New York: Wiley, 1970.

Kessen, W., Salapatek, P., & Haith, M. M. The visual response of the human newborn to linear contour. *Journal of Experimental Child Psychology*, 1972, *13*, 9–20.

Knobloch, H., & Pasamanick, B. Further observation on the behavioral development of Negro children. *Journal of Genetic Psychology*, 1953, *83*, 137–157.

Knobloch, H., & Pasamanick, B. (Eds.) *Gesell and Amatruda's developmental diagnosis.* New York: Harper & Row, 1974.

Locke, J. *An essay concerning human understanding.* London: T. Basset, 1690.

Lowry, R. *The evolution of psychological theory.* Chicago: Aldine, 1971.

Maccoby, E. E., & Jacklin, C. N. *The psychology of sex differences.* Stanford, California: Stanford University Press, 1974.

McCall, R. B., Hogarty, P. S., & Hurlburt, N. Transitions in infant sensorimotor development and the prediction of childhood IQ. *American Psychologist*, 1972, *27*, 728–748.

McGraw, M. B. *Growth: A study of Johnny and Jimmy.* New York: Appleton-Century, 1935.

McGraw, M. B. *The neuromuscular development of the human infant.* New York: Columbia University Press, 1943.

Nelson, K., & Kessen, W. *Visual scanning by human newborns: Responses to complete triangle, to sides only, and to corners only.* Paper presented at the meeting of the American Psychological Association, Washington, D.C., September 1969.

Newton, G., & Levine, S. (Eds.). *Early experience and behavior.* Springfield, Illinois: Thomas, 1968.

Piaget, J. *The origins of intelligence in children.* New York: International Universities Press, 1952.

Pieper, A. *Cerebral function in infancy and childhood.* New York: Consultants Bureau, 1963.

Pikler, E. Some contributions to the study of the gross motor development of children. *Journal of Genetic Psychology,* 1968, *113,* 4–27.

Pikler, E. Data on gross motor development of the infant. *Early child development and care,* 1972, *1,* 297–310.

Postman, L. Association theory and perceptual learning. *Psychological Record,* 1955, *62,* 438–446.

Prechtl, H. F. R. Behavioral studies in the newborn infant. In D. S. Lehrman, R. A. Hinde, & E. Shaw (Eds.), *Advances in the study of behavior.* New York: Academic Press, 1965.

Riesen, A. H. The development of visual perception in man and chimpanzee. *Science,* 1947, *106,* 107–108.

Riesen, A. H. Stimulation as a requirement for growth and function in behavioral development. In D. W. Fiske & S. R. Maddi (Eds.), *Functions of varied experience.* Homewood, Illinois: Dorsey Press, 1961.

Salapatek, P. Visual scanning of geometric figures by the human newborn. *Journal of Comparative and Physiological Psychology,* 1968, *66,* 247–258.

Salapatek, P. The visual investigation of geometric patterns by the one- and two-month-old infant. Paper presented at the meeting of the American Association for the Advancement of Science. Boston, December 1969.

Salapatek, P., & Kessen, W. Visual scanning of triangles in the human newborn. *Journal of Experimental Child Psychology,* 1966, *3,* 155–167.

Schiff, W. Perception of impending collision: A study of visually directed avoidant behavior. *Psychological Monographs,* 1965, *79.*

Shirley, M. M. *The first two years.* Minneapolis: University of Minnesota Press, 1931, 1932.

Stoddard, G. D., & Wellman, B. L. *Child psychology.* New York: Macmillan, 1934.

Terman, L. M. *Mental and physical traits of a thousand gifted children.* Stanford, California: Stanford University Press, 1925.

Walk, R. D. The development of depth perception in animals and human infants. *Monographs of the Society for Research in Child Development,* 1966, *31.*

Walk, R. D. Two types of depth discrimination by the human infant. *Psychonomic Science,* 1969, *14,* 253–254.

Walk, R. D., & Gibson, E. J. A comparative and analytical study of visual depth perception. *Psychological Monographs,* 1961, *75.*

Warren, N. African infant precocity. *Psychological Bulletin,* 1972, *78,* 353–367.

White, B. L. *Human Infants: Experience and psychological development.* Englewood Cliffs: Prentice-Hall, 1971.

Williams, J. R., & Scott, R. B. Growth and development of Negro infants: IV. Motor development and its relationship to child rearing practices in two groups of Negro infants. *Child Development,* 1953, *24,* 103–121.

Wolff, P. H. The causes, controls, and organization of behavior in the neonate. *Psychological Issues,* 1966, *5.*

Chapter

COGNITIVE DEVELOPMENT

Six

INTRODUCTION

We have learned that the neonate is sensitive to many aspects of its environment and is capable of responding to a number of sensory events impinging upon it. We have also discovered that the neonate can perceive some aspects of form, pattern, and distance. Conditionability of the neonate, at least within an operant framework, has been firmly established. There is little question, therefore, that the neonate is capable of receiving physical stimulation from the external environment and differentially responding to such information. What does this level of interaction with the environment mean in terms of the neonate's understanding of the immediate environment? Do these neonatal responses represent meaningless sensations, with little understanding or awareness, or are they vague perceptions to which the neonate attaches some degree of organization and meaning (Gibson, 1966)?

When we speak about the mental processes, activities, and products of knowing, understanding, and thinking, we are referring to cognition and to the general area of cognitive psychology. In the broadest sense, cognition includes all processes involved in the acquisition of knowledge. Cognitive psychologists study not only the content of knowledge but also the mental processes that enable us to acquire and use that knowledge. Cognitive processes, then, include every mental action by which we come to know and represent the world: all the higher mental processes involved in the acquisition, storage, and use of information. Neisser (1967), a pioneer of modern cognitive psychology, defines cognition as "all the processes by which the sensory input is transformed, reduced, elaborated, stored, recovered, and used. It is concerned with those processes even when they operate in the absence of relevant stimulation, as in images and hallucinations" (p. 4). Note that Neisser's definition includes symbolic processes—mental representations and events that involve images and language (symbols) to represent something other than themselves. Symbolic processes allow us to transcend the physical and temporal limits of the world. Thus, we can construct internal representations of the world, in the absence of external stimuli, and transcend time by mental representations of the past and future.

It should now be clear that the study of cognitive psychology consists of such areas as learning, perception, memory, concept formation, reasoning, ideation, thinking, language, intelligence, and emotion. In short, cognitive psychology is everything mental.

While most research activity is still focused on adult human cognition, cognitive development is getting increasing attention. The traditional separation of developmental and cognitive psychologists should end soon, as developmental psychologists become aware of the importance of adult models of cognition, and cognitive psychologists realize the significance of developmental data for the study of adult cognitive patterns and functioning. Our discussion of cognitive development will explore some of the major contemporary findings and theories about early cognitive development. The field of cognitive psychology has grown rapidly since 1967, and there is now a vast amount of literature in a once obscure area of psychology. Research interest and activity in the various areas of human cognition are currently at peak levels. Heavily experimental in its approach, modern cognitive psychology can truly be described as "empirical mentalism" (Reynolds & Flagg, 1977), in sharp contrast to its philosophical and introspective origins.

HISTORICAL PERSPECTIVE

In Chapter One, we mentioned George John Romanes, the nineteenth century pioneer of cognitive psychology who attempted to trace the evolution of mental development. However, the universal questions about mind, thought, and how we come to know and experience the world concerned Greek philosophers 2500 years ago. Such questions have continued to preoccupy the great philosophers, both ancient and modern.

By the end of the nineteenth century, two major views of mental development had taken form: structuralism and the mental processes approach.

Structuralism emphasizes the existence of mental structures such as ideas, images, and sensations. Structuralism states that cognition is the result of the storage of bits of information, that become organized by complex associations with each other. These associations are the essence of learning. The basic philosophical notions of structuralism and association originated with Aristotle and extended into the eighteenth century with the works of John Locke and Rene Descartes. We can see twentieth century versions of structuralism in behaviorism and the more recent learning approaches to cognition.

Structuralism emphasizes the importance of innate structures and organization, environment, and learning in cognitive development. Thus, it is a complex topic to explore. Structural psychology in the early twentieth century attempted to investigate problems in perception and memory by using the techniques of introspection and verbal reports. For structural psychologists like Titchener, consciousness and experience were starting points for psychology, and the only method for studying mental contents was introspection and description by the experiencing individual. As experimental methods designed to determine mental functioning, introspection and verbal reports lack the necessary objectivity, reliability, and validity required for scientific psychology. John Watson's attack on structuralism as unscientific, unobservable mentalism ended introspection as a serious approach in psychology. Watson called for strict empiricism, with directly observable behavior as the only basis for a science of psychology. As a result, the problems of mental representation and mental processes received little attention in psychology during the remaining first half of the twentieth century.

The other major theory of cognition that emerged in the nineteenth century was the mental processes approach. Rather than considering the structure and content of the mind as the structuralists did, the process view emphasized mental operations or cognitive acts such as remembering, feeling, judging, and comparing. This is an approach that considers the dynamics of mental representations rather than static content alone. The nineteenth century German psychologist Franz Brentano was a major advocate of the process approach to cognition. He believed that the dynamics of mental operation should be a primary concern for psychology rather than the static structures of thought which resulted from associative learning.

The study of mental operations actually had begun earlier with the studies of reaction time by F.C. Donders, a Dutch physiologist. In 1868, Donders became interested in measuring the time taken to perform certain mental tasks. He obtained data on three different kinds of reaction times: simple, discrimination, and choice. Donders found that reaction time increased as a function of task complexity. The temporal study of these mental functions was called "mental chronometry" (R. Watson, 1968). In 1885, Ebbinghaus published a monograph on learning and memory experiments that he had performed on himself. These were the first quantified experiments on the higher mental processes of learning and memory. A major twentieth century figure in the mental processes approach to cognition is Jean Piaget. Piaget's developmental psychology is an attempt to trace the development of the operations involved in the growth of thinking, knowledge, and intelligence in children. Piaget's "genetic epistomology" is a major force in modern cognitive psychology.

With the formal establishment of cognitive psychology by Neisser (1967), we see a new area of experimental psychology that reflects its historical origins in both structuralism and mental processes, along with new perspectives, methods, and theories derived from computer science, information theory, and linguistics (Reynolds & Flagg, 1977). Although cognitive psychologists continue to emphasize the study of structure over mental processes, the two approaches are now seen as complementary and perhaps inseparable aspects of cognition. Cognitive psychology is now a vast and vigorous area of research, and cognitive psychologists are almost single-minded about the universal importance of cognition in all of psychology.

THE DEVELOPMENT OF MEMORY

Memory is the fundamental basis for all cognitive development and functioning. While it is true that memory is studied as a subsystem of general cognition, memory and memory processes are universal attributes of the entire cognitive system. Simply stated, memory is the retention (storage) and reactivation (retrieval) of information and events that have been learned or experienced. Underwood (1969) defines memory as the record of an event which consists of a collection of attributes. Underwood states that it is the ensemble of attributes which gives memory psychological meaning, because the absence of attributes would prevent an event from being remembered. Furthermore, the pattern of attributes attached to a memory enables us to differentiate between memories, and so the analysis of memory attributes will lead to our understanding of memory and its development. Underwood identifies seven characteristics of memory in an attempt to provide a topography of memory:

1 *Temporal*: A unique point in time when an event occurs.
2 *Spatial*: An aspect of space or a location in space where an event occurred.
3 *Frequency*: The number of occurrences of an event.
4 *Modality*: The auditory or visual aspects of an event.
5 *Orthographic*: Words and the structural/physical characteristics of words.
6 *Nonverbal associations*: Acoustical or visual images, affect, and contexts associated with an event.
7 *Verbal associations*: Words associated with the occurrence of an event.

If you think about Underwood's list of memory attributes from a developmental perspective, you will note that the differential levels of attribute complexity would result in different patterns of memory characteristics being established at different levels of development. Indeed, Underwood speaks of spatial and acoustical attributes as possibly dominant over others during the early stages of infancy. With increasing maturation and learning, the pattern of memory attributes may change to predominantly verbal associations as language develops in the young child. We would certainly expect the more primitive attributes to be established with early memory because of the cognitive limitations of the young infant. What is significant in the ontogenesis of memory is that the nature and complexity of memory changes with the developmental status of the child.

Infant Visual Memory   Infant memory is implied by a number of behaviors, such as conditioning, habituation, imitation, object permanence (retrieving a hidden object), and preference for novel stimuli. In the preverbal infant, each of these behaviors represents visual memory—the ability to remember some aspect or aspects of what is seen in the absence of a linguistic system and verbal memory processes. Thus, visual memory may be considered a form of memory in which the encoding, storage, and retrieval of information take place without symbolic representation (language). Visual memory is also referred to as image or perceptual memory.

While the evidence for visual memory in neonates and infants is clear, the processes of visual information storage and retrieval remain obscure. Moreover, some researchers deny that visual memory is the first clear evidence for memory in young infants. Bruner (1964), for example, has postulated a developmental sequence of cognitive growth in children which includes a memory system more elemental than visual memory. Bruner describes a series of three stages by which infants and children learn to cognitively represent the environment and remember past experiences. These stages are presented as "modes of representation" that occur in a fixed developmental sequence. Each mode represents a qualitative change in cognitive processing, but each mode remains relatively intact throughout life.

Bruner calls these modes the enactive, iconic, and symbolic modes of representation. Enactive representation is the first cognitive style to develop. It is a process by which past events are represented through the motor responses which characterize, describe, or define the event. Enactive representation is based upon learned responses and habituation. Iconic representation is analogous to visual or perceptual memory. The iconic mode summarizes events by the organization of percepts and images and their various characteristics. The final stage in cognitive growth is the mode of symbolic representation, or the use of words or language to process information.

The discussion of habituation and conditioning in Chapter Four provides evidence for enactive memory in young infants. And as you learned in Chapter Five, neonates and young infants also display iconic memory by their ability to differentially respond to visual stimuli. Nonetheless, it has been hard to distinguish clearly Bruner's three modes of representation, and the data are inconsistent in the support of his developmental sequence (Corsini, 1969). Because both enactive and iconic memory seem to exist in the young infant simultaneously, and because there is much more direct evidence dealing with visual memory, we will limit our discussion to the development of visual memory in infants.

Although research in the development of memory in children has only recently become a major interest, some early developmental studies of visual memory can be found in the literature. The first studies of infant memory were based on the delayed reaction experiment (Hunter, 1917). In this situation, the index of visual memory is the infant's ability to respond to an absent stimulus. The delayed reaction experiment requires the infant to find an object that has been placed out of sight while the infant watches. For example, an infant is given or shown a toy and, while the infant watches, the toy is placed under one of several boxes. After a delay of up to 1 minute, the infant is prompted to find the toy. In this manner, it is possible to assess the degree to which the infant remembers the location of the stimulus object over some period of time. Hunter (1917) found that correct location of the stimulus was a function of the length of delay, and that the ability to delay the correct response increased with age. Hunter postulated that the preverbal infant's ability to delay responding to an absent stimulus represented "kinesthetic" sensory memory. There have been a number of variations of the delayed reaction experiment (Allen, 1931; Buehler & Hetzer, 1935; Skalet, 1931), all of which demonstrate the increasing ability to remember or otherwise respond to a hidden stimulus over longer delays.

Infant visual memory has been investigated primarily through the use of habituation paradigms and studies of attention and perception. Recall that habituation in young infants involves repeated presentation of a stimulus, with decreased visual attention to that stimulus serving as an index of habituation. Typically, it is assumed that repeated stimulus presentation results in a stimulus replica or model in the infant's memory (Sokolov, 1960). Subsequent stimulus presentations are then presumably compared against the model stored in the infant's memory. If there is a match between the present stimulus and the infant's memory model, the infant will no longer orient toward, or attend to, the stimulus. Therefore, if a habituation response is demonstrated, it is interpreted as evidence for a form of visual memory in the infant.

As we noted in Chapter Four, habituation has been found to emerge first in infants between 2 and 3 months of age. Wetherford and Cohen (1973) employed a habituation paradigm in testing two groups of young infants, one of which was 6 to 8 weeks old and the other 10 to 12 weeks of age. Wetherford and Cohen found a habituation response in 10- to 12-week-old infants, with the 12-week-old infants showing more rapid habituation. However, infants of 6 to 8 weeks of age failed to habituate to the repeated stimulus presentations of simple geometric patterns. But Wetherford and Cohen also found that 8-week-old infants preferred to attend to familiar stimuli during the experiment, while the older infants preferred the novel stimulus patterns interspersed among the repeated patterns. The preference for familiar stimuli shown by the 8-week-old infants suggests that some form of stimulus memory has been established despite the absence of habituation. It also suggests that the absence of habituation in infants younger than 10 weeks may have no implications for the presence of visual memory. Visual memory can indeed exist in younger infants in a form adequate for visual attention preference but inadequate for the requirements of habituation, i.e., a "stronger" or more detailed memory model.

The observation of a transition in attentional preference from familiar stimuli at 6 to 8 weeks to novel stimuli at 8 to 10 weeks of age has been replicated by Weizmann, Cohen, and Pratt (1971). Weizmann et al. used a paired-comparison procedure with 4-week-old infants, in which familiar and novel stabiles were presented simultaneously 12 to 24 hours after exposure to the familiar stabile. At 6 weeks of age, infants attended longer to the familiar stabile, and at 8 weeks preferred the novel stabile. These results are interpreted as a preferential shift in stimulus attraction and as evidence of recognition memory of at least 24 hours duration. These findings are consistent with the two-stage preference hypothesis proposed by Hunt (1963). Hunt suggests that the young infant's initial preference for familiar stimuli is based upon the motivating qualities of the newly acquired ability to recognize stimuli. Later in development, mere recognition loses its stimulating qualities for the infant, and attentional preference shifts to novel stimuli because novelty provides new information and experiences which have dominant stimulating and motivating properties.

Several other studies corroborate the findings of a developmental trend from familiar to novel stimulus preferences. In addition, recent research findings indicate that young infants are capable of long-term retention of visual memory. Martin (1975) examined both long- and short-term visual habituation in 2-, 3½-, and 5-month-old infants. One significant finding was the demonstration of visual memory retention in all age-groups 24 hours after the initial stimulus presentation of only 4½ minutes.

Fagan (1973) investigated several parameters of infant visual recognition memory. In a series of five experiments, Fagan used a paired-comparison paradigm in a group of 5- to 6-month-old infants. Infants were shown abstract patterns for a 2-minute familiarization period and then tested for recognition by pairing the familiar stimulus with novel stimuli at various retention intervals. The first experiment demonstrated viewing preferences for novel stimuli over retention periods of 24 and 48 hours. In his second experiment, Fagan discovered recognition memory for black-and-white photographs of a man, a woman, and a baby after retention intervals of 3 hours, 24 hours, 48 hours, 1 week, and 2 weeks, with only a slight decline over time. These data are all the more remarkable considering the initial familiarization period was of a 2-minute duration.

In a third experiment, Fagan exposed infants to lifelike, three-dimensional face masks for 2 minutes and, in a separate condition, to the abstract black-and-white patterns used in the first experiment (see Figure 6-1). Recognition occurred for both the face masks and the patterns when the infants were tested 10 seconds after the familiarization period. However, when the infants were tested 3 hours later, recognition for the patterns was observed, but there was no evidence for memory of the face masks.

This was a surprising finding, inasmuch as Fagan had earlier observed memory retention of 2 weeks. Fagan hypothesized that forgetting occurred in the third experiment because

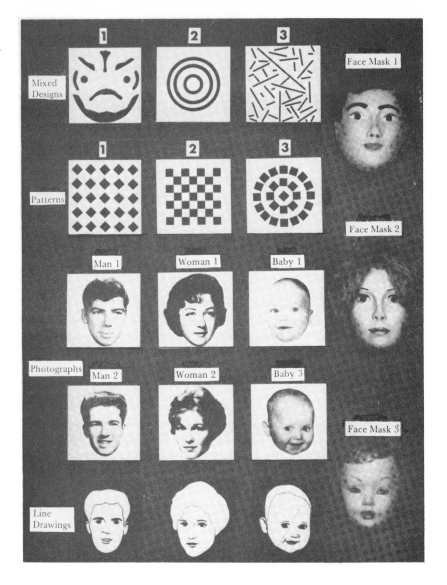

Mixed Designs · 1 · 2 · 3

Face Mask 1

Patterns · 1 · 2 · 3

Face Mask 2

Man 1 · Woman 1 · Baby 1

Photographs · Man 2 · Woman 2 · Baby 3

Face Mask 3

Line Drawings

following the presentation of the masks, the infants were exposed to real faces and this interfered with their later ability to remember the target face mask. Such retroactive interference did not occur with the abstract patterns, so recognition memory remained intact after 3 hours.

Fagan conducted two additional experiments to investigate the effect of retroactive interference on infant memory. In these studies, Fagan used photographs of faces as the stimuli. Immediately following the 2-minute presentation of the target stimulus, infants were exposed for 30 seconds to "interfering" photographs which had either high, medium, or low similarity to the original photograph. The interference conditions were produced by using the original photograph for high similarity, the original photograph rotated 180 degrees for medium similarity, and a line drawing of the original photograph rotated 180 degrees for the low-similarity condition. The results revealed that 3-hour recognition was unaffected by the high- or low-similarity photographs. Total loss of recognition memory did occur under the condition of medium interference. Furthermore, memory loss occurred only when similar stimuli were presented immediately after the familiarization period.

While the existence of infant memory is not challenged, there is an issue over whether interference phenomena disrupt infant memory. Fagan (1977) has replicated his earlier findings of interference, but Cohen, DeLoache, and Pearl (1977) failed to find interference effects in 18-week-old infants. Cohen et al. concluded that infant visual memory is relatively immune to interference effects. On the other hand, McCall, Kennedy, and Dodds (1977) found that interference effects in infant memory depend on the degree to which young infants actually encode a distracting stimulus and that maximum encoding can lead to total interference effects. These authors concluded that the dissimilarity of distracting stimuli may determine the degree of infant encoding rather than affecting the interference process directly.

Collectively, these studies reveal remarkable storage and retrieval capacities in young infants. In addition, infant visual memory is evidently independent of verbal processes and verbal encoding. The emergence of long-term memory ability is an early developmental event, and the disruption of recognition or visual memory in infants seems largely dependent upon immediate interference effects from perceptually similar stimuli. The young infant's memory for static visual stimuli in the absence of any gross motor movements does not fit the theories of Piaget or Bruner, which hypothesize a reliance on motor representation in early memory.

In summary, recognition or visual memory in infants is

established as early as 6 weeks of age. Long-term memory ability also emerges at this time, increasing to a retention period of 2 weeks by approximately 5 months of age. There is also a developmental trend toward more rapid visual habituation with increasing age of the infant, suggesting increased perceptual and memory capacities and cognitive organization. Related to these increasing cognitive skills is the observed developmental shift in attentional preference from familiar to novel stimuli between 6 and 10 weeks of age. This represents a dramatic change in memory capacity. Accompanying this increase in memory processes is the infant's vulnerability to interference effects and forgetting. Attentional behavior in infants, a fundamental requirement for memory development, proceeds from the infant being "captured" by visual stimuli to voluntary and selective attentional behavior with increasing cognitive maturation and experience. As the infant enters the verbal stage of development, symbolic, linguistic activities provide for a change from nonverbal to verbal encoding and storage processes. These events contribute greatly to the speed and efficiency of the basic memory processes that have been established during the first year of life.

Recall Memory We have seen that an infant's capacity for retention of visual experiences develops in the absence of verbal encoding. The evidence also indicates that the rate of information storage and processing (habituation rate) and memory capacity (visual preferences) increase with age. Visual or perceptual memory is the first form of memory to emerge in human infants. It is the simplest form of memory, as it requires only the ability to recognize similarities to previously experienced stimuli. Since infant visual memory develops in the absence of verbal or symbolic activities, it doubtless has the fewest cognitive requirements.

Visual memory capacity continues to increase over the course of development, but its ontogenesis assumes another form with the emergence of memory retrieval skills and increased cognitive functioning. This developmental change involves the transition from simple recognition memory to recall memory. Recall memory refers to the process of retrieval, in which information stored in long-term memory is activated to recognize new information and events or to solve a problem (Posner, 1973). Clearly, memory retrieval capacity is critical for learning, memory, and all cognitive functioning.

It is difficult to investigate recall memory in children less than 3 years old, and there are few studies which clearly identify and assess recall processes in such children. While some researchers argue that delayed responding in infants under 2 years of age represents a form of recall, it is not clear whether this behavior is in fact recall memory or simply a form of recognition memory. That is, the infant may well be responding on the basis of position cues or present stimulus characteristics. If so, then we are observing an example of recognition or visual memory rather than true recall processes.

Piaget's (1954) concept of object permanence may also have implications for the development of recall memory. For Piaget, object permanence means the development of awareness that objects continue to exist even though we are not presently perceiving them. As we have seen, mental representation in infant visual memory depends upon immediate sensory contact. But object permanence or the object concept requires an understanding that objects exist in the absence of any direct sensory experience. For example, with an infant watching, an object is hidden under a box or blanket. Will the infant immediately begin searching for the object, or will the infant forget about it with its disappearance? According to Piaget, the capacity to understand object permanence and the ability to search for hidden objects develop during the latter half of the sensorimotor period, between 8 and 18 months of age. Prior to 8 months, most infants will not respond to an object which has been hidden or made to "disappear" before its eyes.

Object permanence has been shown to depend upon a number of complex factors (Bower, 1974). In short, we may consider this form of memory to be developmentally more complex than recognition memory, but it is not a form of recall memory. Because language development is critically important in the investigation of recall memory, we will examine some findings about the development of recall in children beyond the age of 3.

There have been many developmental studies of recall memory over the past 10 years. In experiments utilizing various stimulus materials and procedures with subjects ranging from

4 to 16 years of age, one general finding is consistently reported. This common observation is that recall memory in older children is superior to that in younger children and that increases in recall performances are associated with increases in age (Cole, Frankel, & Sharp, 1971; Jablonski, 1974). While the mechanisms underlying this improved performance are unclear, older children consistently recall more, whether words, objects, or pictures are used as recall stimuli.

Peek-a-boo! After about 10 months of age, the child no longer needs the visual presence of an object (in this case the researcher) to know that it continues to exist. This knowledge, called object permanence, suggests an important cognitive step: the development of mental systems for the storing and retrieving of information. The first visual appearance of the researcher has been stored in memory to be recalled the next time he peeks around the corner. The result at this stage of development is an amusing game of recognition rather than the repetition of the orienting and attending reflexes of earlier stages each time the researcher reappears.

(Photo by Alice Kandell/Photo Researchers, Inc.)

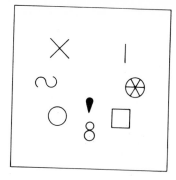

Figure 6-2
The circular array with simultaneous indicator as used by Sheingold (1973).

Jablonski (1974) has noted that the general developmental trend found in recall memory may be related to three different processes. First, increases in recall may reflect an age-related process of physical maturation. Second, observed trends may be an index of some task-dependent processes—that is, memory processes activated by characteristics of the experiment, such as composition of the items to be recalled, organization of the items, item variety, the kind of stimuli used, and what the subject has to do. Jablonski's third suggestion is that recall memory trends in children are an index of the development of storage and retrieval strategies for short- and long-term memory—a learning process, in short.

At this time, the available data do not reveal the mechanisms or processes underlying the development of recall memory. However, the developmental changes in memory do appear to be strongly related to the learning of certain strategies that heavily influence the establishment and operation of the memory system. Consequently, much of the developmental research in memory has studied such learned strategies as rehearsal (covert or overt repetition of the stimuli) and the role of organizational patterns of the stimuli in developmental memory.

Developmental studies of visual memory capacity suggest that observed developmental trends in recall memory depend more upon the acquisition of strategies that help to operate the memory system than they do upon age differences in memory capacity. Sheingold (1973) studied short-term visual memory in four groups of subjects ranging in age from 5 to 21. Subjects were presented with a circular array of eight geometric figures for a duration of 100 milliseconds. At various time intervals after stimulus presentation, a pointer appeared at the location where one of the geometric figures had been displayed (Figure 6-2). The subjects were asked to name the figure that had been in the position indicated by the pointer. This is known as the partial report technique. This procedure is used in assessing memory storage because it does not require the subject to recall all the information presented, which alone may produce memory loss. However, since the subject never knows in advance where the indicator will point, all the information must be stored for successful recall.

Recall memory was tested at delay intervals of 50 to 1000

Figure 6-3
Number of items in visual memory as a function of delay interval for each age group. ("S" represents trials in which the array and the indicator were simultaneously presented.)

(Adapted from Sheingold, 1973.)

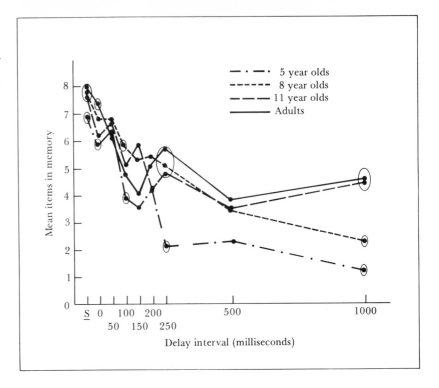

Figure 6-3
Number of items in visual memory as a function of delay interval for each age group. ("S" represents trials in which the array and the indicator were simultaneously presented.)

(Adapted from Sheingold, 1973.)

milliseconds (Figure 6-3). No significant differences in recall were observed between the four age-groups at 50 milliseconds. However, at intervals between 100 and 500 milliseconds, the three oldest groups (8, 11, 21 years) showed the same recall performance. The memory ability of these groups was generally superior to that of the 5-year-old group. At the 1000 millisecond interval, the 21- and 11-year-old groups displayed the same recall performance, which was superior to that of the 5- and 8-year-old groups. At this retention level, the 8 year olds were superior to the 5 year olds.

The similarity of recall memory among the various age-groups suggests that there are no developmental differences in information storage capacity. Developmental differences in recall appear only after longer delays, with older subjects showing superior performance. In the Sheingold study, for instance, both adults and 11 year olds showed an improvement in recall memory performance from 500- to 1000-millisecond intervals, while the 5 and 8 year olds showed a decline. These data suggest that the differences in recall performance may be due to differences in encoding and retrieval processes in older children and adults, such as learned organizational and rehearsal strategies. Other investigators have also obtained data to support the observation that short-term recall memory is similar across a wide age span (Cole et al., 1971; Morrison, 1971; Ornstein, Naus, & Liberty, 1975).

Older children recall generally more than younger ones because they appear better able to store and retrieve items from long-term memory, an advantage acquired by the learning of better strategies for storage and retrieval processes (Cole, et al., 1971). Kingsley and Hagen (1969) and Liberty and Ornstein (1973) have provided evidence that the observed differences in recall memory are not strictly controlled by developmental phenomena such as maturation. These investigators have reported that appropriate training procedures in memory tasks can produce developmental changes in recall patterns in children, sometimes approaching adultlike performance.

Jablonski (1974) has also concluded that children as young as 5 years old employ adult memory processes. However, they are deficient in the ability to spontaneously organize material to be recalled and in the ability to use various mediation techniques, such as rehearsal, that strengthen memory performance. These strategies must be learned, and while recall memory may appear to be age-related or age-dependent under average circumstances, its development can be accelerated by training. The developmental trends in memory that are typically described may be more a function of rearing practices and expectations than of children's capacities.

Developmental memory research currently emphasizes the study of organizational and rehearsal strategies, as these factors have been shown to be critically important in memory development. Consequently, the development of memory is viewed by many researchers as the development of various techniques to "operate" the memory system. Flavell (1971) has asked what memory development is the development of, and has offered the following answer: "It seems in large part to be the devel-

Testing memory. Memory tests, such as the one shown here, provide information about the child's ability to organize and categorize incoming data, to store such data and recall it upon demand, and to know what is stored in order to get at needed information most efficiently. These abilities typically increase with age during childhood and adolescence as the youngster becomes more practiced at processing information.

(Photo courtesy of the Psychological Corporation.)

opment of intelligent structuring and storage of input, of intelligent search and retrieval operations, and of intelligent monitoring and knowledge of these storage and retrieval operations—a kind of 'metamemory,' perhaps" (pp. 272–275).

CONCEPT
DEVELOPMENT

The development of cognitive control is a principal stage in the ontogeny of memory. Cognitive control is the self-regulation of thinking and remembering. It is often referred to as intention, voluntary action, or will. Cognitive control also includes intentional learning, problem-solving, and the integration of various components of cognition toward purposeful behavior. Cognitive control, then, provides for meaningful experiences with the environment and an understanding of its objects and events.

The idea of cognitive control is helpful in understanding concepts and concept development. A concept is typically defined as a collection of stimuli or objects that share one or more common features or characteristics. This definition has its roots in the classical copy theory of concept formation, which defines concepts as abstractions of similarities that exist among a diverse group of objects. Abstraction means the differentiation or discrimination of common stimulus attributes leading to some generality regarding group membership or class of events. So, for example, you might abstract any number of attributes to form the concepts of vehicle, baroque music, or life. These attributes might range from physical stimulus features to functions of the class of the objects.

The point of this argument is to construct a proper perspective of the terms concept and concept development. Blumenthal (1977) has stated this perspective clearly. Blumenthal describes a concept as a psychological event or mental process. He disagrees with the traditional definition of a concept because the attributes picked to construct a concept can be anything an individual is able to create or "dream up." Thus, concepts do not always exist as facts in the environment. According to Blumenthal, concepts are usually "the constructive achievement, or invention, of the perceiver or the thinker" (p. 141). In this perspective, concept development is an active, creative process of learning "principles" about how to organize and structure the environment and our experiences with it.

Concept development thus is characterized by vast individual differences in the style or manner in which individuals learn how to form concepts. These differences are often described as differences in conceptualization systems or cognitive styles (Kagen & Kogen, 1970; Bolton, 1977). Cognitive styles refer to differences in the use of cognitive operations in concept formation and problem-solving, rather than differences in cognitive ability or intelligence. While the relative efficiency of various cognitive styles may be in question, the developmental significance of concept formation is not. Concepts (1) reduce the volume and complexity of information input to manageable proportions, (2) reduce the time and effort required in general interactions with the environment, and (3) provide a preparatory or anticipatory set for future events (Bruner, Goodnow, & Austin, 1956). Concept development therefore provides for more rapid accumulation of knowledge and understanding of the environment. Flavell (1970) has described three major dimensions in which concept formation may vary.

1 *Validity*: The degree to which an individual's conceptualization of a given concept differs from some fixed, standard, popular meaning or interpretation. An individual's concept may not only vary from the standard, but may also vary from time to time as a function of change in the environmental context.

Problem solving or . . . which peg goes in which hole? To resolve this question, the youngster must have concept of shapes. That is, he must recognize those characteristics common to the peg and the hole that make them fit togther. This ability to discern and group common characteristics is crucial to all memory and learning

(Photo by Erika Stone/Peter Arnold, Inc.)

2 *Status*: The degree to which "concept as cognitive object" and "concept as cognitive instrument" are correlated within the individual. Concept status refers to the extent to which a concept has physical referents and/or is conceptualized as an object of thought.

3 *Accessibility*: The extent to which an acquired concept can be used in appropriate situations. Flavell applies the distinction between learning and performance to describe accessibility.

Flavell points out that these dimensions also change during the ontogenesis of concept formation from childhood to adulthood.

Bolton (1977) has summarized from the literature two dimensions underlying individual differences in concept formation, which he describes as attentional deployment and concreteness versus abstractness. Attentional deployment characterizes a cognitive style by the span of attention used in responding to available stimuli, ranging from broad to narrow. The concrete–abstract dimension concerns the degree to which an individual relies upon physical stimulus characteristics or nonphysical, symbolic attributes to form concepts. There is general agreement that cognitive development proceeds from the concrete to the abstract, and insofar as the learning of concepts follows a direction of increasing complexity, this general principle is correct.

Concept Development in Childhood

Early empirical efforts to investigate concept development were based on S–R discrimination learning, in which concept development was viewed as the learning of response equivalence to dissimilar stimuli (Kendler, 1961), or stimulus generalization. The work of Kendler and Kendler (1962) and of Zeaman and House (1963) are representative examples of the learning approach to concept formation and problem solving in children. Kendler and Kendler developed a verbal mediation theory to account for concept formation. They described concept formation as the learning of observable S–R relationships along with the use of some covert verbal representation response (language) that becomes associated with the overt response. Zeaman and House proposed an attentional theory of discrimination learning and concept development. This theory emphasizes attentional responses to external stimulus features chained to some instrumental response, with no necessary reliance on verbal mediation.

A number of developmentalists have decried the sterility of these "classical" learning approaches to concept development. Few concepts fall neatly into the definition of common responses to different stimuli. The S–R approaches to concept development lack the richness of Piaget's approach. Indeed, few recent studies of concept development outside a Piagetian framework can be found in the literature. Consequently, our discussion of concept development will deal with some of Piaget's major theoretical offerings in this area and their empirical foundations. Piaget's general theory of cognitive development will be discussed in some detail later in this chapter.

Preconceptual Development

An understanding of Piaget's approach to concept development requires some discussion of what Piaget describes as preconceptual development (Piaget, 1951, 1954). During the period of infancy, from birth to approximately 2 years, the child progresses through a series of developmental stages that Piaget calls the sensorimotor period. Piaget interprets this first period of cognitive development as the transition from a reflex organism, whose responses to the environment are undifferentiated and nonpurposeful, to one whose sensorimotor actions become organized and purposeful. The perceptual–motor adjustments of the infant are nonsymbolic, representing the development of "practical intelligence" (Flavell, 1963). During this period, the infant acquires basic knowledge about the environment, which serves as the foundation for later concept development. The object concept or object permanence develops during the sensorimotor period, as was pointed out earlier. For Piaget, the ability to recognize objects as having independent, continued existence is a major event because it provides the basis for general cognitive or intellectual development.

The first, primitive concepts formed by the child during the latter stages of the sensorimotor period and earlier stages of the preoperational period (2 to 7 years) are called preconcepts. These preconcepts are characterized by action, imagery, and

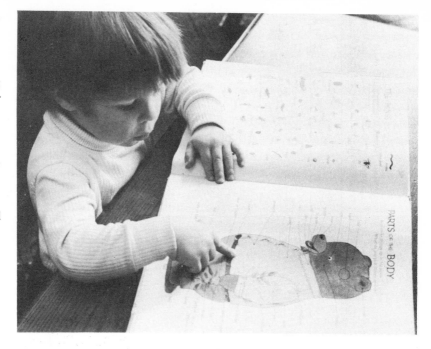

"Bear picks things up in his paws. What do you pick things up with?" This standardized test question measures the child's ability to classify objects according to function and, to some extent, structure. Intelligence—like memory—involves the ability to process and integrate information. Because it is an ability rather than an exact, easily isolated characteristic, the results of testing can be imprecise, inconclusive, and misleading. At best, results of such tests can only be viewed as general indicators of probable cognitive abilities.

(Photo by Suzanne Szasz.)

concreteness rather than by cognitive or symbolic representation (Flavell, 1963). While object identity and permanence are present, their stability fluctuates with various environmental changes in which the object appears. The preoperational child is acquiring "rules" for the logical operations of reasoning and thinking, but they are still faulty and idiosyncratic. Despite the absence of inductive or deductive reasoning, the preoperational child is able to form elementary concepts of various objects and events which can be viewed as preconceptual development and precursors to true concept development. Piaget views the development and use of concepts as dependent upon the object concept, the development of language, and the emergence of imagery, all of which represent preconceptual phenomena in cognitive development.

The Concept of Conservation

The ontogenesis of concepts comprises a major portion of Piaget's observations of cognitive development. Since concept formation involves such complex cognitive processes as logical mental operations and abstract thinking, Piaget's views of concept development have attracted a great deal of theoretical and empirical interest from American psychologists. Of the several concepts that Piaget has studied, the concept of conservation is perhaps the most important and certainly the most extensively investigated. Because conservation plays a principal role in Piaget's theory, we will discuss this concept in some detail to provide an example of Piaget's approach to concept development in general. Comprehensive treatment of Piaget's theory may be found in Flavell (1963, 1970, 1977), Phillips (1975), and Sigel and Cocking (1977). Piaget's theory of cognitive development is technically complex and its terminology is often vague even when it is presented by his major interpreters. For our purposes, it is sufficient to provide only a necessarily selective description for a basic understanding of concept development according to Piaget.

The concept of conservation refers to the ability to understand that certain properties of objects such as quantity, number, volume, area, and weight remain invariant (are conserved) despite transformations in the physical appearance of objects (changing the shape, sectioning objects into pieces, extending objects' parts into space). Just as the development of object permanence is an achievement of monumental importance for all later cognitive development, so is conservation a fundamental requirement for all concept formation and logical thinking in children. For Piaget, the ability to understand and use concepts begins during the period of concrete operations.

The concrete operational period spans the ages between about 7 and 11. During this period, the child's reasoning processes and interactions with the environment first begin to appear rational and organized. The increasing ability to deal with concepts during this developmental period is considered by Piaget to depend upon the ability of the child to think in "logical operations." Logical operations are integrated, organized mental representations, which permit the concrete operational child to think simultaneously about two or more elements of a problem or situation and perceive the relationship between them. Piaget describes cognitive acts such as adding, subtracting, classifying objects, and understanding serial relationships of objects along a continuum of increasing values (seriation) as examples of logical operations.

Such logical operations are necessary precursors to concept

formation for Piaget. But during this period of development, the child's operations are limited by the concrete nature of the situations to which they can be applied in problem-solving and concept formation. That is, the reasoning powers of the child are restricted to actual, observable situations. Hypothetical or possible problems or situations cannot be conceptualized by the concrete-operational child. Piaget refers to this later form of thinking and reasoning as hypothetico–deductive, the highest, most complex level of cognitive development. This form of cognition does not emerge until the period of formal operations, somewhere between 12 and 15 years.

The Conservation Problem

Piaget's research into conservation began between 1935 and 1940 and culminated in several books and articles dealing with the conservation problem (Flavell, 1963). The classical procedure developed by Piaget is to show the child an object and then perform some transformation on that object, as in Figure 6-4. The child is then asked questions concerning the transformation effects on quantity, volume, number, area, and so on.

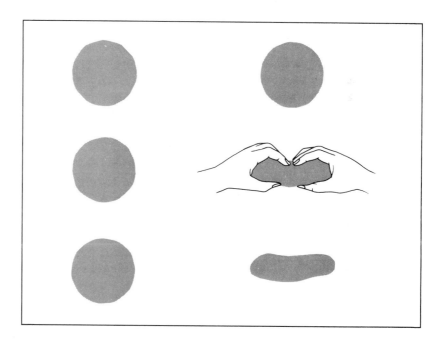

Figure 6-4 (a)
Piaget's conservation of substance problem. The child is shown two equal balls of clay. One is rolled out into a long "sausage," and the child is then asked which one has more clay.

Figure 6-4 (b)
Piaget's conservation of liquid volume problem. The child is asked which container on the bottom shelf has the most water.

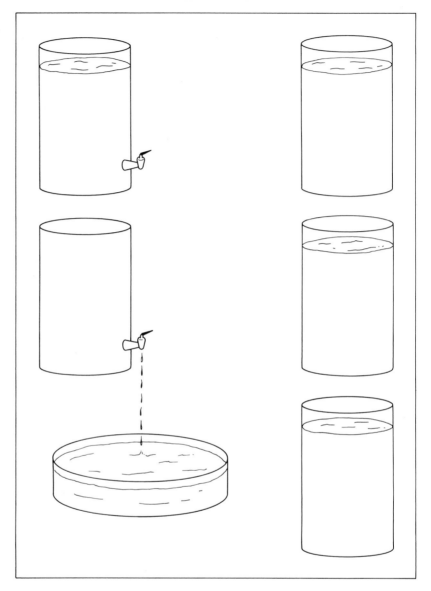

Piaget's studies on various conservations revealed similar developmental trends, moving from total lack of a conservation concept, to differential conservation for some concepts, to total conservation for all concepts. Piaget observed that conservation varied as a function of age and of the particular concept

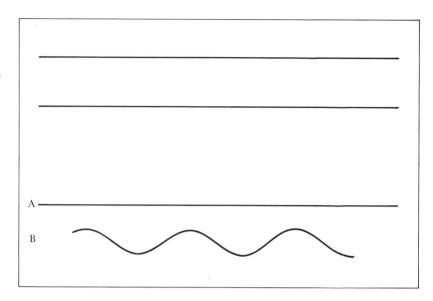

Figure 6-4 (c)
Piaget's conservation of length problem. The child is shown two equal lengths of string. One piece is made wavy and the child is asked which is longer, A or B.

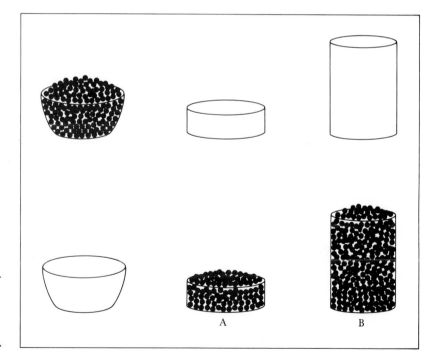

Figure 6-4 (d)
Piaget's conservation of quantity problem. The child is asked to pick up a marble in each hand from the bowl and place one in container A and one in container B until there are no more pairs of marbles and the bowl is empty. The child is then asked which container has more marbles.

involved. Conservation of volume appeared last, at about 12 years of age or beyond (Flavell, 1963). As we learned earlier, the preoperational child is unable to acquire these concepts because of cognitive immaturity and the absence of necessary logical operations. In other words, concept acquisition is subject to the cognitive restrictions and constraints of the developmental period of the child. This is a readiness model of cognitive development which predicts that concept learning is a function of the cognitive level or stage of the child.

Piaget (1970) has described as "hopeless" any attempt to teach children concepts before the appearance of developmentally controlled cognitive structures and operations that permit learning to occur. In fact, Piaget has dismissed learning approaches to concept formation as the "American question." His view that learning is a secondary or perhaps tertiary factor in cognitive development has generated intense reactions from other psychologists who disagree about the nature of concept development. While Piaget's original observations have been replicated by a number of American psychologists (Flavell,

Piaget's conservation of a liquid problem. Understanding conservation, like understanding object permanence, requires the child to go beyond the apparent evidence of his physical senses. In this case, even though it *looks* like there is more water in the tall measuring tube than in the beaker, the actual volume of water is the same in both containers. In other words, the volume of water is conserved. For Piaget, mastery of the overall concept of conservation is a landmark in cognitive development.

(Photo by George Roos/Peter Arnold, Inc.)

1963, 1970), controversy has arisen over the interpretation of the experiments and the teachability of concepts (Brainerd, 1973, 1977; Kuhn, 1974; Sigel & Hooper, 1968).

Concept Training
Several investigators have tried to test Piaget's theory of development empirically by investigating the effects of training on concept development in children. If preoperational children can be taught concepts that Piaget states are restricted to the concrete operational period or beyond, this would challenge Piaget's theory that cognitive development is controlled by internal, self-regulating mechanisms. Most training attempts have been directed toward conservation concepts because of their singular importance in Piaget's theory, although seriation, classification, and spatial concepts have also been investigated.

Brainerd (1977a, b) and Kuhn (1974), among others, have commented on the difficulties that plague laboratory tests of Piaget's theory. There are questions of whether such tests are fair, or equivalent to Piagetian conservation tasks, which are nonstandardized, clinical-style, question-and-answer approaches to children's thinking processes. There are also questions about the criteria for concept acquisition, generalization from one concept to another, and differential biasing of results as a function of the experimental procedure used. For example, Piagetian tasks may increase the probability of data supporting Piaget's theory, while laboratory procedures favor learning as the basis for concept formation. As Ginsburg and Koslowski (1976) state, perhaps clarification of these issues will be reached when investigators become less interested in Piagetian demonstrations, particularly conservation, and more interested in the phenomenon of development itself.

PIAGET'S THEORY OF COGNITIVE DEVELOPMENT

Piaget's theory of cognitive development is the most ambitious and influential statement about child development in contemporary psychology. The complexity and breadth of Piaget's developmental psychology preclude any attempts to summarize the theory without a serious loss of appreciation for the magnitude of the work. Our purpose here is merely to outline Piaget's theory and to give some preliminary understanding of the principles and concepts that characterize Piaget's theory of development. Detailed treatments of Piaget's theory are found in the works of his major interpreters such as Flavell (1963,1977), Inhelder, Sinclair, and Bovet (1974), Phillips (1975), and Sigel and Cocking (1977). If you are more ambitious, you may turn directly to the works of Piaget, with the warning that they are difficult to read and understand— even in English.

Jean Piaget (1896–1980) was a Swiss psychologist who had originally been trained as a zoologist. A gifted observer, scientist, and scholar, Piaget turned his interests early in his career to philosophy and epistemology, the science of the origins, methods, nature, and limits of knowledge. His preoccupation with the origins of knowledge foretold his entrance into the field of child development. Having received some psychological training at various laboratories and psychiatric clinics in Europe, Piaget began working in the laboratory with Alfred Binet in Paris. There, Piaget worked with children, studying their performance on early tests of intelligence. Pursuing his established interest in epistemology, Piaget found the processes leading to problem-solving in children to be more revealing than the tests themselves, particularly those processes leading to incorrect answers (Flavell, 1963).

Piaget subsequently applied clinical methods of interviewing and questioning, which he had learned during his psychiatric training, to learn more about how children solved problems. Piaget's research and publications on child development took him to the University of Geneva as codirector of the J.J. Rousseau Institute. By this time, Piaget had abandoned his scholarly activities as a zoologist, but his biological orientation continued to play a significant role in his theory of development, as we shall see. In 1955, Piaget established the International Center of Genetic Epistemology in Geneva, where his work continued until his death in 1980.

Principles of Genetic Epistemology

As we noted earlier in this chapter, Piaget's theory of development is a process approach to the study of cognition or intelligence. It is concerned with describing the ontogenesis of cognition from infancy to maturity in terms of the dynamic mental processes and functions underlying cognition. Because Piaget's theory deals exclusively with the ontogenesis of knowledge, it is also referred to as genetic epistemology. This term was first used by James Baldwin (1915) to describe a theoretical system in which he postulated three stages of thinking and of interpreting reality.

Piaget described his developmental epistemology as a naturalistic, biological model of an organism–environment interactional system. He related biological adaptation to intellectual–cognitive adaptation, assigning the roots of cognitive development to biological evolution. Cognitive development is inevitable in organisms equipped with structures for adapting to changes in the environment. Innate biological or regulatory mechanisms generate laws of organization (rules of logical operations). For Piaget, these laws have evolved phylogenetically and ontogenetically as a function of living in a lawful universe.

This biological approach predictably leads to the interpretation that the basic properties of cognition or intelligence are constant, species-specific characteristics. Piaget refers to these invariant biological characteristics as functional invariants. The two major functional invariants are cognitive organization and cognitive adaptation. Cognitive organization refers to the orderly system of totalities of cognitive structures and the dynamic relationships among their parts. It is important to remember that cognitive organization changes from one stage of development to the next and that these are qualitative changes in organizational content and structure. Cognitive adaptation is a functional invariant which consists of two processes of singular importance to Piaget's theory: assimilation and accommodation.

ASSIMILATION AND ACCOMMODATION Assimilation and accommodation are two basic processes which determine and control cognitive development. Assimilation is the process by which information from the environment is received and then changed by existing cognitive structures (sets of "rules" for thinking) into a form that can be used and understood. That is, new elements of information are incorporated into genetically preprogrammed cognitive structures at a level and in a form appropriate to the capacities of the cognitive system at that point in development. The assimilation process has been likened to biological assimilation of food via digestion.

Accommodation occurs simultaneously with assimilation. As

stimulus inputs are being assimilated by cognitive structures, the cognitive structures are adjusting (accommodating) to the assimilated material. Accommodation permits change in cognitive structures and thereby alters the individual's knowledge about the environment.

Thus we see a dynamic relationship between assimilation and accommodation. Incoming information is transformed so as to "fit" existing structures, which also change to "fit" the incoming information. The result of accommodation is to produce increases in intelligence. The changes in cognitive structures (accommodation) now permit the assimilation of new information, which makes for new accommodations, and so on. The information that is learned is organized into what Piaget calls a schema. The formation of schemata results in cognition (mental representations), which directs behavior. Feedback information from behavior provides new information for assimilation and accommodation (Figure 6-5).

DEVELOPMENTAL INTERACTIONISM AND CONSTRUCTIVISM Piaget's concept of interaction between innate cognitive capacities and environmental or experiential factors is based on his view that it is impossible to separate the "knowing subject" from the "knowable object" (Inhelder, Sinclair, & Bovet, 1974). Cognitive development can occur only through the child's experiences with the environment. As the child moves about and experiments with the environment, a gradual theory of the world is constructed. In this interactionist interpretation, the role of the environment is minimal. It does not violate Piaget's biological principle that cognition is internally guided and relatively immune to modification or acceleration by environmental influences (learning).

Piaget views the child as an active organism that must create or build what we recognize as human knowledge. The basic assumption of developmental constructivism is that no human knowledge exists preformed in the infant or is inherent in external stimuli. Through actions and experiences with the environment, the child constructs ideas or schemata about the nature of its environment.

EQUILIBRATION Gesell (1946) first used the concept of equilibrium as a self-regulatory mechanism which directed and

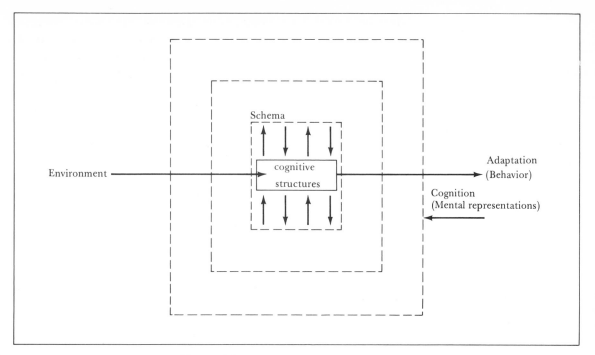

Figure 6-5
A schematic diagram of assimilation and accommodation.

controlled maturation. Piaget postulated the process of equilibrium as the major organizing developmental force behind cognitive change and growth. Knowledge grows as a function of conflict, or disequilibrium, between the existing adaptation level (what the individual knows at any point in development) and the challenge of new situations. Equilibration is a self-regulatory process in which the individual initiates new assimilations and accommodations in order to reduce the unpleasant feelings associated with disequilibrium. When new experiences or information cannot be reconciled with old structures, the child makes further assimilation attempts and generates newly accommodated structures, finally reaching equilibrium and understanding of the new situation. It is the process of equilibration that creates Piaget's stage progression of cognitive development.

STAGE THEORY   If you think about the processes of assimilation, accommodation, and equilibration and their impact on cognitive structures and cognition, you will see that Piaget is describing intellectual development as a series of organizations and reorganizations of cognitive structures. Further, each structural reorganization incorporates all previously existing structures, so nothing is lost in the reorganization process. And because each structural reorganization integrates new information with old information, the result is a new cognitive entity that is qualitatively different from the previous structural organization.

Piaget describes this stage progression of development as a continuous series of events, but the stages themselves are discontinuous and qualitatively separate. We have seen that Piaget's interest lies in the structure of cognition, which emerges in an invariant, predictable sequence. Piaget's observations also have provided normative, descriptive approximations of age-related periods and stages, denoting the average age at which certain cognitive abilities emerge. Piaget uses the term "period" to identify major developmental epochs and refers to the subdivisions of periods as "stages" (Flavell, 1963). While Piaget prefers this usage of periods and stages in his taxonomy of cognitive development, others use these terms interchangeably. A brief description of Piaget's periods of cognitive development is presented in Table 6-1. A more detailed presentation of the stages of the sensorimotor period is shown in Table 6-2. We will not explore Piaget's periods and stages in any detail. Our approach has been to discuss the basic ideas and assumptions of Piaget's system in the belief that this will provide a better understanding of Piaget's theory than do elaborations of periods and stages.

EVALUATION OF PIAGET'S THEORY OF COGNITIVE DEVELOPMENT

The pervasiveness of Piaget's theory throughout much of developmental psychology requires some evaluation of its empirical status. Much of Piaget's theory is cast in terms that are difficult to understand even with help from his interpreters. Many of the mental processes elaborated by Piaget are beyond empirical demonstration at this time, so we must deal with concepts such as cognitive structures, logical operations, schemata, and equilibration only as hypothetical constructs. The universality and invariance of cognitive develop-

Table 6-1
Piaget's Periods of Cognitive Development

PERIOD	GENERAL DESCRIPTION	AGE LEVEL (YR.)
Sensorimotor Period	The child progresses from instinctual reflexive action at birth to symbolic activities, to the ability to separate self from object in the environment. He develops limited capabilities for anticipating the consequences of actions.	0 ½ 1 1½ 2
Preoperational Period	The child's ability to think becomes refined during this period. First he develops what Piaget calls preconceptual thinking, in which he deals with each thing individually but is not able to group objects. The child is able to use symbols, such as words, to deal with problems. During the latter half of this period, the child develops better reasoning abilities but is still bound to the here-and-now.	2½ 3 3½ 4 4½ 5 5½ 6 6½ 7
Period of Concrete Operations	At this time, the child develops the ability to perform intellectual operations—such as reversibility, conservation, ordering of things by number, size, or class, etc. His ability to relate time and space is also matured during this period.	7½ 8 8½ 9 9½ 9½ 10 10½
Period of Formal Operations	This is the period in which the person learns hypothetical reasoning. He is able to function purely on a symbolic, abstract level. His conceptualization capacities are matured.	11 11½ 12 12½ 13 13½ 14 14½ 15

(Adapted from Belkin & Gray, 1977, p. 67. Copyright © 1977.)

ment, as Piaget conceptualized it, contradict what we know about developmental plasticity. While the data reflecting environmental effects on cognitive development are inconsistent, there are many reports of significant variations in cognitive

Table 6-2
Multidimensional View of Development during the Sensorimotor Period

STAGE	DEVELOPMENTAL UNIT	INTENTION AND MEANS—END RELATIONS	MEANING	OBJECT PERMANENCE	SPACE	TIME	CAUSALITY	IMITATION	PLAY
1	Exercising the ready-made sensorimotor schemes (0–1 mo.)								
2	Primary circular reactions (1–4 mo.)		Different responses to different objects					Pseudo imitation begins	Apparent functional autonomy of some acts
3	Secondary circular reactions (4–8 mo.)	Acts upon objects	"Motor meaning"	Brief single-modality search for absent object	All modalities focus on single object	Brief search for absent object	Acts, then waits for effect to occur	Pseudo imitation quicker, more precise. True imitation of acts already in repertoire and visible on own body	More acts done for their own sake
4	Coordination of secondary schemes (8–12 mo.)	Attacks barrier to reach goal	Symbolic meaning	Prolonged, multimodality search	Turns bottle to reach nipple	Prolonged search for absent object	Attacks barrier to reach goal; waits for adults to serve him	True imitation of novel acts not visible on own body	Means often become ends; ritualization begins
5	Tertiary circular reactions (12–18 mo.)	"Experiments in order to see"; discovery of new means through "groping accommodation"	Elaboration through action and feedback	Follows sequential displacements if object in sight	Follows sequential displacements if object in sight	Follows sequential displacements if object in sight	Discovers new means; solicits help from adults	True imitation quicker, more precise	Quicker conversion of means to end; elaboration of ritualization
6	Invention of new means through mental combinations (18–24 mo.)	Invention of new means through reciprocal assimilation of schemes	Further elaboration; symbols increasingly covert	Follows sequential displacement with object hidden; symbolic representation of object, mostly internal	Solves detour problem; symbolic representation of spatial relationships, mostly internal	Both anticipation and memory	Infers causes from observing effects; predicts effects from observing causes	Imitates (1) complex, (2) non-human, (3) absent models,	Treats inadequate stimuli as if adequate to imitate an enactment, i.e., symbolic ritualization or "pretending"

From *The Origins of Intellect: Piaget's Theory*, Second Edition, by John L. Phillips, Jr. W. H. Freeman and Company. Copyright © 1975.)

development as a function of environmental factors (e.g., Almy, 1966; Hunt, 1976).

Similarly, Piaget minimizes the role of experience and environment, a position that is difficult to accept in the light of training experiments in concept development. Piaget's comparative analysis of logical thought processes in children is based on his "highly idealized conception of adult thought" and his tendency to "see nothing but perfect logic and rationality in adult intelligence" (Wohlwill, 1962, pp. 87–112). Piaget's idealized views of adult thinking are simply not realistic. Such exaggerations might well lead to conclusions of qualitative differences between how children and adults think.

Brainerd (1978) strongly argues that Piaget's stage theory is nothing more than descriptive and, contrary to Piaget's claims, does not provide an explanation of cognitive development. Brainerd (1977, 1978) an active critic of Piaget, has reviewed the literature on concept learning and Piagetian development. Brainerd analyzed the available data on concept training experiments and concluded that, contrary to Piaget's theory, children's susceptibility to conservation training does not depend on their developmental stage. Preoperational children have learned the conservation concept and other concepts by such training procedures as simple feedback, learning set, and modeling. Further, Brainerd states that there is no empirical basis for denying that usual learning processes can account for the acquisition of Piaget's stage-related concepts. Brainerd (1977) describes the issue of stage development versus learning as a "pseudo-issue," stating:

It is critical for investigators to recognize that it is impossible, in principle, to address the question of stage versus learning if we continue to operate at a behavioral level. So long as our respective measures of stage and learning are completely behavioral, conjectures about developmental constraints on concept learning will remain untestable. (p. 938)

Brainerd argues that the data reflect the need to consider experiential variables (learning) in cognitive development and concept formation as an alternative to Piaget's views of logical operations as spontaneous, predetermined developments in the concrete operational child. Training studies in concept formation demonstrate that acceleration of cognitive development may be possible. They suggest that the apparent invariance of concept formation which Piaget describes may be partially attributable to common child-rearing practices. Much of the controversy over concept development and training resists resolution because of criteria differences in what constitutes a display of concept responses. Conservation problems presented in the laboratory are not always the same as Piagetian tasks, and there is less subjectivity and interpretation of children's responses in laboratory experiments.

A number of methodological criticisms have focused on Piaget's "clinical methods" and the effects of these procedures on his assessment of cognitive development in children. As we stated earlier, Piaget originally adapted psychiatric clinical interviewing techniques to children's problem-solving in an attempt to obtain information about their thinking processes. Piaget talked with children, asked them questions, and pursued the patterns and logic of their thoughts as he tried to discover systems of reasoning underlying their interpretations of reality. With preverbal children, Piaget used naturalistic observations and subsequent interpretations of behavior patterns. Piaget's clinical method is now known as the "method of critical exploration" (Inhelder et al., 1974).

This procedure has drawn a great deal of criticism (Braine, 1959; Brainerd, 1973a,b; Estes, 1956; Flavell, 1963, 1970). Reported studies suggest that many of Piaget's observations are seriously dependent upon Piagetian methodology and resist laboratory replication. The heavy reliance upon children's language may lead to results that reflect language skills, expression, and vocabulary more than limitations of reasoning processes. Nonverbal approaches often produce results at variance with Piaget's theory. In addition, the method of critical exploration precludes standardized experimental procedures and promotes variations in task presentation and interpretation, verbal exchanges, and outcomes. Related to this problem is the wide range of response interpretation available to the observer using the critical exploration method.

Piaget's theory suggests no sex differences in cognitive development, but the research findings are contradictory. Studies of sex differences in conservation, for example, have shown no sex differences (Boland, 1973; Elkind, 1967; Taloumis, 1975), while others have found sex differences favoring boys

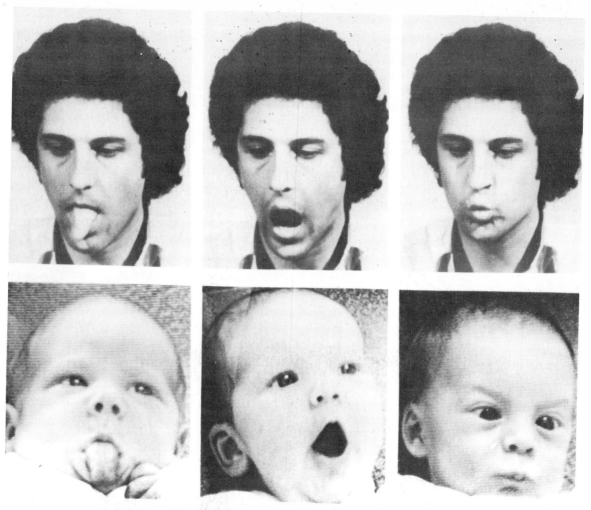

Figure 6-6
Photographs of 2- to 3-week-old infants imitating facial expressions.

(From Meltzoff & Moore, 1977. Copyright © 1977 by the American Association for the Advancement of Science.)

(Burke, 1974; Jordan & Jordan, 1975). Hunt (1975), however, has reported examiner bias and examiner sex effects on the outcome of conservation studies.

A study by Meltzoff and Moore (1977) undermines Piaget's claim that imitation of adult facial gestures cannot appear in infants until 8 to 12 months of age. Prior to this developmental period, Piaget says, the cognitive ability for imitation does not exist. Meltzoff and Moore, however, have reported the demonstration of both facial and gestural imitation in infants between 12 and 21 days old (Figure 6-6). These authors claim that this neonatal imitation is mediated by an abstract representational system and that their findings require a change in our conception of neonatal cognitive capacity. The impact of the Meltzoff and Moore study awaits replication and verification.

The issues and controversies surrounding Piaget's theory are complex and the data are difficult to resolve. While it may indeed be the best theory of cognitive development available (Neimark, 1975), we should maintain the perspective that it is *one* approach to cognitive development. The enormous generation of classic Piagetian studies at times suggests that it is the only theory worthy of such intense investigation. As Ginsburg and Koslowski (1976) emphasize, it is time to go beyond Piagetian orthodoxy and approach cognitive development from a perspective of neo-, pseudo-, or non-Piagetian theories. They call for a "revisionist" movement since it is now clear that continued demonstrations, replications, and refutations will not resolve the controversies over Piaget's system.

THE CUMULATIVE LEARNING MODEL OF COGNITIVE DEVELOPMENT

Gagné (1968) has offered a compelling theory of intellectual development as an alternative to maturational and Piagetian theories. Gagné proposes that intellectual development results from the cumulative effects of learning. Development, for Gagné, is the result of acquiring an ordered set of capabilities, which progressively build upon each other through the processes of differentiation, recall, and transfer of learning. A basic premise in this cumulative learning model of development is that much of what children and adults learn assumes the form of complex "rules," which derive from simpler rules and concepts. The learning of rules and concepts, in turn, depends upon remembering previously learned discriminations and associations (Figure 6-7). Gagné describes a hypothetical cumulative learning sequence in the acquisition of the conservation concept of liquid volume, which is shown in Figures 6-8 and 6-9. Note that Gagné hypothesizes that this developmental sequence begins with the learning of nonmetric

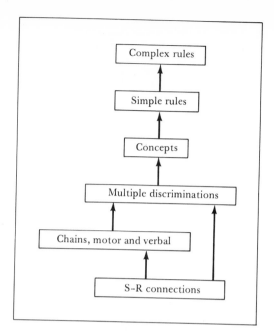

judgments of liquid-volume conservation. This learning then generalizes and transfers to a quantitative concept.

The cumulative learning model proposes that the inability of children to understand liquid–volume conservation reflects a lack of knowledge about containers, volumes, areas, lengths, widths, heights, and liquids. For Gagné, such concept development depends upon the cumulative effects of learning these basic facts rather than on internalized rules of cognitive operations. Gagné believes that Piaget's descriptions of various logical operations are abstractions that, while part of Piaget's thinking, are not in the child's mind. The "magic" in the development of structures of intellectual capability is in learning, memory, and transfer.

Gagné states:

In an oversimplified way, it may be said that the stage of intellectual development depends upon what the learner knows already and how much he has yet to learn in order to achieve some particular goal. Stages of development are not related to age, except in the sense that learning takes time. They are not related to logical structures, except in the sense that the combining of prior capabilities into new ones carries its own inherent logic. (p. 190)

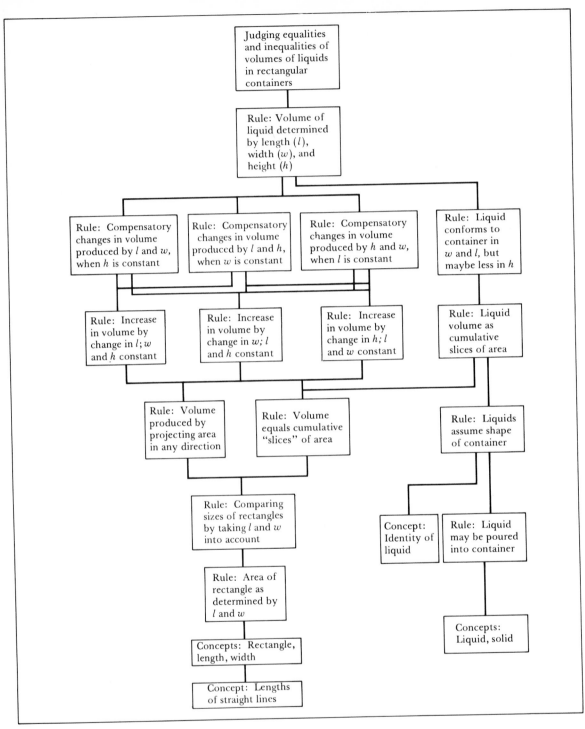

Figure 6-8
A cumulative learning sequence pertaining to the development of nonmetric judgments.

(From Gagné, 1968.)

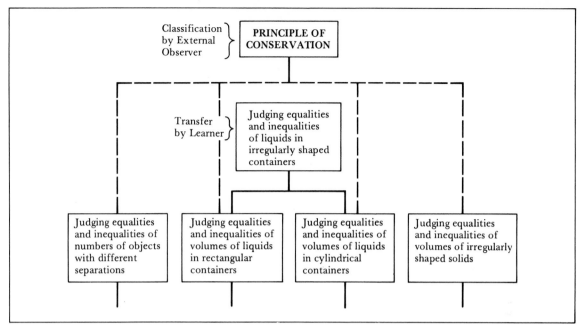

Figure 6-9
The contrast between a principle acquired by the learner through transfer from previously learned priniciples, and a principle of conservation used as a classificatory aid by an external observer.

(From Gagné, 1968.)

REFERENCES Allen, C. N. Individual differences in delayed reaction of infants. *Archives of Psychology,* 1931, *19,* No. 127.

Almy, M. *Young children's thinking.* New York: Teacher's College Press, 1966.

Baldwin, J. M. *Genetic theory of reality.* New York: G. P. Putnam, 1915.

Belkin, G. S., & Gray, J. L. *Educational psychology: An introduction.* Dubuque, Iowa: William C. Brown, 1977.

Blumenthal, A. L. *The process of cognition.* Englewood Cliffs, New Jersey: Prentice-Hall, 1977.

Boland, S. K. Conservation tasks with retarded and non-retarded children. *Exceptional Children,* 1973, *12,* 209–213.

Bolton, N. *Concept formation.* Oxford: Pergamon Press, 1977.

Bower, T. G. R. *Development in infancy.* San Francisco: Freeman, 1974.

Braine, M. D. S. The ontogeny of certain logical operations: Piaget's formulations examined by nonverbal methods. *Psychology Monographs,* 1959, *73,* No. 5.

Brainerd. C. J. Neo-Piagetian training experiments revisited: Is there any support for the cognitive-developmental stage hypothesis? *Cognition,* 1973, *2,* 349–370. (a)

Brainerd, C. J. Judgments and explanations as criteria for the presence of cognitive structures. *Psychological Bulletin,* 1973, *79,* 172–179. (b)

Brainerd, C. J. Cognitive development and concept training: An interpretive review. *Psychological Bulletin,* 1977, *84,* 919–939.

Brainerd, C. J. The stage question in cognitive-developmental theory. *The Behavioral and Brain Sciences,* 1978, *1,* (in press).

Bruner, J. S. The course of cognitive growth. *American Psychologist,* 1964, *19,* 1–15.

Bruner, J. S., Goodnow, J. J., & Austin, G. A. *A study of thinking.* New York: Wiley, 1956.

Buehler, C., & Hetzer, H. *Testing children's development from birth to school age.* New York: Farrar & Rhinehart, 1935.

Burke, E. Training in logical thinking and its effects on the grouping strategies of 8 year old children. *Journal of Child Psychiatry and Psychology,* 1974, *15,* 303–312.

Cohen, L. B., DeLoache, J. S., & Pearl, R. A. An examination of interference effects in infants' memory for faces. *Child Development,* 1977, *48,* 88–96.

Cole, M., Frankel, F., & Sharp, D. Development of free recall learning in children. *Developmental Psychology,* 1971, *4,* 109–123.

Corsini, D. A. Developmental changes in the effect of nonverbal cues on retention. *Developmental Psychology,* 1969, *1,* 425–435.

Elkind, D. Piaget's conservation problems. *Child Development,* 1967, *38,* 15–27.

Estes, B. W. Some mathematical and logical concepts in children. *Journal of Genetic Monographs,* 1956, *88,* 219–227.

Fagan, J. F. Infants' delayed recognition memory and forgetting. *Journal of Experimental Child Psychology,* 1973, *16,* 424–450.

Fagan, J. F. Infant recognition memory: Studies in forgetting. *Child Development,* 1977, *48,* 68–78.

Flavell, J. H. *The developmental psychology of Jean Piaget.* New York: Van Nostrand, 1963.

Flavell, J. H. Concept development. In P. H. Mussen (Ed.), *Carmichael's manual of child psychology* (Vol. 1). New York: Wiley, 1970.

Flavell, J. H. What is memory development the development of? *Human Development,* 1971, *14,* 272–275.

Flavell, J. H. *Cognitive development.* Englewood Cliffs, New Jersey: Prentice-Hall, 1977.

Friedman, S. Habituation and recovery of visual response in the alert human newborn. *Journal of Experimental Child Psychology*, 1972, *13*, 339–349.

Gagné, R. M. Contributions of learning to human development. *Psychological Review*, 1968, 75. 177–191.

Gesell, A. The ontogenesis of infant behavior. In L. Carmichael (Ed.), *Manual of child psychology*, New York: Wiley, 1946.

Gibson, J. J. *The senses considered as perceptual systems.* Boston: Houghton-Mifflin, 1966.

Ginsburg, H., & Koslowski, B. Cognitive Development. In M. R. Rosenzweig & L. W. Porter (Eds.), *Annual Review of Psychology*, 1976, *27*.

Hunt, J. McV. Piaget's observations as a source of hypotheses concerning motivation. *Merrill-Palmer Quarterly*, 1963, *9*, 263–275.

Hunt, J. McV. The utility of ordinal scales inspired by Piaget's observations. *Merrill-Palmer Quarterly*, 1976, *22*, 31–45.

Hunt, T. D. Early number conservation and experimenter expectancy. *Child Development*, 1975, *46*, 984–987.

Hunter, W. S. The delayed reaction in a child. *Psychological Review*, 1917, *24*, 75–87.

Inhelder, B., Sinclair, H., & Bovet, M. *Thinking and the development of cognition.* Cambridge, Massachusetts: Harvard University Press, 1974.

Jablonski, E. M. Free recall in children. *Psychological Bulletin*, 1974, *81*, 522–539.

Jordan, V. B., & Jordan, L. A. Relative strengths of IQ, mental age, and CA for predicting performance on Piagetian tests. University of Denver, 1975, (ERIC Document Reproduction Service, No. ED 111 510).

Kagen, J., & Kogen, N. Individual variations in cognitive processes. In P. H. Mussen (Ed.), *Carmichael's manual of child psychology*, 1970, New York: Wiley, 1970.

Kendler, H. H., & Kendler, T. S. Vertical and horizontal processes in problem solving. *Psychological Bulletin*, 1962, *69*, 1–16.

Kendler, T. S. Concept formation. In P. R. Farnsworth, O. McNemar, and Q. McNemar (Eds.), *Annual Review of Psychology*, *12*, 1961.

Kingsley, P. R., & Hagen, J. W. Induced versus spontaneous rehearsal in short-term memory of nursery school children. *Child Development*, 1969, *1*, 40–46.

Kuhn, D. Inducing development experimentally: Comments on a research design. *Developmental Psychology*, 1974, *10*, 590–600.

Liberty, C., & Ornstein, P. A. Age differences in organization and recall: The effects of training in categorization. *Journal of Experimental Psychology*, 1973, *15*, 169–186.

Martin, R. M. Effects of familiar and complex stimuli on infant attention. *Developmental Psychology*, 1975, *11*, 178–185.

McCall, R. B., Kennedy, C. B., & Dodds, C. The interference effect of distracting stimuli on the infant's memory. *Child Development*, 1977, *48*, 79–87.

Meltzoff, A. N., & Moore, M. K. Imitation of facial and manual gestures by human neonates. *Science*, 1977, *198*, 75–78.

Miranda, S. Visual abilities and pattern preferences of premature and full-term neonates. *Journal of Experimental Child Psychology*, 1970, *10*, 189–205.

Morrison, F. J. A developmental study of the effects of familiarity on short-term visual memory. Unpublished doctoral dissertation. Harvard University, 1971.

Neimark, E. D. Intellectual development during adolescence. In S. Horowitz (Ed.), *Review of research in child development*, 1975, *4*.

Neisser, U. *Cognitive psychology*. New York: Appleton-Century-Crofts, 1967.

Ornstein, P. A., Naus, M. J., & Liberty, C. Rehearsal and organizational processes in children's memory. *Child Development*, 1975, *46*, 818–830.

Pancratz, C., & Cohen, L. B. Recovery of habituation in infants. *Journal of Experimental Child Psychology*, 1970, *9*, 208–216.

Phillips, J. L., Jr. *The origins of intellect: Piaget's theory*. San Francisco: Freeman, 1975.

Piaget, J. *Play, dreams, and imitation in children*. New York: Norton, 1951.

Piaget, J. *The construction of reality in the child*. New York: Basic Books, 1954.

Piaget, J. *The child's conception of the world*. Totowa, New Jersey: Littlefield, Adams, 1965.

Piaget, J. A conversation with Jean Piaget. *Psychology Today*, 1970, *3*, 25–32.

Posner, M. I. *Cognition: An introduction*. Olenview, Illinois: Scott, Foresman, 1973.

Reynolds, A. G., & Flagg, P. W. *Cognitive psychology*. Cambridge, Massachusetts: Winthrop, 1977.

Sheingold, K. Developmental differences in intake and storage of visual information. *Journal of Experimental Child Psychology*, 1973, *16*, 1–11.

Sigel, I. E., & Cocking, R. R. *Cognitive development from childhood to adolescence: A constructivist perspective.* New York: Holt, Rinehart, & Winston, 1977.

Sigel, I. E., & Hooper, F. H. (Eds.). *Logical thinking in children: Research based on Piaget's theory.* New York: Holt, Rinehart, & Winston, 1968.

Sigman, M., & Parmele, A. Visual preferences of four-month-old premature and full-term infants. *Child Development,* 1974, *45,* 959–965.

Skalet, M. The significance of delayed reactions in young children. *Comparative Psychology Monographs,* 1931, 7.

Sokolov, E. N. *Perception and the conditioned reflex.* New York: Macmillan, 1960.

Taloumis, T. The relationship of area conservation to area measurement as affected by sequence of presentation of Piagetian area tasks to boys and girls in grades one through three. *Journal for Research in Mathematics Education,* 1975, *6,* 232–242.

Underwood, B. J. Attributes of Memory. *Psychological Review,* 1969, *76,* 559–573.

Watson, R. J. *The great psychologists* (2nd ed.). Philadelphia: Lippincott, 1968.

Weizmann, F., Cohen, L. B., & Pratt, J. Novelty, familiarity, and the development of infant attention. *Developmental Psychology,* 1971, *4,* 149–154.

Wetherford, M. J., & Cohen, L. B. Developmental changes in infant visual preferences for novelty and familiarity. *Child Development,* 1973, *44,* 416–424.

Wohlwill, J. F. From perception to inference: A dimension of cognitive development. In W. Kessen & C. Kuhlman (Eds.), Thought in the Young Child. *Monograph of the Society for Research in Child Development,* 1962, *27,* 87–112.

Zeaman, D., & House, B. J. The role of attention in retardate discrimination learning. In N. R. Ellis (Ed.), *Handbook of mental deficiency.* New York: McGraw-Hill, 1963.

Chapter

LANGUAGE DEVELOPMENT

Seven

INTRODUCTION

*A*ll children, except for the most severely impaired, acquire language with ease. They do so with a sequential regularity in development that is independent of the particular language learned. The only general requirements for language development are adequate exposure to a linguistic environment and sufficient opportunity for linguistic experience. The facility, motivation, and spontaneity which characterize language acquisition in children reveal a degree of linguistic capacity and a prepared-to-learn quality that are unequaled in the animal kingdom. This statement does not deny the linguistic capacities that have been demonstrated in apes, but rather emphasizes the differences in such capacities between humans and infrahuman primates.

Though the development of general cognitive skills and the capacity for symbolic thinking processes underlie the development of linguistic potential and expression, there is no full and adequate explanation of language acquisition in terms of existing cognitive theories. Learning theories also have failed to explain language development, despite the obvious fact that language is learned. Clearly, the interaction of learning and maturation is necessary for language development, but we are hard pressed to explain how these processes operate and interact in language development. Although a psychological explanation of language development is beyond current knowledge, the normative sequence in the ontogenesis of language has been heavily researched and described.

Language is perhaps the highest expression of cognitive development and complexity. Its psychological and evolutional significance are often obscured by the very familiarity of its emergence in children and its use in every known human society, no matter how primitive. Yet we know very little indeed about language development. The abstract nature and complexity of language seem to defy scientific understanding. Empirical approaches to linguistic development have been inherently limited by both theoretical and methodological problems and constraints.

For some time, language and language development have been recognized as psychological phenomena. The psychological study of language and language acquisition has led to the emergence of two new subspecialties in psychology: psycholinguistics and developmental psycholinguistics. Psycholinguistics is the study of the cognitive processes required for learning and using language (Slobin, 1974). By studying language behavior and comprehension, psycholinguists attempt to discover the various cognitive abilities underlying linguistic functions and how linguistic systems are acquired. Developmental psycholinguistics is concerned with the ontogenesis of language and with the developmental processes underlying language acquisition.

According to Greene (1972), the term, "psycholinguistics," first came into use in the early 1950s, when psychologists began applying linguistic methods to the psychological study of language. Linguistics is the formal study of the structure of language, including phonetics (speech sounds), semantics, syntax, and grammar. There are several branches of modern linguistics that emphasize its interdisciplinary nature: descriptive linguistics (grammar), historical linguistics, anthropological linguistics, sociolinguistics, phonetics, and applied linguistics, all of which have relevance to psychological approaches to language.

The impact of linguistics on cognitive psychology and language development has been monumental. This impact is attributed almost solely to what is often described as the "revolutionary" approach to linguistics developed by the linguist Noam Chomsky (1957, 1965). In the discussion to follow, we will explore the evolution of language, current major theories of language development, and the ontogenesis of language in normal children. As a prelude to our discussion, let us first consider the historical context from which developmental psycholinguistics derives.

HISTORICAL PERSPECTIVE

*T*he record of human history reveals a recurring interest in the origins and diversity of language. The fifth century Greek historian, Herodotus, gave the following account of "The Natural Language of Man":

The Egyptians before the reign of Psammetichus used to think that of all races in the world they were the most ancient; Psammetichus, however, when he came to the throne, took it into his head to settle this question of priority, and ever since his time the Egyptians have believed that the Phrygians surpass them in antiquity and that they themselves come second. Psammetichus, finding that mere inquiry failed to reveal which was the original race of mankind, devised an ingenious method of determining the matter. He took at random, from an ordinary family, two newly born infants and gave them to a shepherd to be brought up among his flocks, under strict orders that no one should utter a word in their presence. They were to be kept by themselves in a lonely cottage, and the shepherd was to bring in goats from time to time, to see that the babies had enough milk to drink, and to look after them in any other way that was necessary. All these arrangements were made by Psammetichus because he wished to find out what word the children would first utter, once they had grown out of their meaningless baby-talk. The plan succeeded; two years later the shepherd, who during that time had done everything he had been told to do, happened one day to open the door of the cottage and go in, when both children running up to him with hands outstretched, pronounced the word "becos". The first time this occurred the shepherd made no mention of it; but later, when he found that every time he visited the children to attend to their needs the same word was constantly repeated by them, he informed his master. Psammetichus ordered the children to be brought to him, and when he himself heard them say "becos" determined to find out to what language the word belonged. His inquiries revealed that it was the Phrygian word for "bread", and in consideration of this Egyptians yielded their claims and admitted the superior antiquity of the Phrygians. (From Herodotus, The Histories, *translated by Aubrey de Selincourt, Penguin Classics, 1954, pp. 102–103)*

The biblical account of the origins of language appears in the Book of Genesis. In Chapter 11, the descendants of Noah repopulated the earth and shared only one language among them. As a monument to their achievements and knowledge, they built a great city with a tower, but God, displeased with what He saw, struck each person with a different language so they could not understand one another and scattered them across the face of the earth. The city and tower were called Babel because all of the languages of the earth were confused there, giving rise to the diversity of human languages.

The questions of the origin of language intrigued the classical philosophers of the seventeenth and eighteenth centuries as they considered language the key to understanding human knowledge and thought. In their philosophical essays, they dealt with questions of the innate (rationalistic) versus the learned (empirical) nature of language. Language was considered, as it is by many today, to be *the* unique human characteristic, separating human from nonhuman by an unbridgeable gap.

The earliest attempts to study language scientifically appeared in various "baby biographies" in the late eighteenth century and the nineteenth century. These were diaries of infant development by such individuals as Teidemann (1787), Taine (1869), Darwin (1877), and Preyer (1881) (see Bar-Adon & Leopold, 1971; Kessen, 1965, for excerpts). These anecdotal, observational descriptions gave way to more systematic, controlled studies of language acquisition in children.

The early work during the first half of the twentieth century consisted mainly of normative, descriptive studies in which language acquisition was carefully recorded, revealing an age-related normative pattern of sequential development. The early normative research concentrated on children's patterns of acquiring language sounds, words, and grammar. There was little if any linguistic theory behind the interpretation of these data (see Brown, 1965; McCarthy, 1954, for reviews of the early literature in language development). Language development was considered a function of maturation and/or learning. Linguistic theory was developing independently in the early twentieth century, largely ignored by psychologists who were much more influenced by the new behaviorism of J. B. Watson. Watson's behaviorism forged the experimental paradigm for most of American psychology through the mid-1950s, ending mentalism and early cognitive approaches to the psychological study of language. For Watson (1924), language, like all other behavior, was the result of conditioning and subject to its principles.

Prior to 1930, textbooks of psychology rarely contained more than a paragraph or two on language (McCarthy, 1954). Quantitative studies of language development only began to appear in the literature in 1926. They described various aspects of linguistic development and achievement in infants and children, laying the foundations for the classical normative data. Research in language structure, semantics, and language disorders attracted increasing attention beginning in the early 1940s, as did the study of the effects of environmental factors on language development. By the mid-1950s, a vast amount of descriptive data on language development had accumulated. Most of this data was free from psychological theory and uninfluenced by the developments in linguistics, which up to that time had been dominated by a behavioristic, empirical, but anti-psychological, approach (Bloomfield, 1933).

Learning approaches to language development expanded and continued to flourish (Bandura, 1971; Mowrer, 1960; Skinner, 1957; Staats, 1968, 1971). But the scientific revolution that dramatically changed the nature of research in linguistics and language development and ultimately created the field of psycholinguistics was launched by Noam Chomsky (1957) with his book, *Syntactic Structures*. Chomsky called his new approach to linguistics generative-transformational grammar. It redefined both the field of linguistics and its research methodology (see Palermo, 1978, for an interesting account of the impact of Chomsky's theory on the study of language). Chomsky's approach was a strong rejection of behavioristic linguistics. He demonstrated the futility of attempts to understand language development in terms of simple learning processes or S–R approaches and showed that learning theory is unable to explain the ability to use language. Chomsky's acerbic review of Skinner's (1959) *Verbal Behavior* has become a classic in the literature.

Chomsky advocated a mentalistic, nativistic approach to linguistics directed toward discovering the cognitive capacities that underlie linguistic creativity—that is, the acquisition of rules which make it possible to generate an infinite number of sentences. Brown (1973), Greene (1972), and Palermo (1978), among others, have described how Chomsky's persuasive arguments forced psychologists to reevaluate their approach to language, precipitating a scientific revolution. We will have more to say about theories of language development in a later section.

Research in developmental linguistics is surging ahead and has come to occupy a major portion of the field in developmental psychology and cognitive psychology. Language development is of central significance to developmental psychology and child development. It may well be the most complex of human developmental phenomena, for linguistic capacity is the culmination of the development of a number of biological and cognitive prerequisites.

THE PHYLOGENESIS OF LANGUAGE

The problem with the title of this section is the uncertainty about whether a phylogenesis of language exists. Is there indeed an evolutionary development of language from infra-human to human organisms? Is language a unique human accomplishment representing an evolutional quantum leap? Or can we identify any elemental precursors to human language development among nonhuman life forms, which would suggest phylogenetic continuity of linguistic capacity? What *about* those linguistic apes? As Roger Brown states it, "In the study of language, one begins to feel the hot breath of chimpanzee" (Brown & Herrnstein, 1975, p. 481). While some psychologists agree that the chimpanzee has demonstrated a rudimentary linguistic capacity, others deny so lofty an evolutional achievement to an ape. Perhaps all linguists and most psycholinguists would maintain that linguistic capacity is a species-specific characteristic of humans. But however heated the arguments may be, the degree and level of linguistic capacity and achievement in chimpanzees remain to be determined by current research programs. As we shall see, the answer to the question of linguistic apes also depends on how language is defined.

C. F. Hockett (1960), an American linguist and anthropologist, proposed a system for tracing the origin and evolution of language. Hockett devised a comparative zoological model, which presumably contained the basic design features of all communicative systems from animal communication patterns to human language. His set of 13 design features of communication is shown in Table 7-1. Only human communication contains all 13 design features, thus qualifying it alone as

Table 7-1
Thirteen Design Features of Communication

	SOME GRYLLIDAE AND TETTIGONIIDAE	BEE DANCING	STICKLEBACK COURTSHIP	WESTERN MEADOWLARK SONG	GIBBON CALLS	PARALINGUISTIC PHENOMENA	LANGUAGE	INSTRUMENTAL MUSIC
1 The Vocal-Auditory Channel	Auditory, Not Vocal	No	No	Yes	Yes	Yes	Yes	Auditory, Not Vocal
2 Broadcast Transmission and Directional Reception	Yes	Yes	Yes	Yes	Yes	Yes	Yes	Yes
3 Rapid Fading (Transitoriness)	Yes, Repeated	?	?	Yes	Yes, Repeated	Yes	Yes	Yes
4 Interchangeability	Limited	Limited	No	?	Yes	Largely Yes	Yes	?
5 Total Feedback	Yes	?	No	Yes	Yes	Yes	Yes	Yes
6 Specialization	Yes?	?	In Part	Yes?	Yes	Yes?	Yes	Yes
7 Semanticity	No?	Yes	No	In Part?	Yes	Yes?	Yes	No (In General)
8 Arbitrariness	?	No		If Semantic, Yes	Yes	In Part	Yes	
9 Discreteness	Yes?	No	?	?	Yes	Largely No	Yes	In Part
10 Displacement		Yes, Always	?	?	No	In Part	Yes, Often	
11 Productivity	No	Yes	No	?	No	Yes	Yes	Yes
12 Traditional Transmission	No?	Probably Not	No?	?	?	Yes	Yes	Yes
13 Duality of Patterning	?(Trivial)	No		?	No	No	Yes	Yes

Eight systems of communication posses in varying degrees the 13 design-features of language. Column 1 refers to members of the cricket family. Column 8 concerns only Western music since the time of Bach. A question mark means that it is doubtful or not known if the system has the particular feature. A blank space indicates that feature cannot be determined because another feature is lacking or is indefinite.

language. Hockett (1963) later added three additional design features he believes are absent from other communication systems: reflexiveness (self-reference), prevarication, and learnability. While Hockett's design features may be useful in attempts to describe and clarify some major aspects of language, such lists of "language universals" are incomplete and reveal nothing about the origin and evolution of language. Interspecies sharing of design features is not an argument for a phylogenesis of language, as Hockett proposes.

Although the fact of animal communication signaling systems is not in dispute, it is difficult to assign linguistic significance to any of these systems. There is no evidence that nonhuman communication systems give valid clues to the phylogenesis of the abstract, symbolic system called human language. Chomsky (1967) has pointed out that if infrahuman communication has any basic properties in common with human language, they are to be found at the level of perceptual and cognitive organization and not at the level of behavioral displays or performance. Others argue that animal communication is part of the perceptual and cognitive activities of the organism and that the functional complexity of these systems has been misunderstood, underestimated, and oversimplified (Menzel & Johnson, 1976). Menzel and Johnson present an interesting case for the similarities and continuities between human and nonhuman communication systems from a functionally oriented, cognitive, and comparative point of view. While this comparative–cognitive approach of Menzel and Johnson seems promising, particularly with the primates, the phylogenetic significance of such data remains problematic.

Comparative Primate Research

Apes have long been known to be our closest relatives. Early scientific curiosity about these interesting creatures focused on what appeared to be the prime factor separating them from humans—language. Comparative studies of the speech-producing abilities of human and nonhuman primates date back to the seventeenth century (Lieberman, 1975). At that time, the larynx was mistakenly considered the primary structure required for speech, and since the chimpanzee appeared to possess a larynx similar to that of humans, it was concluded that apes were capable of articulate human speech. The absence of language in these animals was therefore attributed to lack of intelligence or fine motor control over the speech apparatus. Some eighteenth century philosophers viewed apes as retarded people who might possibly be trained to talk, an idea whose time was to come in the twentieth century.

As Liebermann points out, the belief that apes are capable of human speech production persisted until modern times. It is now known (Lieberman, 1975) that articulate speech ability depends on the shape and functioning of the supralaryngeal vocal tract, which is not well developed in infrahuman primates. Lieberman (1975) has demonstrated that chimps have a limited ability for articulation, defined as the ability to generate the wide range of frequencies necessary for speech sounds (phonetic variation).

The classical assumption of speech ability in chimpanzees was weakened by the ape-rearing experiments conducted between 1932 and 1954. During this time, five major efforts to teach chimpanzees human language appeared in the literature (Kellogg, 1968). Of these, only Hayes and Hayes (1951) reported even limited success. After 6 years of intensive training, the Hayes' chimpanzee, Viki, approximated the sounds of "mama," "papa," "cup," and "up." This seemed to be the upper limit of Viki's linguistic abilities, learned only with the greatest of difficulty, and Viki could not always use the four words correctly. The ape-rearing experiments were a dismal failure. Apes did not appear to have any linguistic capacity, nor, for that matter, any linguistic interests.

The answer to the question of the ape's speech abilities was a resounding "no." Kellogg (1968) concluded that the ape's inability to learn language in a home environment was its greatest deficiency. Eric Lenneberg (1964), a noted psycholinguist, stated that "there is no evidence that any nonhuman form has the capacity to acquire even the most primitive stages of language development" (p. 67). Later, Noam Chomsky (1968) remarked with equal finality that "Anyone concerned with the study of human nature and human capacities must somehow come to grips with the fact that all normal humans acquire language, whereas acquisition of even its barest rudiments is quite beyond the capacities of an otherwise intelligent ape" (p. 59). The evidence for a discontinuity theory of language development seemed clear—such capacities were

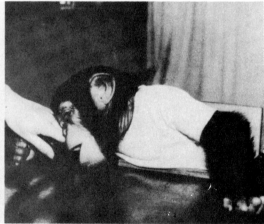

Figure 7-1
Teaching Viki to say "Mama."

(From Hayes & Hayes, 1951. Photos courtesy of The American Philosophical Society.)

unique to humans and had no phylogenetic precursory elements which could be identified among infrahuman primates.

Prior to 1969, there was enough data to justify an assertion of language discontinuity, but perhaps not so strongly worded a statement as we have seen. After all, the ape-rearing experiments were demonstrations of the chimpanzee's inability to produce human articulations, not revelations of linguistic capacity. Until that time, the production of human sounds or words was considered to be the obvious criterion of linguistic ability in apes. The ape-rearing experiments clearly revealed that apes were all but totally lacking in such articulation skills. In other words, apes are not able to spontaneously generate human sounds, for both structural and motivational reasons. Since human speech sounds are beyond the behavioral range of chimpanzees, attempts at speech training place the animal at an insurmountable disadvantage in such experimental tests of linguistic capacity. This represents a classical error in comparative research.

In 1966, Allen and Beatrice Gardner struck upon the idea of an alternative behavioral index to again investigate linguistic ability in apes. Noting the chimpanzee's highly developed manipulatory skills, Gardner and Gardner decided to use a conventional gestural language to demonstrate the presence of language abilities in apes. They chose the American Sign Language (ASL, or the recently adopted term, "Ameslan"), a gestural system of communication used by the deaf in North America. The Gardners obtained a wild-born infant female chimpanzee between 8 and 14 months old, subsequently named Washoe after Washoe County in Nevada. They raised Washoe in a way that maximized social interaction and minimized confinement. All communication to Washoe was in Ameslan, and by using training techniques of imitation, manual "babbling," and instrumental conditioning, they began to teach Washoe Ameslan.

The Gardners (1969) reported that the first phase of "Project Washoe" verified their hypothesis that Ameslan is a feasible medium of communication for the chimpanzee. Washoe had acquired over 30 signs, which she used spontaneously and appropriately by the end of the 22nd month of training. Washoe also spontaneously transferred signs to a wide class of appropriate referents and occasionally combined signs to generate new sentences. In subsequent reports of Project Washoe (Gardner & Gardner, 1971, 1974, 1975), the Gardners described Washoe's remarkable progress in language acquisition. After 51 months of training, Washoe had acquired 132 Ameslan signs in her expressive vocabulary and many more than that in her receptive vocabulary. The Gardners' objective in their project was to determine if a chimpanzee could and would use a human language system to communicate. Washoe was able to ask and respond to questions, combine signs together, and make requests.

Gardner and Gardner (1975), in comparing language acquisition in children and chimpanzees, state, "Any theoretical criteria that can be applied to the early utterances of children can also be applied to the early utterances of chimpanzees. If the children can be said to have acquired language on the basis of their performance, then the chimpanzees can be said to have acquired language to the extent that their performance matches that of the children" (p. 245). The Gardner project was abandoned in 1970 because mature chimpanzees can be difficult and dangerous to manage. Washoe did not retire, however; work with her was continued by Fouts (1975). Other chimpanzees have also been trained in Ameslan in the hope that they would begin "talking" to each other (Fleming, 1974). And the Gardners (1975b) resumed their research with another infant chimpanzee, Mojo.

David Premack also began his pioneering work in 1966 with a 6-year-old mature chimpanzee, Sarah. In a series of reports (1970, 1971, 1972, 1976), Premack has described the results of his efforts to teach a chimpanzee a linguistic system different from that used by Gardner and Gardner. Premack's goal has been to define the fundamental nature of language while trying to determine whether an ape can learn certain elements of a language. Premack established a list of "exemplars," or basic requirements, that an organism must meet as evidence of language acquisition. He provided instructions for teaching the organism the exemplars, which were selected as a partial list of universal features of linguistic structure or functions. Premack was able to construct experimental paradigms for his exemplars in which an ape might demonstrate language capacity. Premack's linguistic exemplars included words, sentences, questions, metalinguistics (using language to teach language), class concepts such as color, shape, and size, the copula (weakened verbal form which links a subject with a predicate: "is," "are," etc.), the quantifiers all, none, one, and several, and the conditional if . . . then.

Figure 7-2
Plastic symbols that varied in color, shape, and size were chosen as the language units to be taught to Sarah. Each plastic symbol stood for a specific word or concept. Premack adopted a "Chinese" convention of writing sentences vertically from top to bottom because Sarah seemed to prefer it. Sarah had to put the words into proper sequence but the orientation of the word symbols was not important.

(From *Teaching Language to an Ape* by A. J. Premack and D. Premack. Copyright October 1972 by Scientific American, Inc. All rights reserved.)

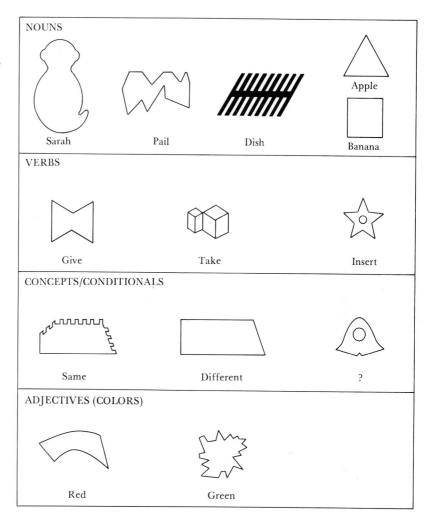

Premack's "words" for the language used with Sarah were pieces of plastic of different sizes, shapes, and colors, which were backed with metal so that they would adhere to a magnetized slate (see Figure 7-2). Sentences were written on the vertical, and Sarah had to get the symbols in the right sequence (Figure 7-3). Sarah's accomplishments were as impressive as Washoe's. She performed various linguistic tasks with 75% to 80% accuracy, a rate comparable with Washoe's accuracy in Ameslan. While she appeared able to engage in

Figure 7-3
Sarah, after reading the message "Sarah insert the apple pail banana dish" on the magnetic board, performed the appropriate actions. To be able to make the correct interpretation that she should put the apple in the dish (not the apple, pail and banana in the dish), the chimpanzee had to understand sentence structure rather than just word order. In actual tests, most symbols were colored.

(Adapted from *Teaching Language to an Ape* by A. J. Premack and D. Premack. Copyright © October 1972 by Scientific American, Inc. All rights reserved.)

some complex linguistic processes when they were elicited by an experimenter, she did not show the spontaneity in initiating conversation demonstrated by Washoe, due perhaps to Sarah's lack of social interaction relative to Washoe. Like Washoe, Sarah became difficult to manage and was replaced by younger animals.

Following the Gardner and Premack projects, a number of other investigators began similar language studies with chimpanzees and gorillas (e.g., Fleming, 1974; Fouts, 1975; Harnad, Steklis, & Lancaster, 1976; see Figure 7-4). Soon there were at least 15 such studies underway to further explore the linguistic competence of apes.

In the midst of these ongoing projects, Terrace (1979) and Terrace, Petitto, Sanders, and Bever (1979) reported the results of a 5-year study designed to carefully evaluate assertions that apes have language capacity. Terrace and colleagues worked with a male chimpanzee named Neam Chimpsky (Nim for short), who was reared in a home environment from infancy and trained in ASL during its first 4 years. All "conversations" between Nim and his teachers were videotaped so that Nim's utterances (signing) could later be analyzed for regularities in

Figure 7-4
Nim signing *shoe* to one of his teachers who is modeling the sign. Dr. Herbert S. Terrace and his group at Columbia University have raised new questions about language acquisition in non-human primates from their work with Nim.

(Photo courtesy of Dr. Herbert S. Terrace.)

grammatical and semantic structure. Terrace et al. based their analysis on the generally accepted belief that language capacity requires the ability to create and understand sentences. Consistent demonstrations of this ability would constitute clear evidence for linguistic competence in apes.

The Gardners, Premack, and others claimed that the language productions of their apes seem to be controlled by a simple set of grammatical rules, and that language acquisition in their apes parallels that of children. However, unlike these earlier researchers, Terrace and his group videotaped more than 20,000 multisign utterances produced by Nim during his 4 years of training. Then they objectively analyzed the videotapes for detailed evidence of grammatical and semantic structure. They found no evidence that Nim could combine symbols to create new meanings or sentences, despite his ability to learn a vocabulary. Further, they found that Nim's combinations of gestures had only a superficial resemblance to a child's early utterances. Unlike a child's early multiword utterances, Nim's multisign utterances were mere repetitions of words, *not* semantic or grammatical elaborations of shorter utterances. For example, although Nim made utterances containing as many as 16 signs, the "sentence" consisted of signs for the following words: *give orange me give eat orange me eat orange give me eat orange give me you.* This does not represent an increase in semantic or grammatical complexity compared to Nim's shorter utterances.

Most of Nim's utterances were also found to have been prompted accidentally by the teacher. Nim simply imitated the teacher's previous utterances, particularly the last one, and interrupted his teachers much more often than a child interrupts an adult's speech. These observations led Terrace et al. to suggest that Nim was less creative than a child in his speech production, which lacked the give-and-take aspect of conversations with young children.

Terrace and co-workers also analyzed films of Washoe and other apes signing with their teachers. Their analyses of these films revealed the same nonhuman pattern of conversation shown by Nim. They concluded that the apes' ability to learn and use vocabulary can be explained by simple, nonlinguistic processes—conditioning processes and problem-solving behavior. They go on to say:

For the moment, our detailed investigation suggests that an ape's language learning is severely restricted. Apes can learn many isolated symbols . . . , but they show no unequivocal evidence of mastering the conversational, semantic, or syntactic organization of language. (Terrace et al., 1979, p. 901)

What can we conclude from these studies about the question of apes and language? Our conclusions will depend on our perspective, as we shall see next.

The Linguistic Competence of Apes

The answer to the question of whether apes have linguistic capacity remains elusive and controversial (see Limber, 1977; Terrace, 1979). Of all the behaviors which we might agree are shared with nonhuman primates, it seems that none is treasured so protectively and so reverently as a human characteristic, and relinquished so grudgingly from this unique status, as language is.

The linguistic capacity of apes cannot be determined without some agreement on the nature of language and its fundamental characteristics, neither of which seems forthcoming at the present time. Attempts to describe the universal properties of language by linguists and psycholinguists have characteristically excluded such capacities from apes (Bronowsky & Bellugi, 1970; Greenberg, 1966; Hockett, 1960; McNeil, 1970). By imposing language requirements such as vocal production and auditory reception, for example, linguists guarantee that no ape can have linguistic potential. Similarly, Chomsky's (1968) abstract structural and semantic properties of language also exclude apes from linguistic consideration. But as Brown (1973) has pointed out, studies with college students have shown that many cannot meet Chomsky's theoretical requirements of the "rudiments" of language. Brown goes on to say that "Chomsky's 'essentials' will certainly keep the animals 'out', but what is the use of that if it is not clear that we ourselves are 'in' " (p. 37)?

Brown (1973) has suggested three properties of language which he considers essential within the context of biological and cultural evolution: semanticity, or meaningfulness; productivity, or sentence construction processes; and displacement, or transmission of information from another time and place. Brown views these linguistic elements as present in the earliest stage of language acquisition in children—Stage I Speech. Brown's analysis of the accomplishments of Washoe and Sarah leads him to conclude that Washoe's performance is similar to that of the simplest stages of linguistic competence in children and that chimpanzees using Ameslan have demonstrated at least some of the rudiments of linguistic capacity. Brown expresses much more caution about the linguistic significance of Sarah's performance in Premack's experiments.

In short, the data suggest that some minimal degree of language capacity or competence exists in apes. Continuity of linguistic capacity does not demand that the apes reach the linguistic skills of humans. Phylogenetic continuity of language capacity requires only the demonstration of some degree of such skills. But it is clear that *some* qualitative differences in language capacity coexist with the quantitative differences between human and nonhuman primates. The fact is, apes do not "have" language in terms of possessing some natural language—at least as far as we know. What they have is the cognitive competence to learn a linguistic system (Ameslan) taught to them by humans. That competence is not comparable to ours and, in fact, pales in the light of human skills.

Brown's (1973) view is that the ape's linguistic competence will be shown to peak at this basic Stage I level (which we will discuss later in this chapter). The quantitative differences in the linguistic attributes shared by humans and apes are very large indeed. And those language characteristics that seem unique to humans represent qualitative differences or discontinuities in the phylogenesis of language. Munn (1971) has pointed to the obvious gap between the human invention of language and the ape's failure to have spontaneously developed a language, a qualitative difference. But even a gap that appears so large in evolution may be due to small intellectual gains or the failure to possess certain unlearned responses such as babbling (Harlow, 1958), or the necessary insight involved in inventing language (Munn, 1971). Such considerations suggest both continuities and discontinuities in the phylogenesis of language capacity.

Brown (1973) also has raised the interesting question of why apes, possessing a level of linguistic skills capable of supporting cultural evolution, do not use these skills to transmit information and build on the experiences of past generations. Perhaps Brown is correct, and we have underestimated the degree to which apes in their natural habitat use their linguistic capacity, most of which is expressed in gestures and body movements. Even if this is true, such linguistic capacity might well meet the needs of a very successful species but fail to meet the requirements of cultural evolution. Some essential cognitive ingredient seems to be lacking in apes, whose general cognitive development has otherwise brought them so close to language expression. Fortunately for the apes, only humans will be tantalized by these observations. While we do not know the answer to the questions raised in this discussion, they will remain fascinating and intriguing in the years to come.

THEORIES OF LANGUAGE DEVELOPMENT

Theories of language acquisition proposed by both linguists and psychologists during this century have come full circle in their theoretical emphasis. Linguistic theory in the early twentieth century was dominated by an approach based on the mentalism of Wundt's structural psychology (Bloomfield, 1914). Two decades later, the mentalistic approach to linguistics was replaced by J. B. Watson's behavioristic, empiricist orientation (Bloomfield, 1933). Psychologists developed neobehavioristic learning approaches to the psychology of language which dominated their investigations through the middle of the century. Chomsky's (1957) theory of generative-transformational grammar returned linguistics to a mentalistic approach. Cognitive theories of language currently proposed by psychologists are also based on the "empirical mentalism" mentioned in Chapter Six. These theories focus on the mental structures and processes assumed to underlie language acquisition. The return to mentalism has not been a smooth trip by any means and not all have taken it.

Theories of language and language development must come to grips with the complexities of language as a phenomenon and the mystery of how children acquire a complex linguistic system so quickly and easily. We can identify three basic approaches to theories of language acquisition: learning theories, biological–nativist theories, and cognitive theories. None of the theories to be discussed accounts for all aspects of language acquisition, and all are therefore incomplete and troublesome as theoretical systems. Nevertheless, they have established the major research approaches to the problem of language development and have determined the nature of the data considered relevant to understanding language.

Learning Theory Approaches

The traditional learning approach to language acquisition and development is exemplified by B. F. Skinner (1957) in his functional analysis of language, *Verbal Behavior.* In keeping with his strict behavioristic orientation, Skinner's approach to the problem of language is to avoid theoretical speculation and focus instead on the function description of stimulus–response events in "language behavior." Skinner's model attempts to account for language as the operation of basic principles of learning. Verbal behaviors are seen as operants, emitted behaviors for which the original stimuli are not immediately obvious or known. For Skinner, operant behaviors are much more important than respondent behaviors which are elicited by known, observable stimuli. Since the learning of all operant behaviors is considered to be under the control of positive and negative reinforcement, verbal behavior now occurs as a function of its reinforcing effects. When a word or a speech sound is emitted (response) and positively reinforced (stimulus), these reinforcing conditions increase the probability of the word or sound being emitted again (response). In this manner, language develops as S–R chains are established from simple to complex levels.

Skinner proposed a set of verbal operants which fall under the control of verbal or nonverbal stimuli. Skinner specified two major classes of utterances, "mands" and "tacts." Mands, derived from words like commands and demands, are controlled by drive states such as thirst, and their emission by the speaker serves to decrease the drive. For example, the word, water, constitutes a mand when emitted in response to the drive state of thirst. Tacts are verbal operants which make contact with physical objects or events through labeling responses. That is, "tacting" refers to the naming of objects or events. Both mands and tacts are controlled by nonverbal stimuli. Skinner also differentiated four other verbal operants which are controlled by verbal stimuli. Echoics are imitations of previously heard speech. Textuals are vocalizations controlled by visual verbal stimuli such as words or other symbols. Social responses and incidental conversation are operants which Skinner calls intraverbals. Autoclitics is Skinner's term for the process of learning grammar and syntax.

When Skinner offered his descriptive model of language as a possible approach to a functional analysis of language development, responses from psychologists and linguists ranged from indifference to caustic criticism. His S–R learning view of language is not generally accepted as a fruitful model for understanding language development.

There have been a number of extensions and variations of traditional learning approaches to the study of language. Some have combined learning principles with various internal mediational (cognitive) processes (i.e., Mowrer, 1960; Osgood, 1963). None of these theories made comprehensive or even adequate attempts to account for language. More recent attempts to describe language acquisition with a learning model are those offered by Staats (1968, 1971) and Whitehurst and Vasta (1975). Staats argues that language acquisition and function are subject to principles of classical and operant conditioning. Mediational processes which link S–R language chains are also conditioned. Language, grammar, and syntax are acquired by the process of differential reinforcement in infants' first vocalizations, their approximations to word production, and ultimately the shaping of speech patterns. In this fashion, language is conditioned and acquired as linear chains of S–R sequences of increasing length. Cognitive processes, along with any biological factors, are minimized. Though it is broader and more detailed in its coverage, Staats' model does not differ significantly from previous strict learning views of language.

Whitehurst and Vasta (1975) have hypothesized a three-stage process of language acquisition. Stage I is comprehension, in which a child grasps the relationship between adult speech and the physical stimuli which are related to it. Comprehension depends upon observational learning and reinforcement. In Stage II, imitation, the child adopts adult speech production by selective imitation. The imitation need not be identical to adult speech, nor is explicit reinforcement necessary for imitation. Stage III is represented by spontaneous language production without imitation. The CIP hypothesis of

Whitehurst and Vasta emphasizes imitation as a key process in language acquisition.

Learning approaches to language development simply fail to deal with the various complexities of language. Among the criticisms leveled at learning theory accounts of language acquisition are the following:

1 Learning theory cannot explain the creativity of word and sentence generation and productivity. Novel utterances by children are not handled well by learning theory models. The number of S–R chains required would approach astronomical figures.

2 The rapid development of language in children exceeds the explanatory power of reinforcement theory.

3 It is unlikely that parental reinforcement schedules even begin to approach the learning conditions laid down by learning theories. Parental reinforcement of language production in children is inconsistent, conflicting, haphazard, and seldom direct in shaping the formal linguistic characteristics of language. If we relied on reinforcement theory, we would have to wonder how any language acquisition could occur under these conditions.

4 Processes like imitation and modeling have not been found to be consistently effective in shaping children's language acquisition (Brown, 1973). In addition, imitation and modeling cease long before linguistic competence is achieved in children.

5 The consistent pattern in the sequential development of language in children is difficult to explain in the context of learning theory, which suggests that each child's language pattern should differ greatly as a function of that child's unique reinforcement history.

Early vocalizations and speech development in children undoubtedly are influenced by explicit reinforcement procedures and simple learning processes. However, it seems difficult to adhere to a strict learning theory account for language acquisition beyond these early stages. The demonstration that verbal behavior can be conditioned under restricted, comparatively barren linguistic circumstances is not convincing evidence for an S–R theory of language development.

The
Biological–Nativist
Approach

As we have seen, the belief that language is a biologically determined, innate human capacity dates back to antiquity. The biological–nativist approach to language holds that linguistic capacity reflects a genetic predeterminism or predisposition to learn and use language. Eric Lenneberg (1967) presented the most detailed and forceful statement of the biological–nativist position in his lengthy theoretical treatise, *Biological Foundations of Language.* Lenneberg's thesis is that behavior is an integral part of an organism's biology and evolution. Thus, language capacity evolved spontaneously and inevitably from the unique biological substrates of human cognition. For Lenneberg, the emergence of speech is under strict maturational (genetic) control. He points to four "hallmarks" as evidence for the maturational control of language emergence: (1) the sequential regularity of the onset of language between the second and third year of life; (2) the relative invariance of environmental opportunity to acquire language and the differential use of such opportunities by the child during early development; (3) the emergence of language before it is of any immediate use to the child; (4) evidence that early vocalizations such as cooing and babbling do not represent practice or learning requirements for later language acquisition. To Lenneberg, these "hallmarks" strongly suggest that the appearance of language primarily depends upon innate maturational phenomena in early human development, ruling out the need for any significant learning factors. Thus, Lenneberg views language as a human developmental event similar to the emergence of walking. It is the manifestation of species-specific cognitive abilities and their biological substrates which make human cognition possible. While Lenneberg's argument is persuasive at certain points, it is conjectural and speculative at others.

McNeill (1966, 1970a, 1970b), a psycholinguist, has elaborated on Lenneberg's biological–nativist position by attempting to describe the innate human capacity for language within the context of Chomsky's linguistic theory. McNeill's argument revolves around the central importance of the sentence concept for language acquisition. In fact, McNeill asserts that the concept of a sentence may be part of the human capacity for language and that the sentence concept is the guiding principle in children's efforts to interpret and organize adult language. McNeill discusses the empirical evidence supporting Chomsky's assumption of linguistic universals by which children discover relationships between sentence structures and their abstract meanings. The rules that relate these "surface" and "deep" sentence structures are called transformational rules (Chomsky, 1957). The nativist position assumes that children are predisposed or innately prepared to generate the rules for understanding the abstract aspects of grammar, syntax, and semantics, which do not appear in overt sentence structure. McNeill argues that this linguistic abstraction capacity is a mentalistic process, not a behavioral one.

Although McNeill (1970b) takes an interactionist position on the role of heredity and environment, his review (1970a) of the contributions of experience to language acquisition is largely negative. He concludes that "our state of knowledge is remote from anything envisioned in behavioristic theories of learning . . . not only is there nothing calling for behavioristic principles of language acquisition, but when situations favorable to response learning are examined, such as imitation or overt practice, one finds no effects that behaviorist principles can explain" (McNeill, 1970a, p. 112). Certainly not all would agree with this summary dismissal of learning theory and the implications of imitation for language acquisition (Clark, 1977). McNeill clearly states that psychological explanations of language acquisition must account for how the innate abilities of children interact with their linguistic experience. This strongly mentalistic, nativist approach to language development is, according to McNeill, forced upon psychological theory and research by Chomsky's (1957, 1965) theory of generative-transformational grammar.

Some of the difficulties facing developmental psycholinguistics involve translating Chomsky's purely linguistic theory of language and grammar into psychological processes, a technically complex task. Moreover, Chomsky by necessity has revised his theory, forcing reformulations in psychological theory and alterations in research approaches in psycholinguistics (see

Greene, 1972; Kaplan, 1972; Macnamara, 1972 for summaries).

| The Cognitive Approach | Cognitive approaches to language are relatively recent attempts to explain linguistic development in terms of principles of cognitive psychology. |

The Cognitive Approach

Cognitive approaches to language are relatively recent attempts to explain linguistic development in terms of principles of cognitive psychology. A basic assumption in such cognitive approaches is that the abstract aspects of language development can be interpreted as, and explained by, cognitive development. McNeill (1970b) has referred to this as the problem of cognition and language, recognizing that cognitive theories of language development cannot be as easily "dismissed" as learning theories. Partly in reaction against the biological–nativist position and purely linguistic approaches to language development, many psychologists continue to interpret language phenomena as an aspect of cognitive ability and nonlinguistic cognitive processing. Sinclair-de-Zwart (1971), for example, views early language development in children as the result of general cognitive abilities. Although Piaget spoke of the emergence of cognitive structures before language and their role in subsequent language development, cognitive theory and approaches did not receive much attention in linguistics and psycholinguistics until about 1970 (Bever, 1970; Bloom, 1970).

Macnamara (1972) has proposed a cognitive basis of language development in infants. Macnamara suggests that infants learn a language by first determining the meaning of words spoken to them and then working out the relationship between the meaning and the language. Meaning, or intent of the speaker, becomes the clue to language rather than the reverse. For Macnamara, word meanings are expressed by a linguistic code (language structures) that relate meaning to the particular sound system of the language. The assumption here is that infants' thought processes or cognitive structures are more developed than their language abilities. This nonlinguistic capability enables the infant to use the meaning of words to learn the linguistic code. Macnamara hypothesizes that children first learn the names of things, then the names for their variable states, conditions, and activities, and finally the names for more permanent attributes such color. These cognitive prerequisites must be present before language is learned. By using nonlinguistic cognitive processes such as problem-solving, cause-and-effect relationships, and concept formation, the child learns the syntax and semantics of language.

Reynolds and Flagg (1977) have developed a cognitive theory of language development that combines features of learning and nativist theories with general cognitive psychology. Their principal assumption is that language acquisition occurs through the use of general cognitive mechanisms—a set of learning principles or inference rules. These rules are seen as representing the human capacity for learning categories and processing information. Reynolds and Flagg hypothesize a cognitive acquisition device (CAD), a mechanism by which children can generate and understand an infinite number of utterances. They emphasize differentiation as the cognitive process underlying language acquisition. By differentiation, Reynolds and Flagg mean some general cognitive mechanism, not specific to language, which enables a child to induce a grammar from both linguistic and nonlinguistic information. In other words, a general learning strategy is implied.

Numerous other psychologists are developing cognitive approaches to language development. While preliminary and tentative in content and scope, cognitive theories of language development offer a feasible psychological approach to this problem. Cognitive psychologists have developed some supporting evidence for their theories, but have a long way to go before they can explain all aspects of language development. This, of course, is true of all theories of language. Nevertheless, Reynolds and Flagg (1977) reflect the confidence that is characteristic of cognitive psychologists:

The conclusion we are forced to draw about linguistic structures is that they are not the result of innate mental categories but rather of active processing of the external world. We should look for the roots of linguistic structures not in the mind or in the genes but in the child's active relationship with the world. Thus linguistic competence is not intuitive but the fruit of some long and dramatic performances nurtured by prelinguistic characteristics at the start and spurred to full flower through the child's cognitive contact with a speaking environment. (p. 365)

With this general introduction to theories of language development, we can now proceed to discuss the ontogenesis of language.

THE ONTOGENESIS OF LANGUAGE

In the process of acquiring language, every child must learn to pronounce the sounds and master the words, their meaning, and the construction of words into sentences. This appears to be an awesome task but, in fact, normal children universally acquire a first language easily and rapidly. The course of language development can be described as a continuous sequence of events, from the prelinguistic period of infancy to adult language. This progression in language development is also characterized by a number of language "periods" through which children pass. These periods apparently emerge in an invariant, predictable order of content and linguistic complexity. Such consistent observations of language periods have resulted in reasonably normative descriptions of language development in children. These descriptions are given in Table 7-2. As chronological age is not an accurate index of language developments, such age-related descriptions of language must be viewed as only approximate time tables. Large individual differences in age are common in the development of language among normal children.

The Basic Elements of Language

Language logically begins with learning to differentiate and produce the basic sounds of a linguistic system. As every student who has studied a second language knows, the basic sound systems of languages may differ greatly, often causing considerable difficulty in mastering their correct pronunciation. The scientific study of speech sounds, called phonology, is a complex science involving the analysis of the physical, sensory, and psychological characteristics of language sound structures. A basic sound in any language is called a phoneme. More precisely, a phoneme is a single class of sounds which has been determined to be significant for a particular language system. American English, for example, requires 34 phonemes or classes of sounds—25 consonant phonemes and 9 vowel

Table 7-2
The Sequence of Emerging Language Behaviors in the Child
(The Times Indicated Are Approximate, Not Normative)

Birth to 6 months	*The infant period.* The child produces such sounds as grunts, cries, shrieks, gasps, chuckling, and cooing (at 4 months).
6 months to 9 months	*The babbling period.* The child produces units of utterances called babbling that differ from one situation to another. These units begin to be acoustically similar to adult utterances because the child sloughs off irrelevant phonemes instead of acquiring new phonemes.
9 months	*The jargon period.* Stresses and intonation patterns in strings of utterance units clearly correspond to those of the adult. Some imitation of general language-like patterns can be identified. Specific morphemes cannot be easily identified by a listener.
9 months to 1 year	*Echolalic period.* This time is characterized by imitation of adult speech sounds.
1 year to 2 years	*The holophrastic period.* The child uses single words to indicate whole phrases or sentences. Preconventional "words" are heard as words by the parents because of reliable use in a given context (for example, using "muk" for milk). The child understands much of what he or she is told and demonstrates comprehension by behaving in an appropriate way (obeying a command or pointing to an object). Vocabulary size increases dramatically toward the end of this period from about twenty words at 18 months to two hundred words at 21 months.
2 years	*The spurt in word development.* Vocabulary size increases from about three hundred words at 24 months to one thousand at 36 months. Two-word and three-word utterances are produced; they are not copies of adult speech. Intonation variation with single words is used: declarative ("doll"), emphatic ("doll!"), and interrogative ("doll?").
3 years	*The sentence period.* At this time the child uses sentences containing grammatical features that anticipate the adult's use of language. The child may use functionally complete but grammatically incomplete sentences ("This one riding horse").
3 to 5 years	The child uses sentences of all types: non-understandable; functionally complete but grammatically incomplete; simple; simple with phrases; compound; complex; and compound-complex.
5 years to maturity	Vocabulary continues to increase. There is increase in length, variety, and complexity of sentences used as well.

(Adapted from DiVesta, 1974. Copyright © 1974 by Wadsworth, Inc. Reprinted by permission of the publisher, Brooks/Cole Publishing Co., Monterey, California.)

Table 7-3
The Phonemes of
American English

CONSONANT PHONEMES

p	(pass)	δ	(this)	n	(no)
b	(but)	s	(so)	rj	(ring)
t	(to)	z	(zero, boys)	l	(love)
d	(do)	š	(should)	w	(wish)
k	(kiss, calm)	ž	(azure)	hw	(when)
g	(go)	č	(church)	y	(yes)
f	(for)	ǰ	(Jim)	r	(run)
v	(value)	m	(more)	h	(how)
θ	(thing)				

VOWEL PHONEMES

i	(bit)	e	(bet)	ae	(map)
i	(children)	e	(above)	a	(not)
u	(put)	o	(boat)	c	(law)

(From DeVito, 1970. Copyright © 1970 by Random House, Inc. Reprinted by permission.)

phonemes (shown in Table 7-3). The phonemic range among the various languages of the world is from 25 to 50. Phonemes, then, represent the most elemental structure of language and the first required learning in language acquisition.

At the next level of structural complexity in language is the morpheme. A morpheme is the smallest meaningful unit of speech sounds that can be produced by combining phonemes. Within a language system, phonemes are combined according to specific rules, and such phoneme combinations result in morphemes. These speech sounds or units cannot be divided into smaller ones without changing or destroying the original meaning of the morpheme. Morphology is the study of the rules by which a language combines morphemes into larger meaningful units of speech. While all words of a language consist of one or more morphemes, not all morphemes constitute a word. For example, the word, dog, is a morpheme, but the word, dogs, consists of two morphemes: /dog/ and the plural indicator /s/. For our purposes, we can say that morphological development leads to the acquisition of the next larger unit of language—words.

The emergence of words leads to the third element of language structure, syntax. In every language, words must be combined into phrases, clauses, and sentences. The rules for combining words in a meaningful sentence are described as syntax. Syntactic development in language acquisition can thus be seen as learning permissible arrangements of words and their relationships for acceptable sentence formation. The rules for syntax are formally known as grammar.

A fourth element of language is semantics, the meanings of words and sentences. The complexity of the semantic dimension of language ranges from relatively simple reference to concrete external stimuli to the extremely abstract. The linguist's concern with semantics deals with how language conveys meaning and in what ways. Children must learn the basic meanings of words, the equivalence of meaning of differently worded sentences, multiple meanings of words, and differences in meaning as a function of language style and context. Semantics is a complex, poorly understood area of linguistics, and semantic development in children similarly is the least understood aspect of language development. Compared to syntactic development, which is relatively complete by age 4 or 5, semantic development is a slow process, extending well into school age (McNeill, 1970b). McNeill suggests some possible reasons for this difference as involving the complexity or abstractness of semantic information and its dependence on intellectual development and maturity.

In summarizing the basic elements of language, we can present its structure and organization as combinations of phonemes that result in morphemes that, in turn, are combined to generate an infinite number of meaningful sentences. This process is determined by complex rules which, when considered together, reveal language acquisition requirements that are indeed formidable. But what is more surprising is the ability of children to master these language requirements and to learn and remember, without apparent effort, the enormous amount of information involved in phonology, morphology, syntax, and semantics.

These considerations of language acquisition have led Chomsky (1957, 1965), who bitterly criticized Skinner and other S–R theorists, to hypothesize a language acquisition device (LAD). Such a LAD would contain information and procedures about languages in general—universal linguistic information. The LAD serves to generate language rules about grammar, syntax, and semantics (Figure 7-5). This hypothetical language processor is similar to the cognitive acquisition device (CAD) discussed earlier. Nativists assume that only some innate mechanism such as the LAD can explain the rapid acquisition of language.

Prelinguistic Development

As we have seen, the acquisition of language begins with phonemic development. While true language first appears in the infant at about 1 year of age, prelinguistic development forms a continuum of events leading to phonological development and language. Prelinguistic vocalizations do not represent phonological development, but such development depends on the ability to produce sounds. Therefore we can view the prelinguistic months as a developmental period during which sound-producing abilities emerge. This view does not imply any necessary relationship between prelinguistic events and language development. Prelinguistic development simply provides the articulatory skills required for the production of sounds. It is independent of the specific emergence of language. Like all developmental phenomena, those skills are the result of maturation and experience.

There are conflicting views about the significance of prelinguistic vocalizations. Learning approaches emphasize the importance of conditioning and discrimination learning in the perception and production of sounds for later language development (Eimas, Siqueland, Jusczyk, & Vigorita, 1971; Staats, 1968; Trehub & Rabinovitch, 1972; Whitehurst & Vasta, 1975). Nativists minimize or dismiss any relationship between prelinguistic vocalizations and language development (Lenneberg, 1967; McNeill, 1970a). Demonstrations of infant instrumental

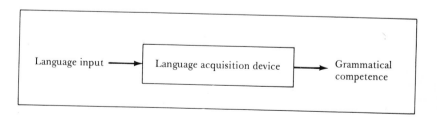

Figure 7-5
Hypothetical language acquisition device.

conditioning in the perception and production of sounds do not establish the developmental importance of such prelinguistic phenomena for language.

Stages in Prelinguistic Development

All normal infants present a similar pattern of vocalizations during prelinguistic development. This pattern emerges as a gradual, continuous progression of events. While there are minor variations in the stages reported (DeVito, 1970; Kaplan & Kaplan, 1971), most psychologists and linguists agree that they universally characterize this period of development.

Stage 1 Reflexive cries, grunts, and random vocalizations predominate during the first 2 months of life.

Stage 2 Between 3 and 5 months of age, a characteristic class of sounds is produced, consisting of /u/ sounds and other vowel sounds. This stage is often referred to as the "cooing" stage.

Stage 3 The babbling stage begins at around 5 months. There is an increase in the range of sounds produced, and repetitions of sounds occur ("dada," "baba") yielding morphemes. Vowel sounds predominate but consonant sounds begin to increase in frequency.

Stage 4 The lallation stage is reached by approximately 6 months of age. The infant begins to imitate its own sounds.

Stage 5 The echolalia stage begins at roughly 9 months of age. Here, the infant begins to imitate the vocalizations of others.

Stage 6 True language appears at about 12 months with the use of words to communicate with others.

Between Stage 2 and Stage 6, there is a developmental trend in prelinguistic vocalization toward phonemic expansion. After the onset of true speech, phonemic contraction occurs, as sounds not present in the child's linguistic environment rapidly drop out of the child's speech productions.

Syntactic Development

With the utterance of the child's first word at about 1 year of age, syntactic development begins. At this time, children use single words, often nouns, to express broad multiple meanings, intents, or actions. These single-word utterances have the meaning of full sentences and are sometimes called holophras-

	AGE IN MONTHS	NUMBER OF CHILDREN	NUMBER OF WORDS	GAIN
Table 7-4 Increase in the Average Size of Vocabulary (Words Understood) as a Function of Age	8	13	0	
	10	17	1	1
	12	52	3	2
	15	19	10	16
	18	14	22	8
	21	14	118	96
	24	25	272	154
	30	14	446	174
	36	20	8896	450
	42	26	1222	326
	48	26	1540	318
	54	32	1870	330
	60	20	2072	202
	66	27	2289	217
	72	9	2562	273

(From Munn, 1974, after Smith, 1926.)

es. The one-word stage of language covers the period between 12 and 18 months and is called the holophrastic stage of language development. The use of holophrases also marks the beginning of the child's vocabulary acquisition. Smith (1926) reports that phrase or sentence construction does not usually appear until the child has a vocabulary or lexicon of 100 to 200 words, a vocabulary size acquired between 18 and 20 months (Table 7-4). Nelson (1977) found that children usually acquire a lexicon of 50 words before they begin to combine two or more words and that 65% of the words are general and specific nouns.

Although the initial vocabulary of a child appears to be highly selective, how and why particular words are acquired over others remain unclear. The end of the one-word stage is sometimes marked by a transitional stage in which two-word utterances are made but with distinct pauses between them (Dale, 1976), pauses which do not occur in later language patterns. Such pauses in the child's earliest two-word sequences may signal the developing ability to use word combinations for more conceptually complex linguistic and environmental relationships. Perhaps the child must take time to process which of several meanings each word must serve, a distinction not made during the holophrastic stage.

THE TWO-WORD STAGE   Between 18 and 24 months of age, children begin to produce multiword utterances regularly, beginning with two-word combinations. The characteristics of two-word utterances were first described by Braine (1963), Ervin (1964), and Brown and Fraser (1964). Their research findings strongly suggest that two-word speech is characterized by semantic completeness or the expression of a complete idea. In addition, these early speech patterns take the form of crude, incomplete sentences. Thus, they are called "telegraphic speech" because they are pared down to the basic message, like telegrams ("doll fall," "doggie gone").

In the early attempts to analyze the structure of two-word speech, it was also observed that the words fell into two classes based on their frequency of usage. These two classes of words are commonly referred to as "pivot" words and "open" words (Braine, 1963; McNeill, 1970), and make up the pivot-open grammar or model of the two-word stage. Pivot words represent a small number of high-frequency words, which are acquired relatively slowly in the child's lexicon. These words are called pivots because the child attaches many other words to them. "Allgone" is a common pivot word to which the child may attach any number of other words to form a two-word utterance. There are many more words in the open class and they are used much less frequently. All nonpivot words in the child's vocabulary are included in the open class. Several researchers have noted that many of these two-word utterances are creative, novel examples of early language expression. For example, Braine (1963) reports utterances such as "allgone sticky" (after washing hands) and "more page" (a request to continue reading). It seems very unlikely that the child has heard or is imitating such speech patterns as these.

A number of criticisms have been raised about the use of pivot grammar to describe early language patterns of children (Bloom, 1970, Bowerman, 1973; Brown, 1973). These criticisms revolve around (1) the lack of generality and consistency in pivot grammar assumptions, which makes it impossible to describe the speech patterns of many children; (2) the simplicity and restrictiveness of pivot grammar; and (3) the inability of pivot grammar to deal with semantics.

THE SENTENCE STAGE We may describe the language period between 3 and 5 years of age as the sentence stage, as this period typically includes the development of appropriate sentence production and usage. The emergence of sentence structure in the child's speech pattern is gradual, beginning with the use of simple declarative sentences. Although functionally complete, their grammatical structure is often incomplete and/or incorrect. As sentence production and variety increases, the child starts to generate negatives, yes–no and "wh-" questions (why, who, what, when, where), and imperatives. Sentences become longer and more complex, with clauses, phrases, and compound sentences appearing by approximately 4 years of age. Vocabulary continues to increase rapidly. Also, children of this age begin to acquire some degree of metalinguistic awareness, the ability to think about and evaluate language (de Villiers & de Villiers, 1974). This ability continues to increase throughout development and adulthood. Overall, language development during this period increasingly approximates adult language patterns. Syntactic development beyond 5 years of age is essentially characterized by grammatical refinements, increases in vocabulary, and semantic awareness.

Roger Brown's Classification of Early Language Development

We have noted that pivot grammar has been criticized as an approach to early syntactic development. The evidence for its claims of universality is very weak, and pivot grammar under-represents the child's knowledge of language (see Brown, 1973 for an excellent review of grammar approaches to language analysis). In 1962, Brown and his students, Bellugi and Fraser, began a longitudinal study of language development in three children, 18 to 27 months of age. They hoped to better describe early language patterns in the search for a universal sequence of language acquisition and to obtain some insight into the structure and meaning of these patterns. The result was a five-stage description of language development (Brown, 1973), shown in Table 7-5. Since chronological age does not accurately reflect language development, Brown decided to

Table 7-5
Stages of Early Language Development for American English

STAGE[a]	MLU[b]	FOCUS[c]	EXAMPLES
I	1.00–2.00	Basic semantic and grammatical rules	
		Nominations	That ball
		Nonexistence	Allgone ball
		Recurrence	More ball
		Attribution	Big ball
		Possession	My ball, Adam ball
		Agent-action	Adam hit
		Agent-action-object	Adam hit ball
II	2.00–2.50	The modulation of meaning	
		Progressive aspect	I walking.
		in, on	in basket, on floor
		Plural	Two balls.
		Past irregular	It broke.
		Possessive inflection	Adam's ball.
		Uncontractible copula	There it is.
		Articles, a, the	That a book. That the dog.
		Past regular	Adam walked.
		Third person regular	He walks. She runs.
		Third person irregular	He does. She has.
		Uncontractible progressive auxiliary	This is going.
		Contractible copula	That's book.
		Contractible progressive auxiliary	I'm walking.
III	2.50–3.00	Modalities of the simple sentence	
		Yes-no questions	{Will Adam go? {Does Eve like it?
		Wh Questions	{Where did Sarah hide? {What did Eve see?
		Negatives	Adam can't go.
		Ellipsis of the predicate	Yes he can.
		Emphasis	He does want to go.

IV	3.00– 3.50	Embedding one simple sentence within another	
		Relative clauses	{ What is that playing the xylophone?
			You got a pencil in your bag.
		Various kinds of subordinate clause	{ I see what you made.
			I went where your office was.
			I want her to do it.
			You think I can do it.
V	3.50– 4.00	Conjunction of one simple sentence with another	
		With no parts deleted	{ We can hear her and we can touch her.
			I did this and I did that too.
		With various redundant constituents deleted once	
		Subject deleted	He's flying and swinging.
		Predicate deleted	No, you and I had some.
		Predicate nominal deleted	John and Jay are Boy Scouts.

[a]Only Stages I and II have received exhaustive analysis; the later stages have been closely analyzed but are not complete.

[b]MLU = mean (or average) length of utterance.

[c]The focus of a stage describes the new frontier that is being explored for the first time in that stage. It is, in effect, the line of advance added onto prior stages, not displacing them.

(From Brown & Herrnstein, 1975, Fig. 7, 9, 9, p. 478. Copyright © 1975 by Little, Brown and Company, Inc., Reprinted by permission.)

Figure 7-6
Mean utterance length and
chronological age for three
children.

(From Brown, 1973. Reprinted by permission.)

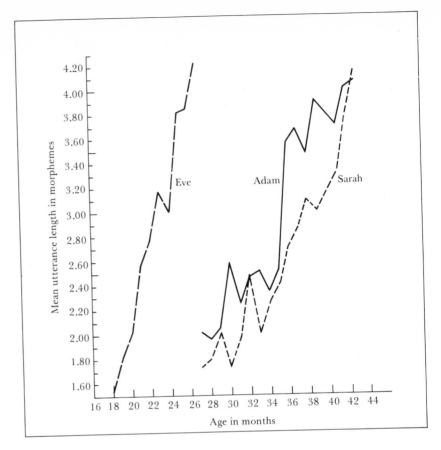

use the mean length of utterance (MLU) as the index of
grammatical development. An MLU is calculated as the average number of words or morphemes produced by a child in a
sample of recorded utterances. Because the MLU increases
with almost every new kind of knowledge, Brown found this
index to be an accurate measure of language development.
The MLU serves as the basis for identifying Brown's five
stages, from 1+ (more than one but less than two words or
morphemes) to 4.0. Table 7-5 contains brief descriptions of
linguistic events in each of Brown's stages. The relationship
between MLU and ages of the three children studied by Brown
is shown in Figure 7-6.

Brown (1973) states that there is good evidence of sequential
and structural universality for Stage I, which can be found in

ten other languages besides American English. Brown believes that the meanings and constructions of Stage I speech derive from what Piaget describes as sensorimotor intelligence. In other words, the intellectual or cognitive requirements for Stage I speech seem to be related to Piaget's descriptions of sensorimotor development. Brown points out that the beginning of Stage I coincides with the end of the sensorimotor period. For Stages II through V, the problems of establishing universality are much more difficult because analysis of the language becomes considerably more complex with increasing complexity of the language patterns. Brown's approach to first-language acquisition is a significant contribution which holds promise for discovering the nature of language acquisition.

FACTORS INFLUENCING LANGUAGE DEVELOPMENT

To this point, our description of the ontogenesis of language has dealt with the emergence of speech patterns among normal children. This sequence of language development can be observed among "average" children reared under more or less "average" environmental conditions. Such conditions provide at least an adequate opportunity to acquire language by exposing children to a linguistic environment and allowing them linguistic practice. While there are striking similarities in language development among normal children, there are also individual differences whose source can be traced. We will examine the major factors which may influence the rate and quality of language acquisition in normal children, excluding physiological or biological impairments which impose sensory or physical restrictions on the child. We will classify the major factors into two groups, sex factors and environmental factors. Environmental factors represent a broad class of situational determinants which may influence language development, including family composition, socioeconomic status, and bilingualism.

Sex Differences

Do boys and girls display differential patterns of language acquisition which are a function of biologically based sex differences? We are referring here to primary differences based on biological factors associated with maleness or femaleness, not to situational determinants such as differential rearing patterns, cultural stereotypy, or differential training or opportunity associated with being a boy or a girl in a given society. A number of studies conducted during the first half of the century strongly suggested that girls are superior to boys in general language development and verbal skills (McCarthy, 1954a; Templin, 1957). These early studies, however, failed to control adequately for environmental factors which confounded the results, and they were based on poor measures of language development from small samples. More recent studies of sex differences in language development reveal few or no inherent sex differences in the course and level of language acquisition (Berko, 1958; Irwin, 1952; McCurry & Irwin, 1953; Menyuk, 1963; Sampson, 1956).

Reports of language superiority in favor of girls generally referred to increased fluency or productivity rather than accelerated language development or increased linguistic ability. The demonstration of the former is not evidence for the latter. McCarthy (1953) attributed these reported sex differences to environmental factors favoring girls, such as differential rearing patterns resulting in greater exposure to, and experience with, language. Reports of sex differences continue to appear in the literature supporting the long-standing view of language superiority in girls (i.e., Schachter, Shore, Hodapp, Chalfin, & Bundy, 1978). But almost all such studies reveal either no sex differences or minor fluency differences in language acquisition between boys and girls (Maccoby & Jacklin, 1974). Given the current evidence, it seems that language acquisition is independent of sex.

Environmental Factors   FAMILY COMPOSITION   Studies involving family composition have concentrated on the effects of siblings on language development. Investigators have reported differences in language acquisition according to the number of siblings in the family, the age spacing between siblings, birth order, and multiple births (twins, triplets, etc.). Findings have been inconsistent, and sibling effects, when found, largely reflect fluency levels, not competence. The direction of sibling effects has often been reported as temporary retardation or delay in

Siblings . . . Although the presence of brothers and sisters in the family is likely to enrich the child's overall environment, it often temporarily retards language development. This is particularly the case when siblings are close together in age and still developing their own individual language skills. The two sisters pictured here are clearly communicating and expressing affection for one another, but their exchange does not appear to involve linguistics.

(Photo by David S. Strickler/Monkmeyer Press Photo Service.)

language acquisition. For example, McCarthy (1954b) has described results of acceleration in language acquisition in only children (singletons) and retarded language development among children of multiple births. The degree of delayed language development seems to vary directly with the number of same-age children in the family. Kim, Dales, Connor, Walters, and Witherspoon (1969) report similar effects between singletons and twins. Moody (1956) found that only children and the youngest or oldest child in the family tend to be low achievers in language development. On the other hand, Irwin (1952) reported no differences in language development between only children and those with older or younger siblings. Lenneberg (1967), on the basis of his analysis of the literature, estimates the frequency of delay in language development among fraternal and identical twins to be 47% and 65%, respectively.

The general assumption underlying observed differences between single children and those with siblings is that single

Father and baby together. Exposure to adults and meaningful interaction with them are of great importance to a child's development of language. Typically, infants begin to imitate the sound of others around them at approximately 9 months of age. Adult speech patterns provide a model for subsequent learning of vocabulary and syntax. The ease with which children learn language and, moreover, the entire process of language acquisition still defy concise explanation.

(Photo copyright © 1980 by Michael Hardy/Woodfin Camp & Associates)

children enjoy relatively enriched language environments and increased exposure to adult patterns of language. Such environments presumably facilitate language development and often do (Nelson, 1977). Children with siblings, especially those of multiple births or closely spaced ages, have less adult contact, and so they have less exposure to adult language and less opportunity or stimulation for language experiences. Blatz, Fletcher, and Mason (1937) reported significant retardation in language acquisition among the Dionne quintuplets compared to only children. This and other examples of language delays are temporary ones among otherwise normal children. Such deficits in language performance are recovered in later childhood. Sibling effects on language are not inevitable. If the quality and quantity of language contact with adults is not reduced, sibling effects will not be observed.

SOCIOECONOMIC STATUS   Socioeconomic status (SES) is a carrier or index variable which alone has no explanatory power as a determinant or independent variable. One must isolate and identify specific independent variables embedded within the general concept of SES. Some independent variables which may (or may not) be related to SES, and which might influence language development, are (1) the frequency and quality of the linguistic environment to which the child is exposed; (2) the level of general stimulation; (3) the number of siblings; (4) parental presence; and (5) parental characteristics. SES is inextricably related to education, intelligence, learning opportunities, and general quality of life. The developmental effects of impoverishment in these areas can be crushing and pervasive.

Research findings generally suggest that children from lower SES groups display lower levels of syntactic construction and communication abilities (see Dale, 1976; Ginsburg, 1972; McCarthy, 1954; Raph, 1965 for reviews). The effects of SES factors on language acquisition may be more or less permanent, depending on the degree and duration of linguistic deprivation. Low SES tends to be related to low educational achievement and therefore to reduced probabilities of significant improvement in language development. The introduction of television may reduce SES differences in language acquisition insofar as it raises the frequency and quality of the child's contact with the linguistic environment (Lenneberg, 1969; Schramm, Lyle, & Parker, 1961).

BILINGUALISM   In her review of the literature on language development, McCarthy (1954a) noted that the studies on bilingualism indicated that children from bilingual homes showed retarded language development, sometimes in both languages. This classical view of bilingualism and its detrimental effects on language acquisition achieved the status of "conventional wisdom." As it turns out, the data from the early studies were confounded by poor methodology, inadequate assessment procedures, failure to consider first and second languages (English was often the second language), and quality

"Hello, out there!" This toddler seems eager to communicate with the outside world, despite the technical difficulties of holding the phone. Her ability to use language will closely reflect the quality and quantity of linguistic experiences in her immediate home environment. From "Dial-A-Story" to "Sesame Street," telecommunications—especially television—have done a great deal to enrich children's linguistic environments, even to the extent of possibly modifying socioeconomic inequalities that might otherwise retard language skill development in lower SES groups.

(Photo by James R. Holland/Stock, Boston.)

of the languages spoken by the parents. In a recent critical review of the literature on second-language learning in children, McLaughlin (1977) thoroughly examined the empirical basis for a number of myths surrounding bilingualism in children. McLaughlin draws the following conclusions concerning second-language learning:

1 There is no evidence for a biologically based critical period for language acquisition. Older children learn a second language more efficiently than younger children under controlled conditions. It remains to be demonstrated that, given the same exposure, children can learn a language faster and better than adults. The possible exception to these findings is phonological acquisition. A native accent is easier to acquire during childhood.

2 Learning a second language involves the same strategies and processes as learning the first language.

3 Studies on second-language learning in children indicate few interference effects from the first language. Children who learn two languages simultaneously show minimal interference if the language learning is kept in balance and properly separated by social context.

4 There is no clear evidence to support the belief that bilingualism has negative (or positive) effects on subsequent intellectual/cognitive functioning or educational achievement.

Reynolds and Flagg (1977) offer similar conclusions. They state that "bilingualism generally serves the needs of the individual well, without any cognitive strain, and in fact may be advantageous both in terms of increased creativity and beneficial social interaction" (p. 406).

In this chapter, we have only been able to suggest the complexities of language and language development. We hope that you have gained some appreciation of language development, while recognizing that what has been described as language development has its roots in the basic developmental phenomena we have covered in the previous chapters.

REFERENCES

Bandura, A. Analysis of modeling processes. In A. Bandura (Ed.), *Psychological modeling*. New York: Lieber-Atherton, 1971.

Bar-Adon, A., & Leopold, W. F. (Eds.), *Child language: A book of readings*. Englewood Cliffs, New Jersey: Prentice-Hall, 1971.

Berko, J. The child's learning of English morphology. *Word*, 1958, *14*, 150–177.

Bever, T. G. The cognitive basis for linguistic structures. In J. R. Hayes (Ed.), *Cognition and language learning*. New York: Wiley, 1970.

Blatz, W. E., Fletcher, M. I., & Mason, M. Early development and spoken language of the Dionne Quintuplets. *University of Toronto Studies: Child Development Series*, 1937, No. 16.

Bloom, L. *Language development: Form and function in emerging grammars*. Boston: M.I.T. Press, 1970.

Bloomfield, L. *Introduction to the study of language*. New York: Henry Holt, 1914.

Bloomfield, L. *Language*. New York: Holt, Rinehart, & Winston, 1933.

Bowerman, M. *Early syntactic development*. Cambridge, Massachusetts: Cambridge University Press, 1973.

Braine, M. D. S. The ontogeny of English phrase structure: The first phase. *Language*, 1963, *39*, 1–13.

Bronowski, J., & Bellugi, U. Language, name, and concept. *Science*, 1970, *168*, 669–673.

Brown, R. *Social psychology*. New York: The Free Press, 1965.

Brown, R. *A first language: The early stages*. Cambridge, Massachusetts: Harvard University Press, 1973.

Brown, R., & Fraser, C. The acquisition of syntax. In U. Bellugi and R. Brown (Eds.), The acquisition of language. *Monographs of the Society for Research in Child Development*, 1964, *29*, No. 1, 43–79.

Brown, R., & Herrnstein, R. J. *Psychology*. Boston: Little, Brown & Co. 1975.

Chomsky, N. *Syntactic structures*. The Hague: Mouton, 1957.

Chomsky, N. Review of *Verbal Behavior* by B. F. Skinner. *Language*, 1959, *35*, 26–58.

Chomsky, N. *Aspects of a theory of grammar*. Cambridge, Massachusetts: M.I.T. Press, 1965.

Chomsky, N. The general properties of language. In F. L. Darley (Ed.), *Brain mechanisms underlying speech and language*. New York: Grune & Stratton, 1967.

Chomsky, N. *Language and mind*. New York: Harcourt, Brace, & World, 1968.

Clark, R. What's the use of imitation? *Journal of child language,* 1977, *4,* 341–358.

Dale, P. S. *Language development: Structure and function* (2nd ed.). New York: Holt, Rinehart, & Winston, 1976.

de Villiers, J. G., & de Villiers, P. A. Competence and performance in child language: Are children really competent to judge. *Journal of Child Language,* 1974, *1,* 11–22.

DeVito, J. *The psychology of speech and language.* New York: Random House, 1970.

DiVesta, J. F. *Language, learning, and cognitive processes.* Monterey, California: Brooks/Cole, 1974.

Eimas, P. D., Siqueland, E. R., Jusczyk, P., & Vigorito, J. Speech perception in infants. *Science,* 1971, *171,* 303–306.

Ervin, S. M. Imitation and structural change in children's language. In E. H. Lenneberg (Ed.), *New directions in the study of language.* Cambridge, Massachusetts: M.I.T. Press, 1964.

Fleming, J. D. Field Report: The state of the apes. *Psychology Today,* 1974, *7,* 31–38, 43–44, 46, 49–50.

Fouts, R. Field report: The state of the apes. *Psychology Today,* 1975, *7,* 31–54.

Gardner, B. T., & Gardner, R. A. Two-way communication with an infant chimpanzee. In A. Schrier and F. Stollnitz (Eds.), *Behavior of nonhuman primates* (Vol. 4). New York: Academic Press, 1971.

Gardner, B. T., & Gardner, R. A. Comparing the early utterances of child and chimpanzee. In A. Pick (Ed.), *Minnesota symposium on child psychology* (Vol. 8). Minneapolis: University of Minnesota Press, 1974.

Gardner, B. T., & Gardner, R. A. Evidence for sentence constituents in the early utterances of child and chimpanzee. *Journal of Experimental Psychology: General,* 1975, *104,* 244–267. (a)

Gardner, R. A., & Gardner, B. T. Teaching sign language to a chimpanzee. *Science,* 1969, *165,* 664–672.

Gardner, R. A., & Gardner, B. T. Early signs of language in child and chimpanzee. *Science,* 1975, *187,* 752–753. (b)

Ginsburg, H. *The myth of the deprived child.* Englewood Cliffs, New Jersey: Prentice-Hall, 1972.

Greenberg, J. H. (Ed.). *Universals of Language* (2nd Ed.). Cambridge, Massachusetts: M.I.T. Press, 1966.

Greene, J. *Psycholinguistics: Chomsky and psychology.* Baltimore: Penguin Books, 1972.

Harlow, H. F. The evolution of learning. In A. Roe & G. G. Simpson

(Eds.), *Behavior and evolution*. New Haven: Yale University Press, 1958.

Harnad, S. R., Steklis, H. D., & Lancaster, J. Origins and evolution of language and speech. *Annals of New York Academy of Science,* 1976, *280.*

Hayes, K. J., & Hayes, C. Intellectual development of a home-raised chimpanzee. *Proceedings of the American Philosophical Society,* 1951, *95,* 105–109.

Hockett, C. F. The origin of speech. *Scientific American,* 1960, *203,* 88–96.

Hockett, C. F. The problem of universals in language. In J. H. Greenberg (Ed.), *Universals of language.* Cambridge, Massachusetts: M.I.T. Press, 1963.

Irwin, O. C. Speech development in the young child: Some factors related to the speech development of the infant and young child. *Journal of Speech and Hearing Disorders,* 1952, *17,* 269–279.

Kaplan, E., & Kaplan, G. The prelinguistic child. In J. Elliot (Ed.), *Human development and cognitive processes.* New York: Holt, Rinehart, & Winston, 1971.

Kaplan, R. M. Augmented transition networks as psychological models of sentence comprehension. *Artificial Intelligence,* 1972, *3,* 77–100.

Kellogg, W. N. Communication and language in the home-raised chimpanzee. *Science,* 1968, *162,* 423–427.

Kessen, W. (Ed.). *The child.* New York: Wiley, 1965.

Kim, C., Dales, R., Connor, R., Walters, J., & Witherspoon, R. Social interaction of like-sex twins and singletons in relation to language development. *Journal of Genetic Psychology,* 1969, *114,* 203–214.

Lenneberg, E. H. A biological perspective of language. In E. H. Lenneberg (Ed.), *New directions in the study of language.* Cambridge, Massachusetts: M.I.T. Press, 1964.

Lenneberg, E. H. *Biological foundations of language.* New York: Wiley, 1967.

Lenneberg, E. H. On explaining language. *Science,* 1969, *164,* 635–643.

Lieberman, P. *On the origins of language: An introduction to the evolution of human speech.* New York: MacMillan, 1975.

Limber, J. Language in child and chimp? *American Psychologist,* 1977, *32,* 280–295.

Maccoby, E. E., & Jacklin, C. N. *The psychology of sex differences.* Stanford, California: Stanford University Press, 1974.

Macnamara, J. Cognitive basis of language learning in infants. *Psychological Review,* 1972, *79,* 1–13.

McCarthy, D. Language development in children. In L. Carmichael (Ed.), *Manual of child psychology* (2nd ed.). New York: Wiley, 1954. (a)

McCarthy, D. Language disorders and parent-child relationships. *Journal of Speech and Hearing Disorders,* 1954, *19,* 514–523. (b)

McCurry, W. H., & Irwin, O. C. A study of word approximations in the spontaneous speech of infants. *Journal of Speech and Hearing Disorders,* 1953, *18,* 133–139.

McLaughlin, B. Second-language learning in children. *Psychological Bulletin,* 1977, *84,* 438–459.

McNeill, D. Developmental Psycholinguistics. In F. Smith & G. A. Miller (Eds.), *The genesis of language: A psycholinguistic approach.* Cambridge, Massachusetts: M.I.T. Press, 1966.

McNeill, D. *The Acquisition of Language: The study of developmental psycholinguistics.* New York: Harper & Row, 1970. (a)

McNeill, D. The development of language. In P. H. Mussen (Ed.), *Carmichael's manual of child psychology.* New York: Wiley, 1970. (b)

Menyuk, P. A. A preliminary evolution of grammatical capacity in children. *Journal of Verbal Learning and Verbal Behavior,* 1963, *2,* 429–439.

Menzel, E. W., & Johnson, M. K. Communication and cognitive organization in human and other animals. In S. R. Harnard, H. D. Steklis, & J. Lancaster (Eds.), Origins and Evolution of Language and Speech. *Annals of the New York Academy of Sciences,* 1976, *280.*

Moody, J. L. An investigation of the differences in language development between elementary school boys and girls of the same chronological age. *Dissertation Abstracts,* 1956, *16,* 2066.

Mowrer, O. H. *Learning theory and symbolic processes.* New York: Wiley, 1960.

Munn, N. L. *The evolution of the human mind.* New York: Houghton-Mifflin: 1971.

Munn, N. L. *The growth of human behavior* (3rd ed.). Boston: Houghton-Miflin, 1974.

Nelson, K. E. Facilitating children's syntax acquisition. *Developmental Psychology,* 1977, *13,* 101–107.

Osgood, C. E. Understanding and creating sentences. *American Psychologist,* 1963, *18,* 735–751.

Palermo, D. S. *Psychology of language.* Glenville, Illinois: Scott, Foresman, 1978.

Premack, A. J., & Premack, D. Teaching language to an ape. *Scientific American,* 1972, *227,* 92–99.

Premack, D. The education of Sarah. *Psychology Today,* 1970, *4,* 54–58. (a)

Premack, D. A functional analysis of language. *Journal of Experimental Analysis of Behavior,* 1970, *14,* 107–125. (b)

Premack, D. Language in chimpanzee? *Science,* 1971, *172,* 808–822.

Premack, D. Language and intelligence in ape and man. *American Scientist,* 1976, *64,* 674–683.

Premack, D. Mechanisms of intelligence: Preconditions for language. In S. R. Harnad, H. D. Steklis, & J. Lancaster (Eds.), Origins and evolution of language and speech. *Annals of the New York Academy of Sciences,* 1976, *280.*

Raph, J. B. Language development in socially disadvantaged children. *Review of Educational Research,* 1965, *35,* 389–400.

Reynolds, A. G., & Flagg, P. W. *Cognitive psychology.* Cambridge, Massachusetts: Winthrop, 1977.

Sampson, O. C. A study of speech development in children of 18–30 months. *British Journal of Educational Psychology,* 1956, *26,* 194–201.

Schachter, F. F., Shore, E., Hodapp, R., Chalfin, S., & Bundy, C. Do girls talk earlier?: Mean length of utterance in toddlers. *Developmental Psychology,* 1978, *14,* 388–392.

Schramm, W. L., Lyle, J., & Parker, E. B. *Television in the lives of our children.* Stanford, California: Stanford University Press, 1961.

Sinclair-de-Zwart, T. Sensorimotor action patterns as a condition for the acquisition syntax. In R. Huxley & E. Ingram (Eds.), *Language acquisition: Models and methods.* New York: Academic Press, 1971.

Skinner, B. F. *Verbal behavior.* New York: Appleton-Century-Crofts, 1957.

Slobin, D. I. *Psycholinguistics.* Glenville, Illinois: Scott, Foresman & Co., 1974.

Smith, M. E. An investigation of the development of the sentence and the extent of vocabulary in young children. *University of Iowa Studies in Child Welfare,* 1926, *3,* No. 5.

Staats, A. W. *Learning, language, and cognition.* New York: Holt, Rinehart, & Winston, 1968.

Staats, A. W. Linguistic-mentalistic theory versus an explanatory S–R learning theory of language development. In D. I. Slobin (Ed.), *The ontogenesis of grammar.* New York: Academic Press, 1971.

Templin, M. C. Certain language skills in children. *Institute of Child Welfare Monograph,* 1957, No. 36.

Terrace, H. S. *Nim.* New York: Knopf, 1979.

Terrace, H. S., Petitto, L. A., Sanders, R. J., & Bever, T. G. Can an ape create a sentence? *Science,* 1979, *206,* 891–902.

Trehub, S. E., & Rabinovitch, M. S. Auditory-linguistic sensitivity in early infancy. *Developmental Psychology,* 1972, *6,* 74–77.

Watson, J. B. *Behaviorism.* Chicago: University of Chicago Press, 1924.

Whitehurst, G. J., & Vasta, R. Is language acquired through imitation? *Journal of Linguistic Research,* 1975, *4,* 37–57.

Chapter

THE ASSESSMENT OF INTELLECTUAL DEVELOPMENT

Eight

INTRODUCTION

We have described the developmental patterns of some major components of intelligence in the preceding chapters. Intellectual development has been represented as the acquisition of sensorimotor, perceptual, learning, cognitive, and language processes. These dimensions of mental ability emerge as basic developmental phenomena to become organized into what we recognize as general intelligence. Thus, the previous chapters have dealt with the empirical and theoretical aspects of intellectual development and ignored intelligence as an abstract concept. While we have examined the development of several components of intelligence and intellectual functioning, we have not considered the level of general intelligence that those isolated developmental events might represent. Attempts to measure the course of intellectual development from birth to maturity require some notion of what intelligence consists. They also require some procedure or instrument to assess the degree to which an individual possesses the defined components of intelligence. Note that the assessment of intellectual development does not tell us anything about the process of development, or how intelligence develops. However, assessment procedures may provide information about the relative rate and current status of intellectual development and functioning under certain conditions.

The widespread use of intelligence tests and IQ scores in psychological and educational practice has stirred bitter polemics over the nature of intelligence and mental testing. The sociopolitical implications of potential test misuse and abuse have inspired both public and scientific clamor over the issue of psychoeducational testing and practices. There are practical, social, and scientific limitations to the assessment of intellectual development, in short. These limitations require some discussion of the problems and issues surrounding the concept of intelligence, its assessment, and their historical background. We will also briefly explore the major instruments used to assess intelligence in infants and children and the mental growth trends that are described by such instruments. The final section of this chapter will deal with the major influences on the course of intellectual development in children, again as revealed by intelligence tests.

HISTORICAL PERSPECTIVE

Interest in the nature of human intelligence and its measurement has its roots in ancient philosophical thinking. More contemporary origins of the measurement and assessment of mental abilities can be found in the history of general psychology, beginning in the latter half of the nineteenth century (see Matarazzo, 1972, for an excellent survey of the historical background on intelligence and intellectual assessment; Reisman, 1966, provides a detailed discussion on the testing movement in the context of the historical development of clinical psychology). Historical attempts to understand the nature of intelligence and to obtain some quantified measures of mental abilities began with the study of individual differences by such psychologists as Sir Francis Galton and J. McKeen Cattell, among others.

Galton was introduced in Chapter Two as a gifted scientist whose consuming belief in the inheritance of intelligence led him to found the eugenics movement in the early twentieth century. In his search to identify individuals best suited for intellectual accomplishment and parenthood, Galton developed a battery of tests of various sensory capacities and acuity. He also used physical measurements and tests of strength. Galton believed that these measures could identify individuals with more or less than normal intelligence. Between 1884 and 1890, Galton maintained an "anthropometric laboratory" where, for a small fee, he provided individuals with a profile of their test results, which supposedly reflected some level of general mental ability.

James McKeen Cattell was an American psychologist who studied with Wilhelm Wundt in Leipzig. Like Galton, Cattell was interested in individual differences, and he was a friend and great admirer of Galton. In 1890, Cattell published a paper entitled "Mental Tests and Measurements," which represented the first formal use of the term "mental tests" (Reisman, 1966). In this paper, Cattell described a battery of 10 tests consisting of reaction time measures, sensorimotor abilities, perceptual tasks, and immediate memory skills. Cattell believed that such mental tests would reveal information about the constancy of intellectual processes and their relationships and that they could be put to practical use in the identification and selection of individuals for various training and educational goals. Cattell recognized the practical and social needs for such diagnostic techniques and their value in the early identification of intellectual superiority and abnormality.

In the following decade, several other psychologists also attempted to measure and diagnose intellectual ability through the use of simple sensorimotor tests. But efforts to discriminate school children's intelligence on the basis of these tests were totally unsuccessful. By the turn of the century, general disillusionment with mental testing began to appear. It became apparent that something as complex as intelligence or mental ability could not be validly assessed or predicted by simple psychophysical or sensorimotor tests.

By 1900, psychologists were still struggling for some understanding of the nature of intelligence and for a working definition which would be generally accepted. Alfred Binet, a French psychologist, had already abandoned the notion that intelligence could be measured by sensorimotor responses. Although he knew that the most fruitful approach to measuring intelligence was to examine complex mental functions such as comprehension, memory, and judgment, he was unable to translate his ideas into an objective, reliable assessment procedure.

In 1904, the Minister of Public Instruction in Paris appointed a commission to develop a procedure which would objectively and reliably differentiate mentally retarded school children from those of normal intelligence. Binet and his physician colleague, Théodore Simon, were among the four appointed members of the commission. The initial result of this effort was the 1905 Binet–Simon Scale, a series of 30 tests arranged in order of increasing difficulty. For example, the first item was to follow a moving object with one's eyes; the last test required defining abstract terms. The 1905 scale tested a broad range of functions, but heavily emphasized judgment, comprehension, and reasoning. The scale was standardized on a group of normal and abnormal children to determine relative difficulty levels of the items. A child's score was simply the number of items passed, an admittedly crude estimate of intellectual status which Binet and Simon offered only as a preliminary instrument.

Continuing their research and development of the original scale, Binet and Simon introduced a refined version in 1908. The 1908 Binet–Simon Scale was longer, with the test items arranged according to chronological age levels, from 3 to 13. The 1908 scale also introduced Binet's concept of mental age as a score on this scale. The mental age score represented the number of items that could be answered correctly by a majority of normal children at each age level. The 1908 scale is considered a major contribution in the history of intelligence testing, born of the pressing social need for the diagnosis of retarded children in order to meet their special education requirements. Binet and Simon revised their scale again in 1911. The 1911 scale included changes and relocations of some of the tests along with the addition of an adult-year level (see Sattler, 1974, for details of the content of the Binet–Simon Scales).

When Binet died in 1911, his scale already had proved of great clinical value to practitioners, who finally were able to discriminate normal and abnormal intelligence. Although the 1911 Binet–Simon Scale contained limitations and weaknesses, both clinically and psychometrically, it was the only useful assessment instrument available, and it was translated into several languages for use in other countries. Henry Goddard, an American psychologist, brought the 1908 scale to America and translated it into English for use with retarded children at the Vineland Training School in New Jersey. However, he did not revise it to correct for cultural differences between Parisian and American children.

The standardized American revision of the 1911 Binet–Simon Scale was introduced by Lewis Terman in 1916 as the Stanford Revision and Extension of the Binet–Simon Intelligence Scale. The 1916 Stanford–Binet Scale represented an extensive revision of everything from test item content to administration and scoring methods. Terman also introduced the intelligence quotient (IQ) as the score obtained on the Stanford–Binet Scale. The IQ concept was adapted from the mental quotient concept developed by the German psychologist William Stern in 1912. The mental quotient was expressed as the ratio between mental age and chronological age. Terman renamed this ratio the intelligence quotient ($IQ = MA/CA \times 100$). IQ scores soon came to represent an estimate of intellectual functioning. The Stanford–Binet Scale underwent subsequent revisions in 1937, 1960, and 1972, each time with increasing psychometric improvements. The impact of the Binet–Simon scales on clinical psychology and the testing movement has been enormous. The Stanford–Binet Scale has long been one of the major instruments for assessing and diagnosing intellectual functioning in America.

When the United States entered World War I in 1917, the government faced the need for objective group tests to screen large numbers of people for suitability, classification, and training in the military services. Individual assessment instruments such as the Binet–Simon Scales were too time consuming and thus totally impractical for such purposes. A group of psychologists led by Robert M. Yerkes was asked to develop a group test of intelligence which could be objectively scored. The result was the Army Alpha and Beta tests for literates and non-English speaking recruits or illiterates, respectively. Following the end of World War I, group tests of intelligence were adopted by industry and colleges for selection purposes. Since 1920, objective group tests of intelligence, aptitude, and achievement for both children and adults have proliferated.

In the mid-1930s, David Wechsler, a clinical psychologist and prominent figure in the history of intellectual assessment, began developing another individual test of intelligence. Reacting against the concept of mental age and notions of IQ constancy, Wechsler introduced the Wechsler–Bellevue Intelligence Scale in 1939. The Wechsler scale consisted of a battery of 11 subtests, verbal and nonverbal, which separately assessed various dimensions of intellectual functioning. In contrast to the Binet scales, the Wechsler was a point scale. An individual's total number of points for correct responses was compared to the total for the standardized sample of that age-group.

In 1949, the Wechsler–Bellevue Scale was revised downward for children between the ages of 5 and 15 and was published as the Wechsler Intelligence Scale for Children (WISC). The adult version was revised in 1955 as the Wechsler Adult Intelligence Scale (WAIS). Finally, in 1967, the Wechsler Preschool and Primary Scale of Intelligence (WPPSI) appeared for use with children between 4 and 6½ years old. Along with the Stanford–Binet, the Wechsler scales have become major instruments for the individual assessment of intelligence for children and adults and have had a major impact on the testing movement in America. For further discussion of these scales, refer to Anastasi (1970), Cronbach (1970), Matarazzo (1972), or Sattler (1974).

During the 1970s, controversy over mental testing, once confined almost entirely within academic circles, boiled over into the public domain. As the furor over IQ scores and their potential abuse grew in intensity, questions about the heritability of intelligence added the element necessary to make the issues explosive. Since 1969, much has been written concerning the problems of mental testing, race, intelligence, and genetics (i.e., Cronbach, 1975). The polemics are now well known, and it appears that they will continue. Perhaps the development of intelligence testing may, as Kennedy (1973) has warned, "become the stone upon which public confidence in psychology stumbles, instead of the rock upon which psychology builds its foundation as a significant scientific discipline" (p. 1).

DEFINITIONS AND THEORIES OF INTELLIGENCE

The Problem of Definition

One of the most common definitions of intelligence is the ability to acquire and use knowledge. This definition may seem clear and straightforward, but like the many other definitions offered in the past, it lacks the necessary precision and rigor required for scientific investigation. Any definition of intelligence must have clear behavioral attributes or referents that can be translated into items or procedures that permit their valid assessment. At this time, innate intellectual capacity or potential cannot be determined or measured. We are restricted to observations of intellectual performance, however that is defined. Therefore, the concept of intelligence, in the biological sense, is an abstraction, a hypothetical construct. We must recognize that in reality we deal with various measures of intelligent behavior, not intelligence as a palpable entity.

The problem of definition thus begins with a theoretical statement of assumptions, describing what are thought to be the structure and attributes of intelligence. This theoretical statement is then incorporated into a test battery designed to assess the degree to which a person possesses the hypothesized attributes. A definition of intelligence is useful if it and the related assessment device reliably discriminate among levels of intellectual functioning. They should also predict outcomes believed to be associated with various levels of intellectual performance as measured. Obviously, different theoretical and psychometric approaches may be equally useful in discriminating and predicting intellectual development and status. The point here is that among the large number of theoretical, empirical, and verbal definitions of intelligence, none can be considered *the* correct one or the *real* one (Miles, 1957). Doubtless there are several kinds or forms of intelligence. And most psychologists would agree that intelligence is something more than any definition has stipulated or assessment device has measured. Remember that IQ scores are an invention—arbitrary numbers designed to reflect the relative performance of individuals on a number of tasks heavily influenced by education, experience, opportunity, and motivation.

Binet's original ideas about intelligence included reasoning and judgment as the "essential activities" of intelligence (Matarazzo, 1972), and he designed his scale as an attempt to measure these attributes. Wechsler viewed intelligence as the global capacity to act purposefully, think rationally, and deal effectively with the environment. Wechsler's broad conception of intelligence is reflected in his scales, which are constructed to tap such dimensions of intelligence as general information, memory, comprehension, judgment, arithmetical skills, and general problem-solving, both verbal and nonverbal. We are already familiar with Piaget's view of intelligence as the process of adaptation to the environment and how his developmental stages reflect changes in those adaptation processes. Piaget, however, is more concerned with qualitative aspects of intellectual development than with formal measurement of intellectual functioning. Uzgiris and Hunt (1975) have developed a scale of perceptual cognitive development based on Piaget's theory of sensorimotor development, but it is still in the experimental stage.

We are still left with the nagging question of what intelligence really is. Perhaps that is how it should be, since we know so little about the answer to that question. Vernon (1969) has described three basic concepts of intelligence. He has called them Intelligence A, Intelligence B, and Intelligence C. Intelligence A refers to innate capacity, the genotype of intelligence. Intelligence B includes definitions that consist of observable behaviors—how an individual adapts to and interacts with the environment, the phenotype of intelligence. Intelligence C is described as what a person does on an intelligence test—an IQ score. Intelligence C represents an operational definition of intelligence. Intelligence A is impossible to determine at this time, B is vague and imprecise, and C is arbitrary and subject to bias. However they are defined and conceptualized, assessment devices can be useful, but they demand conscious decisions about what is to be measured, for what use, and with what recognized limitations.

Theories of Intelligence

While Binet and other applied psychologists were developing their intelligence scales for clinical diagnosis and classification, theoretical psychologists were attempting to delineate empirically the structure of intelligence. By applying various correlational techniques known as factor analysis to existing mental tests, several influential experimental psychologists developed statistical theories of intelligence based on individuals' performances on different mental tasks.

SPEARMAN'S TWO-FACTOR THEORY   Charles Spearman (1904) was a British statistician whose factor analysis of mental test scores and academic performance led him to conclude that intelligence consists of two factors. He found that a common factor seemed to exist in all mental or intellectual performance, regardless of its nature. Spearman labeled this universal component of intelligence the "g" or "general" factor. Spearman's g factor referred to a unitary, universal capacity or trait which underlies all intellectual activity. In addition, Spearman concluded that there are a number of "special" or "specific" capacities, "s" factors, which appear to be unique or specific to a particular test or mental activity. Spearman saw intellectual performance, then, as depending upon some amount of the universal g factor plus whatever amount of s factor was required by the specific tasks. Spearman's major interest was the general factor, and to be intelligent meant that an individual had a large amount of g. In later years, Spearman's theory was weakened by findings of "group" factors falling between g and s factors.

THURSTONE'S MULTIPLE-FACTOR THEORY L. L. Thurstone (1938, 1941) was an American psychometrician who developed a new, multiple-factor analysis to investigate his theoretical assumptions about the nature of intelligence. Thurstone's view of intelligence was that it consisted of several different factors. His factor–analytic procedures enabled him to identify the number and kind of factors which determined performance on a mental test. On the basis of the results of a large battery of tests administered to over 200 college students, Thurstone found seven separate factors or aspects of intelligence that he called primary mental abilities (PMA). The seven factors are spatial, perceptual speed, numerical ability, verbal comprehension, memory, word fluency, and reasoning. Thurstone preferred that an individual's mental abilities not be described as a single IQ score, but rather as separate scores on the primary mental abilities.

GUILFORD'S STRUCTURE-OF-INTELLECT THEORY J. P. Guilford is another American psychometrician whose research on the nature of intelligence led him to reject earlier notions of g, s, and primary mental abilities. Guilford's factor analytic studies of intellectual performance on various intelligence tests confirmed his three-dimensional model or theory of the structure of intellect (Guilford, 1967). Guilford classified intellectual performance into a three-dimensional system according to (1) the kind of mental operation involved, (2) the kind of content or material represented by the mental operation, and (3) the mental products that result when a mental operation is applied to a certain kind of content. Guilford identifies five types of mental operations that may be called into use:

1 Cognition (C)—knowledge
2 Memory (M)—retention of knowledge
3 Divergent Production (D)—generation of logical alternatives

4 Convergent Production (N)—generation of logical conclusions

5 Evaluation (E)—decision of accuracy and adequacy of knowledge

Four types of content are distinguished:

1 Figural (F)—sensory material (sounds, visual images, etc.)
2 Symbolic (S)—letters, numbers, and other conventional signs
3 Semantic (M)—verbal meanings
4 Behavioral (B)—social intelligence, or information from nonverbal contacts

Mental products are analyzed into six alternatives by Guilford:

1 Units (U)—small isolated mental products (words, images)
2 Classes (C)—collection of units
3 Relations (R)—relationships between things
4 Systems (S)—a body of knowledge about something
5 Transformations (T)—changes in products of information
6 Implications (I)—new associations

Guilford's tridimensional model of intellect can be represented as a cube in which all possible combinations of operations, content, and products may be shown. The result is $5 \times 4 \times 6$ or 120 different and separate abilities that are defined by Guilford's structure-of-intellect model, which is shown in Figure 8-1.

While the trend in concepts of intelligence seems to have shifted from general-factor theories to multifactor theories, the evidence continues to support a unitary, general ability factor underlying intellectual performance (Brody & Brody, 1976). Though statistical theories of intelligence have been useful in helping us to better appreciate the complexity of the nature of intelligence, reservations have been expressed about their utility. McNemar (1964), for example, has questioned the wisdom of abandoning the concept of general intelligence. McNemar argues that there is no clear evidence that multifac-

Figure 8-1
Guilford's structure of intellect model.

(From Guilford, 1967.)

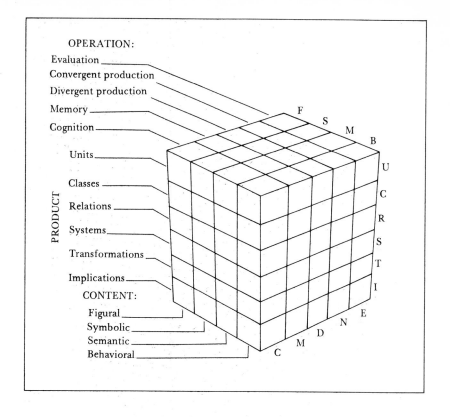

tor measures of intelligence are better predictors than general intelligence tests. McNemar is highly critical of factor analytic approaches to intelligence. McNemar (1964) quips that "the structure of intellect that requires 120 factors may very well lead the British, and some of the rest of us, to regard our fractionization and fragmentation of ability, into more and more factors of less and less importance, as indicative of scatterbrainedness" (p. 872).

In their analysis of statistical theories of intelligence, Brody and Brody (1976) suggest that factor analysis may be a poor procedure for revealing and understanding the structure of human intellect. In many respects, we are not much better off today than Binet was in our attempts to grasp the nature of intelligence. While problems of definition continue to plague psychologists, we can nevertheless outline the general course of intellectual development as revealed by current assessment procedures and describe how intellectual performance on these measures may be affected by a variety of factors.

THE
MEASUREMENT OF
INFANT
INTELLIGENCE

*T*he ability to assess intellectual functioning in young infants and to predict later intellectual performance would be of significant scientific and practical value. Determination of infant intelligence might reveal some basic information about mental capacity in humans and thus enable us to better understand the nature of intelligence and the course of intellectual development. Valid assessment of infant intellectual functioning and the possibility of predicting later development would serve such practical functions as early identification and treatment of intellectual impairments. For these reasons, there has been a long-standing interest in the development of infant scales of intelligence. The development of general behavioral assessment procedures with neonates and infants grew out of the medical tradition of neurological and pediatric examination procedures (St. Clair, 1978). The growth of developmental psychology and the beginning of the testing movement in America spurred interest in the assessment of neonatal and infant behavior. Much of this interest, as we have seen in Chapter Four, focused on studies of maturation and normative development.

One of the earliest attempts to apply mental testing to infants was Kuhlmann's 1912 downward revision of the Binet–Simon Scale (Kuhlmann, 1912). The Kuhlmann–Binet Scale contained tests for infants between 3 and 24 months old. Arnold Gesell (1925), the maturationist, also developed his system of developmental diagnosis (Chapter Four) in an attempt to assess infant intelligence. Today, the most widely used scales of infant intelligence are those developed by Psyche Cattell (1940, 1960) and Nancy Bayley (1969). The Cattell Infant Intelligence Scale is a downward extension of the 1937 Stanford–Binet Scale, but it also includes some items from the Gesell Developmental Schedules. The Cattell scale is designed for infants between 2 and 30 months old. The Bayley Scales of Infant Development are a modern version of an infant mental scale originally published in 1933. They contain mental and motor scales composed of new items and items from the Gesell and Cattell scales. Perhaps the strongest of infant intelligence scales in terms of its empirical basis, the Bayley scale can be used with infants from 1 to 30 months old.

Characteristics of Infant Scales of Intelligence

Scales of infant intelligence are constructed around normative schedules of development. At the preverbal level, infant scales are by necessity limited to sensorimotor development, visual–motor coordination, and directed attention. Test items deal with attending to objects, visual following, simple motor skills, and attending to a voice (Figure 8-2). Once infants acquire language, infant scales can include items designed to measure cognitive abilities such as following simple directions, holding items in memory, solving problems, and various other goal-directed activities. Tasks involving verbal functioning and abstract thinking increase with increasing age levels, and motor tasks decrease.

The nature and content of infant scales of intelligence present special problems in test administration, particularly at the lower levels. Managing young infants and maintaining optimal levels of infants' attention and motivation are demanding tasks. They require skilled, experienced examiners in order

Figure 8-2
Items for the Bayley Scales of Infant Development and the Stanford-Binet Intelligence Scale.

(Photos courtesy of Richard C. LaBarba.)

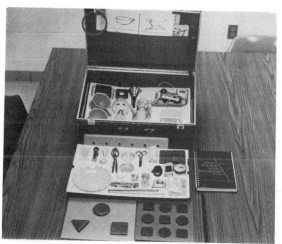 

to obtain valid estimates of mental functioning. In addition to the problems of establishing rapport and motivation, the examiner is also faced with the problems of scoring. Many of the responses to items on infant scales require a rapid, subjective decision from the examiner. The examiner must make a judgment of an infant's behavior by observing a short-lived response to a test item. There is no objective record of the responses under ordinary testing situations. Assuming a competent examiner and accurate scoring, what can be said about an obtained score of intellectual functioning for an infant? When an infant successfully follows a ring or reaches for a cube, is that infant revealing some level of intelligence, or some simple sensorimotor skill? Are these infant responses precursors to later measured intelligence?

Limitations of Infant Scales of Intelligence

Any evaluation of infant scales of intelligence should analyze their validity, or the extent to which they actually measure intellectual functioning. The answer to this question revolves around the consistency of intelligence or intellectual functioning over time. For instance, we might measure the degree to which IQ scores maintain their relative positions in the distribution of intelligence test scores at different ages. While infant scales show good validity in differentiating between age-related performance on scale items from month to month, evidence for the predictive validity of infant scales has been lacking. Predictive validity means that one can successfully estimate later performance on some criterion on the basis of the results of earlier performance on some measuring instrument. For infant scales of intelligence, predictive validity refers to the ability to use IQ scores obtained on an infant scale to predict intellectual performance during later childhood and adulthood. The typical procedure is to obtain correlations between mental test scores of individuals at different ages.

Several studies have described the relationship between scores obtained on infant scales of intelligence and later intellectual performance (Bayley, 1955, 1970; Jones & Bayley, 1941; Lewis & McGurk, 1972; McCall, Hogarty, & Hurlburt, 1972; Stott & Ball, 1965). Among these studies, the Berkeley growth study (Jones & Bayley, 1941; Bayley, 1955, 1970) has provided a significant body of information on the growth and stability of intelligence. The Berkeley growth study is a longitudinal study of 61 infants born in 1928–1929 which continued through age 36. The original group of infants was tested at monthly intervals, beginning at 1 month of age, on a set of various infant scale items which eventually was published as the California First-Year Mental Scale (Bayley, 1933), an earlier version of the Bayley scales. Repeated mental testing of the individuals in the Berkeley growth study continued into adulthood. Bayley's (1955) findings concerning the test–retest relationships between infant scale IQs and IQ scores at 16 to 18 years of age led her to conclude:

These findings give little hope of ever being able to measure a stable and predictable intellectual factor in the very young. I am inclined to think that the major reason for this failure rests in the nature of intelligence itself. I see no reason why we should continue to think of intelligence as an integrated (or simple) entity or capacity which grows throughout childhood by steady accretions. (p. 807)

In 1970, Bayley stated:

The findings of these early studies of mental growth of infants have been repeated sufficiently often that it is now well-established that test scores earned in the first year or two have relatively little predictive validity (in contrast to tests at school age or later), although they may have high validity as measures of the children's cognitive ability at the time. (p. 1174)

Bayley's data on the Berkeley children were consistent with those reported by other investigators. There is no correlation between scores on mental tests administered during the first 6 months of life and mental test scores obtained between the ages of 5 and 18. At 3 to 4 years of age, IQ scores show a low positive relationship with those obtained between 1 and 6 months of age. Measured IQ between 7 and 18 months continue to have low positive correlations with later IQ scores, with correlations reaching a magnitude of approximately .50 between 2 and 3 years of age. After 5 years of age, IQ scores correlate highly with later scores (Tables 8-1 and 8-2).

While some of the correlations shown in Tables 8-1 and 8-2 reach statistical significance, for the most part they are low and account for little of the variance of later IQ scores. Consequently, such low-magnitude correlations do not have much

CHILDHOOD AGE (YEARS)	AGE IN INFANCY (MONTHS)			
	1–6	7–12	13–18	19–30
8–18	.01 (12/4)	.20 (8/2)	.21 (6/2)	.49 (9/2)
5–7	.01 (7/5)	.06 (5/4)	.30 (5/4)	.41 (16/4)
3–4	.23 (7/4)	.33 (5/3)	.47 (6/4)	.54 (16/3)

Note: The Number of Correlations Entering Into the Median and the Number of Different Studies Included are Found in Parentheses.

(From McCall, et al., 1972.)

practical or clinical significance. As you might expect, test–retest correlations increase with increasing age of the first test administration. The failure of infant scales to show any substantial relationship with later intelligence cannot be attributed to poor reliability or sex differences (McCall et al., 1972). Reliability measures of the major infant scales are acceptable, and the predictive validity for both boys and girls is generally similar.

Whatever infant scales of intelligence are measuring, it does not appear to be the same thing that is measured by later intelligence tests. Infant scales may have much greater predictive value with clinical infant populations. Correlations between very low scores obtained by infants with suspected neuropathology and later intelligence and abnormality are in the range of .70–.80 (McCall et al., 1972). Nevertheless, as McCall et al. caution, the diagnostic use of infant scales alone should be avoided. Their clinical value is enhanced when used with other assessment techniques, both medical and behavioral.

There is evidence that predictions from infant IQs may increase slightly when parental socioeconomic status is considered along with test scores (McCall et al., 1972). In addition, some studies indicate that various single test items or clusters of items may have more predictive significance than a total test score. Infant vocalization items from infant scales have been demonstrated to have greater predictive value at later ages for girls but not for boys. Cameron, Livson, and Bayley (1967) have shown impressive correlations between infant vocalization

Table 8-2
Correlations Between
IQs Averaged over
Different Ages and the
Mean IQs at 17 and 18
in the Berkeley Growth
Sample

AVERAGE OF MONTHS OR YEARS	CORRELATION (r)
(months)	
1–3	.05
4–6	−.01
7–9	.20
10–12	.41
13–15	.23
18–24	.55
27–36	.54
42–54	.62
(years)	
5–7	.86
8–10	.89
11–13	.96
14–16	.96

(Adapted from Brody & Brody, 1976.)

in girls from the Berkeley study and later intelligence scores. These authors extracted six items from the Bayley scale which measured early vocalization between the ages of 5½ and 13½ months. These measures reflected the age at which each child *first* passed each test item. As the girls matured, the correlations between IQ and infant vocalization were found to increase. Between 13 and 26 years of age, the correlations reached a range of .40 to .60. At age 26, the correlation with verbal IQ scores reached a magnitude of approximately .74. After the age of 3, such correlations with boys' later IQ scores were primarily negative and nonsignificant, as Figure 8-3 shows. Data from the Fels longitudinal study (McCall et al., 1972) suggest that early social and frolicsome activity in the first-year infant test situation may have inverse predictability for later verbal intelligence in boys ($r = -.36$ at 11 years; $-.26$ at 3½ years; $-.53$ at 2 years).

Many psychologists have interpreted the data on the growth of intelligence from infancy to adulthood as failing to support the notion of general intelligence (the g factor) and simple

Figure 8-3
Girls' vocalization-factor correlations with verbal, performance, and full-scale intelligence scores at ages 6 through 26 years. The bottom line represents a smoothed "base-line" curve of average 10- to 12-month total test scores' correlations with later full IQ. The top smoothed curve indicates the increased prediction available from employing the vocalization-factor scores. Solid dots represent the actual vocalization-factor—full-scale IQ correlations. Fluctuations in the two curves could be due to either fluctuating numbers of subjects or different IQ tests administered at the different ages. Crosses and diamonds illustrate the better prediction by the vocalization factor of later verbal intelligence.

(From Cameron, Livson, & Bayley, 1967.)

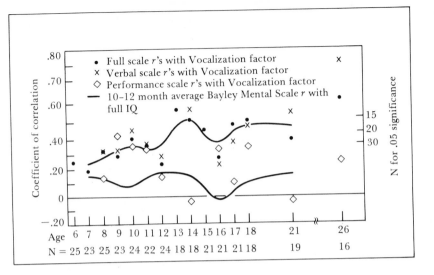

continuity of intellectual development, as Bayley stated in 1955. Some, such as Lewis and McGurk (1972), have taken much stronger positions against the existence of infant intelligence as a measureable, stable, and unitary construct, arguing that infant scales have no generality or implications for future performance. Despite the failures of the infant scales data at prediction and diagnosis, others conclude that there is some evidence to justify further attempts to find continuity between infant mental abilities and later intelligence. They see some promise in differential clusters of infant scale items, if not total scale scores.

In summary, we may attribute the relatively low predictive value of infant scales of intelligence to the following factors:

1 At the preverbal level, infant scales are largely measuring sensorimotor development and skills. Most of these sensorimotor phenomena appear to have few, if any, implications for later intellectual performance in normal children. Among normal children, motor development is not related to intelligence. At these earliest levels of infant development, either sensorimotor processes contain too few cognitive components, or the infant scales are not adequately measuring those existing cognitive abilities which might predict later intellectual performance. Consequently, total scores on infant scales do not reflect the precursors to measured intelligence during later childhood and beyond.

2 The more cognitive items on infant scales, dealing with sustained attention, memory, voluntary vocalization, and social responsivity, are often difficult to score objectively. While such responses may have more predictive value, they are relatively few in number, too general, and superficial. Perhaps more sophisticated, detailed measures of these response capabilities

A child taking the Gesell Test, which measures infant intelligence as a function of overall developmental abilities. This test is useful in diagnosing the current level of such abilities, but—like most intelligence tests administered before the age of 5—the results do not accurately predict later levels of intelligence. The presence of the child's mother (right) probably serves to ease anxiety about the test and its administrators.

(Photo by Mimi Forsyth/Monkmeyer Press Photo Service.)

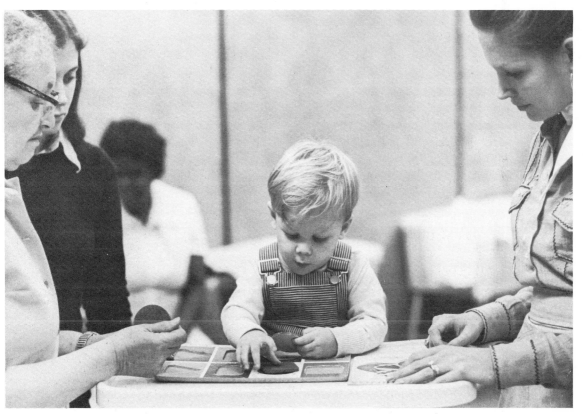

might reveal more overlap with later verbal tests of intelligence. **3** Below the age of 3, there is a great deal of instability and change in mental growth patterns as revealed by performances on infant scales of intelligence. Bayley (1970) reports that fluctuations in an infant's performance on infant scales cannot be attributed to poor reliability of the scales. Rather, these fluctuations in IQ scores in any given infant are due to a number of infant state and motivational variables such as activity level, emotionality, biological/medical conditions, and

Figure 8-4
Individual curves of relative intelligence (standard deviation curves) of five males, birth to 36 years, Berkeley Growth Study cases.

(From Bayley, 1970. Copyright © 1970 by John Wiley and Sons, Inc. Reprinted by permission of publisher.)

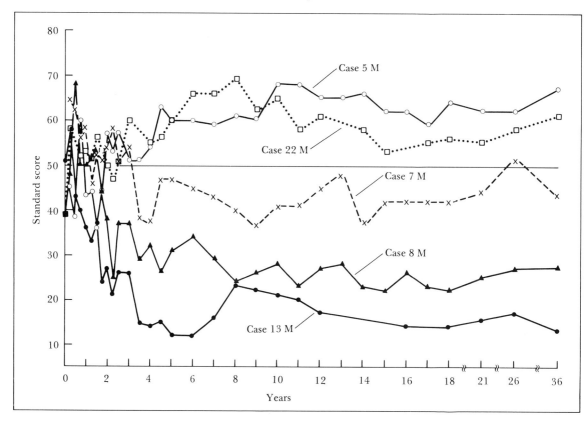

Figure 8-5
IQ fluctuations in one boy.

(From *Wechsler's Measurement and Appraisal of Adult Intelligence,* Fifth Edition, by Joseph D. Matarazzo. Copyright © 1972 by Oxford University Press, Inc. Reprinted by permission.)

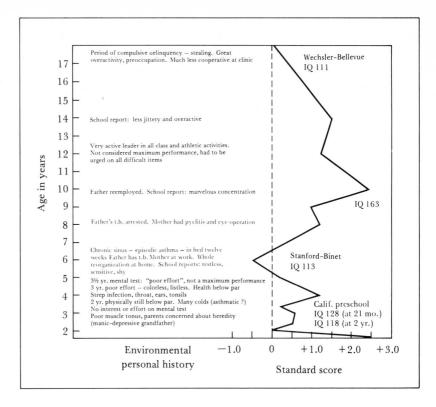

physical/motor developmental status. Such dramatic fluctuations in performance from time to time may seriously depress correlations with later IQ scores (Figures 8-4 and 8-5).

While we have seen that differential item analyses of infant scales can elevate correlations with later intellectual performance, a general evaluation of infant scales of intelligence suggests the modest predictive and practical significance of such measures. Useful predictions of adult intelligence cannot be obtained until 4 to 5 years of age.

TRENDS IN INTELLECTUAL DEVELOPMENT

The expansion of the testing movement during the past 50 years has provided a great deal of data describing intellectual growth and development from birth to maturity. These data on intellectual performance as measured by standardized intelligence tests have revealed information on the degree to which IQ scores (i.e., general intelligence) change with age. Further, they have strongly suggested general trends of intellectual growth, along with enormous individual differences in such trends that can occur under variable conditions of measurement and developmental experiences. Developmental studies of mental test performance have exploded early myths and claims about the concept of fixed intelligence and its stability over age. Current views on intellectual growth are based on data collected from a number of longitudinal studies such as the Berkeley growth study, the Harvard growth study (Dearborn & Rothney, 1963), and the Fels study (Baker, Sontag, & Nelson, 1958).

The various longitudinal studies consistently reported mental growth curves whose general developmental trend was quite different from that described by the earlier cross-sectional studies upon which the Stanford–Binet and Wechsler scales were developed. Traditional views of mental growth, based on cross-sectional data, described intellectual growth and performance as peaking at some time during early maturity or adulthood. After this time, the test results suggested that intelligence began to decline with further age (Figure 8-6). However, more recent longitudinal data suggest a pattern of intellectual development characterized by either continued, but slow, improvement or maintenance of intellectual level into the middle-age period, as shown in Figures 8-7 and 8-8.

We discussed various deficiencies in the classical research designs used in developmental psychology in Chapter One. We noted that different developmental trends often occur as a function of the design used, cross-sectional or longitudinal. A further example, applied to mental growth curves, uses the results reported by Schaie and Strother (1968). Schaie and Strother used an accelerated longitudinal design, described in Chapter One, to examine the test performance of a group of 500 individuals ranging in age from 20 through 70. Schaie and Strother obtained cross-sectional data on their sample, selected at 5-year age intervals. Their measure of intelligence was the Thurstone Primary Mental Abilities Test (PMAT) which was collected in 1956. Seven years later, 302 of the original sample of 500 subjects were retested on the PMAT, the longitudinal component of the study. At this time, the 20 year olds were 27, the 25 year olds 32, etc. Would the cross-

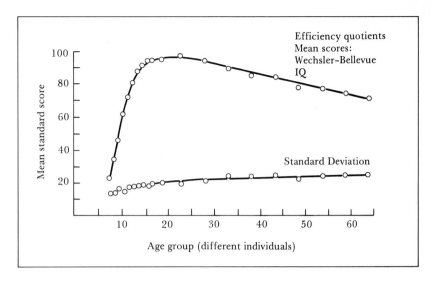

Figure 8-6
Curve of mental growth and decline for Wechsler-Bellevue IQ scores.

(From Honzik, MacFarlane, & Allen, 1948.)

sectional data on intellectual performance obtained in 1956 show the same pattern as the longitudinal data obtained 7 years later? The Schaie and Strother results are shown in Figure 8-9.

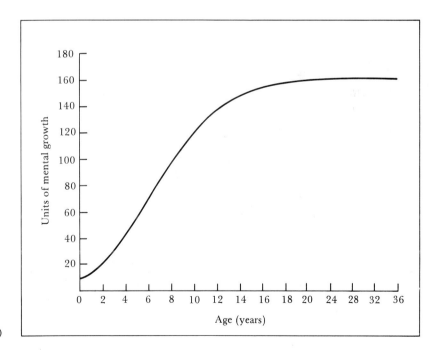

Figure 8-7
Theoretical curve of the growth of intelligence, based on data from the Berkeley Growth Study.

(Adapted from Bayley, 1970.)

Figure 8-8
A general mental growth curve, from the Harvard Growth Study.

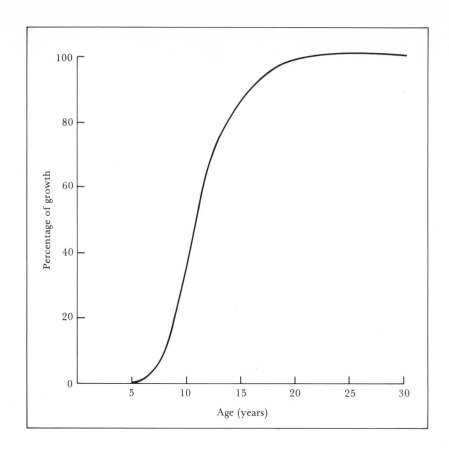

Note that the cross-sectional data reveal general declines in intellectual performance as measured by the PMAT (reasoning, spatial ability, number skills, and verbal meaning). The longitudinal data, on the other hand, show no decline in test performance. The cross-sectional declines can be attributed to generation effects in the original 1956 sample. That is, dramatic differences between the younger and older subjects arise from differential education, health, social, and cultural factors which exist across such age spans and which are generation-related variables. While intellectual performance may decline over age as a function of certain environmental and biological factors, such decline is clearly not an invariant, predictable developmental phenomenon associated with age. Further, such observed declines may be differential in nature, with some mental functions or dimensions of intelligence showing decline,

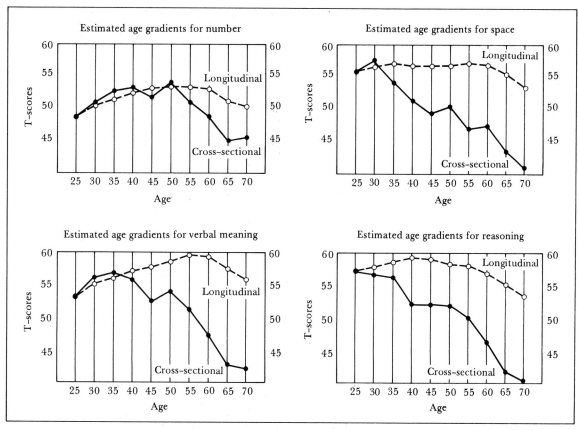

Figure 8-9
Age gradients for intellectual ability.

(From Schaie & Strother, 1968. Copyright © 1968 by the American Psychological Association. Reprinted by permission.)

some remaining stable, and some improving (Schaie, 1974; Schaie & LaBouvie-Vief, 1974). While longitudinal designs are certainly not free from methodological deficiencies, they may reveal developmental trends more accurately than cross-sectional designs.

GENETIC AND ENVIRONMENTAL CONTRIBUTIONS TO INTELLECTUAL DEVELOPMENT

We can conclude that intellectual performance, as measured by IQ tests, is neither constant nor fixed. The data we have discussed concerning individual growth curves and test–retest correlations leave no doubt as to the instability of IQ as we currently measure it. The longitudinal growth studies demonstrate changes in IQ scores ranging from five to 40 points, with average changes being in the range of 10 to 15 points. Large changes are much more common between preschool ages and maturity, with smaller changes occurring after 18 years of age.

To what may we attribute these changes in intellectual performance? What factors can be identified as influencing individual and group differences in intellectual development and as determining adult levels of intellectual functioning and achievement? Clearly, a host of environmental factors can alter intellectual development, resulting in individual and group differences that ultimately affect adult levels of achievement and performance. While environmental influences on intellectual performance and achievement are demonstrable, it is inherently much more difficult to identify the influences of genetics on intellectual performance. A number of complex reasons contribute to this difficulty, as we shall see. In keeping with our general approach to developmental phenomena, we will view intellectual "capacity" and subsequent intellectual development, performance, and achievement as the result of interactions between genetic endowment and environmental/experiential events. The question of hereditary and environmental influences on intelligence has produced perhaps the most bitter controversy in the history of psychology.

Genetics and Intelligence

Long before the mental testing movement began in America, a belief in the hereditary basis of insanity, criminality, and mental retardation was prevalent in both Europe and America. The principal developers of mental tests and the mental testing movement in America, notably Louis Terman, Henry Goddard, and Robert Yerkes, shared Galton's ardent position on the inheritance of intelligence, apparently with equal vigor and enthusiasm. Like Galton, they and other pioneers of the mental testing movement were also active members of various eugenics organizations. As influential psychologists and scientists, they did much to shape social and governmental policies between 1900 and 1930. In their capacity as expert consultants on mental testing and intelligence, they provided "data" substantiating the heritability of intelligence and the "menace" of feeble-mindedness, pauperism, and degeneracy to American society.

The sociopolitical impact of these contributions was heavy indeed. State sterilization laws were enacted largely on the basis of "scientific" documentation offered by psychologists and eugenicists that mental and social degeneracy were genetically determined and therefore untreatable. More important, perhaps, was the effect of the mental testing movement on the passage of American immigration laws. By claiming that IQ data demonstrated the genetic inferiority of southeastern Europeans, various behavioral and biological scientists and eugenics organizations were instrumental in the formulation of new laws restricting the immigration quotas for groups identified as biologically inferior. For a particularly critical and graphic discussion of the sociopolitical impact of early mental testers and the testing movement, refer to Kamin (1974).

Binet designed his original test for purely diagnostic purposes. He made no claims for a genetic basis of intelligence or that his test was a measure of innate intelligence or mental capacity. He did, in fact, react strongly against those who believed that intelligence was fixed by hereditary limitations. But by the time the Stanford–Binet Scale was published by Terman in 1916, the genetic hypothesis of fixed intelligence had become firmly rooted in America. The Stanford–Binet Scale and other mental tests developed during the testing movement were considered by many as measures of innate intelligence and as scientific instruments to identify the genetically inferior.

Contemporary Views of Genetics and Intelligence

The classical interpretation of influences on intelligence and IQ scores claimed that genetic inheritance was virtually the sole basis of individual and group differences in mental ability. Environmental influences were considered of little or no importance by the early hereditarians. Modern versions of the genetic hypothesis of intelligence make similarly strong claims for intelligence being almost exclusively determined by heredity. Between 1900 and 1940, the nature–nurture controversy about intelligence inspired major investigations and heated debate. For the next 30 years or so, interest in the genetic basis of intelligence dissipated for the most part. As the world plunged into war and then raced into the space age, advances in technology and basic scientific research became compelling and absorbing activities. The times had changed and the testing movement was over.

In 1969, Arthur Jensen, an educational psychologist at the University of California, published a controversial paper in the *Harvard Educational Review* entitled "How much can we boost IQ and scholastic achievement?" This paper rekindled the nature–nurture issue of intelligence with an intensity and ferocity unparalleled in the history of modern scientific and public debate (Jensen, 1972; Rice, 1973). In a lengthy and complex review of the literature dealing with the relationship between IQ and scholastic achievement, Jensen (1969) presented his interpretation of the data concerning the heritability of intelligence and the success of compensatory educational programs. Jensen concluded:

1 Blacks consistently score approximately one standard deviation (15 points) below the average of whites on tests of intelligence.
2 The heritability of intelligence is estimated to be approximately 80%.
3 Conventional environmental enrichment programs are generally ineffective in producing long-term changes in IQ.

Jensen's paper was an objective, cautiously moderate, and thoughtful statement of his analysis of the data. The implication of genetic factors in the black-white IQ score differences was offered as "a not unreasonable hypothesis," but Jensen clearly did not exclude environmental factors or their interaction with genetic factors. Eysenck (1971) and later Herrnstein (1971, 1973) took similar positions on the high heritability of intelligence. The severe personal and professional costs of their hereditarian views are well documented by Herrnstein (1973), Jensen (1972), and Rice (1973).

Current estimates of the heritability of intelligence test scores range from zero (Kamin, 1974) to 45% (Jencks, 1972) to 80% (Herrnstein, 1971; Jensen, 1969). Heritability is defined as the proportion of the total variance in a *population* trait that is attributable to genetic factors, usually expressed as h^2. How can such extreme ranges and contradictory interpretations result from different analyses of the same kinds of data? The conflicting conclusions concerning the heritability of intelligence test scores result from which data are used, what kinds of analyses are performed in arriving at heritability estimates, and which studies are considered as acceptable. For extended and objective discussions of these problems and the genetic concept of heritability, see Brody and Brody (1976), Loehlin, Lindzey, and Spuhler (1975), and Scarr-Salaptatek (1975).

Genetic Studies of IQ Heritability

Estimates of the heritability of intelligence test scores are drawn from twin studies, sibling studies, and adoption studies. Each of these designs attempts to control for environmental and genetic factors by manipulating the degree of genetic resemblance among subjects and the degree of environmental influences shared by the subjects. The strongest evidence for the heritability of intelligence comes from studies of identical or monozygotic (MZ) twins reared apart from birth. Since MZ twins have identical genotypes, any differences in intelligence must be attributed to environmental factors. Therefore, if MZ twins are reared in different environments, the degree of relationship between their test scores will provide some estimate of the heritability factor under variable environmental conditions. It is very difficult to find MZ twins who have been separated from birth or during early infancy. There have been only four such studies reported in the literature. Moreover, there is strong evidence that Cyril Burt's influential twin studies are based on fraudulent data (Dorfman, 1978; Jensen, 1978; McAskie, 1978; Wade, 1976). The results are summarized in Table 8-3. The obtained correlations between MZ twins reared apart range from .67 to .88.

The hereditarian position is also supported by kinship studies of fraternal and dyzygotic twins and siblings reared together. Erlenmeyer-Kimling and Jarvik (1963) have summarized the family resemblance data from 52 studies (Figure 8-10). It can be seen that correlations between intelligence test scores of individuals increase with increasing genetic and environmental similarity. The correlation (r) between IQ scores of siblings reared together is approximately .50; for fraternal twins, .53. Jencks (1972), by contrast, reports data from four studies that

Table 8-3
IQ Correlations in Four Studies of Separated MZ Twins

STUDY	NUMBER OF PAIRS	CORRELATION (r)
*Burt (1966)	53	.88
Juel-Nielsen (1965)	12	.68
Newman, Freeman, & Holzinger (1937)	19	.67
Shields (1962)	38	.82
Combined	122	.82

*Burt's data are now generally discredited.

(From *Genetics and Education* by Arthur R. Jensen. Copyright © 1972 by Arthur R. Jensen. Reprinted by permission of Harper and Row, Publishers, Inc.)

yield a mean correlation of .32 between IQ scores of biologically unrelated children reared together. If we turn to the data describing the relationship between IQ scores of children and parents, we find correlational values of approximately .50 between IQ scores of natural parents and their children reared by them (Erlenmeyer-Kimling & Jarvik, 1963; Jencks, 1972). Foster parent and child IQ correlations range from .07 and .37 with a mean of approximately .20.

Munsinger (1975) has critically reviewed and summarized all the published studies of adopted children's IQ development. Munsinger concludes that studies comparing the average IQ of adopted children with that for a normal population cannot be seriously considered until a number of methodological criteria have been satisfied. These methodological considerations include (1) representative sampling, (2) no differential attrition over time, (3) accurate information on biological and adoptive parents, (4) control of early separation and placement of children, and (5) elimination of practice effects of repeated IQ testing and various statistical problems which bias results.

All the studies reviewed by Munsinger fail to meet the majority of these methodological criteria. Munsinger adds that the strongest conclusion that can be drawn from the existing data is that heredity is much more important than environment in producing individual differences in IQ. His analysis suggests that adoptive parents' environment has little effect on the

To what extent is intelligence inherited genetically? The question generates heated scientific and social debate. Contemporary research suggests an increasing positive correlation between genetic similarity and IQ test scores. Rearing identical twins, such as the two shown here, in different environments would control the genetic variable and might resolve the question of the heritability of intelligence. Such situations, however, are rare and, at present, scientists must content themselves with less direct methods of research.

(Photo copyright © 1974 by Susan Richter/Photo Researchers, Inc.)

intellectual growth of their adopted children ($r = .19$), whereas the genetic and environmental contributions of the biological parents have a strong effect on intellectual development ($r = .58$). While the exact nature of the respective quantitative contributions of genetics, environment, and their interaction will remain controversial until additional data are collected, Munsinger states, "The time has come to move beyond arguments about whether heredity or environment affect human intelligence and to begin collecting the data that will lead to an understanding of the biological and environmental mechanisms of IQ development" (p. 658).

CATEGORY		.00	.20	.40	.60	.80	GROUPS INCLUDED
Unrelated persons	Reared apart						4
	Reared together						5
Foster Parent — Child							3
Parent — Child							12
Siblings	Reared apart						2
	Reared together						35
Twins / Two-Egg	Opposite sex						9
	Like sex						11
Twins / One-Egg	Reared apart						4
	Reared together						14

Figure 8-10
Correlations between IQs of individuals showing different degrees of
genetic resemblance and experiencing different degrees of environmental similarity. Data from 52 studies. Median findings are represented by
vertical lines intersecting the horizontal lines, which represent the range
of reported correlations.

(From Erlenmeyer-Kimling & Jarvik, 1963. Copyright © 1963 by the American Association for the Advancement of Science. Reprinted by permission.)

Conclusions on the Heritability of Intelligence

There are many criticisms of the studies which make a case for
the heritability of intelligence. One of the most systematic and
extensive critiques of genetic studies is that of Kamin (1974).
Kamin argues that there are no acceptable data which would
lead one to believe that *IQ test scores* are in any degree heritable.
While Kamin acknowledges the possibility of genetically determined differences in cognitive or intellectual *capacities* which
have yet to be demonstrated, his extreme environmentalist
position is difficult to defend. Even if we dismiss Burt's data,
other twin studies and adopted children's studies strongly
suggest a genetic component of intelligence greater than zero.
Along with others, Kamin reminds us of the methodological
and statistical deficiencies and problems in genetic studies of

intelligence which force us to view the data with caution. However, these considerations would simply decrease heritability estimates from .80 to perhaps .60 or so (Loehlin et al., 1975).

On the basis of the evidence, it seems reasonable to conclude that intelligence test scores are influenced *to some degree* by genetic factors. That is, if we define heritability as some value greater than zero, then intelligence is heritable. But, as has been pointed out by many, the important question is "How heritable?" It must be emphasized that heritability does not mean nor imply strict determinism. Heritability does not mean absence of plasticity or modifiability. Heritability does not mean trait constancy. Heritability does not mean absence of environmental contribution and interaction. Heritability, in short, does not diminish the importance of environment in the development of intelligence.

Environmental Influences on Intelligence

Many environmental factors can influence intellectual development and performance on intelligence tests. These influences may be positive or negative, depending on the nature of the environmental forces acting on the individual. Factors in the environment not only create or prevent various opportunities to acquire knowledge, but they also play a critical role in the development of motivation to learn and achieve.

SOCIOECONOMIC FACTORS AND INTELLECTUAL DEVELOPMENT For some time, it has been known that intellectual development and performance are related to socioeconomic variables and social class differences (McNemar, 1942; Neff, 1938; Stewart, 1947). Similarly, school achievement in children is also positively related to socioeconomic status (Hollingshead, 1949). Socioeconomic class or status is a complex index variable (Chapter One) which contains a number of more or less specifiable independent variables such as family size, rearing patterns, parental education and occupation, general learning opportunities, parental expectancies, and motivational patterns. These variables emerge differentially within SES groups and are usually sustained to some degree throughout childhood.

The impact of these variables is widespread and may affect

The long, hot, urban summer: Children beating the heat with a plastic pool. Socioeconomic factors are known to influence intellectual development and performance. SES is a complex of many variables, including parental educational level and occupation, and parental expectations of their children. Parental variables would seem to be the most important in forming the most pervasive of all socioeconomic influences: motivation. If youngsters feel trapped in an environment deprived of hope, they may simply give up. The consequences of such feelings represent a potential loss for both the individual and society.

(Photo by James H. Karales/Peter Arnold, Inc.)

not only intellectual performance and school achievement, but also personality and adjustment patterns. Emotional adjustment, interests, attitudes, and motivation can play a critical role in intellectual achievement and performance. The data from Bayley and Schaefer (1964), shown in Figure 8-11, are representative of general findings describing the relationship between socioeconomic variables and IQ in children. You can see in Figure 8-11 that, from 2 years of age on, the relationships between IQ and SES factors generally increase in magnitude. This is particularly true for parental education and occupation, which correlate between .40 and .50 with children's IQ. Kagen and Moss (1959) have obtained similar results. Most of these data have been based on white populations. In a study of social-class differentiation in cognitive development among black children, Golden, Birns, Bridger, and Moss (1971) found a similar pattern of relationships between IQ and social class. Between 18 months and 3 years of age, correlations between IQ, SES, and parental education gradually increased to approximately the levels reported for white children.

The important potential contribution of general socioeconomic factors to intellectual development is described in a recent study by Scarr and Weinberg (1976). Scarr and Weinberg investigated 130 black and interracial children adopted by advantaged middle-class white families. The adoptive parents were of well above average intelligence, educational level, and occupational status. When tested on a standardized intelligence test between the ages of 4 and 17 years, the black and interracial children had an average IQ score of 106, one standard deviation above the average IQ score of 90 for black children reared in their own homes in that geographical region. Both this average IQ score and the average school achievement of the children were above that of the average white population but below that of the adoptive parents and that of their natural children. While the Scarr and Weinberg study demonstrates the facilitative effect of an advantaged social and cultural environment on IQ, genetic and environmental contributions were confounded, as the authors point out.

The observed positive relationships between SES factors and IQ are difficult to interpret. Such phenomena do not necessarily weaken hereditarian positions, as it can be argued that people with higher innate intellectual ability are more likely to reach higher educational, occupational, and social class levels. On the other hand, there is no doubt that children of such parents also inherit superior environments and enjoy the advantages of increased learning and cognitive stimulation, better schools, and general cultural enrichment. In addition, such environments are more likely to foster the development

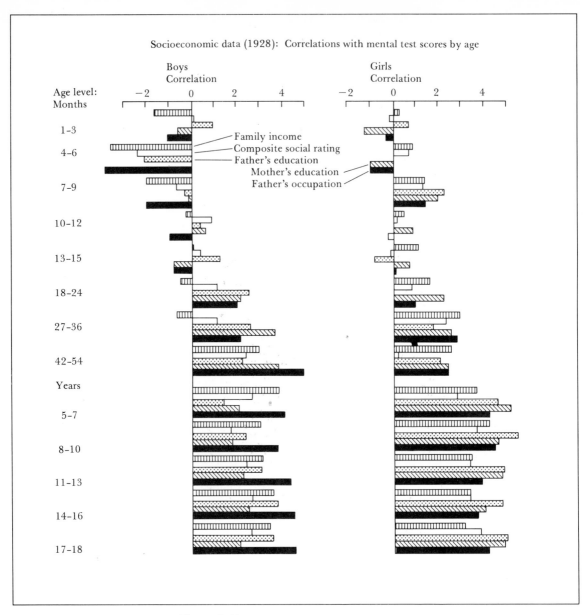

Figure 8-11
Correlation of mental test scores by age, birth to 18 years, with five indicator of parents' socioeconomic status at the time the children were born.

(From Bayley & Schaefer, 1964.)

of motivational and interest patterns conducive to intellectual development. All these factors encourage intellectual achievement and subsequently enhance performances on tests of mental ability.

EARLY ENVIRONMENTAL INTERVENTION AND INTELLECTUAL DEVELOPMENT   One of the more direct ways to assess the degree of environmental impact on intellectual development is to experimentally facilitate the general cognitive, learning, and environmental experiences of a group of children and compare their subsequent intellectual performance with a control group of children reared in their normal environment. There have been several such early stimulation, enrichment, or intervention programs in this country. These programs were designed to prevent the debilitating effects of social, cultural, and cognitive impoverishment, characteristic of low SES children, on intellectual development and educational achievement.

The first such national program was Project Head Start, initiated in 1965. Project Head Start was directed toward the preschool education of low SES children between the ages of 3 and 5. Because Project Head Start was a hasty response to the social needs of the disadvantaged, its design as a social program made it somewhat resistant to evaluation of its effectiveness. The available data, however, indicate short-term, transient effects. That is, children who participated in the early intervention program showed significant IQ gains at the end of the program relative to the control children. However, some 2 to 3 years later, such gains disappeared, and the two groups were found to be comparable in IQ and general achievement (Horowitz & Paden, 1973).

There have been a number of other early intervention programs for preschool children since 1965. These have been reviewed by Brofenbrenner (1975) and Horowitz and Paden (1973). Generally, the results have been disappointing, inasmuch as long-term IQ gains have not been demonstrated. Early intervention seems to result in significant IQ gains during the intervention program, but such gains typically cease after the first year, with "washout" effects after children leave the program. Longitudinal follow-ups on IQ performance reveal no differences between experimental and control groups.

A reported exception to this general washout effect in early intervention projects is the Milwaukee Project (Heber, Garber, Harrington, & Hoffman, 1972). Heber and colleagues have obtained impressive gains in intellectual performance among children placed in an environmental enrichment program from birth to 6 years of age. At 6 years, these children had an average IQ of 121 compared to a control group of children with an average IQ of 87. The two groups of children are now

A group of youngsters using a gallery visit for artistic inspiration. Such culturally enriching experiences provide "food for thought" and serve as intellectual stimuli. Unfortunately, most "early intervention" programs, designed to counteract cultural and social poverty, have had only short-term beneficial effects. Some evidence suggests that the effects last longer when other members of a family, particularly the parents, share in the enrichment program.

(Photo by David Hurn-magnum/Magnum Photo Library Print.)

10 years old, and the experimental group continues to show higher average levels of intellectual functioning relative to the controls (IQ 105 versus 85). The Milwaukee Project provided an infant education center staffed with teachers who administered daily sensory stimulation, sensory training, and cognitive skills building. In addition to the environmental enrichment program for the children, Heber's team set up an intervention program for the mothers of these children. The mothers in the experimental group, originally from the lowest socioeconomic class in Milwaukee and functioning at an IQ level of less than 80, were given extensive training in infant care and vocational competency skills. It appears that combined mother–infant intervention programs, designed to provide specific sensory and skills training, may have more than a temporary influence on intellectual development.

The initial findings on the effectiveness of most other early intervention programs suggest the difficulty of directly manipulating intellectual development. However, such programs continue with better designs and controls. It seems clear from the existing data that such programs must abandon naive, narrow conceptions of cognitive stimulation and intellectual development if the question of intellectual plasticity is to be clearly answered.

PARENTAL FACTORS AND INTELLECTUAL DEVELOPMENT To what degree do parental behaviors and attitudes toward their children's intellectual development affect intellectual achievement and performance? Clearly, these are environmental considerations which can influence children's intellectual development by the early establishment of motivational patterns which facilitate intellectual development and achievement. Additionally, certain parental behaviors may set expectancy levels for performance, which children accept and respond to.

Bayley and Schaefer (1964) studied a number of maternal variables and their correlations with children's intellectual performance, using data from the Berkeley growth study. Their analysis revealed different correlational patterns for boys and girls, as Figure 8-12 shows. Between 5 and 18 years of age, higher correlations between IQ and maternal accept-

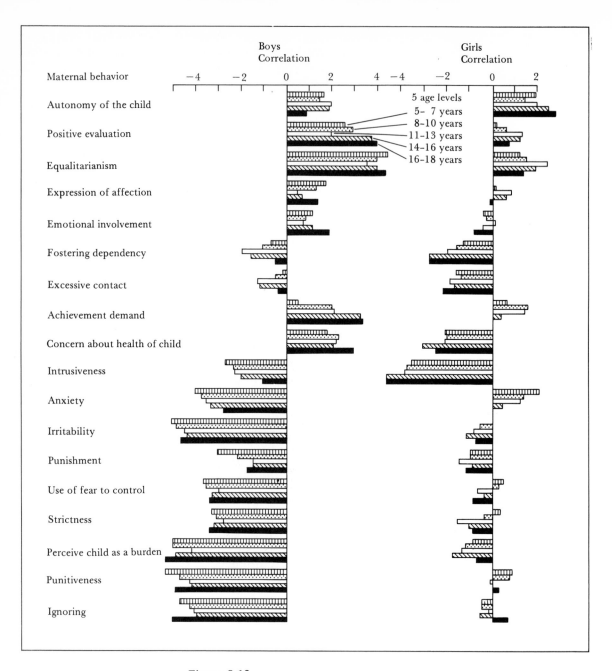

Figure 8-12
Correlations between maternal behavior (0 to 3 years) and intelligence at five age levels (5 to 18 years).

(From Bayley & Schaefer, 1964.)

ance and equalitarianism are found for boys compared to girls. Similarly, maternal demand for academic achievement is more highly positively correlated with their sons' IQ than with their daughters' IQ. Figure 8-12 also shows that stronger negative correlations occur between sons' IQ and maternal variables such as punishment, strictness, and punitiveness. Bayley and Schaefer (1964) also found that these correlational patterns are variable between birth and the school-age years, often showing reversals. Other studies have also shown positive correlations between parental expectations and their children's intellectual development (Kent & Davis, 1957; Wolf, 1964). These data suggest that high parental expectancies, established in a positive atmosphere, may facilitate intellectual development in children by encouraging the development of appropriate, enduring motivational patterns to learn and achieve.

FAMILY CONFIGURATION AND INTELLIGENCE   Several reports have described the tendency of children from large families to have lower IQs than those from small families (Anastasi, 1956; Zajonc, 1976). The reasons for this tendency are poorly understood and cannot be explained by interpretations involving social class factors, parental variables, or genetic background. Zajonc (1976) and Zajonc and Markus (1975) have proposed a new theory of the effects of birth order and family size on intellectual development, called the "confluence model." The confluence model attempts to account for the effects of the intellectual environment within the family and to explain individual differences in intelligence as a function of family configuration. According to the confluence model, the intellectual growth of each member of the family is dependent upon that of all the other members. The rate of intellectual development depends on the family configuration. The family intellectual environment is described as some function of the average absolute level of intelligence among its members, such as mental age, rather than as IQ which is a relative measure. Since each family member makes some absolute contribution to the intellectual environment, that environment constantly changes as children develop and also when children are born into or leave the family.

As a simple example, suppose that the absolute intellectual

The Waltons on the front porch of their Tennessee home. Children from large families tend to have lower IQs than children from small families. There are countless variables in a child's development, and the scientific explanation for this apparent phenomenon is not known. It may be in part a consequence of having to share the various resources of the family—both economic and social—particularly the parents' active attention.

(Photo by Peter Menzel/Stock, Boston)

levels of two parents were 50 units each. The total intellectual environment would be 100. If a child is now born into the family, the intellectual contribution of the newborn would be zero. The average family intellectual environment is now 50 + 50 + 0 divided by 3, or roughly 33. Suppose further that three years later, when the first child now has an intellectual level of say 4, a second child is born. The second-born child enters an intellectual environment of 26 (50 + 50 + 4 + 0 divided by 4). The confluence model therefore predicts that the effects of birth order and family size on intellectual development will depend on the age spacing between siblings. With large enough age gaps between siblings, negative effects on the average family intellectual environment can be neutralized and even reversed.

In a test of the confluence model, Grotevant, Scarr, and Weinberg (1977) were unable to predict intellectual perform-ance among children of different birth ranks in large and small families. As Grotevant et al. point out, although the confluence model fits the population data, it does not account for intellectual patterns within families when both parent and

A family reading together. This sort of close family interaction contrib-utes immeasurably to the child's overall development by reinforcing a whole range of skills and abilities and encouraging a positive self-image. In small families, parents can focus all of their interest and attention on one or two children; in large families, such concern must be shared among all the children, resulting in less individual attention per child. What seems most important from the developmental point of view is that a child have regular interaction with some interested adult or adults. There may be additional benefits if this interaction is with the child's actual parents, although no definitive statement regarding the need for parental interaction can be made at this time.

(Photo copyright © 1980 by Ira Berger.)

child IQ data are available. In short, the confluence model of intellectual development has not yet demonstrated its validity. Although its simplicity is attractive, its failure to consider parental genetic contributions and the extrafamilial intellectual environment (Davis, Cahan, & Bashi, 1977) represent serious problems for the confluence model.

REFERENCES

Anastasi, A. Intelligence and family size. *Psychological Bulletin,* 1956, *53,* 187–209.

Anastasi, A. *Psychological Testing* (Third ed.). New York: Macmillan, 1970.

Baker, C. T., Sontag, L. W., & Nelson, V. L. (Eds.). Mental growth and personality development: A longitudinal study. *Monographs of the Society for Research in Child Development,* 1958, *23,* No. 2.

Bayley, N. *The California first-year mental scale.* Berkeley: University of California Press. Syllabus Series No. 243, 1933.

Bayley, N. On the growth of intelligence. *American Psychologist,* 1955, *10,* 808–818.

Bayley, N. *Bayley scales of infant development: Birth to two years.* New York: Psychological Corporation, 1969.

Bayley, N. Development of mental abilities. In P. H. Mussen (Ed.), *Carmichael's Manual of Child Psychology.* New York: Wiley, 1970.

Bayley, N., & Schaefer, E. S. Correlations of maternal and child behaviors with the development of mental abilities. *Monographs of the Society for Research in Child Development,* 1964, *29.*

Brody, E. B., & Brody, N. *Intelligence: Nature, determinants, and consequences.* New York: Academic Press, 1976.

Brofenbrenner, U. Is early intervention effective: Some studies of early education in familial and extra-familial settings. In A. Montagu (Ed.), *Race and IQ.* New York: Oxford University Press, 1975.

Burt, C. The genetic determination of differences in intelligence: A study of monozygotic twins reared together and apart. *British Journal of Psychology,* 1966, *57,* 137–153.

Cameron, J., Livson, W., & Bayley, N. Infant vocalizations and their relationship to mature intelligence. *Science,* 1967, *157,* 331–333.

Cattell, P. *The measurement of intelligence of infants and young children.* New York: Science Press, 1940; Psychological Corporation, 1960.

Cronbach, L. J. *Essentials of psychological testing* (3rd Ed.). New York: Harper & Row, 1970.

Cronbach, L. J. Five decades of public controversy over mental testing. *American Psychologist,* 1975, *30,* 1–14.

Davis, D. J., Cahan, S., & Bashi, J. Birth order and intellectual development: The confluence model in the light of cross-cultural evidence. *Science,* 1977, *196,* 1470–1472.

Dearborne, W. F., & Rothney, J. W. M. *Predicting the child's development.* Cambridge, Massachusetts: Sci-Art, 1963.

Dorfman, D. D. The Cyril Burt question: New findings. *Science,* 1978, *201,* 1177–1186.

Erlenmeyer-Kimling, L., & Jarvik, L. F. Genetics and intelligence: A review. *Science,* 1963, *142,* 1477–1479.

Eysenck, H. J. *The IQ argument: Race, intelligence, and education.* New York: Library Press, 1971.

Gesell, A. *The mental growth of the preschool child.* New York: Macmillan, 1925.

Golden, M., Birns, B., Bridger, W., & Moss, A. Social-class differentiation in cognitive development among black preschool children. *Child Development,* 1971, *42.*

Grotevant, H. D., Scarr, S., & Weinberg, R. A. Intellectual development in family constellations with adopted and natural children: A test of the Zajonc and Markus model. *Child Development,* 1977, *48,* 1699–1703.

Guilford, J. P. *The nature of human intelligence.* New York: McGraw-Hill, 1967.

Heber, R., Garber, H., Harrington, S., & Hoffman, C. Rehabilitation of families at risk for mental retardation. Madison, Wisconsin. Rehabilitation Research and Training Center in Mental Retardation, University of Wisconsin, 1972.

Herrnstein, R. J. IQ. *The Atlantic,* 1971, *228,* 43–64.

Herrnstein, R. J. *IQ in the meritocracy.* Boston: Little, Brown, 1973.

Hollingshead, A. B. *Elmtown's youth: The impact of social classes on adolescents.* New York: Wiley, 1949.

Honzik, M. P., MacFarlane, J. W., & Allen, L. The stability of mental test performance between two and eighteen years. *Journal of Experimental Education,* 1948, *17,* 320.

Horowitz, F. D., & Paden, L. Y. The effectiveness of environmental intervention programs. In B. M. Caldwell and H. N. Ricciuti (Eds.), *Review of Child Development Research.* Vol. 3. Chicago: University of Chicago Press, 1973.

Jencks, C. *Inequality: A reassessment of the effect of family and schooling in America.* New York: Basic Books, 1972.

Jensen, A. R. How much can we boost IQ and scholastic achievement. *Harvard Educational Review,* 1969, *39,* 1–123.

Jensen, A. R. *Genetics and education.* New York: Harper & Row, 1972.

Jensen, A. R. Sir Cyril Burt in Perspective. *American Psychologist,* 1978, *33,* 499–503.

Jones, H. E., & Bayley, N. The Berkeley Growth Study. *Child Development,* 1941, *12,* 167–173.

Juel-Nielsen, N. Individual and environment: A psychiatric-psychological investigation of monozygotic twins reared apart. *Acta Psychiatrica et Neurologica Scandinavia,* Monographs Supplement, 1965.

Kagan, J., & Moss, H. A. Parental correlates of child's IQ and height: A cross-validation of the Berkeley Growth Study results. *Child Development,* 1959, *30,* 325–332.

Kamin, L. J. *The science and politics of IQ.* Potomac, Maryland: Lawrence Erlbaum Associates, 1974.

Kennedy, W. A. Intelligence and economics: A confounded relationship. Morristown, New Jersey: General Learning Press University Program Module, 1973.

Kent, N., & Davis, D. R. Discipline in the home and intellectual development. *British Journal of Medical Psychology,* 1957, *30,* 27–34.

Kuhlmann, F. A revision of the Binet–Simon System for measuring the intelligence of children. *Journal of Psycho-Asthenics,* Monograph Supplement, 1912, *1,* 1–41.

Lewis, M., & McGurk, H. The evaluation of infant intelligence scores—true or false? *Science,* 1972, *178,* 1174–1177.

Loehlin, J. C., Lindzey, G., & Spuhler, J. N. *Race and intelligence.* San Francisco: Freeman, 1975.

Matarazzo, J. D. *Wechsler's measurement and appraisal of adult intelligence* (5th Ed.). Baltimore: Williams & Wilkins, 1972.

McAskie, M. Carelessness or fraud in Sir Cyril Burt's kinship data? *American Psychologist,* 1978, *33,* 496–503.

McCall, R. B., Hogarty, P. S., & Hurlburt, N. Transitions in infant sensorimotor development and the prediction of childhood IQ. *American Psychologist,* 1972, *27,* 728–748.

McNemar, Q. *The revision of the Stanford–Binet scale.* Boston: Houghton-Mifflin, 1942.

McNemar, Q. Lost our intelligence? Why? *The American Psychologist,* 1964, *19,* 871–883.

Miles, T. R. Contributions to intelligence testing and the theory of intelligence: I. On defining intelligence. *British Journal of Educational Psychology,* 1957, *27,* 153–165.

Munsinger, H. The adopted child's IQ: A critical review. *Psychological Bulletin,* 1975, *82,* 623–659.

Neff, W. S. Socioeconomic status and intelligence: A critical survey. *Psychological Bulletin,* 1938, *35,* 727–757.

Newman, H. H., Freeman, F. N., & Holzinger, K. J. *Twins: A study of heredity and environment.* Chicago: Univ. of Chicago Press, 1937.

Reisman, J. M. *The development of clinical psychology.* New York: Appleton-Century-Crofts, 1966.

Rice, B. The high cost of thinking the unthinkable. *Psychology Today,* December, 1973, 89–93.

Sattler, J. M. *Assessment of children's intelligence.* Phila.: Saunders, 1974.

Scarr-Salapatek, S. Genetics and the development of intelligence. In F. D. Horowitz (Ed.), *Review of Child Development Research*. Vol. 4. Chicago: University of Chicago Press, 1975.

Scarr, S., & Weinberg, R. A. IQ test performance of black children adopted by white families. *American Psychologist*, 1976, *31*, 726–739.

Schaie, K. W. Translations in gerontology—from lab to life: Intellectual functioning. *American Psychologist*, 1974, *29*, 802–807.

Schaie, K. W., & LaBoubie-Vief, G. Generational versus ontogenetic components of change in adult cognitive behavior: A fourteen year cross-sequential study. *Developmental Psychology*, 1974, *10*, 305–320.

Schaie, K. W., & Strother, C. R. A cross-sequential study of age changes in cognitive behavior. *Psychological Bulletin*, 1968, *70*, 671–680.

Shields, J. *Monozygotic twins brought up apart and together.* London: Oxford University Press, 1962.

Spearman, C. "General Intelligence," objectively determined and measured. *American Journal of Psychology*, 1904, *15*, 201–293.

St. Clair, K. L. Neonatal assessment procedures: A historical review. *Child Development*, 1978, *49*, 280–292.

Stewart, N. A.G.C.T. scores of army personnel grouped by occupations. *Occupations*, 1947, *26*, 5–41.

Stott, L. H., & Ball, R. S. Infant and preschool mental tests: Review and evaluation. *Monographs of the Society for Research in Child Development*, 1965, *30*, No. 101.

Thurstone, L. L. Primary mental abilities. *Psychometric Monographs*, No. 1, University of Chicago Press, 1938.

Thurstone, L. L., & Thurstone, T. G. Factorial studies of intelligence. *Psychometric Monographs*, No. 2. University of Chicago Press, 1941.

Uzgiris, I. C., & Hunt, J. McV. *Assessment in infancy: Ordinal scales of psychological development.* Urbana: University of Illinois Press, 1975.

Vernon, P. E. *Intelligence and cultural environment.* London: Metheun, 1969.

Wade, N. IQ and heredity: Suspicion of fraud becloud classic experiment. *Science*, 1976, *194*, 916–919.

Wechsler, D. *The measurement of adult intelligence* (3rd Ed.). Baltimore: Williams & Wilkins, 1944.

Wolf, R. M. The identification and measurement of environmental process variables related to intelligence. Unpublished doctoral dissertation University of Chicago, 1964.

Zajonc, R. B. Family configuration and intelligence. *Science*, 1976, *192*, 227–236.

Zajonc, R. B., & Markus, G. B. Birth order and intellectual development. *Psychological Review*, 1975, *82*, 74–88.

Chapter

EMOTIONAL DEVELOPMENT

Nine

INTRODUCTION

The range, depth, variety, and subtlety of human emotions are unmatched in the animal kingdom. This capacity for human emotional development is expressed not only in normal or adaptive dimensions of emotionality, but also in abnormal or maladaptive forms of emotionality. Emotional capacity and sensitivity are related to phylogenetic level of complexity. Hebb (1972) argues that both the capacity for emotional development and the susceptibility to emotional disturbance are directly related to the phyletic level of intelligence. Humans, therefore, become the most rational and the most emotional of all animals. The general cognitive capacity for interpretation and evaluation of information that results in increased intelligence also results in increased emotional capacity. There is no generally accepted theory or definition of emotion. However, most investigators agree that cognitive capacity is intimately related to emotional capacity and that emotions presuppose the existence of certain cognitive processes such as interpretations or evaluations of stimulus events (Plutchik, 1977). As we shall see, cognitive approaches to emotion and emotional development occupy a major position in current psychological research and thinking.

It is difficult to think about human development without seriously considering emotional development. Emotions continually color human experience, directing and redirecting our perceptions of the world, our thoughts and memories, and all of our behavior. They may serve to organize and facilitate behavior or to disrupt and inhibit behavior. In the course of normal human development, emotional experiences become a pervasive, fundamental component of all cognitive functioning. We may have to agree with Sherrington's (1900) comment that "mind rarely, probably never, perceives any object with absolute indifference, that is, without 'feeling' " (p. 974).

The significance of emotional development for an understanding and appreciation of general human development is obvious. Emotional development involves not only learning emotional responses but also learning to control such responses. The patterns of emotional development and emotional control that are acquired between early childhood and maturity may affect the course of other developmental patterns such as personality and social development. The common experiences and language of emotion greatly contribute to the subjective reality of emotion. However, the problem of studying emotional development and expression as a scientific question has been a thorny one for psychology. The theoretical and empirical basis for an understanding of emotion remain unclear.

There are several reasons for the confusion surrounding emotion and emotional behavior. First, there is no generally accepted definition of emotion. Most of the many definitions available lack the precision and usefulness necessary for scientific study. Second, there are measurement problems. Both physiological and behavioral approaches to emotion have failed to yield any consistently revealing measures or indices of various emotions. Physiological correlates of emotion, such as autonomic nervous system activity, are poorly understood and have been "disappointing" as differential measures of emotions (Strongman, 1973). Similarly, behavioral indices of emotion are extremely variable, inconsistent, and unstable, preventing accurate measurement. A third factor clouding the study of emotion is the problem of interpreting emotional states and responses. That is, it is often difficult for both researchers and subjects to clearly identify or label emotional experiences. Lastly, the general area of emotion and emotional behavior has not been investigated as much as other areas of psychology. This situation may be either the cause or the effect of the first three factors mentioned above. Although emotion has not received much research attention generally, infant emotional development has been an active research area in developmental psychology, as we shall see.

Our discussion of emotional development will be restricted to a psychological approach to "emotions" as used in common language (Mandler, 1975). That is, we will not be concerned with any detailed discussion of the physiological basis of emotional behavior or with the various theories of emotion. Our concern, rather, is with the development and differentiation of emotional behavior in infants and children. Thorough discussions in the general area of emotion, including physiological and theoretical treatments, may be found in Candland, Fell, Keen, Leshner, Plutchik, and Tarpy (1977), Fantino (1973), and Strongman (1973).

We will consider emotion as the perception and interpretation of some external or internal stimulus event, accompanied by a nonspecific physiological state or arousal, leading to an emotional response. This definition is a simple one indeed, offered only for convenience and ease in dealing with the empirical data in developmental psychology. The general problem of definition is complex, unresolved, and, for our purposes, unnecessary for a discussion of development trends in emotional behavior.

HISTORICAL PERSPECTIVE

Philosophical thinking has rarely, if ever, been concerned with emotional development and has touched only slightly on the general problem of emotion. Emotions were considered conditions of the soul, mind, or body by various philosophers from Aristotle to Kant. Human emotions, passions, and appetites were viewed as innate biological faculties, separate from the intellect and reason. Emotional experiences were attributed to biological activities and sensations, and their development was considered an intrinsic human characteristic.

Darwin's long-standing interest in emotion culminated in the first important scientific statement on emotion, *The Expression of the Emotions in Man and Animals,* in 1872. Darwin argues that emotions, like morphology, evolved and that the phylogenesis and ontogenesis of emotional capacity and behavior were subject to the principles of natural selection described in his *Origin of Species.* The significance of Darwin's work for early genetic psychology has been described in Chapter One. Darwin's thesis is that current forms of human emotional expression exist because of their survival value and that the phylogenesis of human emotion has been naturally selected for its contribution to preserving the species. Darwin considered emotional states and their impact on emotional expression to be inherited reactions. While Darwin's primary concern was with physical expressions of emotion such as postures, bodily movements, and facial expressions, his ideas were liberally applied to principles of nineteenth century genetic psychology. Darwin's work on emotion represents the first scientific attempt to explain the origin and development of human emotion.

In the early decades of the twentieth century, another theory of emotion and emotional development was being formulated independently of experimental psychology. Between approximately 1900 and 1939, Sigmund Freud developed his psychoanalytic theory of personality, which in many respects is a theory of emotion and emotional development. Unlike the faculty psychologists of the nineteenth century who segmented mental functioning into isolated events, Freud emphasized the organized, complex interactions of the mind. Freud viewed emotions as often unconscious phenomena generated and maintained by universal psychic systems (id, superego, ego) and the dynamic interaction among these systems, instincts, and anxiety. Like Darwin, Freud believed that human emotion was a product of natural selection and was inherited. For Freud, the origins of emotional experiences lie in the pleasure principle, a principle of tension reduction by which the id attempts to avoid pain and obtain pleasure.

For our purposes, it is important to note that Freud was among the first theorists to emphasize personality and emotional development. He described a series of four psychosexual stages of development, through which all children pass during the first 5 or 6 years of life. These early years were considered critical to, and essentially the formative basis of, later personality development and emotional functioning. This portion of Freud's theory has stimulated many studies of how early experience affects later development in children. In many respects, Freud's ideas directly or indirectly have generated a great deal of research on emotional development in the twentieth century. For instance, Freud's emphasis on the cognitive aspects of emotion has contributed to modern cognitive theories of emotion. We will have more to say about psychoanalytic theory in Chapter Ten. Since most students are at least basically familiar with Freud's theory, we will discuss only briefly Freud's contributions to the study of emotional development.

The common theme of all major philosophical and early scientific ideas about emotion from Aristotle to Freud was that the soul or mind determines emotions and emotional experiences. That is, cognitive events such as perception, interpretation, and evaluation produce and control emotional experiences and the accompanying changes in physical states. This traditional sequence of events was challenged by William James in 1884. James speculated that emotional experiences follow our perception of bodily arousal and are produced by that arousal. Rather than perception producing a cognitive state of emotion which leads to physical arousal and emotional behavior, James was saying that perception leads to physical arousal and behavior which produces some emotional experience. The classical view of the sequence in emotion is:

Perception ---> Cognition ---> Behavior/Arousal
(snake)   (fear)   (run away, tremble, etc.)

James' sequence can be diagrammed as:

Perception ---> Behavior/Arousal ---> Cognition
(snake)   (running, trembling, etc.) (fear)

To put it simply, James' position was that our perception and feeling of bodily changes *is* the emotion (James, 1884). We do not cry because we are depressed over the loss of a fortune; rather, we cry after the loss, and the crying causes the depression. Because the Danish physiologist Carl Lange proposed essentially the same theory at approximately the same time, this sequence is referred to as the James–Lange theory.

While the James–Lange theory of emotion had a significant impact on psychological research in the twentieth century, it has been seriously criticized, most convincingly by Walter Cannon (1929). It has been demonstrated that visceral changes (1) are not required for emotional behavior, (2) do not differ with different emotions, (3) provide relatively poor perceptual feedback, (4) are too slow to produce the rapid emotional experiences that occur, and (5) do not produce emotion when artificially induced in organisms. While James' theory is now generally considered to be incorrect, we mention it because of its historical significance and because James was ultimately interested in the origin, development, and differentiation of emotional behavior (James, 1890).

The development of evolutional–biological views of human emotion generated a great deal of speculation over "primary" human emotions during the first 3 decades of the twentieth century. Many psychologists became preoccupied with attempts to identify innate or original emotions which were instinctive in humans. These lists of primary, inborn emotions were offered as the origins of all subsequent human emotional behavior (Jersild, 1954). The number of innate emotions attributed to the human infant at birth ranged from 3 to almost 20.

Dissatisfied with the growing speculations about the inheritance of emotional reactions, John B. Watson decided to bring the problem into the laboratory (Watson & Morgan, 1917). Watson and Morgan (1917) attempted to identify emotions displayed in human infants under controlled stimulus conditions. Watson and Morgan wanted to "introduce the illuminating concept of habit formation into the realm of emotions" (p. 168). By subjecting infants to several stimulus conditions during the first few months of life, Watson and Morgan identified three emotional reactions which seemed to be reliably "called out" and differentiated by certain stimuli. They concluded that the only emotions which belonged to the "original and fundamental nature of man" were fear, rage, and love. Watson and Morgan recognized that they were using the common language of emotion, but insisted that these observed emotions were reducible to stimulus and response terms. In fact, they were willing to call them "emotional reaction states, X, Y, Z." The stimulus conditions that elicited fear, rage, and love were found to be loss of support, restriction of infant movements, and stroking or rocking, respectively. Watson and Morgan went on to describe how these fundamental emotional responses serve as the basis for the development of all other complex human emotions through conditioning.

The Watson and Morgan study was the first attempt to investigate human emotion scientifically. It ended the vague speculations about the origins of human emotion and generated a great deal of research into infant emotions and emotional development. Indeed, the Watson and Morgan study inspired a number of studies on primary emotions in infants that persisted until approximately 1940. Among the first attempts to replicate the Watson and Morgan study were those of Sherman (1927a, 1927b, 1928). Sherman's results indicated that different groups of observers were unable to reliably identify and differentiate emotional responses of newborn infants subjected to restraint, loss of support, pain, and hunger. Unlike the Watson and Morgan study, the observers in the Sherman studies saw motion picture films of the infants' responses and were unaware of the stimulus conditions applied to the infants.

Sherman found that the observers' ability to identify and differentiate infant "emotional" responses depended on seeing the stimulus conditions eliciting the response. Without such information, observers attributed any number of emotions to an infant reaction, with very little agreement or consistency. When Sherman's observers were asked the reasons for their judgments, many admitted that they made adult interpretations of infants' emotional responses based on their expectations of what should follow a particular stimulus. Had Watson and Morgan done the same? It appears so, for in addition Sherman was unable to find any evidence of the universal emotional responses to the same stimuli that Watson and Morgan had described in their 1917 study. Sherman concluded that whatever emotional responses might exist in the human newborn, they are undifferentiated, characterized only by general activity. Further, he suggested that the term "inherent" should not be applied to infant emotions. Subsequent studies by Bridges (1932), Irwin (1932), Taylor (1934), and Dennis (1940) all failed to find any evidence for the presence of any innate emotional responses in the human infant. Each of these investigators, like Sherman, agreed that the only clear infant response to various emotion-provoking stimuli was a diffuse, undifferentiated one such as motor activity, irritability, or general excitement.

The early work of Katherine Bridges (1930, 1932) is of particular historical significance. She was the first to offer a theory of the ontogenesis of emotions based on longitudinal empirical observations. Over a period of 4 months, Bridges (1932) carefully observed and recorded the daily responses of

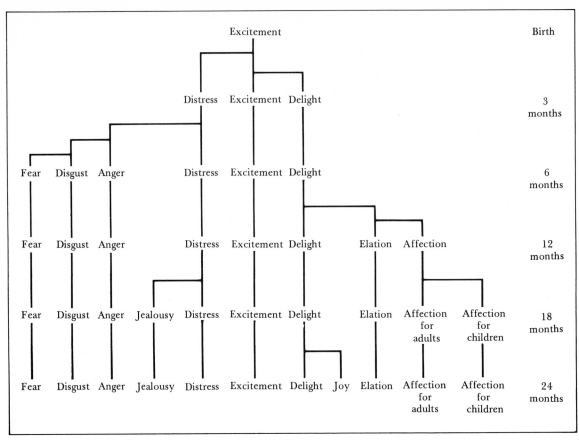

Figure 9-1
The approximate ages of differentiation of the various emotions during the first two years of life.

(From Bridges, 1932.)

62 infants ranging in age from less than 1 month to over 24 months. Her observations led her to conclude that the only original emotion attributable to the infant is general agitation or excitement. Beginning with this general, undifferentiated response, the infant begins to show increasing differentiation of emotional responses under different stimulus conditions. That is, with increasing maturation, learning, and ability to perceive and process information, the infant acquires more and more specific emotional responses, ranging from simple to complex. Bridges attempted to sketch an approximate timetable for emotional development from birth to 2 years of age (Figure 9-1).

By 1940, the issue of primary emotions in humans was no longer popular or scientifically important. Watson's original fear response was viewed as a startle reflex; his rage response as a general reaction to intense pressure or pain; and his love response as a stable or quiescent infant state. Investigators no longer attributed to young infants the complex cognitive abilities required for innate, complex emotional responses. Instead, they turned to more detailed studies of the ontogenesis of emotional behavior and the conditions under which patterns of emotional responses are acquired.

INFANT TEMPERAMENT AND EMOTIONAL DEVELOPMENT

Individual differences in general infant activity and reactivity have been noted in every recorded study of infants, formal and informal, controlled and anecdotal, observational and experimental (i.e., Shirley, 1931; Gesell, 1937). Parents, of course, have always recognized individual differences in their infants' general behavior patterns, beginning in the first weeks of life. Shortly after birth, infants show differences in activity level, responsiveness, arousal patterns, and reaction intensity. Such behavior patterns or styles are referred to as temperament. Are temperamental differences among the infants merely transient, chance variations related to biological states, or do they reflect stable, innate infant characteristics of genetic origins? The data strongly suggest that temperament factors in infants represent genetic predispositions for general emotional reactivity.

Temperament appears to be nonspecific in nature, serving to color, characterize, or propel specific emotional behaviors for any given individual. Thus, temperament contributes both qualitative and quantitative components to a specific emotional response, but there is no direct relationship between temperament factors and specific emotions. Some researchers suggest that the constitutional factors of temperament, interacting with the environment, produce and direct emotional development and personality.

We may consider, then, the concept of temperament as genetic templates that appear in the neonate before specific emotions and that have neural-hormonal bases. Temperament factors produce excitatory or inhibitory effects on central nervous system processes that can influence the behavioral and experiential effect of a given environmental situation (Bridger & Birns, 1968). The survival and development of any temperamental characteristic depends on the degree to which that particular factor is supported and maintained by the environment. That is, the development and stability of infant temperamental dispositions, while initially genetic, is not inevitable or predetermined, but rather a function of interaction effects between these constitutional factors and environment. Assuming that infant temperament is closely related to the innate sensitivity of the central and autonomic nervous systems, such neurophysiological characteristics may be very susceptible to modification by environmental factors.

Temperament in Human Neonates

Bridger and Birns (1968) have reviewed a number of their studies on neonatal temperament and experience, conducted at the Neonatal Behavioral Laboratory at Einstein College of Medicine. These studies were performed on normal, full-term infants between 2 and 5 days old. In their behavioral assessments of neonatal temperament, Bridger and Birns attempted to determine if there were individual differences in response intensity to different stimuli. Then they explored the stability of such response differences and the generality of such responses to different stimuli. They subjected 30 neonates to a soft tone, a loud tone, a cold disc applied to the thigh, and a pacifier inserted into the infant's mouth. Using a rating scale for response intensity to arousing stimuli, they rated observed infant responses from 0 (no response) to 5 (hard crying and intense activation).

The results indicate that infants can be differentiated reliably on general reactivity to stimuli within the first 5 days of life. An infant who responded at a low or high intensity to a particular stimulus responded at that same level to all stimuli. Further, Bridger and Birns found that response intensity to the stimuli remained constant on each day of testing. They report that most babies can be described as slightly, moderately, or intensely responsive, regardless of the modality or nature of the stimulus situation. They interpret their results as evidence for neonatal temperament differences.

In another series of studies, Bridger and Birns (1968) report stable individual differences in neonatal cardiac responses to tactile stimuli. The authors conclude from these data that infants experience different psychophysiological events in response to identical stimulation as a function of individual differences in homeostatic efficiency and autonomic functioning. Because the observed differences occur so shortly after birth, they are considered innate temperamental differences.

Other investigators have also reported stable individual differences in young infants. Nonsocial behaviors such as conditioning and habituation (Friedman, 1975), sleep–wake cycles (Thoman, 1975), and infant states (Thoman, 1975) may all be considered as possible temperamental factors.

Schaffer and Emerson (1964) offer evidence of a different kind in support of infant temperament factors in social behaviors. Schaffer and Emerson examined patterns of response to physical contact among 37 normal infants during the first 18 months of life. They questioned mothers in detail about their infant's behavior when cuddled, carried, held, etc. They explored the consistency of these reactions, the degree of contact-seeking by the infants, the mother's behavior in contact situations, and her reactions to contact avoidance by the infant.

Schaffer and Emerson identified two primary groups among their 37 infants, "cuddlers" and "noncuddlers." The cuddlers sought close physical contact such as holding, hugging, and squeezing, and responded positively to such physical contact. The noncuddlers would not tolerate any close physical contact that involved restraint or restriction of movement. These infants responded to such physical contact by struggling, resisting, and crying. However, the noncuddlers tolerated and enjoyed other forms of contact such as being swung or bounced. Their contact resistance was limited to restraint, and this pattern appeared with anyone, not just the mother.

Schaffer and Emerson also investigated infant reactions to two additional restraint situations. They found that significantly more noncuddlers protested, struggled, and resisted when being dressed and tucked into bed. They also determined that the cuddler/noncuddler response patterns were not related to maternal styles or preferences for infant handling. Schaffer and Emerson concluded that their results revealed a broad, general behavioral characteristic which could not be attributed to maternal or social relationships. In other words, they observed what appears to be an innate temperament

Cuddling . . . Some researchers have grouped infants as cuddlers and noncuddlers, based on the infant's reaction to close physical contact restricting his freedom of movement. This reaction does not appear to be related to the amount of handling and attention an infant receives, leading some researchers to suggest that infants possess certain characteristics of temperament at birth. The infant pictured here is clearly a cuddler and not concerned that the origins of this possibly innate characteristic are unclear.

(Photo by Ken Karp.)

factor. Similar findings have been reported by Brown (1964) and Stone, Smith, and Murphy (1973).

The New York Longitudinal Study of Temperament

Perhaps the most influential and most widely cited longitudinal study of temperament is that of Alexander Thomas, Stella Chess, Herbert Birch, Margaret Hertzig, and Sam Korn, a group of psychologists and psychiatrists who have published a series of reports on their work begun in 1956 in New York City (Thomas et al., 1960, 1963, 1970; Thomas & Chess, 1977). Thomas and colleagues originally studied 80 children of mostly middle and upper class white parents from birth to 2 years of age. They obtained detailed descriptions of the children's behavior through structured interviews with the parents, beginning when the infants were 2 to 3 months old. Analysis of these data led them to identify nine behavioral characteristics which could be scored reliably on a three-point scale of high, medium, and low. Using these nine characteristics to define temperament factors, they were able to produce a behavioral profile of a child.

The temperament factors were (1) activity, (2) rhythmicity, (3) distractibility, (4) approach/withdrawal, (5) adaptability, (6) attention span and persistence, (7) intensity of reaction, (8) threshold of responsiveness, and (9) mood quality. For the Thomas group, temperament refers to behavioral styles which differentiate responses among individuals as a function of intensity, direction, consistency, and quality of expression. Thomas et al. found that temperament profiles were discernable as early as 2 months of age.

The Thomas group then turned to the longitudinal aspects of their study, increasing the number of subjects to 141 children of upper socioeconomic background. The data collected over the first 10 years of life reveal a remarkable degree of stability in temperament profiles first observed at 2 months of age. The data also show that certain temperament attributes tend to cluster together for many of the children, so that Thomas et al. were able to identify three general temperamental types. They described these types as (1) the easy child, (2) the difficult child, and (3) the slow-to-warm-up child. Thomas' temperamental types are described in Table 9-1.

Table 9-1
Temperament Types

TYPE OF CHILD	ACTIVITY LEVEL	RHYTHM-ICITY	DISTRACTIBILITY	APPROACH WITHDRAWAL
	The proportion of active periods to inactive ones.	Regularity of hunger, excretion, sleep and wakefulness.	The degree to which extraneous stimuli alter behavior.	The response to a new object or person.
"EASY"	VARIES	VERY REGULAR	VARIES	POSITIVE APPROACH
"SLOW TO WARM UP"	LOW TO MOD-ERATE	VARIES	VARIES	INITIAL WITHDRAWAL
"DIFFI-CULT"	VARIES	IRREGULAR	VARIES	WITHDRAWAL

TEMPERAMENT of a child allows him to be classified as "easy," "slow to warm up," or "difficult" according to how he rates in certain key categories in the authors' nine-point personality index. The categories are only a general guide to temperament. Of the 141 subjects 65 percent could be categorized, but 35 percent displayed a mixture

Thomas et al. also found that temperament stability and type were not related to parental rearing practices or personality styles. The Thomas group continues to collect data.

IMPLICATIONS OF THE NEW YORK LONGITUDINAL STUDY In summarizing their work, Thomas and Chess (1977) conclude that (1) an "appreciable, but by no means exclusive" genetic component in temperament individuality exists; (2) early identification of infants likely to develop behavior disorders may be possible on the basis of temperament types; and (3) it may be possible to predict general school performance and health status on the basis of infant temperament.

What Thomas et al. are suggesting may have important practical applications in addition to the theoretical implications about the origins of emotionality and personality. In fact, the work of the Thomas group was partially stimulated by the attempt to find answers about individual differences in children which would help parents, pediatricians, teachers, and clinicians to promote and foster healthy development. For

ADAPTABILITY	ATTENTION SPAN AND PERSISTENCE	INTENSITY OF REACTION	THRESHOLD OF RESPONSIVENESS	QUALITY OF MOOD
The ease with which a child adapts to changes in his environment.	The amount of time devoted to an activity, and the effect of distraction on the activity.	The energy of response, regardless of its quality or direction.	The intensity of stimulation required to evoke a discernible response.	The amount of friendly, pleasant, joyful behavior as contrasted with unpleasant, unfriendly behavior.
VERY ADAPTABLE	HIGH OR LOW	LOW OR MILD	HIGH OR LOW	POSITIVE
SLOWLY ADAPTABLE	HIGH OR LOW	MILD	HIGH OR LOW	SLIGHTLY NEGA- TIVE
SLOWLY ADAPTABLE	HIGH OR LOW	INTENSE	HIGH OR LOW	NEGA- TIVE

of traits. Such a child might, for example, be rated "easy" in some ways and "difficult" in others.

(From *The Origin of Personality* by A. Thomas, S. Chess, and H. G. Birch, Copyright ©
August 1970 by Scientific American, Inc. All rights reserved.)

some time, Thomas and co-workers had become interested in such questions as why children reared by the same parents or under similar family environments differ so dramatically in personality development and general adjustment. They had noted, along with others, the lack of any consistent or predictable relationship between general personality development and parental rearing patterns, family characteristics, or general environmental quality. This inability to predict the general developmental outcome in children was attributed to the omission of the child's individual temperamental characteristics and his or her style of responding to vigorous environmental demands.

Because children may differ in temperament and in behavioral patterns of activity and reactivity, they may react quite differently to similar parental rearing patterns or child-training procedures. Thomas et al. suggest that their data indicate that parental or environmental demands that strongly conflict with a child's temperamental characteristics and capacities may place that child under "heavy and even unbearable stress." What this means is that an understanding of a child's temperament characteristics is crucial in determining how parents and teachers should handle a child, what demands and expectations should be placed on a child, and how such demands and expectations should be formulated and carried out. Thomas et al. go on to say that detailed knowledge of a child's temperamental characteristics would be of great significance in establishing healthy parent–child and teacher–child relationships and in helping to prevent the development of behavioral and learning problems in children. Thus, established parental rearing patterns on weaning, toilet training, and discipline training that might have been successful on an "easy" child may utterly fail when applied to a "slow-to-warm-up" or a "difficult" child, leading to any number of potential problems in development. Similarly, fixed teaching techniques and rigid teacher discipline patterns in the classroom may be beyond the temperamental capacities of a child to respond in the expected manner or direction, resulting in possible academic failure or behavioral problems in school.

Thomas et al. suggest that patterns of teaching and discipline must meet not only the learning capacities of a child, but also the temperament style of the child. Clearly, these notions argue against "cookbook" approaches to parenting styles and teaching programs. The adoption of any single approach to child rearing or parenting techniques is inappropriate without serious consideration and awareness of a child's temperamental characteristics and capacities. If Thomas et al. are correct, there is no "one way" to rear children, or to discipline them, or to teach them. Such notions are based on simplistic interpretations of normative data and incorrect generalizations about how children behave at different ages. Thomas, Chess, and Birch (1970) conclude the following:

Theory and practice . . . must take into full account the individual and his uniqueness: how children differ and how these differences act to influence their psychological growth. A given environment will not have the identical functional meaning for all children. Much will depend on the temperamental makeup of the child. (p. 9)

The data on infant temperament are strongly suggestive. However, much more information is required to reveal the interaction processes between the infant and its environment which contribute to the reported stability of temperament factors. While all the investigators cited above acknowledge the importance of environmental factors in supporting such characteristics, the nature and source of those factors remain unclear. Although the innate character of temperament factors may be defended with some confidence, approximately one-third of the children in the Thomas et al. study show variability and inconsistency in their temperament profiles. In addition, other data reveal relatively few correlations between behavioral traits observed during early childhood and traits observed in adolescence (Kagan & Moss, 1962).

LEARNING, MATURATION, AND EMOTIONAL DEVELOPMENT

The first empirical demonstration of a conditioned emotional response was reported by Watson & Rayner (1920) in their classic study of Albert B. ("Little Albert"). Watson's earlier study of original infant emotions with Morgan in 1917 led him to believe that human emotions were the result of conditioned reflexes occurring in the early home life of the child. Conditioned emotional responses, built upon fear, rage, and love, served to establish these emotions and their "compounds" of more complex emotions.

To test this theory, Watson and Rayner obtained a normal, healthy infant, Albert B., when he was about 9 months old. First, they gave Albert a number of "emotional" tests to determine the presence of a fear response to a white rat, a rabbit, a dog, a monkey, masks with and without hair, and burning newspapers. Albert showed no fear response to any of these objects. When tested with a sudden loud sound made by striking a steel bar with a hammer, however, Albert displayed a strong fear response. After debating the ethics of experimentally inducing fear in a young child, Watson and Rayner decided to proceed with the study on the assumption that similar conditioning would naturally occur anyway.

When Albert was 11 months old, Watson and Rayner began their conditioning procedures. In a series of trials on two separate days, they presented a white rat to Albert. Each time he reached for the rat or touched it, they produced a loud sound behind him with the hammer and steel bar. In 10 trials, a strong fear response to the rat was conditioned. Albert was similarly conditioned to a rabbit and dog. One month later, when he was 1 year and 21 days old, Albert was presented with a Santa Claus mask, sealskin coat, white cotton, rat, rabbit, and dog. Albert continued to be fearful of the animals, but with much less intensity than originally observed. In addition, Albert had generalized his fear response to the mask, cotton, and coat, showing mild distress and crying at the sight of them.

Watson and Rayner had planned to "detach" or remove the conditioned emotional responses in Albert, but he was taken away before they could decondition him. However, Watson did discuss four possible procedures for the removal of fear: (1) habituation or fatiguing of the reflex, (2) reconditioning by simultaneous presentation of the fear stimulus and stimulation of the erogenous zones, (3) reconditioning by feeding candy or food during stimulus presentation, and (4) providing "constructive" activities around the stimulus by social imitation (watching others handle the fear stimulus). Watson and Rayner, then, demonstrated that under simple conditioning procedures, emotional reactions could persist for at least a month, although much diminished in intensity. Watson believed that the persistence and intensity of emotional responses in children were a function of the nature and consistency of the conditioning processes present in the home environment.

Three years later, Mary Cover Jones (1924) had a chance to put Watson's treatment ideas to a test. A 34-month-old boy named Peter was brought to her with a number of fears remarkably similar to those induced in Albert. Peter was afraid of rats and rabbits, and his fears extended to fur coats, feathers, and cotton. Jones used the techniques of reconditioning with simultaneous presentation of food and fear stimulus, along with social imitation, and reported that Peter's fear responses had disappeared or greatly diminished. Jones' demonstration provided the first strong support for Watson's theory of emotional conditioning. Harold Jones (1931) replicated the findings of Watson and Rayner by conditioning a fear response in a 15-month-old boy. Jones used a bell as the neutral stimulus and mild electric shock to induce a fear response to the sound of the bell.

While learning factors were increasingly recognized as potent influences in emotional development, it was also apparent that such learning conditions seldom occurred in such a clear form outside the laboratory. Less intense and more subtle forms of stimuli often fail to produce emotional conditioning in children (Bregman, 1934). The ontogenesis of emotion involves more covert forms of learning in most natural home situations (Venn & Short, 1973). The increasing specificity of emotional responses is directly related to general cognitive development and the acquisition of knowledge about situations which come to have more or less emotional significance for a child. Emotional responses may be acquired through direct parental training and conditioning, by imitation of others, and by trial-and-error methods.

What, then, is the role of maturation in emotional development? Early views of emotional development held that certain emotional responses appeared in children as response itself matured (Gesell, 1929; Valentine, 1930). Current views of the role of maturation no longer attribute the emergence of any emotion to some specific, innate maturational event or process directly controlling the development of an emotional reaction. Rather, the data strongly suggest that the importance of maturation for emotional development lies in its preparatory role for general emotional responsivity. Thus, the capacity for emotional development is innate in terms of the biological and physiological requirements necessary for emotional expression. However, it is incorrect to speak of the maturation of specific emotions such as fear. What provides for emotional development is the maturation of fundamental processes underlying the capacity for emotional experience. These processes include perceptual and attentional capacities, conditionability or learning capacity, symbolic capacity, and language capacity. In other words, we are talking about general cognitive development. This position may be defended by referring to studies that demonstrate the increasing effectiveness of more and more stimuli in eliciting emotional responses as a function of increasing maturation and learning (Lewis & Rosenblum, 1974; Skarin, 1977). We may say that a child's susceptibility to an emotional response in a given situation and the complexity of that response are directly related to the child's general and cognitive developmental level. In the normal course of development, increasing behavioral competence results in the attachment of emotional value or significance to an ever-widening range of stimuli. Stimuli which have no emotional eliciting power in early stages of development come to generate a variety of emotional responses later in development (Bridges, 1932; Jersild, 1954; Kagan, 1971; Lewis & Rosenblum, 1974). We find the same general pattern among infrahuman organisms (Hebb, 1972).

THE DEVELOPMENT OF FEAR, SMILING, AND LAUGHTER

*T*he ontogenesis of specific emotions is one of the most extensively studied topics in infant development. Early studies of infant emotional behavior were descriptive, normative accounts of age-related emotional responses over the course of childhood. Contemporary research is characterized by experimental attempts to determine the nature and etiology of basic emotional patterns in infancy. There are a number of reasons for this current emphasis on research in emotional development. Among these are (1) the theoretical and applied implications of early emotional development for later child development and rearing practices; (2) the importance of early emotional development for personality development; and (3) the need for information on infant reaction to parents and strangers as a result of the increasing development and use of day care centers for infants and young children (Haith & Campos, 1977).

We will explore the development of fear, smiling, and laughter because these topics have received most of the research attention in developmental psychology. These emotional patterns are strikingly apparent during infancy, and they have empirical and theoretical significance for a number of developmental phenomena, such as cognitive development and personality–social development. Another area of infant research which has received much attention is infant attachment behavior. We will discuss this topic in Chapter Ten, which deals with personality and social development.

Theoretical Considerations in Fear Development

There are several theories that propose to explain the development of fear in infants. While none of the major theories can account adequately for all observed aspects of infant fear responses, they have served to stimulate and guide research efforts. We will discuss three major theoretical approaches: the ethological approach, the learning approach, and the cognitive approach.

THE ETHOLOGICAL APPROACH TO FEAR Ethologists are behavioral biologists who study the behavior of organisms under natural conditions. The ethological approach to behavior stresses the organization and function of specific behavior patterns observed in real-life situations and attempts to explain behavior within the framework of evolutional theory. Thus, ethologists explain fear in terms of its biological adaptiveness for the organism. They view fear as a product of evolution, a response pattern selected for its high survival value for the species. The ethologists propose that fear has a genetic basis and that there are biological structures that serve as innate releasing mechanisms (IRM) for eliciting fear under certain specific conditions (Hess, 1970). Further, fear responses are explained as adaptive, unlearned reactions to unfamiliar stimuli that protect the infant from potentially harmful situations by strengthening the infant's attachment to the mother (Bowlby, 1973; Freedman, 1961). The data for this interpretation of infant fear development are not very convincing. Fear of strange or unfamiliar stimuli is not universally observed among infants, varies with the situational determinants, and is not necessarily related to infant attachment (Lewis & Brooks, 1974; Rheingold & Eckerman, 1973).

THE LEARNING APPROACH TO FEAR Earlier, we outlined the conditioning or learning model of fear. It is easy to argue that conditioning plays a significant role in emotional development in general, and, more specifically, in the development of fear. Conditioned emotional responses (CER) have been demonstrated repeatedly in laboratory experiments with animals, and there is little doubt that fear can be conditioned (Miller, 1948). But if the learning approach to fear accounts for the variability of the emergence and development of fear in infants, the nature of the learning process involved is not clear. Fear, like other emotional responses, is seldom the product of powerful, overt conditioning experiences involving pain or trauma. Difficulties in experimental control and lack of detailed information on infants' past experiences make it hard to determine the etiology of observed fear responses. Are such responses due to simple, direct conditioning, generalization, more complex conditioning phenomena, parental conditioning of attachment bonds, or imitation and incidental learning? Or does learning occur through cognitive events, such as evaluation of the situation based on learned perceptual stim-

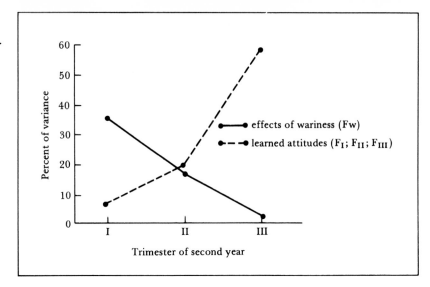

Figure 9-2
Major determinant's of babies' differing emotional reactions.

(From Bronson & Pankey, 1977.)

ulus dimensions of familiar-novel or expectancy-discrepancy?

Bronson has shed some light on the complexity of fear development with his proposal of a dual process interpretation of infants' early aversive reactions to strangers (Bronson, 1978; Bronson & Pankey, 1977). Bronson observed 40 infants in various novel situations, both social and nonsocial, in an attempt to determine the mechanisms of avoidance behavior (Bronson & Pankey, 1977). Through repeated observations during the second year of life and a follow-up assessment at 3½ years of age, Bronson found two distinct, unrelated mechanisms of the fear response in children. The data suggest that between 12 and 20 months of age, most aversive reactions are due to an inherent "wariness of the unfamiliar," to the sheer unfamiliarity of the immediate situation. After 20 months, aversive reactions appear to be a product of learning, as the child associates novel situations with similar ones experienced in the past (Figure 9-2). Bronson also states that emotional responses based on associative learning appear to be cumulative in their effect, while the effects of differences in wariness among children are relatively transient.

Bronson (1978) also found the dual process mechanisms operating in infants between 3 and 9 months old. His data analysis suggests that up to approximately 6 months of age, infants' aversive reactions to adult strangers can be attributed to wariness or uneasiness about the unfamiliar. At about 9 months, stranger reactions begin to reflect prior, learned, disturbing experiences. Bronson argues that this learning factor has been overlooked in previous studies of infant fear reactions and that positive and negative social evaluations, learned and accrued by the infant, may be the major determinants in establishing emotional and social reactions.

THE COGNITIVE APPROACH TO FEAR   Cognitive approaches to fear development assume an ability to differentiate between the familiar and unfamiliar. This cognitive ability is viewed as a necessary precondition, whose development precedes the emergence of the fear response. Recognition of a new or strange stimulus leads to a state of arousal that in turn results in some specific emotional response. Cognitive interpretations of fear include the incongruity hypothesis, the perceptual–recognition hypothesis, and the discrepancy hypothesis. All are similar notions involving some comparative processing of external events and internal representation (memory) by the organism. The result is a cognitive evaluation of familiar-unfamiliar, recognizable–strange, or expectancy-discrepancy.

Hebb (1946) was the first to state the relationship between the perceptual incongruity of a stimulus and fear. Hebb demonstrated that fear responses in chimpanzees were dependent upon perceptual patterns that are learned and accumulated through normal experiences and rearing. When stimuli that represent a gross violation of these perceptual patterns, such as a model of a monkey's head or a chimpanzee death mask, are presented to normally reared animals, they exhibit strong fear responses. However, in infant chimpanzees and in animals reared under conditions of perceptual restriction, no fear responses were observed to these stimuli. In the absence of learned perceptual patterns of expectancy typical to the species, there is no perceived incongruity and thus no fear response.

There have been several variations of the cognitive-evaluative hypothesis of fear (Lewis & Rosenblum, 1974). All share the common hypothesis that infant fear development depends upon the establishment of a schema, concept, cognition, or perceptual pattern of the familiar or expected people, objects, and events in the infant's environment. While cognitive approaches to fear development are widely accepted, they fail to account for the variable development of fear and the observations of infants' positive or neutral responses to the unfamiliar.

The Development of Fear

Historically, the study of emotional development has meant the study of negative reactions in infants. Most early theoretical and empirical efforts in emotional development were concerned with the onset of fear and anxiety (i.e., Jersild, 1954). The descriptive studies during the first half of the twentieth century and the later experimental studies all seemed to confirm a common developmental event. During the second-half year of life, typically between 7 and 9 months of age, the normal human infant displays a strong fear of strangers and the unfamiliar.

This observation was so consistent that the emergence of stranger distress or fear came to be considered a "developmental milestone" denoting normal infant development. Positive, affiliative, or neutral reactions to strange people or events were viewed as a sign of abnormal development if they appeared during the second-half year of life. Contemporary research findings now strongly suggest that phenomena such as stranger distress or fear are by no means universal, invariant developmental events. The use of terms such as "8-month anxiety" (Spitz, 1950) to describe a predictable pattern of infant development is no longer accepted as accurate. Nor is it correct to describe the absence of a stranger–fear response as a sign of abnormal or delayed development, since there is no evidence to support such a notion.

Rheingold and Eckerman (1973) have strongly criticized the commonly stated position that infants inevitably show stranger fear or distress in the second-half year of life. Their review of the literature clearly points to serious limitations of previous research in this area. Rheingold and Eckerman describe three general methodological deficiencies in the infant fear literature: (1) the lack of behavioral detail about the infant's response to a stranger, particularly with regard to the frequency, duration, and sequence of the behaviors used as indices of fear; (2) the absence of baseline information on how infants behave toward familiar and unfamiliar persons; and (3) the experimenters' disregard and omission of the infant's positive responses to a stranger, even though infants often show friendly responses. Rheingold (1974) has further questioned studies that have confounded fear of strangers with maternal separation, so that one cannot be sure whether the infant is showing stranger fear or reacting to the mother's departure.

Rheingold also is critical of weaknesses in operational definitions of fear, statistical analyses, and observer agreements about an infant's behavior. She has raised the interesting question of whether the infant's response is due to a strange person or to strange procedures. Rheingold maintains that the behavior of the unfamiliar person presented to the infant in an experimental situation is usually stereotyped, contrived, and stilted—in short, unnatural. Therefore, what appears strange to the infant is not the stranger, but his or her strange *behavior*. Rafman (1974) has reported such findings. Unfamiliar women who were trained to behave like the mother did not elicit fear responses among infants.

Rheingold and Eckerman also present data that add to the doubts about the generality of the concept of stranger fear. They found no evidence of stranger fear in 24 normal infants between 8 and 12 months old. Instead, they observed acceptance of, and friendliness toward, unfamiliar adult females who were introduced while the mother was present. No sex differences were found in the responses of the 12 male and 12 female infants. A number of other studies support the position of Rheingold and Eckerman (see Rheingold & Eckerman, 1973). Moreover, their review of the literature clearly indicates that none of the research findings reveal fear of the stranger as the majority response among infants. More recent studies also support these findings (Bretherton & Ainsworth, 1974; Corter, 1976; Ross, 1975; Ross & Goldman, 1977; Trause, 1977; Ricciuti, 1974).

Although it has been demonstrated that the onset and development of fear in infants are neither universal nor predictable, several studies continue to show a developmental trend from positive responses during the first-half year of life to more negative responses to strangers during the second-half year (Gaensbauer, Emde, & Campos, 1976; Ricciuti, 1974; Sroufe, Waters, & Matas, 1974). Most of these responses, however, are only mild distress reactions and only appear under certain situational conditions. Campos, Emde, Gaensbauer, and Henderson (1975) investigated both cardiac and behavioral responses of 5- and 9-month-old infants to strangers. Campos et al. found that at 5 months, infants behave positively to male adult strangers and also show cardiac deceleration, an index of attention or attentiveness. At 9 months of age, infants tended to cry or whimper in the presence of strangers and manifested cardiac acceleration, a sign of distress or defensiveness. Campos et al. interpreted their findings as evidence for a developmental shift in stranger response from attentiveness to fearfulness. They also found that cardiac acceleration, but not behavioral distress, was reduced at 9 months when the mother was present. Not all cardiac accelerations were due to distress, however. In some conditions of positive affect such as laughing and smiling, some of the infants also showed cardiac acceleration.

Similar findings were reported by Skarin (1977) in a cross-sectional study of 32 infants between 5 and 12 months old. Older infants responded more negatively to a stranger than did younger infants, but their responses were affected by situational determinants such as familiarity of the setting, mother's presence, and sex of the stranger (males were more threatening). Skarin interpreted his results as evidence for developmental changes in cognitive organization that take place between 7 and 9 months of age, but he emphasized the significance of situational factors, their interactive effects, and the differential importance of such factors at different age levels for stranger fear.

Bronson (1971) has introduced the term "wariness" as a substitute for infant fear or distress. Although not always an accepted or popular concept, it has received considerable research attention (e.g., Lewis & Rosenblum, 1974). Wariness has been defined as a mild negative reaction consisting of a worried face, frowning, gaze aversion, and a "cry face." Wariness has often been considered a simpler response than fear, but Rheingold and Eckerman (1973) question this assumption and suggest it is even more complex than fear.

Sroufe (1977) has recently reviewed the literature dealing with infant wariness of strangers. He concludes that the concept of wariness is an empirically useful and valid concept

Fear and wariness . . . This infant is the reluctant participant in a well-baby examination at the Stanford Medical Center in Stanford, California. Note the worried look, the frown, the so-called "cry face"—all identifying characteristics of wariness. Efforts to study fear in children have been hampered by the many variables influencing children's reactions to experimental situations. As a result, studies of the ontogenesis of fear have produced no definitive results. It *is* known, however, that infants tend to exhibit a greater wariness in their response to strangers during the second 6 months of life than in the first, indicating the development of the child's ability to differentiate between what is familiar and what is alien.

(Photo by David Powers/ Stock, Boston.)

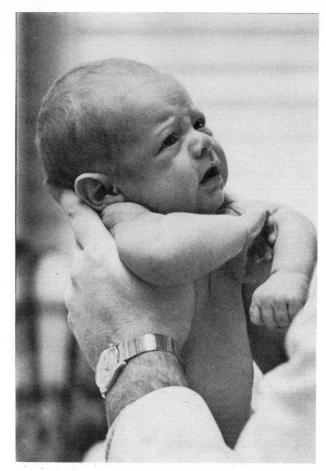

which reveals consistent developmental trends. Sroufe views negative reactions to strangers as a general phenomenon which becomes common by 8 or 9 months of age. He notes that stranger wariness is strongly affected by situational determinants. To Sroufe, this shows significance for developing an organized view of infancy which could integrate cognitive, social, and emotional development. Here, Sroufe is arguing for a systems approach to the study of emotional development. Rather than consider each specific emotional pattern in infancy as an isolated phenomenon, we should try to learn how such responses are integrated into the overall developmental status

Crying . . . Fear and the crying it usually produces have been the most studied aspect of emotional development in children. Emotional development in children generally reflects a child's increasing ability to control his own behavior and to interact more successfully with the world around him. Whether such development is innate, learned, or the product of cognition is still a subject of much debate in the scientific community. Increasingly, researchers seem to favor a systems approach to understanding child development; that is, an approach that attempts to integrate the varied aspects of a child's physical, cognitive, intellectual, emotional, and social growth.

(Photo by Susan Berkowitz.)

of the infant. In this way, we may determine the multiple developmental processes contributing to the response and how they interact.

In summary, what may we say about the developmental course of fear? Obviously, a controversy has surfaced over the nature and significance of fear development. We have learned that the onset of fear is variable, unpredictable, and certainly not necessarily a developmental milestone in normal infant development. Both negative and positive reactions to the unfamiliar may be observed, depending on the presence or absence of several situational factors. These situational or contextual factors operate both independently and interactively to determine the type, direction, and intensity of emotional responses. In other words, there are strong qualifications underlying the appearance of the fear response during infancy.

Consequently, we cannot make any normative statements describing fear development. While the data are complex, it seems clear that emotional reactions to the unfamiliar are ultimately determined by multiple developmental processes and events which require careful analysis.

Fear may have no special developmental significance for human development, except as an index of the growing perceptual competence of the infant and of the increasing cognitive capacity of the infant to understand, evaluate, and control its behavior. After all, there is no particular reason why negative reactions should dominate developmental research as they have in the past. They are no more important to development than positive reactions and are probably no more revealing about developmental phenomena.

Speaking of the concept of fear of the stranger, Rheingold and Eckerman (1973) state:

It catches the dramatic nature of its apparently sudden appearance in the occasional infant. As a landmark it satisfies man's desire to divide wholes into parts and stages. . . . To use a term because it is simple and easy does an injustice to the full panoply of the infant's response to an unfamiliar person; his responses are modulated by a host of past experiences and present conditions. The term allows no room for the interest, curiosity, and pleasure he often accords new events of all kinds, including people; it obscures the richness and variety of his behavior. (pp. 218–219)

Theoretical Considerations in Smiling and Laughter Development

Although historically neglected as topics of study except for Darwin's (1872/1961) classic work on emotion, the development of positive emotions such as smiling and laughter has drawn increasing research attention during recent years. The developmental trends of smiling and laughter are different from, and much less controversial than, those discussed in fear development. While we lack a complete understanding of smiling and laughter as developmental phenomena, their significance for an integrated conceptualization of cognitive, emotional, and personality–social development remains of central interest to developmental psychologists. Before we turn to the development of smiling and laughter, therefore, we will consider the major theoretical approaches that have guided the research in these areas.

Ethological, learning, and cognitive interpretations dominate the theoretical approaches to the development of smiling and laughter. Again, as with fear development, none of these theoretical positions fully accounts for the developmental course of these behaviors, but they continue to generate most of the research in this area of emotional development. The meaning of smiling and laughter during early development, the relationship between early and later forms of these behaviors, their function for the infant, and their significance to general principles of development all remain unknown (Sroufe & Waters, 1976). Since the theoretical formulations and assumptions about the development of smiling and laughter are basically the same as those presented for the development of fear, we need to refer to them again only briefly.

THE ETHOLOGICAL APPROACH TO SMILING AND LAUGHTER   Ethological theory interprets the onset of smiling and laughter as an adaptive function that has high survival value for the infant. Inherited responses with evolutional origins, smiling and laughter ensure and facilitate the formation of attachments between infant and caretaker (Bowlby, 1969; Freedman, 1974). Smiling plays a major role in attachment, and laughter strengthens social bonding insofar as common feelings and emotional expressions bind people together. Ethologists argue that the human face is the most powerful stimulus for eliciting social smiles in infants and that the eyes and then the full face are innate releasing mechanisms for infant smiling (Freedman, 1974; Spitz & Wolf, 1946). Some ethologists have proposed that infant smiling serves the function of appeasement, but such notions attribute too much cognitive awareness to the infant and cannot account for the variability of infant smiling (Sroufe & Waters, 1976). However intriguing they may be, ethological interpretations cannot deal with the data suggesting that infant recognition of faces, and attention to them, may account for smiling, and that nonsocial stimuli can also elicit smiling and laughter (Sroufe & Waters, 1976).

THE LEARNING APPROACH TO SMILING AND LAUGHTER   Learning accounts of the origin and development of smiling and laughter claim that the conditionability of the young infant forms the basis for the acquisition of these behaviors. Smiling and laughter have been shown to be susceptible to learning through instrumental conditioning, classical conditioning, and social conditioning (Rothbart, 1973; Sroufe & Waters, 1976). However, as Sroufe and Waters point out, several investigators have obtained results which seriously weaken conditioning and reinforcement as adequate explanations of smiling and laughter. The development of these behaviors simply does not depend exclusively on overt learning conditions.

THE COGNITIVE APPROACH TO SMILING AND LAUGHTER The view that the development of smiling and laughter is a function of cognitive development, reflecting underlying cognitive processes, is probably the most influential theory today. Cognitive theory has drawn considerable research interest and has developed strong empirical support in the current literature (Macdonald & Silverman, 1978; Rothbart, 1973; Sroufe & Waters, 1976). Basically, the cognitive approach to smiling and laughter describes the infant as an information-processing organism (Kagan, 1971) that actively attends to stimuli, interprets their meaning, and develops schemata or cognitions of stimuli. With the development of memory (recognition and recall), the infant comes to understand various aspects of the environment. The final result is smiling, laughter, or some other emotional response, depending upon the general context of the situation.

Sroufe and Waters (1976) have developed a tension-release hypothesis which combines cognitive, physiological, and social interpretations of smiling and laughter. They propose that smiling and laughter are related to a tension-release mechanism that has a physiological basis. Beginning with the infant's capacities for orienting and attending to novel stimulus situations, Sroufe and Waters document the complex motoric, sensory, and autonomic reactions (tensions) that occur simultaneously when the infant confronts novelty, change, or termination of stimulation.

Orientation and attention are important adaptive responses. However, it is equally important that mechanisms exist for terminating these initial responses so that the infant can make further, tension-releasing responses to the situation. These mechanisms involve the expression of negative or positive affect. Smiling or laughter permits the infant to release tension while remaining oriented toward the stimulus situation. At the same time, smiling or laughter contributes to further cognitive and emotional growth by maintaining the novel or provocative stimulation. If the environmental context is perceived as an insecure one, the infant displays fear or some negative, avoidance reaction, which is also tension releasing and seeks to end the interaction. In either case, the emotional responses modulate arousal levels for the infant, permitting further adaptive responding to the environment. Moreover, the infant's active participation in these developmental events is supported by the social environment.

For Sroufe and Waters, then, the infant becomes increasingly active and responsible in creating and mastering its own experiences. The social–emotional aspects of development become inseparable from the cognitive components because the relationship is a reciprocal one. Cognitive development facilitates exploration, social development, and emotional development. At the same time, social–emotional development facilitates cognitive development by promoting increased cognitive stimulation from caretakers and individual exploration. Clearly, this approach attempts to integrate emotional and cognitive development into a unified system, rather than studying separate systems in isolation.

The Development of Smiling

The onset of smiling precedes laughter by approximately 4 weeks and can be observed in newborn infants. Smiling in the neonate and very young infant once was attributed to gas or gastric distress, but this has been shown to be untrue (Emde & Koenig, 1969). These earliest smiles are now described as reflexive, endogenous, or spontaneous smiles since they almost always occur during sleep and in the absence of any known external stimulus (Emde & Koenig, 1969; Gewirtz, 1965; Wolff, 1963). The data (summarized by Sroufe & Waters, 1976) suggest that reflexive smiles are correlated with transient, spontaneous central nervous system activity and cannot be considered as social or otherwise meaningful responses to the environment.

The first alert smile which can be elicited when the infant is awake and attentive occurs at about 3 weeks of age (Wolff, 1963). From this point on, smiling becomes an increasingly frequent response. At first, it takes vigorous external stimulation to produce a smile. But gradually, smiling becomes less dependent on external stimulation, more selective, and increasingly self-produced and voluntary. Between 5 and 8 weeks of age, the human face begins to elicit smiling, and by approximately 12 weeks social smiling to faces and voices has developed (Table 9-2). Kagan (1971) reports that face-specific smiles peak at 4 months of age, after which they decline because they are recognition responses which eventually lose their attention, tension, or arousal value. However, the evidence does not suggest that human faces are superior to other stimuli in

Table 9-2
The Development of Smiling

AGE	RESPONSE	STIMULATION	LATENCY	REMARKS
Neonate	Corners of the mouth	No external stimulation		Due to central nervous system fluctuations
Week 1	Corners of the mouth	Low level, modulated	6–8 sec	During sleep, boosting of tension
Week 2	Mouth pulled back	Low level, modulated; voices		When drowsy, satiated
Week 3	Grin, including eyes	Moderate level, voices	4–5 sec	When alert, attentive (nodding head with voice)
Week 4	Grin, active smile	Moderate, or moderately intense	Reduced	Vigorous tactile stimulation effective
Weeks 5–8	Grin, active smile, cooing	Dynamic stimulation, first visual stimulation	3 sec or less	Nodding head, flicking lights, stimulation that must be followed
Weeks 8–12	Grin, active smile, cooing	Static, visual stimulation, moderately intense	Short	Trial by trial effects, effortful assimilation, recognition; static at times more effective than dynamic

(From Sroufe and Waters, 1976.)

Smiling . . . The ability to smile appears to be an innate human characteristic, although *alert* smiling—that is, smiling as an intentional response to an external stimulus—typically begins after 3 weeks of age. Environmental factors also influence the appearance and frequency of smiling in babies. Institutionalized children have shown the slowest rate of smiling development, while children receiving close, individual attention from adults, such as is likely to occur in small, nuclear families, experience the most rapid rate of smiling development. The smiling baby pictured here is undoubtedly reacting to the familiar, encouraging presence of her mother as well as the floating, shimmering soap bubbles.

(Photo by Lance C. Brambeck.)

Figure 9-3
Frequency of smiling among infants raised in three different environments.

(From Gewirtz, 1965. Reprinted by permission.)

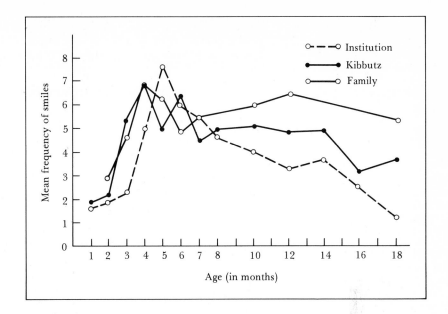

eliciting smiling during the first year of life (Kagan, 1971; Stayton, Ainsworth, & Main, 1973).

Smiling appears to be an innate human capacity, and its development is intimately correlated with general cognitive development. Nevertheless, the patterns and rates observed in the development of smiling may be affected by environmental conditions, such as child-rearing patterns and learning or experimental factors. Gewirtz (1965), for example, investigated the frequency of smiling among children reared in three different child-rearing settings in Israel: a kibbutz, a normal family, and a residential institution. Gewirtz found that the patterns and rates of frequency of smiling which emerged differed as a function of the social setting (Figure 9-3). Institutionalized children showed the slowest rate of development of smiling and the most rapid rate of decline between 5 and 18 months of age.

Emotional development in general is extremely variable, and environmental factors that can affect cognitive, intellectual, and social development are also likely to affect emotional development. The direction, severity, and stability of such alterations in emotional development will depend on the exact nature of the environmental factors.

The Development of Laughter

Since Washburn's (1929) first observations of infant laughter, there have been some conflicting reports about the onset of laughter in infants. Washburn's longitudinal observations of 15 infants during the first year of life placed the onset of laughter between 12 and 16 weeks of age, depending on the type and intensity of the social stimulation. However, laughter always appeared later than smiling. Other investigators (Wolff, 1963; Church, 1966) have reported the onset of infant laughter as early as 5 to 9 weeks of age. In the most extensive observations of infant laughter to date, Sroufe and Wunsch (1972) studied laughter in infants from 4 to 12 months of age under various stimulation conditions, while trained observers recorded the infant responses. Sroufe and Wunsch report the emergence of laughter at approximately 16 weeks of age. They also note age changes in the amount of laughter and in the kind of stimulation which is effective in eliciting laughter. These developmental trends in laughter are shown in Table 9-3.

At 4 months of age, only vigorous, intrusive tactile and auditory stimulation elicits laughter (i.e., vigorous kissing of the stomach and "I'm gonna get you" game). From the fourth to the sixth month, laughter occurs to less intense but more interesting tactile and auditory stimulation. During the second

Table 9-3
The Development of Laughter

AGE	RESPONSE	STIMULATION	LATENCY	REMARKS
Month 4	Laughter	Vigorous tactile and auditory stimulation	1–2 sec	Tactile, auditory
Months 5–6	Laughter	Intense auditory stimulation, as well as tactile	Immediate	Includes stimuli that may have previously caused crying
Months 7–9	Laughter	Social, visual stimulation, primarily dynamic	Immediate	Tactile and auditory stimuli decline in effectiveness
Months 10–12	Laughter	Visual, social	Immediate or in anticipation	Includes visual incongruities, active participation of the infant

(From Sroufe and Waters, 1976.)

Laughter . . . Always appearing later than smiling, laughter usually first occurs between 12 and 16 weeks of age. Like smiling, a child's initial laughter is usually a response to vigorous physical stimulation, such as tickling. In the second-half year of life, however, laughter tends to become more of a voluntary response to visual and aural stimulation—particularly in social situations. This is yet another index of a child's increasing awareness of the outside world. Chris, pictured here at 10 months of age, is responding with glee to the visual and aural stimulation provided by the photographer.

(Photo by Anestis Diakopoulos/Stock, Boston.)

6 months, the trend is away from laughing at vigorous stimulation and toward laughter at social and visual stimulation, with increasing infant participation in the stimulus situation. Between 9 and 12 months, the infant begins to laugh in anticipation of social stimulation. Sroufe and Wunsch (1972) note the developmental similarity of smiling and laughter; in both, cognitive development interacts with the infant's active participation in novel experiences.

The study of early emotional responses such as fear, smiling, and laughter has revealed that these are important cognitive–social developmental events. We have also seen that emotional development parallels cognitive development. In fact, these developmental systems are so closely related that we can argue for emotional development as an index of cognitive development. We have seen early emotional development as an integrated pattern of interrelated events, not just a collection of isolated developmental phenomena. By viewing these behaviors within a systems approach, we may gain further insight into the development of other emotional behaviors and learn how they too are integrated with other developmental systems.

REFERENCES

Bowlby, J. *Attachment and loss.* New York: Basic Books, 1969.

Bregman, E. O. An attempt to modify the emotional attitudes of infants by the conditioned response technique. *Journal of Genetic Psychology,* 1934, *45,* 169–196.

Bretherton, I., & Ainsworth, M. D. S. Responses of one-year-olds to a stranger in a strange situation. In M. Lewis and L. A. Rosenblum (Eds.), *The Origin of Fear.* New York: Wiley, 1974.

Bridger, W. H., & Birns, B. Experience and temperament in human neonates. In G. Newton and S. Levine (Eds.), *Early experience and behavior.* Springfield, Illinois: Thomas, 1968.

Bridges, K. M. B. A genetic theory of the emotions. *Journal of Genetic Psychology,* 1930, *37,* 514–527.

Bridges, K. M. B. Emotional Development in early infancy. *Child Development,* 1932, *3,* 324–341.

Bronson, G. Infants' reactions to an unfamiliar person. Paper presented at the meeting of the Society for Research in Child Development, Minneapolis, April, 1971.

Bronson, G. Aversive reactions to strangers: A dual process interpretation. *Child Development,* 1978, *49,* 495–499.

Bronson, G., & Pankey, W. B. The distinction between fear and wariness. *Child Development,* 1977, *48,* 1167–1183.

Brown, J. L. States in newborn infants. *Merrill-Palmer Quarterly,* 1964, *10,* 313–327.

Campos, J. J., Emde, R. N., Gaensbauer, T. & Henderson, C. Cardiac and behavioral interrelationships in the reaction of infants to strangers. *Developmental Psychology,* 1975, *11,* 589–601.

Candland, D. K., Fell, J. P., Keen, E., Leshner, A. I., Plutchik, R., & Tarpy, R. M. *Emotion.* Monterey, California: Brooks/Cole, 1977.

Cannon, W. B. *Bodily changes in pain, hunger, fear, and rage.* New York: Appleton-Century-Crofts, 1929.

Church, J. (Ed.), *Three babies: Biographies of cognitive development.* New York: Random House, 1966.

Corter, C. M. The nature of the mother's absence and the infant's response to brief separations, *Developmental Psychology,* 1976, *12,* 428–434.

Darwin, C. *The expression of the emotions in man and animals.* Chicago: University of Chicago Press, 1961. (Originally published, 1872).

Dennis, W. Infant reaction to restraint: An evaluation of Watson's theory. *Transactions of the New York Academy of Science,* 1940, *2,* 202–218.

Emde, R. N., & Koenig, K. L. Neonatal smiling and rapid eye movement states. *American Academy of Child Psychology,* 1969, *8,* 57–67.

Fantino, E. Emotion. In J. A. Nevin (Ed.), *The study of behavior.* Glenview, Illinois: Scott, Foresman, 1973.

Freedman, D. G. The infant's fear of strangers and the flight response. *Journal of Child Psychiatry and Psychology,* 1961, *4,* 242–248.

Freedman, D. G. *Human infancy: An evolutionary perspective.* Hillsdale, New Jersey: Lawrence Erlbaum Associates, 1974.

Friedman, S. Infant habituation: Process, problems and possibilities. In N. R. Ellis (Ed.), *Abberant development in infancy: Human and animal studies.* Hillsdale, New Jersey: Lawrence Erlbaum Associates, 1975.

Gaensbauer, T., Emde, R., & Campos, J. "Stranger" distress: Confirmation of a developmental shift in a longitudinal sample. *Perceptual and Motor Skills,* 1976, *43,* 99–106.

Gesell, A. The individual in infancy. In C. Murchinson (Ed.), *The foundation of experimental psychology.* Worcester, Clark University Press, 1929.

Gesell, A. Early evidence of individuality in the human infant. *Scientific Monthly,* 1937, *45,* 217–225.

Gewirtz, J. L. The cause of infant smiling in four childrearing environments in Israel. In B. M. Foss (Ed.), *Determinants of infant behavior* (Vol. 3). London: Methuen, 1965.

Haith, M. M., & Campos, J. J. Human infancy. In M. R. Rosenzweig and L. W. Porter (Eds.), *Annual Review of Psychology, 28,* 1977, 251–293.

Hebb, D. O. On the nature of fear. *Psychological Review,* 1946, *53,* 259–276.

Hebb, D. O. *Textbook of psychology.* Philadelphia: Saunders, 1972.

Hess, E. H. Ethology and developmental psychology. In P. Mussen (Ed.), *Carmichael's manual of child psychology.* New York: Wiley, 1970.

Irwin, O. C. Infant responses to vertical movement. *Child Development,* 1932, *3,* 167–169.

James, W. What is an emotion? *Mind,* 1884, *9,* 188–205.

James, W. *Principles of psychology.* New York: Holt & Company, 1890.

Jersild, A. T. Emotional development. In L. Carmichael (Ed.), *Manual of child psychology.* New York: Wiley & Sons, 1954.

Jones, H. E. The conditioning of overt emotional responses. *Journal of Educational Psychology,* 1931, *22,* 127–130.

Jones, M. C. A laboratory study of fear: The case of Peter. *Journal of Genetic Psychology,* 1924, *31,* 208–315.

Kagan, J. *Change and continuity in infancy.* New York: Wiley, 1971.

Kagan, J., & Moss, H. A. *Birth to maturity: A study in psychological development.* New York: Wiley, 1962.

Lewis, M., & Brooks, J. Self, other, and fear: Infants' reactions to people. In M. Lewis and L. A. Rosenblum (Eds.), *The origins of fear.* New York: Wiley, 1974.

Lewis, M., & Rosenblum, L. A. (Eds.). *The origins of fear.* New York: Wiley, 1974.

Macdonald, N. E., & Silverman, I. W. Smiling and laughter in infants as a function of level of arousal and cognitive evaluation. *Developmental Psychology,* 1978, *14,* 235–241.

Mandler, G. *Mind and emotion.* New York: Wiley, 1975.

Miller, N. E. Studies of fear as an acquirable drive. I. Fear as motivation and fear reduction reinforcement in the learning of new responses. *Journal of Experimental Psychology,* 1948, *38,* 89–101.

Plutchik, R. Cognitions in the service of emotions: An evolutionary perspective. In D. K. Candland, J. P. Fell, E. Keen, A. I. Leshner, R. Plutchik, and R. M. Tarpy (Eds.), *Emotion.* Belmont, California: Wadsworth, 1977.

Rafman, S. The infant's reaction to imitation of the mother's behavior by the stranger. In T. G. Decarie (Ed.), *The infant's reaction to strangers.* New York: International University Press, 1974.

Rheingold, H. L. General issues in the study of fear. In M. Lewis and L. A. Rosenblum (Eds.), *The origins of fear.* New York: Wiley, 1974.

Rheingold, H. L., & Eckerman, C. O. Fear of the stranger: A critical examination. in H. W. Reese (Ed.), *Advances in child development and behavior.* New York: Academic Press, 1973.

Ricciuti, H. N. Fear and the development of social attachments in the first year of life. In M. Lewis and L. A. Rosenblum (Eds.), *The origins of fear.* New York: Wiley, 1974.

Ross, H. S. The effects of increasing familiarity on infants' reactions to adult strangers. *Journal of Experimental Psychology,* 1975, *20,* 226–239.

Ross, H. S., & Goldman, B. D. Infants' sociability toward strangers. *Child Development,* 1977, *48,* 638–642.

Rothbart, M. K. Laughter in young children. *Psychological Bulletin,* 1973, *80,* 247–256.

Schaffer, H. R., & Emerson, P. E. Patterns of response to physical contact in early human development. *Journal of Child Psychology and Psychiatry,* 1964, *5,* 1–13.

Sherman, M. The differentiation of emotional responses in infants: I. Judgments of emotional responses from motion picture views and from actual observation. *Journal of Comparative Psychology,* 1927, *7,* 265–284.(a)

Sherman, M. The differentiation of emotional responses in infants: II. The ability of observers to judge the emotional characteristics of the crying of infants, and of the voice of an adult. *Journal of Comparative Psychology,* 1927, *7,* 335–351.(b)

Sherman, M. The differentiation of emotional responses in infants: III. A proposed theory of the development of emotional responses in infants. *Journal of Comparative Psychology,* 1928, *8,* 385–394.

Sherrington, C. S. Cutaneous sensations. In E. Schafer (Ed.), *Textbook of physiology.* New York: Pentland, 1900.

Shirley, M. M. *The first two years: A study of twenty-five babies.* Minneapolis: University of Minnesota Press, 1931.

Skarin, K. Cognitive and contextual determinants of stranger fear in six- and eleven-month-old infants. *Child Development,* 1977, *48,* 537–544.

Spitz, R. A. Anxiety in infancy: A study of its manifestations in the first year of life. *International Journal of Psycho-Analysis,* 1950, *31,* 138–143.

Spitz, R. A., & Wolf, K. M. The smiling response: A contribution to the ontogenesis of social relations. *Genetic Psychology Monographs,* 1946, *34,* 57–125.

Sroufe, L. A. Wariness of strangers in the study of infancy development. *Child Development,* 1977, *48,* 731–746.

Sroufe, L. A., & Waters, E. The ontogenesis of smiling and laughter: A perspective on the organization of development in infancy. *Psychological Review,* 1976, *83,* 173–189.

Sroufe, L. A., Waters, E., & Matas, L. Contextual determinants of infant affective response. In M. Lewis and L. A. Rosenblum (Eds.), *The origins of fear.* New York: Wiley, 1964.

Sroufe, L. A., & Wunsch, J. P. The development of laughter in the first year of life. *Child Development,* 1972, *43,* 1326–1344.

Stayton, D. J., Ainsworth, M. D. S., & Main, M. B. Development of separation behavior in the first year of life: Protest, following, and greeting. *Developmental Psychology,* 1973, *9,* 213–225.

Stone, L. J., Smith, H. T., & Murphy, L. B. *The competent infant.* New York: Basic Books, 1973.

Strongman, K. T. *The psychology of emotion.* New York: Wiley, 1973.

Taylor, J. H. Innate emotional responses in infants. *Ohio State University Studies,* 1934, *12,* 69–81.

Thoman, E. B. Early development of sleeping behavior in infants. In N. R. Ellis (Ed.), *Abberant development in infancy: Human and animal studies.* Hillsdale, New Jersey: Lawrence Erlbaum Associates, 1975.

Thomas, A., & Chess, S. *Temperament and development.* New York: Brunner-Mazel, 1977.

Thomas, A., Chess, S., & Birch, H. The origin of personality. *Scientific American,* 1970, *223,* 102–109.

Thomas, A., Chess, S., Birch, H., & Hertzig, M. E. A longitudinal study of primary reaction patterns in children. *Comprehensive Psychiatry,* 1960, *1,* 103–112.

Thomas, A., Chess, S., Birch, H., Hertzig, M. E., & Korn, S. *Behavioral individuality in early childhood.* New York: New York Century Press, 1963.

Trause, M. A. Stranger responses: Effects of familiarity, stranger's approval and sex of infant. *Child Development,* 1977, *48,* 1657–1661.

Valentine, C. W. The innate bases of fear. *Journal of Genetic Psychology,* 1930, *37,* 394–420.

Venn, J. R., & Short, J. G. Vicarious classical conditioning of emotional responses in nursery school children. *Journal of Personality and Social Psychology,* 1973, *38,* 249–255.

Washburn, R. W. A study of the smiling and laughing of infants in the first year of life. *Genetic Psychology Monographs,* 1929, *6,* 397–537.

Watson, J. B., & Morgan, J. J. B. Emotional reactions and psychological experimentation. *The American Journal of Psychology,* 1917, *28,* 163–174.

Watson, J. B., & Rayner, R. Conditional emotional reactions. *Journal of Experimental Psychology,* 1920, *3,* 1–14.

Wolff, P. Observations on the early development of smiling. In B. M. Foss (ed.), *Determinants of infant behavior.* II. London: Methuen, 1963.

Chapter

PERSONALITY AND SOCIAL DEVELOPMENT

Ten

Up to this point, we have described basic developmental events that occur universally in the course of normal human development. In discussing the ontogenesis of various developmental phenomena, we have emphasized the etiology and fundamental processes of development. While we have considered different developmental events and processes separately, we have noted that, in fact, many of these developmental systems appear and develop more or less simultaneously. We have seen that the onset of certain developmental events sometimes varies, and yet there is considerable overlap in the emergence of psychological processes. It is also apparent that increasing psychological organization becomes superimposed upon general development as it proceeds from relatively simple to more complex processes and behaviors. Increasingly complex cognitive development requires the integration of sensorimotor, perceptual, linguistic, intellectual, and emotional systems. Such system integration makes possible the psychological or cognitive organization that results in adaptive, purposeful behavior.

In the course of normal development, the common systems that ultimately become integrated are those we defined as true developmental phenomena in Chapter One. These are the common systems that emerge under nonspecific environmental conditions. While these developmental events appear in all normal members of the species, we have noted that individual differences emerge in the expressivity and quality of their functioning. Individual differences arise in response to factors ranging from genetic constitution to differential learning and environmental conditions and from the continual interaction of all such factors. Over the years, individual variations in developmental patterns and the manner in which these developmental processes are integrated and organized result in the total system of behavior that we recognize as personality. But unlike the basic developmental variables, personality and social development involve few common or universal patterns. While we all share the basic components of personality, their integration and organization are unique products of individual development.

The concept of personality is an abstraction that attempts to describe the consistent and regular aspects of individual human behavior. That is, personality refers to the unique, global integration of behavioral systems that results in characteristic responses or response styles to situations. From a developmental perspective, we may view personality as the development, integration, and organization of individual biological and psychological processes and their interaction with the environment. What ultimately emerges is a mature expression of developmental individuality. Since development occurs in a social environment, personality development is a consequence of the individual's interactions and experiences with the social environment—the acquisition of social perceptions, social behaviors, and social sensitivity to oneself and others.

In this chapter, we will build upon the material of the last chapter and examine some basic patterns of infant social behavior. We will explore the manner in which some major elements of personality may emerge under various environmental conditions. We will also discuss the role of early experience on personality development, including the research with animal models of development. But first we will look at the historical background from which current theory and research have derived.

HISTORICAL PERSPECTIVE

Prescientific ideas about personality and personality development were constructed from constitutional views of human development. For example, the Greco-Roman physician Galen (1 A.D.) believed that personality was related to four "body humours"—blood, phlegm, yellow bile, and black bile. The predominance of one of these resulted in a sanguine (cheerful), phlegmatic (sluggish), choleric (easily angered), or melancholic (depressed) personality style. In the eighteenth and nineteenth centuries, other forms of constitutional or hereditarian views of personality development were proposed. Phrenologists such as Gall spoke of mental faculties, traits, or character types that comprised personality. They claimed that the development of personality characteristics depended on inherited patterns of development of the various brain areas possessing the personality functions. They also claimed that these developed areas raised bumps on the skull that they could identify and interpret.

Darwin's theory of evolution spawned further speculations concerning human development, as we saw in Chapter One. In the latter part of the nineteenth century, Haeckel and Hall invoked recapitulation theory to account for personality development (cited in Grinder, 1967). The human mind was said to pass through stages similar to the development of the prehuman and human species. While Hall believed that personality development was also influenced by society, he relied primarily on heredity as the basis of personality.

Constitutional theories of personality resurfaced in the twentieth century with the work of Ernst Kretschmer (1925) and William H. Sheldon (1942). Kretschmer was a German psychiatrist who studied the relationship between physique and normal and abnormal personality. After a lengthy series of measurements and analyses, Kretschmer identified three basic physiques or body types: asthenic (tall and thin), athletic (muscular), and pyknic (short and fat). Kretschmer then studied the physiques of 260 psychotics and found a "biological affinity" between manic-depressive psychosis and the pyknic physique. He also found an association between schizophrenia and the asthenic and athletic body builds.

Some 20 years later, the American physician and psychologist W. H. Sheldon (1942) formulated his theory of physique and temperament, in which he stated the importance of biological–hereditary factors and physical structure as primary determinants of personality. He identified three dimensions of physique or somatotypes similar to those of Kretschmer: ectomorph, mesomorph, and endomorph. Sheldon derived three primary components of temperament, which he called cerebrotonia (shy, self-conscious), somatotonia (love of physical adventure and activity), and viscerotonia (love of comfort, sociability, and gluttony). He subsequently found high correlations between his somatotypes and temperament components. Sheldon's work has been controversial (Hall & Lindzey, 1970) and modern researchers do not consider physique to be a major determinant of personality development. In short, such constitutional psychologies have contributed little to our understanding of personality development.

The major influence on the study of personality development in the twentieth century has been Sigmund Freud's theory of psychoanalysis. Freud was the first theorist to emphasize the great importance of infancy and early childhood to personality formation. Freud interpreted personality development as consisting of three psychosexual stages of development through which every child passes during the first 5 years of life. These are the oral, anal, and phallic stages, so named to indicate the major zones of psychic activity and tension. Freud viewed these early years and experiences as critical for personality development and considered them the period during which personality is essentially established. According to Freud, personality development results from tensions caused by a complex set of inconsistencies between biologically inborn needs and later growth processes, frustrations, conflicts, and threats, which occur during the psychosexual stages. In response to increases in tension, the individual learns new ways to reduce tension. Learning how to deal effectively with tension and anxiety by rational and irrational methods results in personality development. After 5 years of age, the child enters the latency period of relative calm and stability. At adolescence, the individual passes through the last stage of personality development, the genital stage. During this stage, the person becomes socialized, rational, and stabilized as the personality is finally organized. The resolution of conflicts and tensions and the development of various complexes and defense mechanisms during early personality development determine the ultimate nature and direction of adult personality.

We commented on the contributions of psychoanalytic theory to developmental psychology in Chapter One. The most significant legacy of psychoanalysis has been its emphasis on early experiences and early child development. Freud's theory generated a great deal of research on the influence of early experiences on later personality development. Attempts to validate empirically psychoanalytic concepts relating psychosexual development, infant rearing, nursing, and mothering patterns to later personality development were generally unsuccessful (Anderson & Anderson, 1954; Caldwell, 1964; Orlansky, 1949; Sears, 1943). Modern psychoanalytic theory has moved away from the classical emphasis on biological and instinctual aspects of development toward a greater emphasis on environmental and social factors, and the impact of Freudian theory on contemporary thinking and research in personality development has considerably diminished (Zigler & Child, 1972). Current research in personality and social development is dominated by cognitive, ethological, and learning approaches, with an emphasis on early infant attachments and the impact of culture and the family on personality and social development.

ORIGINS OF SOCIAL BEHAVIOR

*D*uring the first few months of life, infants do not show any true social behavior. However, developing motor, perceptual, cognitive, and affective systems are giving the infant an increasing capacity for discrimination, differentiation, and understanding of its environment and active interaction with it. While the young infant differentially orients, attends, and vocalizes to environmental stimuli, it responds equally to social and nonsocial stimuli. The onset of active smiling and laughter between about 12 and 16 weeks of age, accompanied by increasing preference for human contact and stimulation, marks the beginning of social behavior and responsiveness for the infant. Even these first and simplest forms of interpersonal responses are characterized by social reciprocity, a process of stimulus interchange (Schaffer, 1971) between the infant and another person. These events are precursors to the development of social bonds.

The Development of Attachment

An attachment is an enduring affectional bond formed between two people. Under ordinary conditions, the infant's first attachment is to the mother or other immediate caretaker. This initial social bond develops into a strong and almost exclusive attachment. As affectional ties develop toward others, the infant establishes additional attachments. Attachment is a

Mother and son. Infants are born with the ability to form attachments; normally this ability manifests itself toward the mother or caretaker. The origins of attachments are disputed, but research evidence suggests that the mechanism of attachment is a selective and reciprocal process whereby the infant and the mother form a close affectional bond. It has been hypothesized that the nature and quality of such early attachments profoundly affects the child's later social adjustment.

(Photo by Jean-Claude Lejeune.)

selective social response that develops over the first months of life. As far as we know, human infants are not born with any specific instincts for maternal attachment; they have only the general capacity to form such bonds. Social bonding and attachment is not unique to humans, of course. Many species of animals display strong patterns of social behavior and bonding.

Ainsworth (1964, 1969) has described the "hallmark" of attachment as behavior that promotes closeness or contact. She defines attachment behaviors as those that produce proximity and contact with someone to whom a person is attached. Included among the attachment behaviors of an infant are "signaling" behavior (smiling, vocalization), orienting behavior, locomotion (following, approaching), and active physical contact (hugging, clinging). For Ainsworth, attachments are the products of infant activity and responsiveness to maternal attempts at social contact and stimulation and of maternal responsiveness to the infant's initial attachment behaviors. In other words, the development of attachments depends upon reciprocal, interactive social responses between the infant and mother (see Table 10-1). The long-term stability and integrity of these conditions of early social relationships may strongly affect later social–personality development.

Trends in the Study of Attachment

Attachment is a relatively new term, first introduced by John Bowlby (1958), a British psychiatrist. Bowlby used the term to describe the nature of an infant's ties to its mother. Before that time, early social relationships were studied as topics of dependency, socialization, or, more generally, as maternal-infant relationships. Although early infant social behavior has been studied from a variety of perspectives, the earlier work shared a common view of the nature of maternal–infant relationships. Infants were viewed as passive recipients of parental socializing influences, unable to take any meaningful, active part in their own social development. Maternal–infant relationships were considered unidirectional bonds, established and maintained exclusively by the mother. Starting with Bowlby (1958), however, investigators began questioning this basic assumption about the nature of maternal–infant relationships.

Bell (1968), for example, noted that the socialization literature was based almost entirely on parent–child correlations and that such correlations could also be interpreted in terms of the effects of children on parents. Korner (1965, 1971, 1973) has suggested that neonatal behavior patterns may contribute to maternal responsiveness. Similarly, Sander (1969) has shown that individual differences in neonatal sleep–wake cycles interact complexly with caretaking regimes. A general

	PATTERN		DESCRIPTION
Table 10-1 Patterns of Attachment	1. Differential crying	1.	The infant cries when held by someone other than the mother, and stops when taken by the mother.
	2. Differential smiling	2.	The infant smiles more readily and more frequently in interaction with his mother than other people.
	3. Differential vocalization	3.	The infant vocalizes more readily and more frequently in interaction with his mother than other people.
	4. Visual-motor orientation	4.	When apart from his mother, but within visual proximity, the infant maintains a continuous orientation toward her.
	5. Crying when mother leaves	5.	The infant cries when his mother leaves his visual field and contact is broken.
	6. Following	6.	The baby, once able to crawl, attempts to pursue his mother on her departure from his contact.
	7. Scrambling	7.	The baby climbs over his mother, exploring her person, and playing with her face, her hair, or her clothes.
	8. Burying the face	8.	The baby, whether in the course of scrambling over the mother or after returning to her following exploration, buries his face in her lap.
	9. Exploration from mother as a base	9.	The infant takes little excursions away from his mother, returning from time to time for brief periods.
	10. Clinging	10.	The infant displays excessive holding and grasping, particularly in the presence of strangers.
	11. Lifting arms in greeting	11.	The baby raises arms, smiling and vocalizing toward mother after an absence.
	12. Clapping hands in greeting	12.	The baby claps hands in response to maternal reappearance.
	13. Approach through locomotion	13.	With the advent of crawling, the infant terminates greeting responses by crawling to the mother as swiftly as possible.

(Adapted from Ainsworth, 1964.)

trend in the study of maternal–infant relations has now emerged which views early social relationships as an interactive, reciprocal process in which the infant plays an active role in establishing social bonds.

Theoretical Perspectives of Attachment

PSYCHOANALYTIC THEORY Contemporary approaches to the study of attachment have been a development of, or a reaction to, psychoanalytic formulations. Freud's treatment of early infant attachments was incomplete and often contradictory (Ainsworth, 1969). But many of Freud's basic assumptions continue to influence current thinking and research. The psychoanalytic view of the newborn infant is that of a narcissistic organism driven by instincts for gratification. As the agent of the infant's primary oral gratifications, the mother becomes the first love object ("anaclitic love"). Maternal love is established within 6 to 8 months. Modern psychoanalytic theory has diverged from its classical Freudian roots by emphasizing cultural factors in personality–social development. However, it remains crisis-oriented for the most part, and it is still difficult to test with experimental procedures.

SOCIAL LEARNING THEORY Learning theories have been influential in the study of attachment in the United States. Modern social learning approaches to attachment are represented in the work of investigators who have adopted an operant learning framework of infant development (Bijou & Baer, 1965; Gewirtz, 1969, 1972). The social learning interpretation of the development of maternal–infant relationships sees the mother as acquiring a singular bond with her infant through the provision of primary reinforcers. Bijou and Baer (1965) describe the process as follows:

The mother herself will, as a stimulus object, become discriminated as a 'time' and 'place' for either the addition of positive reinforcers to the baby's environment or the subtraction of negative reinforcers from it . . . Thereby, she acquires positive reinforcing functions, and lays the foundation for the further social development of her infant. (p. 123)

Social learning theorists generally agree that development is subject to the basic concepts and processes of operant learning principles. They argue that the consequences of infant behavior are the primary determinants of development. Considerable evidence indicates that social responses in infants and children can be operantly conditioned (e.g., Cairns, 1972; Gewirtz, 1972). Despite this evidence for the conditionability of social behavior, a number of criticisms have been leveled at the social learning approach. It is seen as a limited, narrow approach to complex developmental phenomena, intent on demonstrations of behavior shaping rather than etiology and developmental processes. Evidence of conditionability is not evidence for etiology. Further, the subsequent development and maintenance of responses in the absence of any clear external reinforcers is not explained by social learning theory. Ainsworth (1969) argues that the operant approach emphasizes environmental influences to the exclusion of organismic contributions to development. Thus, in her view, learning approaches perpetuate the wearisome heredity–environment controversy which has been abandoned in favor of an epigenetic or interactional approach to development. Others, such as Escalona (1968) and Lewis (1972), have stressed the need to study individual differences in infant sensitivities and characteristics that may interact with learning effects to influence the developmental course of attachment. There have been some efforts to integrate organismic and learning variables, however. For example, Cairns (1972), an operant theorist, has outlined his attempt to synthesize psychobiological and social learning approaches to attachment phenomena.

COGNITIVE THEORY   Cognitive theory, exemplified by Piaget (1969), would interpret the development of attachment as a function of the level of cognitive development (Piaget did not explicitly deal with attachment). Social development and attachment are not seen as independent developments but rather as the product of social schemata constructed by the infant. The infant establishes maternal relationships by acquiring knowledge about the social object—mother. As assimilation and accomodation of the mother continues, the infant develops the concept of maternal permanence as an independently existing person–object and eventually forms an affective component to its social schemata. As these affective components are formed, infant attachment develops. While many of Piaget's notions concerning attachment are difficult to test, Bell

(1970) did find that object permanence seems to be a prerequisite for infant attachment. She also found that person permanence emerges before object permanence. Although Bell found a relationship between patterns of cognitive and social development, the nature and direction of the relationship remain unclear.

ETHOLOGICAL THEORY   Currently, the single most influential position in the study of attachment is Bowlby's (1958, 1969) ethological theory. Bowlby's theory is an outgrowth of psychoanalytic tradition, a modernization of Freudian theory that draws on contemporary biological and social science, especially ethology. Bowlby's central assumption is that human attachment has biological, evolutionary roots. Because of evolutionary pressures to protect the young from predators in presocietal eras, certain biological and behavioral species characteristics were selected for their high survival value in promoting and maintaining the proximity of caretaking adults. Human infants are, therefore, considered to have inherited behavior systems, both instinctive or species-specific and modifiable (plastic), which ensure attachment and probable survival. These behavioral systems initially include sucking, crying, smiling, looking, vocalization, and listening. As the infant matures, additional behavior systems such as crawling and walking emerge. These attachment behaviors come under an innate control system that provides feedback information to the infant so that attachment behavior can be "goal-corrected" as required.

For Bowlby, the mother has evolved as the prime figure of initial attachment for which the infant is programmed. Bowlby has much to say about the consequence of infant attachment in terms of the infant's predictable response patterns to maternal separation. Bowlby identifies four phases in the development of attachment (described in Table 10-2):

1 Undiscriminating social responsiveness
2 Discriminating social responsiveness
3 Active initiative in seeking proximity and contact
4 Goal-corrected partnership

Eventually, the child's tendencies to explore conflict with attachment, so that the latter becomes less easily identified after

Table 10-2
Bowlby's Phases of Attachment

PHASE	APPROXIMATE AGE OF ONSET AND DURATION	BEHAVIORAL CHARACTERISTICS
Undiscriminating social responsiveness	0–3 months	Orienting behaviors (visual fixation and tracking; listening) Contact-promoting behaviors (sucking and grasping) Contact-promoting signaling behavior (smiling, crying, vocalizations)
Discriminating social responsiveness	3–6 months	Clear discrimination of familiar vs. non-familiar figures Differential smiling, crying, vocalizations
Active initiative in seeking proximity and contact	6–24 months	Increase in proximity- and contact-promoting behaviors (locomotion, following, greeting responses) Goal-corrected sequences (use of feedback from attachment figure) Beginnings of object permanence
Goal-corrected partnership	24–36 months	Inferences about attachment figure's set-goals and plans egocentrism Beginnings of reciprocity in child-figure relationships

about 3 years of age. Bowlby's theory of attachment has received wide acknowledgment (Ainsworth, 1973; Maccoby & Masters, 1970) and has provided strong impetus for observational, naturalistic studies of attachment, with a subsequent de-emphasis of experimental research.

ATTACHMENT RESEARCH

There has been extensive research on the development of attachment since Bowlby's formulations appeared in 1969. We will examine some of this data in order to gain a contemporary perspective on the concept of attachment and its development. More detailed discussion may be found in Ainsworth (1973), Cohen (1974), and Sroufe and Waters (1977).

Among the most widely cited naturalistic studies supporting Bowlby's theory are those of Schaffer and Emerson (1964) and Ainsworth (1967). In their Glasgow study, Schaffer and Emerson followed a group of 60 Scottish infants from early infancy

Figure 10-1
The developmental course of attachments.

(From Schaffer & Emerson, 1964.)

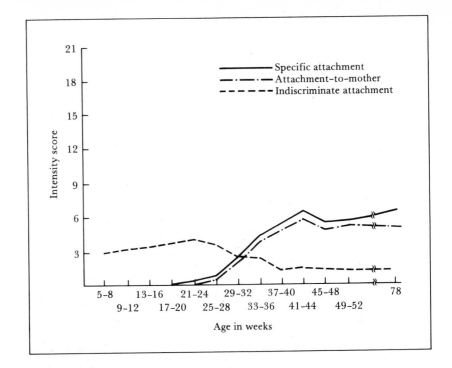

to 18 months of age. Through monthly maternal interviews and observations of infant responses to approach situations, Schaffer and Emerson identified age trends in infant attachment (Figure 10-1). Specific attachments emerged at approximately 7 months, most commonly to the mother first, but not always. Observations of some infant attachments to the father, along with the observation that 29% of the sample formed multiple, specific attachments simultaneously, are not in accord with Bowlby's theory. Bowlby stresses the initial, single attachment to the mother as the first species-specific attachment response to appear. Although there were large individual differences, the development of attachment was observed by Schaffer and Emerson to follow Bowlby's phases in general.

In the Uganda study, Ainsworth (1967) conducted a short-term longitudinal study of 28 unweaned infants. Through maternal interviews and infant observations, Ainsworth found the development of attachment to follow the pattern described by Bowlby. Ainsworth also differentiated three groups of infants: the "secure attached" ($N = 16$), the "insecure attached" ($N = 7$), and the nonattached ($N = 5$). The infants in the insecure group often cried, were demanding, and chose to remain close to the mother rather than explore.

Despite the important and revealing data of naturalistic studies, the critical test of a theory lies in experimental procedures which allow for control and manipulation of variables. Serious questions have been raised concerning the reliability of naturalistic studies (Cohen, 1974), the small number of subjects, and the correlational nature of many infant attachment studies (Masters & Wellman, 1974). Moreover, other observational studies have not supported the position of Bowlby and Ainsworth. For example, Willemsem, Flaherty, Heaton, and Ritchley (1974) concluded that attachment may be more a function of situational variables than species-specific maternal bonding. They found no differential attachment patterns between mother and father and pointed to the importance of infant motivational states in the study of attachment. Tracy, Lamb, and Ainsworth (1976) also found situational variables to be important in infant attachment behaviors. The behavioral uniformity often described in early attachment studies appears less real than was originally assumed. In fact, infant expression of phases and behaviors is subject to a good deal of variation (Ainsworth, Bell, & Stayton, 1972).

Bowlby has argued, incorrectly, that the infant's response to maternal separation is predictable and is characterized by stages of acute distress, depression, and detachment. Studies of stranger reactions of infants (discussed in Chapter Nine) do not support these notions or the idea that there is a necessary relationship between attachment and fear. Like emotional reactions and development, infant attachment is complexly determined. Its course of development is influenced by a number of infant and situational variables.

Sroufe and Waters (1977) argue for an organizational concept of attachment. They suggest abandoning the trait model of attachment, which is unable to deal with the inconsistent research findings. Rather, they propose that the conflict between situational influences and individual differences may be resolved by focusing on the functions, outcomes, and situational sensitivity of attachment and on the cognitive components that organize and control it. Sroufe and Waters claim an organizational approach will provide the integration needed for more productive future research in this area.

*O*f all the areas in developmental psychology, none is more fascinating or challenging than the concept of early experience and its role in human development. We briefly discussed some aspects of early experiential effects in Chapters Four and Five. The critical-period hypothesis, which is often invoked to explain early experiential effects, was also introduced in the discussion of teratology in Chapter Three. We will now examine in more detail the concepts of early experience and critical periods in the broader context of personality–social development.

The research findings and their implications for human development are complex and sometimes controversial. Because much of the significant data comes from laboratory research, our presentation of early experiential effects on personality–social development will include both infrahuman and human studies. There is a vast literature on early experience, and we can cover only the most salient studies related to our discussion. For a more detailed coverage, turn to Ambrose (1969), Newton and Levine (1968), Rutter (1972), and Thompson and Grusec (1970).

The Problem of Early Experience and Critical Periods

Sigmund Freud was the first psychologist to dwell on the significance of early infant and childhood experiences for later personality development and functioning. For Freud, early experience involved psychodynamic events resulting from conflicts between instinctual impulses and the restrictions and demands of reality. Freud considered early psychosexual development to be of singular importance in personality formation and thus to be a period when the child is most vulnerable to permanent effects produced by various environmental experiences. In the psychoanalytic tradition, the notion of early experiential effects tends to focus on negative, unhealthy, or traumatic experiences that have pathological outcomes for the individual.

By the middle of the twentieth century, laboratory studies of the effects of early experience on a variety of animals were well under way. Psychologists began to look at the developmental impact of early experience from almost every conceivable way, under conditions of both environmental deprivation and enrichment. Psychologists and ethologists both used the critical-periods hypothesis in their attempts to explain the effects of early experience on various developmental patterns of behavior in animals. Although not consistent, the data suggested that the immature organism is a plastic psychobiological system capable of being modified by experiential events, both social and nonsocial. Laboratory studies with animals ranging from rodents to nonhuman primates suggested that the critical aspects of early experience involve stimulation input (or lack of it) during the period when the organism's behavioral systems are still immature and developing.

Early theoretical formulations of the critical-period hypothesis attempted to piece together the rapidly accumulating, diverse data from human and nonhuman studies. J. P. Scott (1962) suggested that there were three major kinds of critical periods: one is the optimal period for the formation of basic social relationships, the second is optimal for learning, and the third period is critical for "infantile" stimulation. Scott's third period includes various sensory stimulation effects on physiological processes during the early stages of immaturity and then on psychological processes during the later stages of immaturity.

Scott viewed these critical periods as representing developmental processes and adopted an embryological interpretation of critical periods and processes. He proposed a general principle of biological and behavioral organization to account for critical periods of development. His principle states that once a system becomes organized, either through cellular differentiation or learning, it becomes increasingly difficult to reorganize the system. Organization inhibits reorganization, in short. Since organization can be optimally modified only when systems are being actively organized, Scott saw this organization principle as an explanation of critical periods.

Caldwell (1962) argued that the critical-period hypothesis had been prematurely applied to the study of human infant attachment. She pointed out the vague, undefined nature of the hypothesis as a scientific construct. Furthermore, she noted that the evidence did not justify its indiscriminate use in describing various developmental phenomena, particularly human development. Caldwell spoke for more cautious and controlled experiments to clarify the nature of critical periods, their variability from one behavioral system to another, and the processes underlying any observed effects. In a similar vein, Denenberg (1964, 1968) criticized Scott's hypothesis of critical periods for early stimulation, arguing that the data do not support such generalizations as Scott had suggested. The work of Denenberg and others suggested that critical-period effects in rodents are a complex function of the amount of stimulation input along with various parameters of the independent and dependent variables employed. Denenberg also argued that there may be as many critical periods as there are behavioral systems and variables.

As the true complexity of the critical-period concept was revealed, along with the inability to generalize from animal to human critical periods, the concept lost much of its earlier appeal. Whereas there is evidence for critical-period phenomena in animals under certain stimulation conditions and for certain behavioral events, there is little evidence of critical periods for behavioral development in humans (Rutter, 1972; Scott, Stewart, & DeGhett, 1974), if one defines the term as a specific period of development beyond which some behavioral phenomenon will not develop. Current research activities emphasize functional relationships between early stimulation and developmental outcomes, rather than attempting to demonstrate critical periods in the traditional sense.

Animal Studies of Early Experience and Social Development

Of all the laboratory experiments demonstrating the effects of early experiential manipulations on later development, the most relevant to human development are those dealing with nonhuman primates. Because they are closest to humans on the evolutionary scale, nonhuman primates may share some basic developmental processes with us and thus may contribute to our understanding of human development. The human infant differs from the nonhuman primate infant in terms of behavioral capacity and general level of development. But nonhuman primate studies have stimulated a great deal of research and thinking about early experience and development in humans. For these reasons, we will confine our discussion of animal studies to the nonhuman primates.

Researchers have turned to nonhuman primates in order to study systematically the effects of early social experiences on subsequent behavior and development. Obviously, early social experiences cannot be readily manipulated with human infants for ethical reasons. One must search for such conditions as they already exist or have existed in actual situations (quasi-experiments). Further, considerations of experimental control and the relatively rapid maturation of nonhuman primates make these organisms an ideal model for developmental study. These animals possess strong patterns of maternal–infant bonds and a large repertoire of social behaviors, including social aggression, which appear to be unlearned response patterns. Thus their development can be observed under abnormal conditions of infant social environments constructed in the laboratory.

Studies of early experience and social development in non-human primates have typically been deprivation studies, in which general or social environmental stimulation has been restricted or withheld from the young organism. Therefore, such studies take the form of isolation, maternal deprivation, or maternal separation paradigms. Much of the early work on social separation in monkeys was stimulated by the work of Bowlby and earlier psychoanalytic researchers on attachment and maternal deprivation in human infants.

Social Separation and Affectional Systems in Monkeys

The principal figure in the study of social separation in monkeys is Harry Harlow. Harlow's (1958) publication of "The Nature of Love" was the first in a series of now-classic studies on the effects of maternal and social deprivation in Rhesus monkeys (for a recent review of the literature on social separation in monkeys, see Mineka & Suomi, 1978). Here, Harlow presented his paradigm of the "surrogate mother," reviewed in detail by Harlow and Zimmerman (1959). Harlow credited the idea of the infant monkey's contact needs to Van Wagenen (1950), who had observed strong attachment behavior of infant monkeys to a soft cloth placed in the cage. Harlow's original experiment was designed to study the role of nursing in infant–mother attachment. Eight infant monkeys, separated from their mothers at birth, were placed in two experimental conditions with two surrogate mothers, one made of terrycloth and the other of wire (Figure 10-2). One-half of the animals were fed from the cloth mother and one-half from the wire mother. The cloth mother was found to be preferred over the

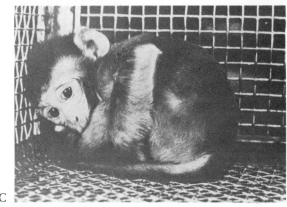

Figure 10-2
Infant monkeys with wire and terry cloth surrogate mothers (A, B). Terrified infant in absence of surrogate (C).

(Photos courtesy of H. F. Harlow, University of Wisconsin Primate Laboratory.)

wire mother, regardless of which provided nourishment.

From these data, Harlow hypothesized the concept of "contact comfort" as essential to normal development in these animals. In later studies, Harlow and colleagues (1962, 1963, 1965, 1971) further investigated attachment, fear, and social development as functions of maternal separation and isolation. They found that contact comfort was not the only essential variable in normal development, as other, more complex maternal–infant variables emerged. They conducted studies in which infant monkeys were subjected to periods of total isolation of 3, 6, and 12 months duration (Harlow, Dodsworth, & Harlow, 1965). The monkeys isolated with a surrogate mother for the first 3 months of life were basically unimpaired when allowed to interact with peers. At 12 to 24 months of age, they were indistinguishable from controls. Both 6 and 12 month complete isolates were severely impaired in their social behavior, displaying developmental disruptions in species-specific patterns of social, motivational, and sexual behaviors. Infants totally isolated from all social contacts for the first 12 months of life were almost hopelessly damaged. Harlow, Harlow, and Hansen (1963) discovered that female Rhesus monkeys reared under total isolation conditions and then made pregnant forcibly ("motherless mothers") failed to develop normal maternal behavior patterns. These mothers were indifferent when their infants were removed from their cages and violently abused their infants when they approached for attachment or feeding (Figure 10-3).

Mason (1968) has described the general outcome of these social separation studies as the primate deprivation syndrome. The primate deprivation syndrome includes the development of (1) abnormal postures and movements, (2) motivational disturbances, (3) poor integration of motor patterns, and (4) deficiencies in social communication (Table 10-3).

During the first 20 years of nonhuman primate research, several variables were shown to determine the effects of social separation in monkeys (Mineka & Suomi, 1978). These include the species of the animal, age, sex, duration and number of separations, preseparation history, separation environment, and peer interaction. These variables interact in a complex, unknown manner to determine how a given animal will respond to separation. Harlow's earlier claims about the critical

Figure 10-3
Infant monkeys with
"motherless mothers." Ma-
ternal punitive behavior
(A); indifference of motherless mother toward her infant (B).

Table 10-3
The Primate Deprivation Syndrome

	SYMPTOM	BEHAVIORAL CHARACTERISTICS
1.	Abnormal Postures and Movements	Repetitive, stereotyped rocking and swaying, self-clasping, digit-sucking
2.	Motivational Disturbances	Excessive fearfulness or aggressiveness, lack of exploratory behavior, failure to respond to sexual stimulation from peers
3.	Poor Integration of Motor Patterns	Absence of certain postures or movements or a failure to form certain movements into larger integrated patterns; i.e. inadequate sexual behavior
4.	Deficiencies in Social Communication	Fails to respond to social communication signals of threats, of sexual behavior, of alarm, etc.

(From Mason, 1968.)

importance of "mother love" for normal development have been reconsidered. The critical variables appear to be the amount and level of stimulation input to the infant organism. For example, Mason (1968) reported that infant monkeys reared with a robot surrogate mother, which moved randomly about the cage, did not develop the abnormal postures and movements associated with the primate deprivation syndrome. Robot mothers apparently provide a variety of stimulation inputs via different sensory modalities, which is not possible with a stationary surrogate mother (Figures 10-4 and 10-5).

Meier (1965) also obtained results contradicting some of Harlow's data. Meier found that socially isolated female monkeys were able to mate successfully and conceive. Socially isolated males were also able to mate satisfactorily and in three out of four cases sired offspring. Meier accounted for these differences in terms of increased visual and auditory stimulation for his animals relative to Harlow's. Individual cages in Meier's laboratory were closer together than in Harlow's, providing more visual–auditory contact for the infant monkeys. Meier suggested that perhaps such stimulation was more important for the development of normal sexual behavior than tactile stimulation. As it turns out, Meier seems to have been correct.

In their review of the literature on social separation in monkeys, Mineka and Suomi (1978) conclude that there is

Figure 10-4
Monkey with robot surro-
gate mother.

(From Mason, 1968.)

enormous variation in response to maternal separation. They view the most important determinants of separation responses and recovery to be the preseparation history of the animal and the nature of the separation environment. Also, it is not clear to what extent the long-term effects of social separation are a consequence of separation as opposed to other traumatic events experienced by the animal. Clearly, the data are complex and no easy generalizations or firm conclusions are available.

Figure 10-5
Two contrasting reactions
of infant monkeys to hu-
mans. The robot-reared
monkey (*left*) shows curiosity while the stationary-
reared monkey (*right*) is
fearful.

(From Mason, 1968.)

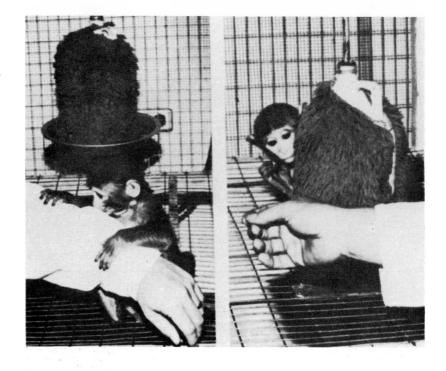

But, just as clearly, the laboratory data strongly suggest the importance of adequate levels of social and sensory stimulation for development of the young organism. Such stimulation input is particularly important at or around the time of maturation of infant response systems (Suomi & Harlow, 1978).

Interestingly, the stimulation resulting from being raised exclusively with peers (with mother absent) is as effective in producing healthy development as is being raised by a mother. If duplicated by others, such findings would challenge many cherished beliefs of lay persons and behavior scientists alike (Suomi & Harlow, 1978). While generalization of such developmental events from monkeys to humans is indeed risky, we can at least generalize about the complexity of the animal data. Certainly, it seems reasonable to assume that the relationship between early experience and personality–social development in humans is even more complex and intricate than what we have observed for monkeys.

EARLY SOCIALIZATION AND PERSONALITY DEVELOPMENT

*f*ollowing Zigler and Child (1972), we shall use the term, socialization, to describe the process by which an individual acquires and develops specific patterns of socially relevant behaviors and experiences. Socialization includes all aspects of child-rearing by which the individual comes to learn about his or her culture or society and the knowledge, expectations, and behavior necessary for responsible and appropriate functioning within that society. Among the socializing agents included in this process are specific characteristics of parent–infant interactions and their quality, duration, and intensity; child-rearing practices; parental discipline patterns; and interactions and experiences with other social agents such as teachers and peers. Obviously, the process of socialization is highly variable, and the behavioral contents of socialization are dependent on what children experience and learn about social values, judgments, and expectations.

A number of investigators have attempted to relate early socialization patterns and experiences of infants with later personality development (Anderson & Anderson, 1954; Caldwell, 1964). The importance of infant socialization for personality development has been heavily emphasized in both classical and modern psychoanalytic theory. In these theoretical contexts, specific personality traits and general personality functioning have been assumed to have their origins in early socialization patterns. Thus, great etiological significance is attributed to such infant experiences as feeding patterns, attachment, toilet training, and mothering. In an early critical review of the literature on infant care and personality development, Orlansky (1949) concluded that the effects of such early infant experiences on personality development have been exaggerated and that there is no empirical basis to support such contentions. Orlansky went on to state, "It is contended that personality is not the resultant of instinctual infantile libidinal drives mechanically channeled by parental disciplines, but rather it is a dynamic product of the interaction of a unique organism undergoing maturation and a unique physical and social environment" (p. 39).

Subsequent investigations of the effects of different infant nursing regimens, weaning, toilet training, and parental discipline styles (Sears, Maccoby, & Levin, 1957; Sewell, 1952) on later childhood personality and adjustment revealed no relationships. In both of these studies, the style of mothering (i.e., attitudes, warmth, acceptance) was found to be more important for personality development than any specific pattern of infant care. More recent studies by Heinstein (1963) and Hetherington and Brackbill (1963) also undercut psychoanalytic claims about the relationship between early socialization patterns and later personality development. Similarly, specific patterns of infant attachment have not been found to be consistently related to personality characteristics such as dependency (Maccoby & Masters, 1970). For example, infant attachment patterns characterized by multiple mothers or mothering (Leiderman & Leiderman, 1974; Yarrow, 1964) have not been shown to have deleterious effects on later personality functioning or general adjustment. In summary, the psychoanalytic view of the infant as a vulnerable organism sensitively susceptible to a variety of "traumatic" experiences of long-lasting personal impact has not been substantiated.

The significance of early socialization processes and experiences for subsequent personality development lies in the general quality of those events and the degree to which they predict consistent rearing patterns in the years to come. In this respect, the effects of early socialization are cumulative in nature. There appears to be no reasonable basis for adhering to any single trauma theory of early development or to a crisis interpretation of programmed socialization patterns (Erikson, 1950) which are not observed in reality. Personality–social development is probabilistic in nature, ultimately depending upon complex development processes beyond infancy and early childhood no less than on those occurring earlier.

Parental Discipline Styles and Personality–Social Development

Numerous studies have explored the effects of child-rearing practices and parental attitudes on personality–social development. The most ambitious, and perhaps the most influential, are those of Diana Baumrind (1966, 1967, 1971, 1975, 1977). Baumrind investigated patterns of parental authority and their effects on the social behavior and personality characteristics of 146 nursery school children. Baumrind used the term *instrumental competence* to refer to socially responsible and independent behavior. She defined instrumental competence as behavior

Mother scolding daughter for having a messy room. The expression of parental authority has a profound influence on a child's social and moral development. Offspring of authoritative parents—parents who are tolerant without being permissive, who are firm but reasonable—seem to be the most successful in finding and coping with their place in the world.

(Photo copyright © 1980 by Paul Fortin/Stock, Boston.)

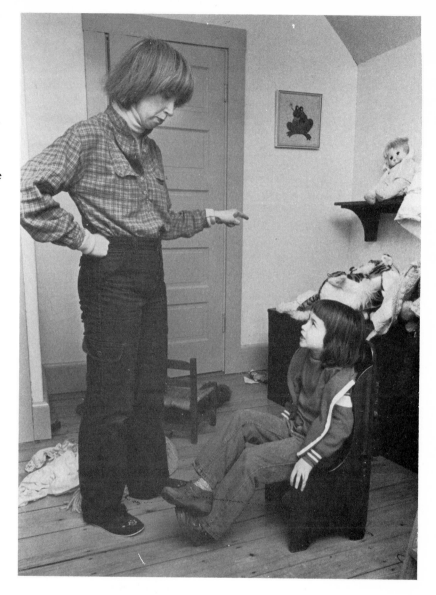

which is friendly rather than hostile, cooperative rather than resistive, achievement rather than nonachievement oriented, dominant rather than submissive, and purposeful rather than aimless.

Baumrind assessed parental behavior patterns and styles by interviews, standardized test data, and observations of parent–child interactions. She identified three major patterns of parenting: authoritarian, authoritative, and permissive. She also found several subpatterns of these major parental styles, which reflected various mixtures of the three basic patterns. Baumrind described the major patterns of parental authority as follows:

1 The authoritarian parent follows an absolute standard of conduct in the attempt to shape and control the child's behavior and attitudes. Obedience is valued as a virtue, and disobedience or self-will is met with punitive measures. The child is taught respect for work, order, and tradition. Discussion is discouraged, with the expectation that the child will accept the parent's word for what is right.

2 The authoritative parent also attempts to control the child's behavior but in a manner characterized by open discussion and reasoning with the child. Although firm in expectations, the authoritative parent does not restrict the child's individuality or self-will by demanding blind adherence to some external set of standards.

3 The permissive parent makes few demands of child responsibility and social conduct. Control and obedience are avoided, and the child is permitted to regulate his or her own behavior with few or no limits or imposed standards to guide behavior. The permissive parent is available as an accepting, benign resource person, not a socializing agent.

Data on parent characteristics and on the personality–social development of the children were independently collected from parents, teachers, and observations of the children. Observers of the children did not know the parents' characteristics, and vice versa. Children of authoritarian parents were observed to be relatively discontented, withdrawn, and distrustful. Children of authoritative parents, on the other hand, were self-reliant, self-controlled, contented, and socially responsible. They displayed the highest level of instrumental competence. Children of permissive parents were the least competent, controlled, and self-reliant of all (Table 10-4).

On the basis of her extensive research in this area, Baumrind (1977) has suggested that personality–social development is facilitated by (1) adult modeling of socially responsible and

Table 10-4
**Baumrind's Patterns of Paternal Authority
and Children's Levels of Competence**

PARENTAL PATTERN OF AUTHORITY	LEVEL OF CHILDREN'S INSTRUMENTAL COMPETENCE
Authoritative: firm but warm and nonrejecting; willing to explain and reconsider rules	Competent; self-reliant, self-controlled, explorative, and content
Authoritarian: detached, controlling, restrictive, and overprotective; unwilling to discuss or reconsider rules	Less competent; discontented, withdrawn, and distrustful
Permissive: noncontrolling and nondemanding; does not set firm rules	Least competent; dependent, aimless, and irresponsible

(From Baumrind, 1971.)

self-assertive behavior; (2) firm but reasoned discipline policies which reinforce socially responsible behavior and which punish deviant behavior; (3) accepting but not overprotective parental attitudes, where parental approval is conditional on the child's behavior; (4) high parental demands for achievement and parental conformity without relinquishing the child's rights for independence and self-assertion; and (5) provision of a complex and stimulating environment for the child where divergent as well as convergent thinking is fostered.

The implications of Baumrind's research findings are that social maturity, independence, and general sociopersonality development are not inhibited by firm but democratic parental control. Indeed, such instrumental competence is fostered. Effective parents were found to include frequent punishment, corporal or otherwise, in their discipline styles. When punishment is appropriate in time and context, consistent, and combined with information about correct or expected behavior and reinforcement, punishment becomes an effective means of controlling behavior and is not psychologically damaging to the child.

Maternal Deprivation in Human Infants

In the early decades of the twentieth century, much concern was expressed over the alarming mortality rate among children living in institutions and the frequency of psychological disturbance among such children (Thompson & Grusec, 1970). As increasing attention was drawn to this state of affairs, Margaret Ribble (1944) a psychoanalyst, published an account of her clinical observations of 600 infants. Ribble suggested that the infant's helplessness and immature physiological organization demanded adequate mothering to provide the infant's needs for tactile, auditory, and kinesthetic stimulation. The absence of continued maternal or substitute caretaker contact, according to Ribble, resulted in the development of biological and psychological symptoms of deterioration which Ribble described as "marasmus."

Shortly after Ribble's publication, René Spitz, also a psychoanalyst, published the first of four influential papers describing a longitudinal study of institutionalized children (Spitz, 1945, 1946a,b; Spitz & Wolf, 1949). Spitz reported the results of a comparative development study among infants raised in two different kinds of institutions. One institution, which Spitz called "Nursery," was a New York State prison for delinquent girls. Infants ($N = 122$) born in this institution were cared for by their mothers until they were approximately 1 year old. These girls were described as adequate mothers despite Spitz' comments that they were maladjusted, criminal, or retarded. Infants in Nursery received a good deal of attention, affection, and social interaction and stimulation.

The other institution was called "Foundling Home." This group originally consisted of 91 infants who were institutionalized because their mothers were unable to care for them. They were breast-fed for the first several months by their mothers, who were present in the institution but who had little other contact with their children. Five to eight nurses cared for the infants but gave them relatively little social contact. Infants remained in cribs with sheets hung over the sides, and no toys were available to them. Hollows had been worn into the mattresses, restricting the infants' movement.

At the end of the first year, Spitz reported a decline in average developmental quotient scores (relative performance on sensorimotor and cognitive tasks) from 132 to 72 among the Foundling Home infants, and to 45 by the end of the second year. Developmental quotient scores of Nursery infants and a control group of noninstitutionalized infants remained essentially the same. In addition to the developmental retardation observed in the Foundling Home, Spitz also described a variety of psychogenic disorders that developed among these infants. These included poor physical health, high susceptibility to disease, weight loss, disturbed emotional patterns, retarded skeletal and motor development, and poorly developed social behavior. Spitz referred to this pattern of debilitation as "hospitalism."

Nursery infants who were separated from their mothers for 3 months during the second-half year of life were reported to develop a syndrome of "anaclitic depression," characterized by a drop in developmental quotient scores, listlessness, and weeping. They recovered when reunited with their mothers. On the basis of his observations, Spitz concluded that infants who are separated from their mothers during the first year of life develop symptoms of psychological and physical disorders which may be irreversible.

By 1950, several other investigators had confirmed Spitz's findings on the effects of institutionalization and maternal deprivation. In 1951, at the request of the World Health Organization of the United Nations, Bowlby published a monograph on the developmental effects of maternal deprivation. Reviewing all the available data up to that time, Bowlby (1951) stated that infants deprived of maternal care and love are "almost always" physically, intellectually, and socially retarded. He concluded, "It is now demonstrated that maternal care in infancy and early childhood is essential for mental health. This is a discovery of which the importance may be compared to that of the role of vitamins in physical health, and is of far-reaching significance for the prevention of mental ill-health" (p. 69).

The worldwide impact of Bowlby's conclusions was monumental. It brought about vast social reforms in the institutional care of children. But unlike the general public, many scientists challenged Bowlby's conclusions and the data upon which they were based. The maternal deprivation hypothesis quickly became a matter of intense controversy.

The Maternal Deprivation Controversy   Following Bowlby's World Health Organization monograph, a number of reviews and experiments began to appear in the literature (see Casler, 1968; O'Connor, 1968; Rutter, 1972;

Thompson & Grusec, 1970; and Yarrow, 1964 for major and extensive critical treatments of the literature on maternal deprivation). Pinneau (1950, 1955), a psychologist, was among the first to evaluate critically the reports of Ribble and Spitz and to raise serious questions about the maternal deprivation hypothesis. In a stinging and devastating review of Spitz's series of reports, Pinneau (1955) pointed out methodological deficiencies, inconsistencies, and contradictions so serious in scope and number as to seriously challenge Spitz's data and conclusions. Specifically, Pinneau pointed to (1) inconsistencies in the numbers of children reported in the study; (2) contradictory descriptions of parents, child care, and conditions in the institutions; (3) differences in cultural, racial, and socioeconomic background between groups (the Foundling Home was reportedly in Mexico, but its exact location remains unknown); (4) the questionable validity of the developmental scale used to obtain developmental quotients; and (5) selective sampling bias in the Foundling Home resulting from loss of children through adoption. Stone (1954), in his presidential address to the New York State Psychological Association, referred to Pinneau's critique, stating, "I commend you his article as a kind of hydrogen bomb perfection of destructive criticism; not a paragraph is left standing for miles around" (p. 14).

In discussing the evidence for maternal deprivation effects, O'Connor (1968) points out that 11 studies on maternal deprivation were published between 1956 and 1962. Four of these show deleterious effects, four show no significant effects, and three show significant recovery at later ages following debilitating effects in infancy. O'Connor concludes that the evidence clearly shows a great deal of variability in the response to maternal deprivation, even among those studies that report deprivation effects. The observation that effects are often temporary suggests that reported maternal deprivation effects in infants are more likely due to prolonged sensory deprivation rather than to maternal deprivation as interpreted by psychoanalytic theory (loss of maternal love, essentially).

In another review of the literature, Casler (1968) evaluated two major hypotheses about the effects of institutionalization: (1) the maternal deprivation hypothesis, which is the original psychoanalytic position that the absence of a loving mother or mother substitute is the cause of developmental disruption;

and (2) the perceptual deprivation hypothesis, which attributes deterioration to the deprivation of general perceptual and social stimulation, for which a large body of supporting data is offered. Casler states that the studies supporting the maternal deprivation hypothesis contain serious methodological flaws that undermine any interpretation of the data. He lists seven major problems of these studies:

1 Failure to control for age of separation. Infant effects may be related to disruption of an already existing maternal–infant bond rather than to maternal deprivation.
2 Failure to adequately describe post-separation environment in terms of child–nurse ratio, feeding regimen, etc., so that infant stimulation levels may be assessed independently of maternal deprivation.
3 Failure to describe the reasons for institutionalization.
4 Failure to describe prenatal histories and environments of institutionalized children.
5 Failure to control for selective sampling bias operating after institutionalization. Since the healthiest and most responsive children are more likely to be adopted, those who remain the longest are likely to be least desirable for one reason or another (i.e., poor health, unresponsiveness).
6 Failure to control for deprivation effects due to massive environmental changes and sudden reduction in sensory and social stimulation when an infant is removed to an institution.
7 Failure to control for post-institutionalization environment (i.e., foster homes).

Each of these confounding variables, if uncontrolled, may account for the observed effects that are attributed to maternal deprivation. Summarizing the data supporting the maternal deprivation hypothesis, Casler concludes that there is no strong evidence to attribute the deficiencies found in maternally deprived children to maternal deprivation itself. Further, Casler reports studies of deprived children who suffered no ill effects. In 1956, Bowlby conceded that "some of the workers who first drew attention to the dangers of maternal deprivation resulting from separation have tended on occasion to overstate their case" (cited in Casler, 1968, p. 585).

The concept of maternal deprivation has served a significant scientific and clinical role in the study of both personality development and general development. It has forced us to specify clearly the nature of early experiential events and their underlying processes. The research generated by Spitz's original work has made an important contribution to developmental psychology, both theoretically and empirically.

LATER SOCIALIZATION AND PERSONALITY DEVELOPMENT

Through the process of socialization, children begin to learn the basic rules and standards necessary for the development of the reasoning, judgment, and conduct required for social interactions. As the child's network of social interactions and experiences expands, the number and complexity of social demands increase. New people and new social situations introduce new socialization skills that are required for adequate personality–social development and functioning. These later socialization processes are not a simple transmission of information from one generation to another. What each child extracts from various socialization agents is largely dependent on individual experiences (Brown, 1965). As Brown states, the system of norms, rules, and values that governs the child's socialization changes as the child grows older, and the product can be unique and sometimes revolutionary. In the discussion to follow, we will examine some socialization phenomena of later childhood and the attempts to trace their developmental patterns.

Moral Development

Morality and its development, for centuries a topic of philosophical thought, has been studied by psychologists for almost 50 years. Moral development is concerned with the processes by which children learn principles of right and wrong or good and bad behavior. Most of the research attention in moral development is directed toward the development of moral reasoning and moral conduct. Moral reasoning involves how the child learns and adopts rules and standards by which moral decisions and actions are made. Moral conduct refers to actual behavior in situations demanding some moral or ethical act. The first deals with cognitive processes of judgment and reasoning while the second is concerned with specific moral behaviors in specific social situations.

Cognitive Theories of Moral Development: Piaget and Kohlberg

The developmental study of moral reasoning and judgment originated with Piaget (1932). Piaget views morality as consisting of the child's respect for social rules and sense of equality and justice toward people. The cognitive structures of social rules are learned from parents and other adults and are assimilated out of the child's submission to authority. The child's sense of justice is acquired through social experiences, wherein the child learns about self-government, autonomy,

Peers . . . Social experiences in which the child learns about what his peers expect and/or will tolerate are important to the overall process of socialization. Such experiences provide feedback on particular modes of behavior and ideas that may reinforce or conflict with information acquired earlier from adults. In either case, the child's awareness of others is enhanced, and dealing with conflicting ideas of parents and friends probably advances moral development.

(Photo by Richard C. LaBarba.)

Table 10-5
Kohlberg's Moral Stages

LEVEL	STAGE
I. Premoral: Moral values reside in external, quasi-physical events, or in bad acts. The child is responsive to rules and evaluative labels, but views them in terms of pleasant of unpleasant consequences of actions, or in terms of the physical power of those who impose the rules.	1. Obedience and punishment orientation. Egocentric deference to superior power or prestige, or a trouble-avoiding set. Objective responsibility.
	2. Naively egoistic orientation. Right action is that which is instrumental in satisfying the self's needs and occasionally others'. Awareness of relativism of values to each actor's needs and perspectives. Naive egalitarianism and orientation to exchange and reciprocity.
II. Conventional Role Conformity: Moral values reside in performing the right role, in maintaining the conventional order and expectancies of others as a value in its own right.	3. Good-boy/good-girl orientation. Orientation to approval, to pleasing and helping others. Conformity to stereotypical images of majority or natural role behavior. Action is evaluated in terms of intentions.
	4. Authority and social-order maintaining orientation. Orientation to "doing duty" and to showing respect for authority and maintaining the given social order for its own sake. Regard for earned expectations of others. Differentiates actions out of a sense of obligation to rules from actions for generally "nice" or natural motives.

and individual social-rule formation. These two components of morality represent a shift in moral development, according to Piaget. Piaget's investigations of moral reasoning in 4- to 12-year-old children led him to identify two stages of moral development. The first and more primitive stage he called heteronomous morality—obedience to external moral rules imposed by others. It is seen in children 4 to 7 years old. Piaget's second stage, called autonomous morality, arises from

LEVEL	STAGE

III. Self Accepted Moral Principles: Morality is defined in terms of conformity to shared standards, rights, or duties apart from supporting authority. The standards conformed to are internal and action-decisions are based on an inner process of thought and judgement concerning right or wrong.

5. Contractual legalistic orientation. Norms of right and wrong are defined in terms of laws or institutionalized rules which seem to have a rational basis. When conflict arises between individual needs and law or contract, though sympathetic to the former, the individual believes the latter must prevail because of its greater functional rationality for society, the majority will and welfare.

6. The morality of individual principles of conscience. Orientation not only toward existing social rules, but also toward the conscience as a directing agent, mutual trust and respect, and principles of moral choice involving logical universalities and consistency. Action is controlled by internalized ideals that exert a pressure to act accordingly regardless of the reactions of others in the immediate environment. If one acts otherwise, self-condemnation and guilt result.

(Adapted from Kohlberg, 1969.)

peer interactions between 10 and 12 years of age. In this stage, the child develops and follows internal moral rules.

KOHLBERG   Piaget's work provided most of the theoretical foundations for Kohlberg's doctoral dissertation on moral development in children (Graham, 1972). Kohlberg (1969, 1976) has elaborated and extended Piaget's stages of moral reasoning and development. His investigations of responses to moral dilemmas presented to children, adolescents, and adults resulted in the formulation of six universal stages of moral development (Table 10-5). Kohlberg's data (Turiel, 1969) drew him to the conclusion that:

1 The six moral stages are an invariant sequence.
2 Movement from one stage to the next results from a restructuring of the preceding stage.
3 Restructuring occurs when the child is confronted with conflicting rationales.

For both Piaget and Kohlberg, moral reasoning and development are primarily determined by cognitive maturation, with relatively little formative input from the environment.

Empirical support for cognitive stage approaches to moral development has been inconsistent at best (Hoffman, 1975). Piaget's theory has been criticized as too simplistic (Isaacs, 1966). Others have found that moral reasoning may be accelerated or acquired by imitation or social learning, or as a function of reinforcement (Bandura, 1969; Constanzo, Coie, Grumet, & Farnell, 1973; Simpson, 1974). Kurtines and Greif (1974) are critical of the methodology used in research on Kohlberg's theory. Most of the criticism is directed toward Kohlberg's moral judgment scale as a weak instrument, lacking standardization in administration and having too complex a scoring system. Kohlberg's theory has been influential in the study of moral development, but much more research is required to clarify the question of universal stages of moral development (Kurdek, 1978). Empirical observations of variability and modifiability in children's moral development continue to plague cognitive stage theories (Hoffman, 1977; Keasey, 1973).

Social Learning Theory

The common-sense approach to moral development (and other socialization processes) simply sees the child learning the rules, values, and traditions of his or her society. This approach characterizes the social learning theory of Bandura and associates (Bandura, 1977; Bandura & Walters, 1964). Bandura has modified traditional operant learning principles to form a "sociobehavioristic" approach to social phenomena such as socialization and personality development. Within this framework, Bandura and colleagues stress the role of observational learning, imitation, and modeling in the development of social behavior and personality. Through principles of reinforcement, generalization, and discrimination, social training and development are established.

In social learning theory, punishment serves primarily to inhibit a child's undesirable behavior so that the responses may be replaced by more appropriate behavior, which is then reinforced. According to Bandura, modeling of adult social behaviors requires the child to attend to, remember, and reproduce the model's behavior. The final requirement is

Johnny and the Law . . . The fact that socially acceptable templates of behavior exist is not in question, and friendly encounters with agents of authority may provide a child with guidance as to appropriate models of behavior. The child's ultimate acceptance of such models or templates, however, seems to depend upon the consistency with which acceptable behavior is reinforced and nonacceptable behavior is punished.

(Photo by Owen Franken/Stock, Boston.)

reinforcement of the child's behavior. That reinforcement may be external or internal (vicarious reinforcement). Modeling is mediated by the child's imaginative and verbal systems, an idea similar to Aronfreed's (1968) concept of a "cognitive template." Bandura argues against the generality of moral development, noting the evidence of marked inconsistency and specificity of moral behavior. He suggests that modeling of socializing agents is sufficient to explain moral development and judgment. Consistency in moral development is observed in children only when parental models exhibit consistency in moral conduct across a variety of situations (Bandura & McDonald, 1963).

While social learning theory has many appealing aspects, it has not escaped criticism. The de-emphasis of cognitive processes does not sit well in contemporary psychology. And just because observational learning in moral development can be demonstrated, that does not constitute evidence that it is the basic process underlying development. The learning of complex moral reasoning and behavior is not likely to occur through observational learning alone. Moral development is clearly an important consideration in developmental psychology because of its significance to the individual's general functioning and its impact on others. However, we are far from understanding the nature and conditions of its development.

Prosocial Behavior

After years of research concentration on negative aspects of social and personality development, psychologists have recently turned to positive forms of behavioral development. Thus, research on childhood aggression and anxiety has decreased, while there has been a burgeoning of research on prosocial behavior (Bryan, 1975; Bryan & London, 1970; Hoffman, 1977; Rushton, 1976; Staub, 1975). Prosocial behavior is any behavior that has positive social consequences (Wispé, 1977). Any number of behaviors fall within this definition, including altruism, cooperation, sharing, friendship, and helping. Since altruism has been the primary focus on prosocial investigations, we will restrict our discussion to an examination of its development in children.

ALTRUISM Altruism is variously defined, but, typically, the term is used to describe selfless helping behavior that is voluntary and not motivated by external reward. Hoffman (1975) has hypothesized an intrinsic altruistic motivation that is independent of egoistic, selfish motives and also has developed a theoretical model for the development of such a motive. Basically, Hoffman's model states that empathy to another's distress, interacting with a cognitive sense of the other person, provides the basis for altruism. Hoffman argues that the human capacity for empathy serves as a built-in mechanism for altruism and that its development is dependent upon cognitive development, particularly the development of a sense of others. A child's empathic distress emerges out of the development of person permanence, the first stage in the development of a cognitive sense of others. In the second stage, the child acquires the concept of role taking, an awareness of the feelings of others, and some sense of the emotional states of other people. This is seen to occur between 2 and 4 years of age. The third step in the development of the sense of others is the child's concept that the other person has a personal identity and feelings. This stage emerges between 6 and 9 years of age. While provocative, Hoffman's model is difficult to test empirically and seems far in advance of our actual data on altruism in children.

ELICITING CONDITIONS OF ALTRUISTIC BEHAVIOR The most extensively studied aspect of altruistic behavior in children has been the conditions that tend to promote altruistic behavior. Given the complexity of this behavior, this is not very surprising. Berkowitz and Daniels (1963) view the development of altruistic behavior in terms of learning "social responsibility norms" or "norms of giving." This approach assumes that the child learns and believes the norms by which altruistic behavior develops. Some research has demonstrated children's belief in altruistic norms (Bryan & Walbeck, 1970) and rules (Midlarsky & Bryan, 1975), but the research is generally equivocal (Rushton, 1976).

A number of studies have demonstrated the positive effects of modeling on altruistic behavior (Bryan & London, 1970; Rushton, 1976; Yarrow, Scott, & Waxler, 1973), but little is known about the processes involved. Interestingly, it has been shown that modeling is more powerful in eliciting altruistic behavior than preaching or exhortation (Grusec, Saas-Kortsaak, & Simutis, 1978). Although an active area of research, the study of prosocial behavior and its development is relatively young and requires much more systematic investigation and conceptualization.

In summary, personality–social development is the culmination of human development. And as the final outcome of so

Pouring milk for little brother . . . Altruism is generally defined as voluntary, selfless helping. Like most aspects of social development, altruism appears to be a pattern of behavior modeled after the behavior of significant individuals, such as parents, siblings, grandparents, or peers. What is most important from the viewpoint of moral development is that the child has become aware of the presence of others, of their needs or desires, and is willing to act on those needs or desires without the promise of reward—immediate or long-range. This awareness is fundamental to loving and to a whole range of other positive and constructive human emotions.

(Photo by Burk Uzzle. Copyright © 1967 by Magnum Photos.)

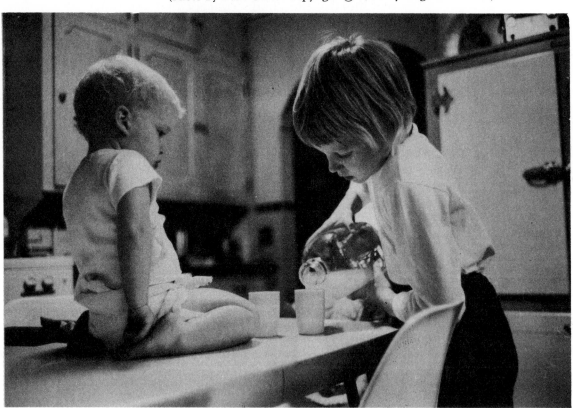

many complex developmental events, it is an awesome process. The unique complexity of personality–social development remains an unsolved puzzle to challenge the developmental sciences. Ultimately, our understanding of the development of personality and social behavior will rely on our knowledge and understanding of the developmental foundations upon which they rest.

REFERENCES

Ainsworth, M. D. S. Patterns of attachment behavior shown by the infant interaction with his mother. *Merrill-Palmer Quarterly,* 1964, *10,* 51–58.

Ainsworth, M. D. S. *Infancy in Uganda: Infant care and the growth of love.* Baltimore: Johns Hopkins University Press, 1967.

Ainsworth, M. D. S. Object relations, dependency, and attachment: A theoretical review of the infant–mother relationship. *Child Development,* 1969, *40,* 965–1025.

Ainsworth, M. D. S., Bell, S. M., & Stayton, D. J. Individual differences in the development of some attachment behaviors. *Merrill-Palmer Quarterly,* 1972, *18,* 123–144.

Ainsworth, M. D. S. The development of infant–mother attachment. In B. M. Caldwell and H. N. Ricciuti (Eds.), *Review of child development research.* Chicago: University of Chicago Press, 1973.

Ambrose, A. (Ed.). *Stimulation in early infancy.* London: Academic Press, 1969.

Anderson, H. H., & Anderson, G. L. Social development. In L. Carmichael (Ed.), *Manual of child psychology* (2nd Ed.). New York: Wiley, 1954.

Aronfreed, J. *Conduct and conscience.* New York: Academic Press, 1968.

Bandura, A. Social learning of moral judgments. *Journal of Personality and Social Psychology,* 1969, *11,* 275–279.

Bandura, A. *Social learning theory.* Englewood Cliffs, New Jersey: Prentice Hall, 1977.

Bandura, A., & McDonald, F. J. The influence of social reinforcement and the behavior of models in shaping children's moral judgments. *Journal of Abnormal and Social Psychology,* 1963, *67,* 274–281.

Bandura, A., & Walters, R. H. *Social Learning and Personality Development.* New York: Holt, Rinehart, & Winston, 1964.

Baumrind, D. Effects of authoritative parental control on child behavior. *Child Development,* 1966, *37,* 887–907.

Baumrind, D. Child care practices anteceding three patterns of preschool behavior. *Genetic Psychology Monographs,* 1967, *75,* 43–88.

Baumrind, D. Current patterns of parental authority. *Developmental Psychology Monographs,* 1971, *41,* No. 1, Part 2.

Baumrind, D. *Early socialization and the discipline controversy.* Morristown, New Jersey: General Learning Press, 1975.

Baumrind, D. Socialization and instrumental competence in young children. In E. M. Hetherington and R. D. Parke (Eds.), *Contemporary readings in child psychology.* New York: McGraw Hill, 1977.

Bell, R. Q. A reinterpretation of the direction of effects in studies of socialization. *Psychological Bulletin,* 1968, *75,* 81–95.

Bell, S. M. The development of the concept of the object as related to infant–mother attachment. *Child Development,* 1970, *41,* 291–311.

Berkowitz, L., & Daniels, L. Responsibility and dependency. *Journal of Abnormal and Social Psychology,* 1963, *66,* 429–436.

Bijou, S. W., & Baer, D. M. *Child development.* New York: Appleton-Century-Crofts, 1965.

Bowlby, J. *Maternal care and mental health.* Geneva: W.H.O. Monograph Series, No. 2, 1951.

Bowlby, J. The nature of the child's tie to his mother. *International Journal of Psychoanalysis,* 1958, *39,* 350–373.

Bowlby, J. *Attachment and loss,* Vol. 1. New York: Basic Books, 1969.

Brown, R. *Social Psychology.* New York: The Free Press, 1965.

Bryan, J. H. Children's cooperation and helping behaviors. In E. M. Hetherington (Ed.), *Review of child development research.* Chicago: University of Chicago Press, 1975.

Bryan, J. H., & London, P. Altruistic behavior by children. *Psychological Bulletin,* 1970, *70,* 200–211.

Bryan, J. H., & Walbeck, N. Preaching and practicing generosity: Children's actions and reactions. *Child Development,* 1970, *41,* 329–353.

Cairns, R. B. Attachment and dependency: A Psychobiological and social learning synthesis. In J. L. Gewirtz (Ed.), *Attachment and dependency.* Washington, D.C.: Winston, 1972.

Caldwell, B. M. The usefulness of the critical period hypothesis in the study of affiliative behavior. *Merrill-Palmer Quarterly,* 1962, *8,* 229–242.

Caldwell, B. M. The effects of infant care. In M. Hoffman and L. Hoffman (Eds.), *Review of child development research,* Vol. 1. New York: Russell Sage Foundation, 1964.

Casler, L. Perceptual deprivation in institutional settings. In G. Newton and S. Levine (Eds.), *Early experience and behavior.* Springfield, Illinois: Thomas, 1968.

Cohen, L. J. The operational definition of human attachment. *Psychological Bulletin*, 1974, *81,* 207–217.

Constanzo, P. R., Coie, J. D., Grumet, J. F., & Farnell, D. A reexamination of the effects of intent and consequence on children's moral judgment. *Child Development,* 1973, *44,* 154–16.

Denenberg, V. H. Critical periods, stimulus input, and emotional reactivity. A theory of infantile stimulation. *Psychological Review,* 1964, *71,* 335–351.

Denenberg, V. H. Considerations of the usefulness of the critical period hypothesis as applied to the stimulation of rodents in infancy. In G. Newton and S. Levine (Eds.), *Early experience and behavior.* Springfield, Illinois: Thomas, 1968.

Erikson, E. *Childhood and society.* New York: Norton, 1950.

Escalona, S. *The Roots of individuality.* Chicago: Aldine, 1968.

Gewirtz, J. L. Mechanisms of social learning: Some roles of stimulation and behavior in early human development. In D. A. Goslin (Ed.), *Handbook of socialization theory and research.* Chicago: Rand-McNally, 1969.

Gewirtz, J. L. On selecting attachment and dependence indicators. In J. L. Gewirtz (Ed.), *Attachment and dependency.* Washington, D.C.: Winston, 1972.

Graham, D. *Moral learning and development.* New York: Wiley-Interscience, 1972.

Grinder, R. *A history of genetic psychology.* New York: Wiley, 1967.

Grusec, J. E., Saas-Kortsaak, P., & Simutis, Z. M. The role of example and moral exhortation in the training of altruism. *Child Development,* 1978, *49,* 920–923.

Hall, C. S., & Lindzey, G. *Theories of personality* (2nd ed.). New York: Wiley, 1970.

Harlow, H. F. The nature of love. *American Psychologist,* 1958, *13,* 673–685.

Harlow, H. F. The maternal affectional system. In B. M. Foss (Ed.), *Determinants of infant behavior* II. London: Metheun, 1963.

Harlow, H. F. *Learning to love.* San Francisco: Albion, 1971.

Harlow, H. F., Dodsworth, R. O., & Harlow, M. K. Total isolation in monkeys. *Proceedings of the National Academy of Science,* 1965, *54,* 90–97.

Harlow, H. F., & Harlow, M. K. Social deprivation in monkeys. *Scientific American,* 1962, *207,* 136–146.

Harlow, H. F., Harlow, M. K., & Hansen, E. W. The maternal affectional system of Rhesus monkeys. In H. Rheingold (Ed.), *Maternal behavior in mammals.* New York: Wiley, 1963.

Harlow, H. F., & Zimmerman, R. R. Affectional responses in the infant monkey. *Science,* 1959, *130,* 421–432.

Heinstein, M. I. Behavioral correlates of breast-bottle regimes under varying parent-infant relationships. *Monographs of the Society for Research in Child Development,* 1963, *28,* No. 4.

Hetherington, E. M., & Brackbill, Y. Etiology and covariation of obstinacy, orderliness, and parsimony in young children. *Child Development,* 1963, *34,* 919–943.

Hoffman, M. L. Developmental synthesis of affect and cogintion and its implications for altruistic motivation. *Developmental Psychology,* 1975, *11,* 607–622.

Hoffman, M. L. Personality and social development. In M. R. Rosenzweig and L. R. Porter (Eds.), *Annual Review of Psychology,* 1977, *28.*

Isaacs, S. *Intellectual growth in young children.* New York: Schocken, 1966.

Keasey, C. B. Experimentally induced changes in moral opinions and reasoning. *Journal of Personality and Social Psychology,* 1973, *26,* 30–38.

Kohlberg, L. Continuities and discontinuities in childhood and adult moral development. *Human Development,* 1969, *12,* 93–120.

Kohlberg, L. Moral stages and moralization. The cognitive development approach. In T. Likona (Ed.), *Moral development and behavior.* New York: Holt, Rinehart, & Winston, 1976.

Korner, A. F. Mother-child interaction: One or two-way street? *Social Work,* 1965, *10,* 47–51.

Korner, A. F. Individual difference at birth: Implications for early experience and later development. *American Journal of Orthopsychiatry,* 1971, *41,* 608–619.

Korner, A. F. Sex differences in newborns with special reference to differences in the organization of oral behavior. *Journal of Child Psychology and Psychiatry,* 1973, *14,* 19–29.

Kretschmer, E. *Physique and character.* New York: Harcourt, 1925.

Kurdek, L. A. Perspective taking as the cognitive basis of children's moral development: A review of the literature. *Merrill-Palmer Quarterly,* 1978, *24,* 3–28.

Kurtines, W., & Greif, E. B. The development of moral thought: Review and evaluation of Kohlberg's approach. *Psychological Bulletin,* 1974, *81,* 453–470.

Leiderman, P. H., & Leiderman, G. F. Affective and cognitive consequences of polymatric infant care in the East African Highlands. In A. Pick (Ed.), *Minnesota symposium on child development,* Vol. 8. Minneapolis: University of Minnesota Press, 1974.

Lewis, M. State as an infant-environment interaction: An analysis of mother-infant interaction as a function of sex. *Merrill-Palmer Quarterly,* 1972, *18,* 95–121.

Maccoby, E. E., & Masters, J. C. Attachment and dependency. In P. H. Mussen (Ed.), *Carmichael's manual of child psychology*. New York: Wiley, 1970.

Mason, W. A. Early social deprivation in the nonhuman primates: Implications for human behavior. In D. C. Glass (Ed.), *Environmental influences*. New York: Rockefeller University Press and Russell Sage Foundation, 1968.

Masters, J. C., & Wellman, H. M. The study of human attachment: A procedural critique. *Psychological Bulletin*, 1974, *81*, 217–237.

Meier, G. W. Other data on the effects of social isolation during rearing upon adult reproductive behavior in the rhesus monkey (*Macaca mulatta*). *Animal Behavior*, 1965, *13*, 429–452.

Midlarsky E., & Bryan, J. H. Training charity in children. *Journal of Personality and Social Psychology*, 1975, *5*, 408–415.

Mineka, S., & Suomi, S. J. Social separation in monkeys. *Psychological Bulletin*, 1978, *85*, 1376–1400.

Newton, G., & Levine, S. (Eds.). *Early experience and behavior*. Springfield, Illinois: Thomas, 1968.

O'Connor, N. Children in restricted environment. In G. Newton and S. Levine (Eds.), *Early experience and behavior*. Springfield, Illinois: Thomas, 1968.

Orlansky, H. Infant care and personality. *Psychological Bulletin*, 1949, *46*, 1–48.

Piaget, J. *The moral judgment of the child*. New York: Harcourt, 1932.

Piaget, J. *The psychology of the child*. New York: Basic Books, 1969.

Pinneau, S. R. A critique of the articles by Margaret Ribble. *Child Development*, 1950, *21*, 203–228.

Pinneau, S. R. The infantile disorders of hopitalism and anaclitic depression. *Psychological Bulletin*, 1955, *52*, 429–452.

Ribble, M. A. Infantile experience in relation to personality development. In J. McV. Hunt (Ed.), *Personality and the behavior disorders*. New York: Ronald Press, 1944.

Rushton, J. P. Socialization and the altruistic behavior of children. *Psychological Bulletin*, 1976, *83*, 898–913.

Rutter, M. *Maternal deprivation reassessed*. London: Penguin, 1972.

Sander, L. W. Regulation and organization in the early infant-caretaker system. In R. Robson (Ed.), *Brain and early behavior*. London: Academic Press, 1969.

Schaffer, H. R. *The growth of sociability*. London: Penguin, 1971.

Schaffer, H. R., & Emerson, P. E. The development of social attachments in infants. *Monographs of the Society for Research in Child Development*, 1964, *29*, No. 3.

Scott, J. P. Critical periods in behavioral development. *Science,* 1962, *138,* 949–958.

Scott, J. P., Stewart, J. M., & DeGhett, V. J. Critical periods in the organization of systems. *Developmental Psychobiology,* 1974, *7,* 489–513.

Sears, R. R. Survey of objective studies of psychoanalytic concepts. *Social Science Research Council Bulletin,* 1943, *51,* 156–170.

Sears, R. R., Maccoby, E. E., & Levin, H. *Patterns of child rearing.* Chicago: Row, Peterson, 1957.

Sewell, W. H. Infant training and the personality of the child. *American Journal of Sociology,* 1952, *58,* 150–159.

Sheldon, W. H. *Varieties of temperament.* New York: Harper & Row, 1942.

Simpson, E. L. Moral development research. A case study of cultural bias. *Human Development,* 1974, *17,* 81–106.

Spitz, R. A. Hospitalism: An inquiry into the genesis of psychiatric conditions in early childhood. *Psychoanalytic Study of the Child,* 1945, *1,* 53–74.

Spitz, R. A. Hospitalism: A follow-up report. *Psychoanalytic Study of the Child,* 1946, *2,* 113–117. (a)

Spitz, R. A. Anaclitic depression. *Psychoanalytic Study of the Child,* 1946, *2,* 313–342. (b)

Spitz, R. A., & Wolf, K. M. Autoeroticism. Some empirical findings and hypotheses on three of its manifestations in the first year of life. *Psychoanalytic Study of the Child,* 1949, *34,* 85–120.

Sroufe, L. A., & Waters, E. Attachment as an organizational construct. *Child Development,* 1977, *48,* 1184–1199.

Staub, E. *The development of prosocial behavior in children.* Morristown, New Jersey: General Learning Press, 1975.

Stone, L. J. A critique of studies of infant isolation. *Child Development,* 1954, *25,* 9–20.

Suomi, S. J., & Harlow, H. F. Early experience and social development in Rhesus monkeys. In M. E. Lamb (Ed.), *Social and personality development.* New York: Holt, Rinehart, & Winston, 1978.

Thompson, W. R., & Grusec, J. E. Studies of early experience. In P. H. Mussen (Ed.), *Carmichael's manual of child psychology.* New York: Wiley, 1970.

Tracy, R. L., Lamb, M. E., & Ainsworth, M. D. S. Infant approach behavior as related to attachment. *Child Development,* 1976, *47,* 571–578.

Turiel, E. Developmental processes in the child's moral thinking. In P. Mussen, J. Langer, and M. Covington (Eds.), *Trends and issues in developmental psychology.* New York: Holt, Rinehart, & Winston, 1969.

Van Wagenen, G. The Monkey. In E. J. Farris (Ed.), *The care and breeding of laboratory animals.* New York: Wiley, 1950.

Willemsem, E., Flaherty, D., Heaton, H., & Ritchley, G. Attachment behavior of one-year-olds as a function of mother vs. father, sex of child, session, and toys. *Genetic Psychology Monographs,* 1974, *90,* 305–324.

Wispé, L. A. (Ed.). *The psychology of sympathy and altruism.* Cambridge, Massachusetts: Harvard University Press, 1977.

Yarrow, L. J. Maternal deprivation: Toward an empirical and conceptual reevaluation. *Psychological Bulletin,* 1964, *58,* 459–490.

Yarrow, M. R., Scott, P. M., & Waxler, C. Z. Learning concern for others. *Developmental Psychology,* 1973, *8,* 240–260.

Zigler, E., & Child, I. L. (Eds.) *Socialization and personality development.* Reading, Massachusetts: Addison-Wesley, 1972.

Glossary

Abstraction The differentiation or discrimination of common stimulus attributes, leading to some generality regarding group membership in a group or class of events.

Accelerated longitudinal design See *convergence approach*.

Accessibility In concept formation, the extent to which an acquired concept can be used in appropriate situations. See also *status, validity*.

Accommodation In Piaget's theory, the adjustments made by existing cognitive structures to incoming information. See also *assimilation*.

Adolescence The developmental period extending from age 13 to age 18.

Agenesis Failure of body tissue to develop.

Agent specificity The production by teratogens of characteristic and predictable patterns of defects.

Allele (allelomorph) A member of a gene pair located at a specific point on homologous chromosomes; a gene (as one of a pair).

Altruism Selfless helping behavior that is voluntary and not motivated by external reward.

Amniocentesis A medical procedure used to determine the presence of chromosomal abnormality in a fetus, or its sex.

Anaphase The third phase of mitosis. See also *prophase, metaphase, telophase*.

Articulation The ability to generate the wide range of sound frequencies necessary for speech.

Assimilation In Piaget's theory, the process by which information from the environment is received and then changed by existing cognitive structures into a form that can be used and understood. See also *accommodation*.

Asthenic Kretschmer's term for a tall, thin physique. See also *athletic, pyknic*.

Athletic Kretschmer's term for a muscular physique. See also *asthenic, pyknic*.

Attachment An enduring, affectional bond between two people; in infants, it consists of signaling behavior (smiling, vocalization), orienting behavior, locomotion (following, approaching), and active physical contact (hugging, clinging).

Attending reflex A response to a stimulus that consists of fixation and processing of the stimulus as a function of its complexity, novelty, and significance.

Authoritarian parenting According to Baumrind, a pattern of parenting in which absolute standards are followed in attempting to shape and control the child's behavior and attitudes. See also *authoritative parenting, permissive parenting*.

Authoritative parenting According to Baumrind, a pattern of parenting in which there is an attempt to control the child's behavior through open discussion and reasoning with the child. See also *authoritarian parenting, permissive parenting*.

Autoclitics Skinner's term for the process of learning grammar and syntax.

Autogenous A term used to describe behavior that is self-generated, instinctive, or free from any environmental influence.

Autonomous morality According to Piaget, a stage of moral development characterized by obedience to internal moral rules. See also *heteronomous morality*.

Autosome (autosomal chromosome) Any chromosome that is not a sex chromosome.

Baby biography A diary of infant development kept in order to study language scientifically.

Behavioral embryology The study of the origin and development of the nervous system and behavior, especially the relationship between neurobehavioral development and later psychological development.

Behavioral genetics The branch of genetics that is concerned with the relationship between the genotype and the developing behavioral phenotype.

Binocular disparity In an organism with stereoscopic vision, the slight difference between the visual field as perceived by the right and left eyes.

Body humour According to Galen (1 A.D.), a bodily substance (blood, phlegm, yellow bile, black bile) that, if it predominates, results in a particular personality style (cheerful, sluggish, easily angered, depressed).

Canalization The restriction of alternate phenotypic outcomes to a single, genetically determined path of development.

Capacitation The process (whose details are unknown) by which sperm cells acquire the ability to fertilize after remaining in the female genital tract for several hours.

Cephalocaudal A term used to describe a response pattern or developmental trend that begins in the neck region and spreads downward through the trunk.

Cerebrotonia Sheldon's term for a shy, self-conscious temperament. See also *somatotonia, viscerotonia*.

Child development The study of the child as a developing person, specifically, of the changes that occur as the child grows to maturity.

Childhood The developmental period extending from birth to the age of 13.

Child psychology The part of developmental psychology that is concerned with behavioral development during childhood; the study of child behavior and psychological processes.

Chromatin Within a cell the structural network that comprises the chromosomes.

Chromosome A threadlike strand of cellular material that carries genes and transmits hereditary traits.

Chromosome deletion A chromosome anomaly characterized by partial loss of a chromosome.

Chronological age The length of time that an individual organism has lived. See also *ontogenetic age*.

Classical conditioning Learning processes that involve the temporal pairing of an originally neutral (conditioned) stimulus with an already effective (unconditioned) stimulus to evoke a reliable response.

Classical designs   A term used to refer to standard, traditional research designs. See also *multivariate*.

Co-dominance   A condition in which each of a pair of alleles fully expresses its trait in the heterozygote.

Codon   A unit of the genetic code.

Cognition   All the mental processes involved in the acquisition, storage, and use of information.

Cognitive acquisition device (CAD)   A hypothetical mechanism, proposed by Reynolds and Flagg, with which children can generate and understand an infinite number of utterances.

Cognitive adaptation   In Piaget's theory, the processes by which intelligence is increased. See also *assimilation, accommodation*.

Cognitive approach   In developmental psycholinguistics, the view that language is an aspect of cognitive ability.

Cognitive control   Self-regulation of thinking and remembering; also referred to as intention, voluntary action, or will.

Cognitive organization   In Piaget's theory, the orderly system of cognitive structures (sets of "rules" for thinking) and the dynamic relationships among the parts of those structures.

Cognitive psychology   The study of mental processes such as memory, reasoning, and thinking.

Coital age   The estimated age of an embryo or fetus, calculated from the probable time when the parents engaged in coitus.

Comprehension-Imitation-Production (CIP) hypothesis   A learning approach to language development that proposes a three-stage process: (1) comprehension, which depends on observational learning and reinforcement; (2) selective imitation; and (3) spontaneous language production without imitation.

Concept   A collection of stimuli or objects that share one or more common features.

Concept development   An active, creative process of learning the principles by which one can organize the environment and one's experiences with it.

Conditioned response   (1) A response that, after paired associations of stimuli, is elicited or intensified by a stimulus that did not previously elicit it; (2) a response emitted under the control of environmental circumstances that did not previously control it.

Conditioned stimulus   A stimulus that is neutral before being paired with an unconditioned stimulus, whereupon it evokes a conditioned response.

Confluence model   A theory, proposed by Zajonc and Markus, that explains individual differences in intelligence as a function of family configuration (i.e., birth order, family size, an age spacing between siblings).

Conservation   In concept formation, the ability to understand that certain properties of objects, such as volume, remain invariant despite transformations in the physical appearance of those objects.

Constructivism   Piaget's assumption that knowledge is not inherent either in the infant or in external stimuli but must be constructed through actions and experiences with the environment.

Continuity model   A model that describes development in terms of quantitative changes, with complexity of function increasing in small degrees. See also *discontinuity model*.

Contralateral response A response (contraction) in the direction opposite to the side stimulated.

Controlled observation See *naturalistic observation*.

Convergence approach A research design that combines the cross-sectional feature of sample selection with the longitudinal feature of follow-up of individual subjects over time.

Correlational research method A nonexperimental research approach in which the investigator attempts to measure the relationship between two or more events or situations.

Correlation coefficient The numerical value of a correlation, which can range from +1.00 to −1.00; does not imply causation.

Critical period hypothesis The hypothesis that there are certain periods of development in which an organism is most susceptible to specific environmental influences (or the lack of them).

Cross-sectional design A classical research design that involves the comparison of two or more groups of subjects (e.g., subjects of different ages) at the same point in time. See also *longitudinal design*.

Crown-rump (CR) length The head-to-tail or sitting-height length of an embryo or fetus.

Cultural recapitulation Hall's belief that cultural as well as phylogenetic stages of development are repeated in ontogenesis. See also *recapitulation, theory of*.

Cumulative learning model Gagné's proposal that intellectual development results from the cumulative effects of learning, in which an ordered set of capabilities is built up through the processes of differentiation, recall, and transfer of learning.

Cytoplasmic division (cytokinesis) Cleavage of the cytoplasm and subsequent cell division.

Delayed reaction experiment An experimental situation in which an infant is required to find an object that is placed out of sight while the infant watches.

Deoxyribonucleic acid (DNA) A form of nucleic acid found in the nucleus of a cell and structured in such a way as to provide genetic information. See also *ribonucleic acid*.

Dependent variable In an experimental design, the behavioral event or response that is affected by the manipulation of an environmental condition, process, or event (the independent variable).

Development The series of changes that occur in an organism over the course of its life as a result of growth, maturation, and learning. See also *growth, maturation, learning*.

Developmental diagnosis A framework formulated by Gesell and Amatruda to provide early diagnosis of developmental defects and deviations.

Developmental interactionism Piaget's concept of interaction between innate cognitive capacities and environmental or experiential factors.

Developmental psycholinguistics The study of the ontogenesis of language and the developmental processes underlying language acquisition.

Developmental psychology A branch of psychology that attempts to understand the origins, emergence, and course of psychological processes—specifically, the behavioral changes associated with age changes in humans—and to integrate them into a coherent picture.

Developmental variable A universal behavioral change that is part of the process by which behaviors originate and become established. See also *differential variable*.

Differential variable A non-developmental behavioral change that occurs as a result of particular environmental influences. See also *developmental variable*.

Differentiation approach The view of perceptual learning that holds that infants innately possess all the capacities and skills necessary for perceptual competence, but must learn to differentiate among stimuli.

Dihybrid cross A breeding cross involving two phenotypic traits determined by two gene pairs.

Diploid number The number of chromosomes in a somatic cell. See also *haploid number*.

Discontinuity model A model that describes development in terms of qualitative changes that tend to occur in a relatively discrete manner. See also *continuity model*.

Discrepancy hypothesis A variant of the cognitive-evaluative hypothesis of fear.

Disequilibrium In Piaget's theory, the conflict between the individual's existing adaptation (or knowledge) level and the challenge of new situations.

Dishabituation Recovery of the attentional reflexes when a new stimulus is presented after habituation has occurred.

Displacement Transmission of information from another time and place; according to Brown, one of the essential properties of language. See also *semanticity, productivity*.

Dizygotic twins Simultaneously born offspring who develop from two separate zygotes, each of which is the product of a different sperm and ovum; fraternal twins. See also *monozygotic twins*.

Dominant gene A gene that directs the formation of a specific enzyme that will effect the expression of a specific trait; dominant alleles express their effects over recessive alleles. See also *recessive gene*.

Dysgenesis Incomplete or excessive tissue development.

Echoics Skinner's term for a class of utterances that imitate previously heard speech.

Echolalia stage The stage of prelinguistic development in which the infant begins to imitate the vocalizations of others.

Ecological approach See *naturalistic observation*.

Ectoderm The outer germinal layer of the embryonic disc, from which the skin, sense organs, and nervous system develop. See also *endoderm, mesoderm*.

Ectomorph Sheldon's term for a tall, thin physique. See also *mesomorph, endomorph*.

Embryology The branch of biology that deals with the origin and development of individual organisms.

Embryonic disc The form taken by the fertilized ovum after implantation in the uterine wall; a flattened, disc-shaped mass of cells.

Emotion The perception and interpretation of some external or internal stimulus event, accompanied by a nonspecific physiological state of arousal, leading to an emotional response.

Empiricism The belief (following Locke) that knowledge is furnished to the mind through the senses. See also *nativism*.

Enactive representation Bruner's term for a mode of cognitive representation in which past events are represented through the motor responses that characterize, describe, or define the event. See also *iconic representation, symbolic representation*.

Endoderm   The inner germinal layer of the embryonic disc from which the digestive, respiratory, and glandular systems and the genito-urinary tract develop. See also *ectoderm, mesoderm*.

Endomorph   Sheldon's term for a short, fat physique. See also *ectomorph, mesomorph*.

Enrichment approach   The view of perceptual learning as beginning from zero and being progressively enriched through experience and learning.

Environment (prenatal)   Everything outside the prenatal organism, including the amniotic fluid, the uterus, the maternal body, and the environment outside the mother.

Epigenesis   In prenatal development, the emergence of structure and function through a patterned series of transformations and reorganizations.

Epigenetic event   An event that occurs during embryonic development and involves the creation of a new structure.

Epigenetic landscape   Waddington's term for a model of development.

Epiphenomenon   An accidental residual of another event or process.

Equilibration   In Piaget's theory, a self-regulatory process in which the individual initiates new assimilations and accommodations in order to reduce the unpleasant feelings associated with disequilibrium.

Error of potentiality   The idea that although simpler elements may make up more complex systems, the functions and characteristics of those systems may not be found in the elements that preceded them.

Ethology   A field of biology that deals with the behavior of organisms under natural conditions.

Etiology   The scientific study of causes, origins, or reasons.

Eugenics   Improvement of the human species by selective breeding.

Euphenics   Improvement of the phenotype by environmental treatment of genetic defects.

Experimental designs   A category of research approaches characterized by manipulation of independent variables and observation of their effect on some dependent variable or variables. See also *quasi-experimental designs*.

Expressivity   The degree to which a particular trait is displayed. See also *penetrance*.

Functional invariant   According to Piaget, a constant, species-specific biological characteristic.

Gamete   See *germ cell*.

Gene   The basic unit of heredity; the hereditary material that determines some biological trait.

Generative-transformational grammar   A term used to refer to Chomsky's linguistic theory.

Genetic code   The sequence of three bases carried by tRNA and ordering the synthesis of a specific protein.

Genetic epistemology   A term used to refer to Piaget's theory of cognitive development through a series of stages and periods.

Genetic psychology   A term formerly used to refer to what is now called developmental psychology.

Genetics   A branch of biology that deals with heredity and variation in plants and animals and the processes by which hereditary characteristics are transmitted from parents to offspring.

Genome   A single pair of chromosomes, of which one is of paternal origin and the other of maternal origin. Also refers to complete complement of chromosomes.

Genotype The genetic composition of an individual. See also *phenotype*.

Germ cell (germ plasm) A reproductive cell. See also *somatic cell*.

G factor According to Spearman, a unitary, universal capacity or trait that underlies all intellectual activity.

Grammar The rules of syntax.

Growth Quantitative changes in the dimensions or volume of tissues, organs, and structures.

Habituation A mechanism that selectively terminates the attentional reflexes in the face of irrelevant or insignificant stimuli.

Haploid number The number of chromosomes in a germ cell. See also *diploid number*.

Heritability (h^2) The proportion of the total variance in a population trait that is attributable to genetic factors.

Heteronomous morality According to Piaget, a primitive stage of moral development characterized by obedience to moral rules imposed by others. See also *autonomous morality*.

Heterozygous (heterozygote) Possessing different forms of a particular allele.

Holandric A term used to refer to a sex-linked gene located on the Y chromosome.

Holophrase A single-word utterance with the meaning of a full sentence produced by a child at about one year of age.

Holophrastic stage The stage of language development in which the child produces holophrases (single-word utterances with the meaning of a full sentence).

Homozygous (homozygote) Possessing identical forms of a particular allele.

Hospitalism Spitz's term for the psychogenic disorders that develop in institutionalized infants who are deprived of maternal contact.

Hypothetico-deductive reasoning In Piaget's theory, the highest, most complex level of cognitive development.

Iconic representation According to Bruner, a mode of cognitive representation in which events are summarized by the organization of percepts and images and their characteristics. See also *enactive representation, symbolic representation*.

Incomplete dominance See *intermediate inheritance*.

Incongruity hypothesis A variant of the cognitive-evaluative hypothesis of fear.

Independent assortment, law of Mendel's second law, which states that whenever two or more pairs of contrasting characters (i.e., traits) are brought together in a hybrid, the genes for each character separate independently during meiosis.

Independent variable In an experimental design, an environmental condition, process, or event that is manipulated by a researcher so as to observe its effect on some behavioral event or response (the dependent variable).

Individuation, theory of Coghill's theory that prenatal behavioral development is a process of individuation, or differentiation in which discrete, local reflexes develop from an integrated overall pattern of activity. See also *integration, theory of*.

Infant neuropsychiatry See *developmental diagnosis*.

Inheritance of acquired characters, law of One of Lamarck's laws of evolution, which states that all environmentally produced acquisitions or losses of organs are preserved by hereditary transmission to the offspring, provided that they are common to the parents. See also *use and disuse, law of*.

Instrumental conditioning Learning processes in which the response rate of a specific behavior is modified by the consequences of the response.

Integration, theory of Windle's theory that specific reflexes are the first basic units of prenatal behavior to appear in higher vertebrates, and that later patterns of behavior result from the integration of earlier reflexes. See also *individuation, theory of*.

Intelligence quotient (IQ) The score obtained on the Stanford–Binet Scale; the ratio between mental age and chronological age.

Intelligence test A test whose purpose is to determine a person's ability to acquire and use knowledge.

Intermediate inheritance (incomplete dominance) A condition in which the heterozygote shows a blending of alleles.

Interphase A term used to describe the resting, nondividing cell.

Intraverbals Skinner's term for social responses and incidental conversation.

Karyotype (chromosome complement) A photograph of the appearance (size and structure) of a set of chromosomes.

Kinesthesis Awareness of the location in space of parts of the body.

Lallation stage The stage of prelinguistic development in which the infant begins to imitate its own sounds.

Language acquisition device (LAD) A hypothetical mechanism, proposed by Chomsky, that contains universal linguistic information and generates language rules.

Learning Changes in behavior that result from training, practice, or experience.

Learning approach In developmental psycholinguistics, the view that language consists of a set of conditioned responses for which the original stimuli may not be obvious or known.

Learning theory The belief that experiential and environmental factors influence the sequence and form of development. See also *maturation theory*.

Lexicon A vocabulary (e.g., the vocabulary of a child).

Linguistics The study of the structure of language, including phonetics, semantics, syntax, and grammar.

Logical operations In Piaget's theory, integrated, organized mental representations that permit a person to think simultaneously about two or more elements of a problem and perceive the relationship between them.

Longitudinal design A classical research design that involves the measurement of a single group of subjects at two or more points in time (i.e., at different ages). See also *cross-sectional design*.

Looking chamber An apparatus used to test the visual interests of infants, which consists of a crib within a box from whose ceiling objects may be hung; the observer watches the infant through a peephole.

Looming The rapidly increasing change in the optical size of an approaching object that occurs before collision with that object.

Low birth weight A birth weight below 2500 grams.

Mands Skinner's term for a class of utterances controlled by drive states.

Manipulation A term used to refer to the ability of a researcher to isolate, control, and systematically vary an independent variable in order to observe its effect on a dependent variable.

Marasmus Ribble's term for the biological

and psychological symptoms of deterioration that develop in infants who are deprived of continuous caretaker contact.

Maternal deprivation hypothesis The hypothesis that the absence of a loving mother or mother substitute is the cause of developmental disruption in institutionalized infants. See also *perceptual deprivation hypothesis*.

Maturation The anatomical and physiological development of organs and organ systems; the process by which they become operational.

Maturation theory The belief that development "unfolds" in an invariant, universal pattern that is not influenced by learning, training, or experience. See also *learning theory*.

Mean length of utterance (MLU) The average number of words or morphemes produced by a child in a sample of recorded utterances; used by Brown as an index of grammatical development.

Mechanical mirror (learning) theory of human development A theory of development that states that behavioral development is controlled by, and is a function (reflection) of, the physical and social environment.

Meiosis The process by which germ cells divide, in which chromosomes are separated and their number reduced from diploid to haploid.

Memory The storage and retrieval of information and events that have been learned or experienced.

Menstrual age The estimated age of an embryo or fetus, calculated from the beginning of the mother's last menstrual period.

Mental age score On the Binet–Simon Scale, the number of items that could be answered correctly by a majority of normal children at a particular age level.

Mental processes approach The theory of cognition that emphasizes mental processes such as remembering, judging, and comparing. See also *structuralism*.

Mental quotient See *intelligence quotient*.

Mental test See *intelligence test*.

Mesoderm The middle germinal layer of the embryonic disc, from which the musculoskeletal, cardiovascular, excretory, and reproductive systems develop. See also *endoderm, ectoderm*.

Mesomorph Sheldon's term for a muscular physique. See also *ectomorph, endomorph*.

Messenger RNA (mRNA) The form of RNA that carries the genetic message from the nucleus of the cell to the cytoplasm.

Metalinguistic awareness The ability to think about and evaluate language.

Metalinguistics The use of language to teach language.

Metaphase The second phase of mitosis. See also *prophase, anaphase, telophase*.

Method of critical exploration A term used to describe Piaget's "clinical method," an adaptation of psychiatric interviewing techniques to research on children's problem solving.

Mitosis The process by which a somatic cell divides and forms two identical daughter cells.

Model A systematic structure of ideas that is designed to assist in the testing of scientific principles and the understanding of empirical events. Models may be stated in logical, mathematical, or physical terms.

Modifier gene A gene that alters or otherwise influences the phenotypic expression of other genes.

Molecular genetics The branch of genetics that is concerned with the structure of genetic material and the biochemical mechanisms of genetic processes.

Monohybrid cross A breeding cross involving a single phenotypic trait determined by a single gene pair.

Monosomy A chromosome anomaly in which one chromosome is missing.

Monozygotic twins Simultaneously born offspring who develop from a single zygote; identical twins. See also *dizygotic twins*.

Moro reflex A startle reaction in which the newborn extends its forearms and fingers and then returns them to its chest.

Morpheme The smallest meaningful units (speech sounds) in a language system; produced by combining phonemes.

Morphology The study of the rules by which a language combines morphemes into larger meaningful units of speech.

Motherless mother In primate research, a female monkey reared in total isolation and made pregnant forcibly.

Motion parallax The apparent movement of objects that occurs when the head or eyes move.

Motion perspective General changes in object movement that accompany movement by the observer.

Motor primacy theory Preyer's theory that prenatal motor behavior is first autogenous and later reactive.

Multivariate A term used to refer to research designs that consider several variables simultaneously. See also *classical designs*.

Mutation A sudden, spontaneous change in a gene or chromosome.

Myogenic response The response of muscle neurons when stimulated directly.

Nativism The belief (following Kant) that knowledge and ideas of the world and space are innate and divinely endowed. See also *empiricism*.

Nativist approach In developmental psycholinguistics, the view that children are predisposed or innately prepared to generate the rules for understanding the abstract aspects of grammar, syntax, and semantics.

Naturalistic observation A nonexperimental research approach in which behavior is observed under realistic, nonlaboratory conditions and carefully recorded.

Neurogenic response The response of motor neurons when stimulated directly.

Nondisjunction The failure of a pair of chromosomes to separate during meiosis.

Normative research method A nonexperimental research approach characterized by the gathering of observational data on the average ages at which certain behaviors appear in normal children.

Norm of reaction The notion that different genotypes react differently to the same environment and that different environments may affect the same genotype differently.

Nuclear division See *mitosis*.

Object permanence The awareness that objects continue to exist even when they are not currently in view.

Ontogenetic activity A behavior that a child may or may not acquire as a function of learning, opportunity, or advantage. See also *phylogenetic activity*.

Ontogenetic age The accumulation of experiences that are unique to the individual organism. See also *chronological age*.

Ontogenetic psychology The study of psychological development in individual organisms; according to Munn, one of two major branches of developmental psychology. See also *phylogenetic psychology*.

Ontogeny   The development of an individual organism. See also *phylogeny*.

Open words   All nonpivot words in the child's lexicon. See also *pivot words*.

Operant conditioning   See *instrumental conditioning*.

Organic lamp (autogenetic) theory of human development   A theory of development in which development is viewed as an unfolding of inherent characteristics and potentials in a predetermined direction.

Orienting reflex   A response to a stimulus that serves to maximize reception; consists of orientation of the receptors toward the stimulus source, arrest of ongoing activity, and certain physiological changes.

Ovulation   The liberation of an ovum from the ovary and its capture by the fallopian tube.

Ovulation age   The estimated age of an embryo or fetus, calculated from the approximate time of ovulation following the mother's last menstrual period.

Palmar reflex   A grasping reflex in response to pressure against the palm.

Pangenesis   Darwin's idea that reproductive cells are composed of atomic-sized "gemmules" that originate from all body cells and are capable of reproducing those cells.

Parsimony, principle of   Morgan's principle that an action may not be interpreted as an outcome of a higher psychic faculty if it can be interpreted as an outcome of a faculty that is lower on the psychological scale.

Partial report technique   A procedure used in assessing memory storage in which subjects are asked to name which of several figures has previously been displayed at a particular location.

Penetrance   The frequency of expression of a trait in an organism possessing the genetic combination for that trait. See also *expressivity*.

Perception   The ability to extract information selectively from the environment.

Perceptual deprivation hypothesis   The hypothesis that the lack of general perceptual and social stimulation is the cause of developmental disruption in institutionalized infants.

Perceptual-recognition hypothesis   A variant of the cognitive-evaluative hypothesis of fear.

Perinatal factor   A condition or state that arises between the thirtieth week of pregnancy and the second week after birth.

Period of concrete operations   In Piaget's theory, the period from age 7 to age 11.

Period of the embryo   The second stage of human prenatal development (from the beginning of the fourth week to the end of the eighth week). See also *pre-embryonic period, period of the fetus*.

Period of the fetus   The third stage of human prenatal development (from the beginning of the ninth week to birth). See also *pre-embryonic period, period of the embryo*.

Period of formal operations   In Piaget's theory, the period in which the person's conceptualization capacities mature, beginning at about age 11.

Permissive parenting   According to Baumrind, a pattern of parenting in which few demands are made on the child for responsibility and proper behavior. See also *authoritarian parenting, authoritative parenting*.

Personality   The unique, global integration

of behavioral systems that results in an individual's characteristic response styles.

Person permanence   See *object permanence*.

Phenocopy   An individual who, as a result of certain events, displays a particular trait but does not possess the genotype for that trait.

Phenotype   A characteristic of an individual that is observable and measurable. See also *genotype*.

Phoneme   A class of sounds that has been determined to be significant for a particular language system; the most elemental structure of language.

Phonology   The scientific study of speech sounds.

Phrenology   A nineteenth-century theoretical system that associated various mental faculties and behaviors with skull protruberances.

Phylogenetic activity   A behavior that is acquired by, and common to, all normal children. See also *ontogenetic activity*.

Phylogenetic psychology   The study of the evolution of psychological processes in organisms; according to Munn, one of two major branches of developmental psychology. See also *ontogenetic psychology*.

Phylogeny   The development of a species. See also *ontogeny*.

Pivot words   A small number of high-frequency words that are acquired relatively slowly and to which the child attaches other words. See also *open words*.

Plantar reflex   Flexion of the toes in response to stimulation.

Plasticity   The degree to which developmental phenomena are influenced by experience, functioning, and learning.

Pleiotropism   A condition in which one gene influences more than one phenotypic trait.

Polygene   A set of genes that individually have a small effect on a particular trait but jointly have an additive or multiplicative effect on that trait, with the result that the phenotypic expression of the trait is quantitative rather than discrete.

Preconcepts   The primitive concepts formed by the child during the late sensorimotor and early preoperational periods; characterized by action, imagery, and concreteness.

Predetermined epigenesis   The view of prenatal development that stresses genetically controlled maturation of the organism. See also *probabilistic epigenesis*.

Pre-embryonic period (period of the ovum)   The first stage of human prenatal development (approximately the first three weeks of life). See also *period of the embryo, period of the fetus*.

Preformationism   The belief that the kinds and numbers of living things were fixed by special creation, and that embryonic life forms are complete, so that growth is simply a process of enlargement.

Prehension   Visually controlled and directed reaching to grasp an object.

Prematurity   Birth at less than 37 weeks menstrual age.

Preoperational period   In Piaget's theory, the period from age 2 to age 7.

Prepotent genotype   According to Waddington, a genotype that follows a narrow path allowing for little deviation in its expression in the developing organism.

Probabilistic epigenesis   The view of prenatal development that stresses environmental factors as determinants of the maturation of the organism. See also *predetermined epigenesis*.

Productivity   In linguistics, sentence construction processes; according to Brown, one of the essential properties of language. See also *semanticity, displacement.*

Prophase The first phase of mitosis. See also *metaphase, anaphase, telophase.*

Prosocial behavior Any behavior that has positive social consequences.

Proximodistal A term used to describe a response pattern or developmental trend that begins near the body axis and spreads outward to the extremities.

Psychoanalytic theory of human development Freud's theory of development, in which inborn impulses strive for expression and come into conflict with environmental pressures and controls; the result is a compromise that reduces internal conflict and leads to more or less healthy development.

Psycholinguistics The study of the cognitive processes required for learning and using language.

Pyknic Kretschmer's term for a short, fat physique. See also *asthenic, athletic.*

Quasi-experimental designs A category of research approaches in which the investigator cannot manipulate the independent variable but can nevertheless determine its relationship to some dependent variable or variables. See also *experimental designs.*

Recall memory The process of retrieval, in which information stored in long-term memory is activated to recognize new information or solve a problem.

Recapitulation, theory of The theory that "ontogeny recapitulates phylogeny," that is, the development of the individual repeats the development of the species.

Recessive gene A gene that either fails to direct the formation of an enzyme or produces a defective enzyme; a recessive gene cannot be expressed in a heterozygote that possesses its dominant allele. See also *dominant gene.*

Recognition memory See *visual (recognition) memory.*

Reflex An unlearned, automatic response that involves a localized, discrete reaction by an organism to a specific eliciting stimulus.

Rehearsal Covert or overt repetition of stimuli in order to remember them.

Reinforcement In operant conditioning, the consequence of a response.

Ribonucleic acid (RNA) A form of nucleic acid found in both the cytoplasm and the nucleus of a cell and responsible for carrying the genetic message from the nucleus to the cytoplasm. See also *deoxyribonucleic acid.*

Rooting reflex A neonatal reflex, consisting of head movements toward the stimulus, that can be elicited by tactile stimulation of the area around the mouth.

Schema In Piaget's theory, the product of the process of organizing incoming information.

Segregation, law of Mendel's first law, which states that a hybrid organism from two different parental varieties possesses both types of parental genes, which separate in the gametes of the offspring.

Semanticity Meaningfulness; according to Brown, one of the essential properties of language. See also *productivity, displacement.*

Semantics The meanings of words and sentences.

Senescence The onset of old age (usually at about age 60).

Sensorimotor development The integration of sensory and motor functioning so that sensory information becomes coordinated with motor acts.

Sensorimotor period In Piaget's theory, the period from infancy to about age 2.

Sensory deprivation A technique used in

studies of environmental influences on maturation that involves depriving the organism of normal levels of stimulation.

Sentence stage The stage of language development in which the child begins to produce sentences.

Sequential strategy A multivariate research design that combines longitudinal and cross-sectional methods.

Sex-influenced gene A gene whose expression may occur in members of either sex but is more common in members of one sex.

Sex-limited gene A gene whose expression occurs only in members of one sex, such as beards in males or breast development in females.

Sex-linked gene A gene, usually located on the X chromosome, that produces sex-linked traits such as color blindness and hemophilia.

S factor According to Spearman, a capacity that appears to be unique to a particular test or mental activity.

Short-term longitudinal design See *convergence approach*.

Singleton An only child.

Socialization All aspects of child rearing by which the individual learns about his or her society, and the knowledge, expectations, and behavior necessary for appropriate functioning within that society.

Social reciprocity The process of stimulus interchange between an infant and another person.

Somatic cell (somatoplasm) Any cell that is not a reproductive cell. See also *germ cell*.

Somatotonia Sheldon's term for a temperament characterized by love of physical adventure and activity. See also *cerebrotonia, viscerotonia*.

Somesthetic deprivation Depriving an organism of stimulation by touch, temperature, pressure, and sensation of movement.

Special creation, doctrine of The belief that all the generations of individuals destined to exist were produced at the moment of divine creation.

Stage theory See *genetic epistemology*.

State An index of level of arousal.

Status In concept formation, the extent to which a concept has physical referents and/or is conceptualized as an object of thought. See also *accessibilty, validity*.

Structuralism The theory of cognition that states that it is a product of the storage of bits of information, which become organized by association with each other; emphasizes innate structures, environment, and learning. See also *mental processes approach*.

Surrogate mother In primate research, a simulated mother monkey made of wire or terrycloth; sometimes a robot is used.

Symbolic representation According to Bruner, a mode of cognitive representation in which language is used to process information. See also *enactive representation, iconic representation*.

Syntax The combination of words in a meaningful sentence.

***Tabula rasa* (blank slate)** Locke's term for the condition of the mind at birth, that is, a blank slate to which all knowledge is furnished through experience alone.

Tacts Skinner's term for a class of utterances that name objects or events.

Telegraphic speech The two-word utterances produced by children between 18 and 24 months of age to express complete ideas.

Telophase The fourth and final phase of

mitosis. See also *prophase, metaphase, anaphase*.

Temperament An individual's unique patterns of activity, responsiveness, arousal level, and reaction intensity.

Tension-release hypothesis The hypothesis, proposed by Sroufe and Waters, that smiling and laughter are related to a tension-release mechanism with a physiological basis.

Teratogen An environmental factor (e.g., a virus or a drug) that produces a developmental defect.

Teratogenesis A sequence of abnormal developmental events.

Teratology The branch of embryology that deals with the etiology and manifestation of abnormal structural and functional development in prenatal and postnatal organisms.

Textuals Skinner's term for a class of utterances controlled by visual verbal stimuli.

Texture gradient A change in object texture that occurs as a function of distance.

Tonic neck reflex (TNR) A neonatal reflex in which the extremities on one side of the body are extended and those on the other side are flexed.

Transfer RNA (tRNA) The form of RNA that is responsible for the production of the polypeptide chain by which amino acids are bonded together to form proteins.

Transformational rules In Chomsky's theory, the rules that relate "surface" and "deep" sentence structures.

Translocation A condition in which a chromosome becomes attached to a nonhomologous chromosome during meiosis.

Transmission genetics The branch of genetics that is concerned with describing the patterns of inheritance of genetic material and tracing the transmission of biological similarities and variation from one generation to another.

Trihybrid cross A breeding cross involving three phenotypic traits determined by three gene pairs.

Trisomy A chromosome anomaly in which an extra chromosome is present.

Two-word stage The stage of language development in which the child produces two-word utterances or telegraphic speech.

Unconditioned response A response that occurs without learning or experience (i.e., reflexively).

Unconditioned stimulus A stimulus that evokes a reliable response without conditioning.

Use and disuse, law of One of Lamarck's laws of evolution, which states that the presence, size, and strength of any organ is dependent on the length of time over which it is used and the degree to which it is used. See also *inheritance of acquired characters, law of*.

Validity In concept formation, the degree to which an individual's conceptualization of a given concept differs from some standard or popular conceptualization of it. See also *accessibility, status*.

Vestibular stimulation Stimulation of the inner ear.

Viscerotonia Sheldon's term for a temperament characterized by love of comfort, sociability, and gluttony. See also *cerebrotonia, somatotonia*.

Visual cliff An apparatus used to determine depth perception, which consists of a glass-topped table under which a textured surface can be placed at various distances from the table top.

Visual (recognition) memory The ability to

recognize similarities to previously experienced stimuli; the simplest form of memory.

Wariness In infants, a mild negative reaction consisting of a worried face, frowning, and gaze aversion.

Word A unit of language consisting of one or more morphemes.

Zygote A fertilized egg; the first cell of a new individual.

Name Index

Numbers in italics refer to the pages on which the complete references are listed.

Subject Index

Discontinuity model of
    development, 14–16
DNA, *see* Deoxyribonucleic acid
Dominant gene, 64, 66–68
    inherited defects, 90, 94
    sex-influenced, 80
    sex-linked inheritance, 79
Donders, F. C., 272
Down's syndrome, 96–99
Drugs
    obstetric, effect on infants,
        161–163
    phenocopy, drug-induced, 75
    teratogenicity of, 142, 146–148
Dugdale, Richard, 86–87
Dysgenesis, 144

E

Early menopause syndrome, 102
Echoics, in language
    development, 336–337
Echolalia stage, in language
    development, 348
Ectoderm, 114–115
Ectomorph, 463
Egg cell (ovum), 50, 77
    viability, 121
Electroencephalogram patterns of
    fetus, 134
Embryology, 37
Embryology, behavioral, *see*
    Behavioral embryology
Embryonic age, 120–122
Embryonic development
    critical periods, 144–145
    neural function and
        stimulation, 177–178
    teratogenic susceptibility of
        embryo, 143–144
Embryonic disc, 114
Embryonic growth, 112–113,
    115–116
Emotion, 419
Emotional development, 416–459
    fear, 436–445
    historical perspective, 419–425

infants, 425–433
    learning and maturation,
        433–436
    smiling and laughter, 445–454
Empathy, in altruism, 501
Empiricism, 246–247, 249
Enactive representation, 274–275
Endocrine imbalance,
    teratogenicity of, 142, 152
Endomorph, 463
Entoderm, 114
Environment, 12, 18–19, 32, 45,
    184
    and antisocial behavior, 105,
        107
    and cognitive development,
        300, 305
    early intervention, and
        intellectual development,
        404–407
    and genetic expression, 72–75
    influence on intelligence,
        397–412
    interaction with genes, 81, 85
    intrauterine, and prenatal
        development, 140–161
    in Lamarck's evolutionary
        theory, 35
    and language development,
        321, 342, 356–361
    and maturation, 175, 185–202
    and motor development, 238
    and perceptual development,
        247, 249, 261–262
    and prehensile development,
        243–244
    and smiling, 451
    and temperament, 426,
        432–433
Environmental enrichment
    programs, and intellectual
    development, 405–407
Environmentalism, 85
Environmental restriction,
    185–195
Environmental stimulation,
    195–202
Enzyme, 61–62, 64

Epigenesis, in embryology, 120,
    124–126
Epigenetic landscape, 81
Epistemology, 246–247; *see also*
    Genetic epistemology
Equilibration, in Piaget's theory,
    300–301
Error of potentiality, 124
Ethology, 32
    attachment, 471–472
    fear, 436–437
    smiling and laughter, 446
Etiology, 4
Eugenics, 88, 370, 394
Euphenics, 93
Evolution, biological, 32, 34–41
    attachment, 471
    and cognitive development, 299
    and language development, 339
Experiential factors, in
    maturation, 176, 185–202
Experimental child psychology, 6
Experimental research methods,
    21, 30
Expressivity, in genetics, 73

F

Factor analysis, in theories of
    intelligence, 376–379
Family composition
    and intelligence, 409–412
    and language development,
        356–359
Fear, 433–434, 436–445
Females
    language development,
        355–356
    maternal factors in intellectual
        development, 409
    motor development, 236–238
    sex chromosomes, 76–79
    sex-linked inheritance, 79–80
Fertilization of egg cell, 50, 55,
    77–78, 120–121
Fetal alcohol syndrome, 150

maternal contraction of rubella, 151

and perinatal anoxia, 154–156

phenylketonuria, 90–92

Mental tests, 369–374, 395; *see also* Intelligence tests

Mesoderm, 114–115

Mesomorph, 463

Messenger RNA, 61–63

Metabolic disorders

Lesch-Nyhan syndrome, 93–94

phenylketonuria, 90–93

Tay-Sachs disease, 94

teratogenicity of, 142, 150

Milwaukee Project, 406

Mitosis, 51–53, 60

Model, in research and study, 13

Modeling, in development of social behavior, 498–501

Modifier gene, 73–74

Molecular genetics, 57–64

Mongolism, *see* Down's syndrome

Monkeys, maternal and social deprivation studies, 478–484

Monohybrid inheritance, 67–70

Monosomy, 95

Monozygotic twins, intelligence, 397

Moral development, 494–502

Morgan, C. Lloyd, 38

Moro (startle) reflex, 134, 225, 425

Morpheme, 345–346

Morphology, in linguistics, 345–346

Mothers and mothering, *see* entries under Maternal

Motor behavior, prenatal, 122

Motor development, 220–244

differential, 233–239

and environmental restriction, 193–194

gross, 229–233

origins in neonatal reflexes, 223–229

mRNA, *see* Messenger RNA

Multiple births, and language development, 356–359

Multiple-factor theory of intelligence, 377–378

Multivariate research designs, 27–28

Mutation, 60

Myogenic response, fetal, 128

N

National Collaborative Perinatal Project, 162

National Institute of Neurological and Communicative Disorders and Stroke, 162

Nativism, 246–247, 249

language development biological–nativist approach to, 339–341, 347

Naturalistic research methods, 32

Natural selection, 35–36, 53

Nature–nurture controversy, 84–85, 184

in intellectual development, 395–396

NCPP, *see* National Collaborative Perinatal Project

Negative correlations, 30

Neonates

behavior patterns and maternal responsiveness, 467

cognition, 269

conditioning, 209–211

emotions, 422–424

habituation, 207–208

looming avoidance response, 260

perception, 245, 249–251, 254

psychoanalytic view of, 469

reflexes, 223–229

smiling, 448

temperament, 425–427

visual memory, 274

Neural function and stimulation, in embryonic development, 177–178

Neurogenic response, fetal, 128

NINCDS, *see* National Institute of Neurological and Communicative Disorders and Stroke

Nitrogen base, of DNA, 59–60

Nonexperimental research methods, 30–32

Normative research methods, 31

in motor development, 222

Norm of reaction, in genetics, 73

Nucleic acid, 49, 59

Nucleolus, 49

Nucleotide, 59–60

Nucleus, cell, 49, 52, 59

Nutrition, and prenatal development, 152–154

O

Object permanence, 281, 290–291, 470–471

Obstetric medication, effect on fetus, 161–164

Old age, 7, 9

Ontogenetic activities, 197–198

Ontogenetic age, 11

Ontogenetic psychology, 6–7

Open words, 350

Operant conditioning, *see* Instrumental conditioning

Oral stage, of personality development, 464

Organic lamp theory of development, 16, 19

Organization, biological and behavioral, in social development, 476

Orienting reflex, 205, 208, 245

Ovulation, and prenatal age, 121

Ovum, *see* Egg cell

Oxygen deprivation, perinatal, and development, 154–156

P

Palmar reflex, 132, 225

Pangenesis, hypothesis of, 36, 47

Parameter, 187

Parental factors, and IQ of
  children, 403, 407–409
Parenting
  discipline styles, and social
    development, 486–489
  parent–child interactions, and
    social development, 485–489
  and temperament, 431–431
Parsimony, principle of, 38–39
Partial report technique, 283
Pattern perception, 253–256
Pavlovian conditioning, *see*
  Classical conditioning
Penetrance, in genetics, 73
Perceptual development,
    220–223, 244–262
  environment, 261–262
  historical perspective, 246–249
Perceptual memory, *see* Visual
  memory
Perinatal factors in development,
    152–161
Permissive parent, 488–489
Personality, 430, 460–509
  definition, 462
  early experience and, 475–484
  early socialization and
    developments of, 485–494
  historical perspective, 462–465
  later socialization and
    development of, 494–503
Phallic stage, of personality
  development, 464
Phenocopy, 75
Phenotype, 48, 67–68, 70–75,
  81–82
Phenylketonuria, 90–93
Phocomelia, 75
Phoneme, 343, 345–346, 348
Phonology, 343, 346
Phosphate group, of DNA, 59
Phrenology, 86, 463
Phylogenetic activities, 197–198
Phylogenetic psychology, 6–7
Physique, and personality,
  463–464
Piaget, Jean, 19, 249, 272, 281,
  290–294, 296–308, 341, 375,

470, 495–498
Pivot words, 350
PKU, *see* Phenylketonuria
Placental weight, 113
Plantar reflex, 132, 225
Pleasure principle, 420
Pleiotropism, in genetics, 74
PMA, *see* Primary mental abilities
Polygene, 71–72
Polypeptide chain, 59, 61–62, 64
Positive correlations, 30
Practical intelligence, 290
Practice, effects of, in
  development of skills,
  197–200
Precocious motor development,
  235
Preconceptual development,
  290–291
Predetermined epigenesis,
  124–126, 171
Predictive validity, of infant IQ
  scores, 382–385
Preference hypothesis, 276–277
Preformationism, 34–35, 124
Prehension, 239–244
Prelinguistic development,
  347–348
Premature infants, 156–159
  survival of, 126–127
Prenatal care, and fetal
  development, 136–37
Prenatal development, 110–169
  behavioral embryology, history
    and concepts in, 122–126,
    137–140
  embryonic age, 120–122
  embryonic growth, 112–113
  intrauterine influences on,
    140–161
  maturation, 171–172
  ontogeny of fetal behavior,
    128–137
  periods of development,
    114–120
  study of, 126–128
Preoperational period, in child
  development, 290–291, 296

Preschool educational programs,
  and intellectual development,
  404–407
Preyer, William, 122
Primary mental abilities, 377
Primary Mental Abilities Test,
  390–392
Primate deprivation syndrome,
  480, 482
Primates, nonhuman
  early experience and social
    development, 477–484
  linguistic capacity, 322,
    324–335
Probabilistic epigenesis,
  1125–126, 171
Prosocial behavior, 500–502
Protein, in genetic processes, 49,
  57, 59, 64
Proximodistal progression, in
  motor development, 230
Psychoanalytic theory, 16–18,
  420, 464–465, 469, 475,
  485–486, 492
Psychoeducational testing,
  369–374
Psychogenesis, 122
Psycholinguistics, 318, 321
Psychological maturation, 172
Psychosexual stages of
  development, 464–465, 475
Punishment, 489, 499
Purine base, of DNA, 59
Pyknic body type, 463
Pyrimidine base, of DNA, 59

Quasi-experimental designs, in
  developmental research,
  21–22
Quinine, 148

Race differences
  in intelligence, 396, 403

in motor development, 238–239

Radiation, teratogenicity of, 142, 145

Recall memory, 280–286

Recapitulation, theory of, 37–38, 40–41

Recessive gene, 64, 66–68
  inherited defects, 90–94
  sex-influenced, 80
  sex-linked inheritance, 79

Reflexes
  fetal, 122, 130, 132, 134, 137–139
  infant, 205–208
  neonatal, 223–229
  smiling, 448

Reinforcement, in conditioning, 203–204
  in attachment, 469
  in language development, 337–338
  in moral development, 498–500

Research methods, 20–32

Respiratory reflex, 134

Retina, 250

Ribonucleic acid, 59, 61–63

Ribosome, 61–63

RNA, *see* Ribonucleic acid

Robot mother, and primate deprivation syndrome, 482

Romanes, George John, 38

Rooting reflex, 224–225

Rubella, 150–151

S

Schema, in Piaget's theory, 300

Segregation, law of, in Mendelian genetics, 67–68

Semantics, 346–347

Sensorimotor development, 223, 290
  prehension, 239–244

Sensory deprivation, 186–187
  and perceptual development, 261–262

Sentence concept, in language acquisition, 339–340

Sequential motor development, 230, 232–233

Sex chromosome, 55, 57, 75–79, 90
  anomalies, 101–106

Sex determination, 75–79

Sex differences
  in cognitive development, 306–307
  in language development, 355–356
  in motor development, 235–238

Sex-influenced gene, 80

Sex-limited gene, 80

Sex-linked inheritance, 79

Sexual behavior, and social isolation, 480, 482

Sexual reproduction, 53–57

Sheldon, W. H., 463–464

Shirley, Mary M., 182

Siblings
  IQ scores, correlation between, 397
  language development, 356–359

Sickle-cell anemia, 64

Sign language, *see* Gestural language

Simon, Théodore, 371–372

Simpson, James, 161

Skinner, B. F., 18, 336

Smiling, 445–451

Smoking, teratogenicity of, 148–149

Social development, 460–509
  early experience and, 475–484
  historical perspective, 462–465
  maternal and social deprivation studies, 478–484, 489–494
  origins of social behavior, 465–474
  socialization and personality development, 485–503

Social learning
  attachment, 469–470
  moral development, 498–500

Socioeconomic factors
  and intellectual development, 401–404
  and language development, 359
  and motor development, 239

Somatic cell, 47, 49–50, 53
  mitosis, 51–53

Somatotonia, 463

Somatotype, 463–464

Spatial perception, 256

Spearman, Charles, 376–377

Special creation, doctrine of, 34–35

Sperm cell, 50, 77
  viability, 121

Spontaneous abortion, 95, 141

Stage theory, in Piaget's system, 301–302, 305

Stanford-Binet Scale, 372–373, 390, 395

Startle reaction, *see* Moro reflex

Stentence stage, in language development, 351

Sterilization laws, 88

Steroid hormones, 146–147

Stimulation input, and social development, 476–477, 482, 484

Stimulus deprivation, and maturation, 176

Stimulus preference, in infants, 276–277

Stimulus-response, 18
  in concept development, 289–290
  in language development, 336–339

Stockard, C. R., 144–145

Structuralism, 271–272

Structure-function relationship, 125, 171, 176, 183

Structure-of-intellect theory of intelligence, 377–378

Subcortical control of fetal reflexes, 134

Sucking reflex, 134, 225

Surrogate mother, 478, 480, 482

Symbolic processes, in cognition, 270, 274

A   1
B   2
C   3
D   4
E   5
F   6